Criminal Intimacy

Criminal Intimacy

Prison and the Uneven History of Modern American Sexuality

REGINA KUNZEL

The University of Chicago Press
Chicago and London

REGINA KUNZEL is professor of history and gender, women, and sexuality studies and the Paul R. Frenzel Land Grant Chair in Liberal Arts at the University of Minnesota. She is the author of *Fallen Women, Problem Girls: Unmarried Mothers and the Professionalization of Social Work, 1890–1945.*

The University of Chicago Press, Chicago 60637
The University of Chicago Press, Ltd., London
© 2008 by The University of Chicago
All rights reserved. Published 2008
Printed in the United States of America

17 16 15 14 13 12 11 10 09 08   1 2 3 4 5

ISBN-13: 978-0-226-46226-4 (cloth)
ISBN-10: 0-226-46226-9 (cloth)

Library of Congress Cataloging-in-Publication Data

Kunzel, Regina G., 1959–
    Criminal intimacy : prison and the uneven history of modern American sexuality / Regina Kunzel.
        p.   cm.
    Includes bibliographical references and index.
    ISBN-13: 978-0-226-46226-4 (hardcover : alk. paper)
    ISBN-10: 0-226-46226-9 (hardcover : alk. paper)
    1. Prisoners—Sexual behavior—United States. 2. Prison violence—United States. 3. Rape—United States. I. Title.
    HV8836.K86 2008
    306.7086'9270973—dc22

                                                    2007036400

♾ The paper used in this publication meets the minimum requirements of the American National Standard for Information Sciences—Permanence of Paper for Printed Library Materials, ANSI Z39.48–1992.

For my father Fritz Kunzel,
in loving memory

CONTENTS

Illustrations follow page 190

ACKNOWLEDGMENTS

This book has taken a long time to think through, research, and write. I have received a great deal of support over more than a decade's time, and it is a pleasure and privilege to acknowledge its many sources here.

Several institutions provided the gifts of time, space, and intellectual community. I am grateful for generous sabbaticals from Williams College, one spent at the Oakley Center for Humanities and Social Sciences as I was just beginning to explore this project. I also thank the Radcliffe Institute for Advanced Study, where I spent a year in the lively and generative company of Virginia Drachman, Mary Maples Dunn, Drew Gilpin Faust, Helen Horowitz, Ellen Moore, Kenda Mutongi, Thomas Lewis, Christina Rathbone, Brenda Shaughnessy, Cathy Silber, and others. My thanks, too, to the University of Minnesota's Department of Gender, Women, and Sexuality Studies for housing me as an affiliated scholar as I was finishing a draft of this book.

Like all historians, I owe an enormous debt of gratitude to the staffs of libraries and archives. I'd like to single out for special mention Mimi Bowling at the New York Public Library, Sarah Hutcheon and Jane Knowles at the Schlesinger Library, Terence Kissack, formerly at the GLBT Historical Society in San Francisco, Joan Krizack at Northeastern University Library's Archives and Special Collections, Brenda Marston at Cornell University's Human Sexuality collection, Fred Romanski at the National Archives, and Liana Zhou and Shawn Wilson at the Kinsey Institute. The interlibrary loan staff at Williams College, headed by Alison O'Grady, was wonderfully resourceful at tracking down even the most obscure sources and bringing them to the Berkshires. I also benefited from advice and citations passed along by archive-savvy friends and colleagues. Chad Heap was very generous with references and advice about navigating Chicago archives. Brad Verter shared his encyclopedic knowledge of underworld narratives and loaned me books from his own incredible library. Margot Canaday tutored me in the workings of the National Archives and in filing Freedom of Information Act requests. Naomi Murakawa shared her expertise on race, incarceration, and public policy. And Terence Kissack regularly sent materials relating to sex in prison my way.

I was very fortunate to work on this book in the company of smart and supportive friends and colleagues at Williams College. Thanks to my colleagues in the history department and beyond, especially Ondine Chavoya, Robert Dalzell, Charles Dew, Peggy Diggs, David Eppel, Ed Epping, Alexandra Garbarini, Rip Gibson, Cheryl Hicks, Liza Johnson, Katie Kent, Roger Kittleson, Tom Kohut, Gretchen Long, Brian Martin, Karen Merrill, Kenda Mutongi, Carol Ockman, Mark Reinhardt, Mérida Rua, Stefanie Solum, Peter Starenko, Karen Swann, Chris Waters, Ben Weaver, Carmen Whalen, Scott Wong, and Jim Wood. I feel honored and grateful to have been a part of this community for so many years. I finished this book as I began my new position at the University of Minnesota, where I have already benefited from engaged questions and comments from new colleagues, including Anna Clark, Susan Craddock, Jigna Desai, Lisa Disch, Sara Evans, Andreas Gailus, Amy Kaminsky, Elaine Tyler May, and Kevin Murphy.

I also wish to thank Williams students Lisa Ja Young Ahn and Matthew Ellis for research assistance. Undergraduates at the time, they've both gone on to great things. Thanks also to Daniel Kukla for his eleventh-hour help with archival research.

Doug Mitchell, my editor at the University of Chicago Press, is often the recipient of gushing thanks in authors' acknowledgments, and with good reason. I thank him here for his unstinting support and enthusiasm, his long-standing confidence in me and in this project, and for some truly wonderful meals. Thanks, too, to Tim McGovern, Sandy Hazel, and Rob Hunt, all of whom helped shepherd the book into press. I am grateful to Yvonne Zipter for her discerning care with the manuscript and her skillful copyediting.

An earlier version of chapter 3 was published as "Situating Sex: Prison Sexual Culture in the Mid-Twentieth Century," *GLQ: A Journal of Lesbian and Gay Studies* 8, no. 3 (2002): 253–70. My thanks to Duke University Press for permission to reprint this text here. Some portions of chapter 6 appear in "Lessons in Being Gay: Queer Encounters in Gay and Lesbian Prison Activism," *Radical History Review* 100 (Winter 2008): 11–37. My thanks to Duke University Press for permission to reprint this text as well.

I owe many thanks to those who read early versions of one or more chapters. Ondine Chavoya, Jeffrey Escoffier, Alexandra Garbarini, Timothy Gilfoyle, David Halperin, Lisa Henderson, Janice Irvine, Katie Kent, Terence Kissack, Molly McGarry, Kevin Murphy, Jana Sawicki, Siobhan Somerville, Dara Strolovitch, and Chris Waters all read drafts of chapters at various stages and offered comments that helped me develop my ideas. I began this book in close conversation with Molly McGarry, and I'm grateful for her enthusiasm for it over the years. Kevin Murphy, my old friend and new colleague at the University of Minnesota, was also present from the beginning of this project and has seen it, and me, through to the end. I owe special thanks to David Halperin and Joanne Meyerowitz, both of whom, from the start, posed questions I couldn't answer (and probably haven't still). My work and my life would be much poorer without Siobhan Somerville's buoying friendship, intellectual engagement, and true generosity in reading my work at every stage. Any imaginative leaps here are probably ones she encouraged me to take.

I cannot overstate my gratitude to friends and colleagues who put aside their own work to read the entire manuscript and offer comments, suggestions, and prodding critique that made this a much better book. My sincere thanks to Margot Canaday, Estelle Freedman, Joanne Meyerowitz, Kathy Peiss, Siobhan Somerville, and Dara Strolovitch for the generous gifts of their time and intelligence and for the inspiring example of their scholarship.

Beyond providing help both intellectual and practical, Dara Strolovitch offered reassuring support, true kindness, and the best company. This book was written and finished under her watch. I am so grateful to have her in my life.

My father and my mother, in different ways, both nurtured my appreciation for the study of the past. My father had a keen interest in history and a skeptical view of incarceration. He was also a great lover of books. I dedicate this one to him, with deep love and gratitude.

In prison, inmate John Rosevear observed, "time accumulates a new dimension."[1] The essence of incarceration was forced spatial confinement, of course, but many prisoners experienced it as temporally rupturing as well. Prison's strange ability to distort conventional understandings of time as orderly, linear, and rationally clocked found blunt and telling expression in prison vernacular. Time, to prisoners, was something to be "done"; prison time could be "hard" or "easy." For some, incarceration took place in a strange and disorienting time out of time; for others, it suspended time altogether. Time in prison could assume a physical dimension and exert a material, sometimes malicious force and pressure. "In prison," inmate George Harsh wrote, "time is a leaden-footed, creeping bastard."[2]

Historical as well as individual time can seem weirdly aslant in prisons, refusing to conform to cultural shifts and changes as they are understood to proceed in the larger world. Perhaps most striking among prison's apparent anachronisms was the sexual life of prisoners—the subject of intense anxiety, fascination, and scrutiny even as it was treated as a closely guarded secret of carceral life. From its early-nineteenth-century origins, the American prison was observed to cultivate sexual practices, norms, and identities that existed in an increasingly eccentric relationship to those developing beyond bars. Marked by the participation of putatively "normal" or otherwise heterosexual people in same-sex

sex, prison sexual life failed to synchronize with dominant notions of sexuality—tracked by historians as emerging in the nineteenth century and solidifying in the twentieth—which held sexual acts and desires to be expressions of sexual identity. Indeed, one of the most important and defining assumptions of the sexual regime that announced itself as "modern" was the belief that the object of sexual desire reflected an individual's essence. Who one desired, and what one did sexually and with whom, came to define, importantly, who one *was*. Sex, as Michel Foucault proposed famously, came to be understood as the "truth of the self."[3]

Some sexual acts and actors, however, confound this historical narrative. Prisons attracted special interest as places where participation in same-sex sex often failed to confer or connote a (homo)sexual identity, but they were far from alone. Sexual practices similarly unmoored from sexual identity have long been observed in other sex-segregated settings, such as the armed services, aboard ship, in logging camps, and in boarding schools. Although historian Allan Bérubé was primarily interested in the formative role of the mass mobilization of the Second World War in forging gay and lesbian identity and community in his path-breaking book, *Coming Out under Fire*, much of the sexual life he documented—from the furtive, drunken gropings of servicemen on weekend passes to the intimate ties established in the terror of combat—involved many who would not have identified as homosexual and who would presumably go on to live heterosexual lives.[4] Likewise the culture of "smashing" and intense romantic attachments among girls and young women observed in boarding schools and colleges in the nineteenth and early twentieth centuries, a tradition apparently so thoroughly institutionalized and so widely practiced as to constitute a veritable norm.[5]

At some points, such non-identity-based same-sex practices were exposed as being much more widely represented in the population as a whole. Alfred Kinsey proposed to mid-twentieth-century Americans that sexual behavior must be disentangled from sexual identity when he argued that the startling diversity of their sexual practices was more accurately represented by a continuum than by a homo/heterosexual binary.[6] It was certainly more comforting, however, to conceive of such practices as bounded within a specific site or circumstance and explained by its peculiar constraints. Locating prison as *the* home of what came, by the mid-twentieth century, to be termed "situational homosexuality" may, in fact, have worked to relieve the pressure to acknowledge and consider sexual instability in other less stigmatized and more dispersed domains.

Far more than other sites, the prison attracted sustained attention to its apparently renegade and dissident sexualities that failed to map neatly according to dominant identity categories. Observers who noted prisoners' apparent refusal to abide by a changing sexual logic and epistemology sometimes expressed that sense of dissonance in temporal terms, casting prisons either as sexually retrograde or as beyond the bounds of history altogether. Some located prison sexual practices in time immemorial. In his influential 1940 study of inmate community life, sociologist Donald Clemmer declared "abnormal sex conduct" among prisoners a "natural phenomenon" because "it has appeared not in any one time or place but has existed since the facts of man's behavior have been recorded by man."[7] Others called on historical analogies, the distant past of ancient Greece or Rome among the most popular, to evoke the *longue durée* of sex in prison and to conjure its anachronistic, asynchronistic nature. Early-twentieth-century prison reformer Thomas Mott Osborne, for instance, declared that "degenerates" had posed a problem in prison "since the days of ancient Greece."[8] In his popular 1933 prison memoir, *Prison Days and Nights*, Victor Nelson opened his chapter, "Men without Women" with a similar observation that "since the days of Ancient Greece, and very likely long before that, students of human behavior have known that wherever men or women are deprived for very long of the normal means of sexual satisfaction, they almost invariably resort to such substitutes as masturbation, oral copulation, sodomy, and various bodily and mechanical substitutes."[9] More than half a century later, anti–prison rape activist Stephen Donaldson compared the sexual life he experienced behind bars to "that found to prevail in ancient Rome." Sex in men's prisons, Donaldson observed, was organized according to "the dominance-enforcement model," whereby "the sexual element expresses and symbolizes a previously imposed power relationship, the desires of the passive partner are irrelevant, the rulers are prohibited from taking a passive role, and sexual penetration of an adult male is viewed as the natural fruit of conquest."[10]

Although Donaldson disparaged academics as "armchair theorists" who arrived at their analyses at a comfortable distance from prison life, he relied on the work of historians of sexuality to make this argument and to venture this historical comparison.[11] In the last twenty years or so, historians have produced a rich and sophisticated body of scholarship dedicated to proving that sexuality has a history, that the meanings attributed to sexual practices are historically and culturally made rather than biologically given. The insistence on the incommensurability of past and present understandings of sex has helped dismantle notions of sexuality as self-evident, transhistorical, and natural and has exposed the historically

specific and contingent character of present-day understandings and experiences of sexuality. Historians point to the concept of sexual identity,
heterosexual and homosexual, as constituting the most distinctive marker
of modern sexuality. More than anything else, its emergence delineated a
sexual present from a sexual past.

Tracking and explaining change over time is the historian's métier. Historians have accordingly explored and debated the circumstances that gave
rise to the formation of modern sexual identities, including the decline
of a family-centered economy and the rise of industrial capitalism, the
new possibilities of urban life, and sexological attention to "inversion."[12]
Sexual practices and norms in prison, however, apparently produced by
spatial rather than temporal circumstances, can seem peculiarly, even ob-
stinately, ahistorical. Apparently unmoored from identity and resistant to
the taxonomic pressures of the twentieth century, these sexual practices
and their practitioners can seem to stand curiously outside time.

No doubt in part for this reason, and with very few exceptions, historians have declined to consider sex in prison as an interesting, important, or
even relevant subject in the larger project of the history of sexuality.[13] In
the rare moments in which they reference it, some historians have resorted
to representational strategies remarkably similar to those ventured by observers in earlier periods, depicting it either as strangely anachronistic or
beyond the proper purview of history altogether. Some accept the notion
of sex in prison as transhistorical, the inevitable consequence of heterosexual deprivation, presumably governed by biological drive rather than
cultural and social forces, and therefore unilluminating and unmeaning-
ful to the questions that concern historians. Vernon Rosario, for instance,
proclaims that historians of sexuality have little interest "merely in any
same-sex sexual activity (for example, the 'situational' homosexuality of
prisoners or sailors restricted to a single-sex environment). It is the more
elusive issue of same-sex *desire* or sexual *orientation* ('true' homosexuality
or 'gayness'),") he writes, "that is the matter of concern."[14] Other scholars
invoke familiar historical analogies to capture prison sexual culture's apparent asynchronicity. The prison experience of Jack Abbott, for instance,
appears to historian David Halperin "uncannily reminiscent" of the sexual
system of classical Athenian society.[15] Abbott wrote in his correspondence
with Norman Mailer about performing the "active," penetrative role in
sex with other men in prison who were feminized in the process, professed ignorance of "the clinical term 'homosexual,'" and claimed to have
experienced sex in prison as "a natural sex that emerged within the society
of men."[16] In Abbott's account of prison, as in ancient Greece, Halperin

writes, sex "did not express inward dispositions or inclinations so much as it served to position social actors in the places assigned to them," reflecting and reinforcing a hierarchy among men.[17]

While historians of sexuality have paid little attention to prisons and prisoners, historians of the prison have paid scant attention to sex and sexuality. Historians have made powerful claims for the historicity of the prison—an institution (not unlike modern sexuality) that has become endowed with an aura of inevitability, but one with surprisingly recent origins that has undergone important changes over the course of its relatively short history. As historians Norval Morris and David J. Rothman write, "In the popular imagination, institutions of incarceration appear so monumental in design and so intrinsic to the criminal justice system that it is tempting to think of them as permanent and fixed features of Western societies." Morris and Rothman thus envision that "the most novel contribution" of their edited volume, *The Oxford History of the Prison*, "will be its demonstration that prisons do have a history."[18] In the now expansive historical literature on the prison, however, as in the scholarship on sexuality, the sexual life of prisoners has received little attention.[19] When sex is observed in histories of the prison (often only to be hurriedly brushed past) it is typically represented as an inevitable aspect of prison life, part of the underground culture created by inmates confined in single-sex institutions, understandably born of heterosexual deprivation.

In this book, I make a claim for the payoffs (and acknowledge the productive challenges) of cultivating historical curiosity about sexual desires and practices assumed either to have no history or to confound our historical assumptions. Although same-sex sexual acts have long been part of prison life, they have been understood in radically different ways and have provoked varying responses at different historical moments. If prison sexual life stands in an oblique relationship to sexual practices and beliefs prevailing in the outside world, the discourses that took shape around and in response to it were firmly entrenched in and richly illuminating of the assumptions of their particular historical context.

Criminal Intimacy examines the shifting concerns, anxieties, and fascinations about sex in prison and tracks the different strategies to ease those anxieties employed from the institution's beginnings in early-nineteenth-century America through the late twentieth century—strategies that helped explain, tame, or ignore sex in prison. Exploring those shifts, I argue, exposes the fretful labor involved in the making of modern sexuality and its distinctive fictions, stable and fixed sexual identity primary among them. The relationship of prison sexual practice to "modern" sexuality emerges as neither marginal nor oppositional but, rather, as disquieting, sometimes ironically buttressing, and always revealing of its fissures and fault lines.

Among the rewards of a historical examination of prison sexual culture is the illumination of an unexpectedly plural, varied, and contradictory sexual world. Reflecting further on Jack Abbott's prison experience, Halperin proposes that, even late in the twentieth century, "there are . . . sectors of our own societies to which the ideology of 'sexuality' has failed to penetrate."[20] Attention to the sexual life produced and practiced by prisoners alerts us to the racialized and classed specificity of the sexual regime we call "modern"; it exposes its marked unevenness and qualifies in significant ways its reach and scope. Prisoners have always comprised a diverse population housed together in unusually intimate circumstances, and they brought (and bring) with them different ways of thinking about and expressing sex and sexuality. Prisons were thus places where different sexual cultures and ideologies, shaped importantly by class, gender, race, ethnicity, age, and place, converged and sometimes clashed. In spite of the diversity of their populations, American prisons have always been disproportionately occupied by poor and working-class people and by people of color; this book illuminates as well the intertwined histories of criminalized race and class and criminalized sexuality.

Attending to the multiple sexual cultures that inmates brought with them to prison as well as the distinctive sexual culture made by prisoners behind bars exposes the limits of the trajectory that historians have posited, from a premodern regime in which sexual acts were not linked to identity to a modern one in which sexual object choice bears a privileged relationship to identity and selfhood. It reveals that historical narrative, depending as it does on the occlusion of some forms and practices of sexuality, to be falsely even and misleadingly totalizing. Exploring the ways in which sex in prison has been represented also lays bare the developmental model implicit in that acts-to-identities telos, according to which sexual expressions that do not follow that story line are characterized as lagging behind. Prisons were often represented as hermetic institutions in which residues of past and more primitive sexual cultures persisted and thrived. And as in other iterations of that developmental narrative, the primitivism of prison sex was often cast in classed and racialized terms.[21]

Region, class, and race complicate the story of modern sexuality, or what historians have sometimes termed "sex as we know it"—often shorthand for the presumed present-day hegemony of a homo/heterosexual binary against which a less familiar and more exotic sexual past can be counterposed.[22] Postcolonial theorists and anthropologists have noted the ways in which that narrative has constrained thinking about sexuality among non-Western and diasporic populations. Martin F. Manalansan, for example, offers a powerful challenge to assumptions about the progressive development of a gay world and a uniform gay modernity in his ethnographic study of Filipino immigrants in New York City.[23] Historians, too, have begun to problematize the neat narrative that posits a move from sexual acts to sexual identities. In his study of the postwar rural and small-town South, historian John Howard finds that "gay identity in Mississippi (surely as elsewhere) existed alongside multiple queer desires that were not identity based or identity forging." Howard moves further to propose that "throughout the twentieth century, queer sexuality continued to be understood as both acts *and* identities, behaviors *and* beings. It was variously comprehended—depending in part on race and place—along multiple axes and continuums as yet unexamined by historians."[24]

Sex in prison was not unique in exposing the false coherence that historians have sometimes granted to modern sexuality. But sexuality and the prison were bound together in several important, distinctive, and possibly mutually constitutive ways that warrant closer attention. First, unlike other examples of apparent sexual instability, the prison was a site of enduring fascination—simultaneously cordoned off and a place of intense interest. In part due to its compelling grip on the American imagination, the prison distilled anxieties about the indeterminacy of sexual identity and came by the mid-twentieth century to be understood as the archetypal and iconic site of sexual mutability. As a consequence, efforts to explain the persistent enigma of same-sex sexual desires and practices among incarcerated men and women reached beyond the prison to reckon with the meaning of human sexuality itself.

The prison, identified by Foucault as the quintessential symbol of the development and deployment of modern technologies of disciplinary power, was also a privileged site for the observation, study, and burgeoning production of knowledge about sex and sexuality.[25] Criminality and sexual perversion had long been understood to exist in a tautological relationship, such that attention to one naturally and inevitably invited attention to the other. The relationship between incarceration and sexual knowledge had more instrumental underpinnings as well. Because the prison was organized around the imperatives of surveillance and classification, it was uniquely situated to license and even encourage the observation of human behavior, sexual behavior included. Frank Tannenbaum, a labor activist and social reformer who served several prison and jail sentences in the early twentieth century, characterized the prison in 1920 as "the greatest laboratory of human psychology that can be found. It compels men to live social lives . . . under unsocial conditions, and it therefore strains to the breaking-point those things that come naturally to people in a free environment."[26] Indeed, prisons were construed as "laboratories," nearly from their beginning, offering uncommon opportunities for observation and human experimentation. Experiments, often invasive and sometimes dangerous, could be carried out using prisoners as subjects. Investigations deemed otherwise impractical or impossible were pursued behind bars.[27]

Many valued the prison as a laboratory of sexual deviance in particular. Prisons seemed to showcase sexual deviance in abundance; they also made available a population for its scientific study, and investigators took ready advantage of a literally captive subject pool. Prisoners' participation in studies of sexuality, as in many other kinds of investigations and experiments, could be coerced or compelled and often was. Psychiatrist Samuel Kahn was far from alone in drawing on prisoners as subjects but was more candid than most in detailing the methods he used to obtain their cooperation. Kahn needed homosexuals to interview for his 1937 study, *Mentality and Homosexuality*, and he acknowledged that his position as physician at the penitentiary on New York's Welfare Island granted him "a great array of material denied to the average worker in the field."[28] Those who "were not suggestible and who were strong willed," Kahn wrote, were simply "threatened with such suggestions as prolonging their time in institutions, transferring to state institutions, etc."[29] Through Kahn's work and that of many others who used prisoners as subjects, the prison was not simply reflective of the shifting understandings of homosexuality in America; it was deeply implicated in them.

Investigators turned to prisons and prisoners to study the causes and dynamics of deviant sexuality. But as observers came to acknowledge, implicitly and sometimes explicitly, the essence of the problem of prison sex was less the practice of homosexuality among prisoners than its implications for the nature of *hetero*sexuality. Indeed, much of what was at stake in the anxiety over homosexuality in prison concerned its potential to reveal heterosexual identity as fragile, unstable, and, itself, situational. This book, then, looks to one of the most marginalized of American spaces—the prison—and its most stigmatized practice—same-sex sex—to illuminate questions about the cultural and ideological center and the making of the normal. Historians have recently insisted that heterosexuality is as historically constructed as its marked counterpart and have called for a history of heterosexuality.[30] But while deviant sexuality—forced out of hiding, interrogated, surveyed, and policed—leaves a paper trail, the normal covers its tracks. Indeed, the power of the normal depends on making invisible its own constructedness. On studying whiteness, for instance, film scholar Richard Dyer joins many others in noting the difficulty of capturing a subject that so effectively deflects attention from itself that it "seems not to be there as a subject at all."[31] Heterosexuality is at least as elusive. But naturalization does not happen naturally; it requires cultural work. One way to subject the social process of normalization and the categories of identity and experience defined as normal to historical scrutiny it is to examine responses to what might be considered their border problems. Sex among prisoners constituted one such problem that threatened to erode the border of heterosexuality. Efforts to evacuate prison sex of its corrosive meaning for the broader culture, at times intense, expose the framing beneath the edifice of heterosexuality at a key moment in its construction.

:::

Criminal Intimacy examines the sexual world made by prisoners through the course of the nineteenth and twentieth centuries, as well as the efforts to grapple with its meaning and consequences. The question I have been asked most consistently in the course of working on this book has been about the sources available to write such a history. The concern behind the question, of course, is that sources that speak to such a tabooed subject, one presumably protected by powerful institutional interests, must be very scarce. There is a correspondingly curious tendency on the part of people writing about sex in prison, evident from the early nineteenth century through the early twenty-first, to suggest that the subject had never before been broached or even acknowledged. Many accounts of sex in prison began with this claim, often followed by shocked exposé and ethnographic detail. Recent examples of this rhetorical strategy can be found in the discussion surrounding the National Prison Rape Elimination Act of 2003, declaring sexual violence in men's prisons "long ignored," the "most-silent crime," and a "dirty secret."[32]

But like many secrets, the subject of prison sex was an all but open one, almost from the beginning. And like many forms of supposed repression, sex in prison enjoyed an expansive discursive life. Many disciplines and forms of knowledge were applied to the problem of sex between prisoners. Indeed, prisons embraced with enthusiasm all of the emergent professional social sciences of the twentieth century, including psychology and psychiatry, social hygiene, and sociology, and provided opportunities for these new forms of expertise to be developed, deployed, and authorized. This book chronicles the shift in authority over matters both criminological and sexual, from religious reformers to medical doctors, and later to psychologists, psychiatrists, and sociologists. The inherent drama of prison life and the intrigue of life lived behind bars also attracted a wide array of purveyors of popular culture, giving rise to literary, cinematic, and documentary genres both high and low. I have thus been able to draw on a broad range of sources over a long expanse of time, authored by prison reformers, correctional administrators, physicians, psychiatrists, sociologists, social workers, journalists, fiction writers, and filmmakers.

I also draw extensively on representations of prison life written by prisoners themselves. To the extent possible, I have tried to gain access to their point of view and to reconstruct their experiences of and ideas about sexual life in prison, in order to contribute to a larger project that historian Patricia O'Brien has called "the history of the prison from the inside out."[33] The prison was a powerfully imagined space; it also exerted an undeniably material presence and often brutal force in the lives of prisoners. I have tried to do justice to both the discursive and the material histories of incarceration, recognizing the ways in which they are mutually constituted. In so doing, however, I hesitate to summon prisoners to speak the authentic truth of prison life against the more distanced and mediated representations posed by outsiders (although many of them represented themselves in that way). Surely prisoners had a fundamentally different relationship to carceral life than those who were not imprisoned, and it is crucial to keep in mind their profound disempowerment and disenfranchisement. But the circulation of knowledge about prison sexuality was much more fluid than suggested by a model of insiders versus outsiders or one of oppression met by resistance. Prisoners and prison observers, to borrow historian Ann-Louise Shapiro's words, did not represent "two opposing interpretative communities"; rather, they were in constant conversation.[34] Popular and social scientific representations often drew from prisoners' representations, and vice versa. Prisoners participated in constructing the imaginary of prison life, not just in experiencing its reality. They did not stand outside of the discourses about prison and representational strategies surrounding same-sex sex behind bars but were themselves producers of knowledge about prison life.

Neither did prisoners comprise a homogeneous group who spoke in one voice. "Prisoner" is not a coherent identity category, and prisons have always housed diverse communities of inmates who spoke about different experiences, in different voices, and from different perspectives. There are also good reasons to approach prisoners' representations of prison and, especially, their representations of sex behind bars and their relationship to it, with considerable caution and sometimes skepticism. Historians of institutions of social control have learned to read against the grain of the official record and to refuse to take administrators and other professionals at their word, and that critical approach is crucial to historical research on the prison. But prison officials were not the only ones with agendas. Prisoners, too, had every reason to be cagey about the subject of sex and to represent it in strategic, self-serving, or self-protective ways. They were justifiably suspicious of prison administrators and of those they took to be on the side of administrators. As Stephen Donaldson reminds us, "Outlaws . . . are accustomed to secrecy and resistant to prying." Prisoners were justifiably suspicious when it came to matters sexual, as Donaldson noted, since so much was at stake: "Without exception, all sexual activity on the part of prisoners is prohibited by disciplinary codes in each institution, and these codes, unlike state and federal sodomy laws, are frequently enforced with punitive sanctions, including solitary confinement, loss of 'good time,' and denial of parole."[35] At the same time, prisoners have participated in a long history of autobiographical and fiction writing, and both the highly literate and the unlettered have offered powerful and often eloquent testimony to the experience of incarceration and the texture of life behind bars, including its sexual life.[36] I call on that rich material, attending at the same time to the context and circumstances in which it was produced and the audience for which it was intended.

If prisoners were not a homogenous group, neither was the prison a singular entity. That term is used to refer to a wide variety of institutions, including state and federal penitentiaries, minimum, moderate, and maximum security facilities, city and county jails, adult and juvenile reformatories, and penal farms. The experience, philosophy, and architecture of incarceration varied widely by region as well as over time. The prison constituted a literal space and was part of a larger penal system and carceral imaginary. I have tried to be attentive to those differences, while at the same time casting a wide net in considering the representation and experience of sexual life in places of criminal incarceration broadly construed.

I also make an effort to examine the sexual life of both incarcerated men and women, tracking the consonances and dissonances in the sexual cultures of men's and women's prisons and in the representations of and by male and female prisoners. In our current age of mass incarceration, women constitute the fastest growing population in the prison system. But throughout the nineteenth and most of the twentieth centuries, women represented a very small percentage of prisoners. In part for that reason, and perhaps in part due to the discomfort caused by the idea of female criminality, women prisoners received far less attention than did their male counterparts. Indeed, much writing on the prison and prisoners simply assumes that prisoners are male. I have tried not to replicate that assumption in this book, but my imbalanced consideration of men and women reflects both the lopsidedness in the sources available and the asymmetries in the gendered histories themselves.

While this book proceeds in chronological order, beginning in the early nineteenth century and ending in the late twentieth, the subject of sex in prison and its reckonings fails to track neatly according to a conventional historical chronology. The lines of historical demarcation are not sharply distinct when it comes to prison sex, its meanings, and its representations, and I avoid imposing a stronger sense of periodization than is warranted by the evidence. I have tried to attend to the continuities as well as discontinuities in this history, and that commitment can sometimes confound the historian's desire for a timeline.

Chapter 1 thus covers a relatively broad sweep of time, from the early national period to the Progressive era. The book opens in the first decades of the nineteenth century, with the beginning of the widespread practice of incarceration in the early United States and the birth of the modern prison. Exploring the contemporaneous history of the emergence of the prison and concern about sex between prisoners and locating apprehension about sex among prisoners and the sexual possibilities of prisons centrally in the early history of the prison more generally, I argue for their mutually constitutive relationship.

Throughout the first century of its existence, the prison was recognized as a place where perversion was regrettably rampant. By the twentieth century's early decades, the prison gained notoriety as home to perverts. Prison observers in this period took advantage of the new conceptual tools supplied by sexologists to understand homosexuality in its congenital and acquired varieties, as they appeared to take shape behind bars. Chapter 2 examines the importance of the prison in the production of knowledge about sexual identity at the moment of its supposed founding.

Sex between prisoners had long posed a problem of institutional discipline; by the 1940s and 1950s, with the growing influence of the practice of classifying individuals primarily according to sexual object choice and heightened fears of sexual deviance, it posed an epistemological problem as well. Chapter 3 charts the strategies at midcentury to come to terms with the apparent instability of sexual identity in prison. It also explores the burgeoning representations of sex in prison in popular culture and the significant hold that prison sex came to have on the American imagination.

Tracking the convergences and divergences in the new representations of the sexual cultures of male and female prisoners that appeared in the 1960s and 1970s illuminates the distinctly gendered contours of those cultures as well as the different and distinctly gendered fascinations and fears they each elicited. Chapter 4 examines the representation of sex in women's prisons and the attempts to make sense of lesbianism judged to be widespread in women's prisons. Chapter 5 analyzes the newly urgent attention to sexual violence in men's prisons in this period, argues for its inextricability from ideas about race, and considers anxieties about the politicization and criminality of black men in particular.

Prison sexualities refuse normative categories—of heterosexuality, certainly, but of homosexuality as well. The final chapter explores encounters between the sexual culture in the making by newly politicized lesbian and gay activists in the 1970s and 1980s and that of the prison. It examines the understandings, misunderstandings, and sometimes awkward alliances forged between queer prison insiders and outsiders and traces the shifting understandings of "situational" and "true" homosexuality in the context of a newly solidified lesbian and gay identity and the emergence of gay identity politics. In the process, it exposes the participation of gay and lesbian activists in producing and enforcing the homo/heterosexual binary as well as in promoting newly normative understandings of what it meant to be "gay."

A logic of contamination and infection often structured discussions of prison sexuality. When prisoners in the early 1980s began to get sick and die from diseases that would come to be attributed to HIV/AIDS, that logic assumed strikingly literal form. The epilogue explores how ways of thinking about sex in prison, established over the course of two centuries, hampered the ability and willingness to address the HIV/AIDS epidemic in prisons in the 1980s and 1990s. At the same time, reckoning with the epidemic forced a reconsideration of the meaning of sex in prison and its practitioners, unconstrained by notions of sexual identity, which ramified beyond prison walls.

The tendency of prison to unsettle notions of "true" sexuality in all its forms goes some distance toward explaining the seemingly endless fascination and anxiety it elicited, fueling conversation and contestation over the course of nearly two centuries. What people in different periods made of prison's apparently queering effects—the different kinds of trouble that prison sex made for people in different historical moments—is, in broadest strokes, the subject of this book.[37] Among the most common strategies for accommodating prison sex, especially after the mid-twentieth century, was to assert that the lives of prisoners had nothing to do with the lives of those outside prison walls. If anything, the impulse to isolate the prison from meaning, consequence, or correlative in the outside world has intensified in recent years—ironically so, given that the number of incarcerated Americans has expanded so astonishingly in the last twenty-five years, to well over 2 million at the time of this writing.[38] In tracing the preoccupation, at times intense, to come to terms with the meaning and consequences of the sexual life of prisoners, this book gives lie to the notion that the prison ever existed in a space or time apart.

CHAPTER ONE

"An Architecture Adapted to Morals"

The modern American prison was conceived, in the words of an early prison reformer that ring with irony today, as an "architecture adapted to morals."[1] The idea of incarceration as a way to redeem as well as to punish criminals was the invention of the early nineteenth century and of a Christian, reformist, and even utopian imagination. Many of the earliest prison reformers were closely affiliated with churches, some as ministers. The word "penitentiary," of course, derives from an understanding of the prison as a place of penitence, atonement, and self-transformation, and those goals were central to the earliest conception of the carceral mission.

The story of the emergence of the penitentiary has been told by Michel Foucault as marking a shift in the grip of punishment from its violent hold on the prisoner's body to new demands on the mind and soul.[2] Still, the prisoner's body was a site of urgent concern for the first prison philosophers, architects, reformers, and administrators, and remained so. From the prison's beginnings in the early nineteenth century and extending into the twentieth, prison officials struggled with a vexing paradox: the new philosophy and architecture of incarceration that they endowed with so many redemptive virtues seemed to be uniquely adapted to, and even encouraging of, vice. Even more troubling, rather than the consequence of a correctable flaw, the problem seemed to inhere in the design of the prison itself. "Immorality," prison reformer

15

Thomas Mott Osborne noted with resignation in 1916, "springs from the very nature of the institution."[3]

Osborne offered this uncharacteristically defeatist comment from the vantage point of nearly a century's worth of prison reform efforts and their repeated, cyclical failure.[4] But many noted this distressing feature of prison life, one that struck at the essence of the institution, almost from its inception. The practice of incarceration, collecting together people convicted of crimes into a sex-segregated environment, seemed inevitably to give rise to immorality in myriad forms. The Boston Prison Discipline Society's first annual report in 1826 documented the many "vices of prisoners" observed in the Commonwealth's early prison, including "drunkenness, gambling, profane swearing, fighting, combinations against society, insurrections, [the making of] false keys." "Unnatural crime"—among the most common of nineteenth-century terms to denote same-sex sexual practices—concluded this baleful list.[5]

Writings by early prison administrators and reformers suggest that concern about and even obsessive preoccupation with the possibility of sex between prisoners, especially between the male inmates that constituted the vast majority of prisoners, structured ideas about the modern prison and determined its first architectural designs and administration. Rather than peripheral to the workings of the early carceral regime or the regrettable by-product of sex-segregated incarceration, same-sex sex was constitutive of the modern prison, informing the preoccupations of its designers, determining its modes of scrutiny, and structuring the inmate culture that would come to take shape there. Sex was constitutive of the modern prison; the prison, I argue, was constitutive, in turn, of important shifts in understanding sex. Cloistered and private by design, prisons paradoxically made same-sex sex newly visible, public, and available for observation. Prisons accordingly demanded new ways of accounting for and representing same-sex sex, as ventured by the first penological "experts" as well as by early prisoner-scribes and autobiographers.

Sex and the Design of the Nineteenth-Century Prison

Charting a history of the prison works against the grain of the deeply taken-for-granted, almost naturalized status that prisons have acquired in a remarkably short period of time. Indeed, the concept of imprisonment as the primary form of punishment is today imbued with such self-evidence and seeming inevitability it can be surprising even to recall that it has a history. Prior to the early nineteenth century, however, imprisonment was rarely used to punish convicted criminals. The jails and prisons that had existed for several centuries in England and served as models for the early American colonists were, for the most part, places of brief detention for debtors, witnesses to crimes, and those awaiting trial or execution. People convicted of relatively minor crimes were punished by the imposition of fines, public humiliation in the stockades, and corporal punishment including branding, flogging, and mutilation. The English Criminal Codes inherited by the colonists listed a great number of capital crimes for more serious offenses. Treason, murder, robbery, burglary, arson, sodomy, rape, and witchcraft were all felonies punishable by death.[6]

The prison was envisioned as an enlightened, humane, and progressive alternative to capital and corporal punishments and shaming practices common in colonial America. While neither execution nor public punishment disappeared in the early republic, they were increasingly overshadowed by incarceration, especially in the northeastern and mid-Atlantic states.[7] In 1794, in response to petitions from Quaker reformers, Pennsylvania substituted imprisonment for the penalty of death for all crimes except premeditated murder. New York followed suit in 1795. Those states commissioned the construction of prisons—Auburn Penitentiary in upstate New York was built between 1816 and 1819, and Eastern State Penitentiary in Philadelphia was approved by the state legislature in 1821 and opened in 1829—which became models, in architectural design and penological philosophy, for most of the prisons built in the United States, Europe, and throughout the Americas during the nineteenth century.

These early prisons in Pennsylvania and New York were at the center of a vibrant transatlantic and trans-American conversation about the new idea of the penitentiary and the new philosophy of incarceration.[8] Their fame extended far beyond the world of prison reformers. Eastern State and Auburn penitentiaries were among the most popular tourist sites in the new nation, attracting distinguished European visitors including Charles Dickens and Alexis de Tocqueville, the latter commissioned by the French government in 1831 to study the American penal system, in collaboration with Gustave Auguste de Beaumont. Although these new American prisons drew on European antecedents, they were understood by contemporaries to be novel in aim and design. "Europeans traveled to the new world to examine an American creation," historian David Rothman writes, "not to see a minor variant on an old world theme."[9]

Central to these model prisons were the ideals of isolation, solitude, and separation—as techniques of disciplinary control and forms of punishment, certainly, but also, in the minds of early prison philosophers, as opportunities for rehabilitation through remorseful self-reflection. Prison architects and planners in New York and Pennsylvania differed over how best to achieve the goal of isolating prisoners from one another. The designers of the Philadelphia prison were committed to a program of radical separation, and the inmates at Eastern State Penitentiary were held in strict solitary confinement in individual cells, twenty-four hours a day. The fortress-like prison building was circular, with high perimeter walls and seven cell-lined corridors radiating outward from a central observatory rotunda. Each cell opened onto its own small walled exercise yard. Prisoners were supplied with a Bible and with tools and materials for work in their cells, where they ate, lived, and slept alone. With the rare exception of carefully screened visitors, they were allowed to see no human being. Since prisoners were handed their meals through a small slot in their cell door, they rarely if ever even saw prison staff. Most important, they were never to lay eyes on their fellow inmates. When new prisoners were taken to their cells, they were hooded in order to conceal their identities. Prisoners unable to recognize each other, it was hoped, would be able to leave behind their criminal associations and would return to the streets having formed no new ones.

Eastern State Penitentiary was not modeled on Jeremy Bentham's famous Panopticon, another circular prison design proposed in 1791. In that design the prison overseer, located in a central tower, would command an unobstructed view of every backlit cell, arranged, in Foucault's words, like "so many small theatres, in which each actor is alone, perfectly individualized and constantly visible," and creating an impression among inmates of omniscient surveillance.[10] Although different in architectural plan, the Philadelphia prison aspired to Bentham's ideal of total observation, control, and disciplinary efficiency. Prisoners could be viewed at any time through the small holes in their cell doors but could see neither fellow prisoners nor their keepers. In the minds of Pennsylvania prison planners, that surveillance and separation rendered unnecessary the brutal corporal punishment of prisons in the past and inculcated the desired habits of self-scrutiny and self-discipline.

In contrast to Philadelphia's program of total isolation, New York's Auburn Penitentiary pursued what came to be known as the "congregate system." Auburn prisoners slept alone in tiny individual cells by night and worked together in groups by day. At all times, however, they were held to a strict code of absolute silence, forbidden even to exchange glances with fellow inmates and commanded to move about the prison with eyes cast downward.[11] "The bodies of the prisoners are together," prison reformers Enoch Cobb Wines and Theodore Dwight observed in their 1867 investigation, "but their souls are apart; and, while there is a material society, there is a mental solitude."[12]

The relative merits of what became known as the "Philadelphia system" and the "Auburn system," named after the two prisons in which they were most famously applied, were matters of heated and acrimonious debate among prison administrators, reformers, and other observers in the early to mid-nineteenth century. Critics of Philadelphia's solitary system charged that the total isolation of Eastern State Penitentiary violated human nature to the degree that it drove prisoners insane. Charles Dickens visited the Philadelphia prison in 1842 and published a scathing condemnation of its solitary system in his travel account, *American Notes*. "This slow and daily tampering with the mysteries of the brain" resulting from the prison's system of total solitude, Dickens proposed, was "immeasurably worse than any torture of the body."[13]

The Auburn model seemed by comparison to offer a modest concession to the human need for sociability, allowing prisoners the comfort of each other's company, however silent and surveyed, while they worked side by side during the day and marched in lockstep. Auburn also offered the practical advantage of its more economically constructed tiered-cell design and the promise of greater profits from its system of congregate convict labor. Auburn's rule of silence, however, was enforced with the lash, and critics of the New York system condemned the flogging of prisoners as an unfortunate relic of a more brutal and bloody past, inconsistent with "the spirit of an enlightened age."[14] Others believed that corporal punishment, while effective in an immediate sense in soliciting the prisoner's submission, failed to produce more meaningful and lasting change. As William Crawford reported to the British government in his detailed investigation and comparison of the competing American prison systems in 1835, "the whip inflicts immediate pain, but solitude inspires permanent terror."[15]

While the distinctions between these two rival penal philosophies and prison designs were matters of great importance for their partisans in the first half of the nineteenth century, the similarities of their most fundamental and guiding philosophies are more striking than their differences in retrospective view. Both systems held isolation and separation to be paramount. Prisoners were to be isolated from the tempting pleasures and contaminating dangers of the outside world. At least as important, they were to be separated from the corrupting influence of each other's company. Early prison reformers and keepers decried what they often termed "the intercourse of criminals" permitted by the unsupervised congregation of inmates.

Imbued with broad meaning in this period, "intercourse" was used by prison reformers and administrators to refer to any verbal exchange or interaction between and among prisoners. Its dangers were many. Inmates who were allowed to intermingle and converse might foment plans for insurrection and escape. Free exchange among prisoners also allowed them to teach each other the tricks of their respective criminal trades. Boston prison reformers recalled the evils of the "old Prisons" of Europe and colonial America, in which "old thieves taught young thieves . . . how to pick pockets and pick locks; how to burn houses and break stores; how to make and set the matches; how to make the false keys; where were the most exposed places, and the richest plunder; who kept money in their houses; in what part of the room it was kept; when the men of the house were away from home."[16] Prison administrators and reformers also worried that inmates who were allowed to congregate would form underworld associations behind bars that they might continue to pursue on the streets on their release.

Nineteenth-century prison officials were especially anxious to curtail opportunities for intercourse of any sort between male and female prisoners. Mere conversation between male and female inmates was understood to be "a monster evil," inevitably "corrupting and pernicious."[17] Such opportunities were abetted by the long-standing practice of housing men and women in adjacent quarters in the same institution. Prison reformers had been appalled by the access that male and female inmates were granted each other in early modern European prisons and jails, some of which supported a thriving traffic in prostitution. A reform movement for separate women's institutions began in the United States in the 1870s, driven, in part, by the concern about female vulnerability to rape, coercive sex, and harassment by male prisoners and guards. But, as inspectors Wines and Dwight pointed out, "in most of the states, there are not female convicts enough to warrant the erection and maintenance of prisons for them alone."[18] Many prisons in the later nineteenth and early twentieth centuries continued to confine men and women under the same roof, providing possibilities for their interaction, consensual as well as coercive. The New York Prison Association's 1845 report charged, for instance, that "too many opportunities exist for a *promiscuous intercourse of the sexes*" in the City Penitentiary on Blackwell's Island in Manhattan's East River.[19] Thirty years later, a state investigation reported that the

Blackwell's Island prison still permitted "too much intermingling of male and female prisoners."[20] An inmate in the Tennessee State Penitentiary decades later still, Horace Woodroof recalled that in the 1920s, "the presence of female prisoners in the prison occasionally caused a sex problem." Though the women's section was "completely isolated and boarded off by a high wooden fence," and women and men worked in separate factories, Woodroof noted, "hot-blooded male prisoners made desperate attempts to break into the no-man's-land" and occasionally made "actual contact" with female prisoners. "A man would manage to climb the fence into the female section, or they would meet somehow during work in the mills."[21] Pregnancies were not uncommon in nineteenth-century prisons, and they stood as embarrassing testimony to the inability of prison officials, regardless of their commitments to sexual separation, to segregate male and female prisoners successfully.[22]

Sex between male and female inmates, often housed adjacently but separately, usually took some ingenuity and resourcefulness. Prisoners had easier access, of course, to members of their own sex. Concern about sex between prisoners haunted administrators of early prisons, although evidence of that concern, and even acknowledgement of the possibility of sex between prisoners, can be difficult to detect in their published reports. While prison officials had a robust vocabulary at their disposal to articulate alarm about the corrupting contact between male and female prisoners, the linguistic conventions of the day were markedly limited when it came to identifying and condemning sex between women or between men. Prison reformers and administrators often resorted to innuendo and suggestion, presumably comprehensible to their contemporaries because of a distinctive equivocation reserved for these particular acts. What is often taken by historians to be a form of Victorian reticence or evidence of sexual repression was, in fact, an expressive (if limited and deliberately unspecified) vocabulary unto itself that made it possible to name same-sex sexuality, paradoxically, by announcing its unnamability. Sodomy (along with bestiality, with which it was sometimes linked) was specified in many colonial legal codes as the "crime not fit to be named"; to refer to a crime as something so horrible that it could not be identified was thereby to identify it.[23] This telling refusal of specificity—apparent in references to unutterable abominations, unspeakable acts, and unmentionable vices— appeared in prison writing throughout the nineteenth century.

Concern about the sexual possibilities in sex-segregated institutions was in large part responsible for fueling the early-nineteenth-century obsession with isolating prisoners from each other. The system of perfect

solitary confinement envisioned at Pennsylvania's Eastern State Penitentiary and upheld for a time after its completion, valued as a practice that reformers hoped would encourage reflection, remorse, and ultimately moral
reclamation, also offered the more practical advantage of prohibiting sex
between prisoners. But total isolation raised vexing sexual problems of
its own. An early-twentieth-century history of the Philadelphia prison
noted that "the separate system of confinement did not make possible any
irregular sex practice except masturbation."[24] Few nineteenth-century
prison officials, however, especially those in the early decades of the century, would have taken much heart in that exception. Freighted with consequence in this period, masturbation was believed to exact a serious toll
on the physical health and welfare, as well as on the moral constitution of
the "self-abusing" individual. By the early nineteenth century, masturbation was understood to be a disease of the body as well as the soul and
was held accountable for a range of physical and mental ailments including epilepsy, blindness, impotency, loss of memory, rickets, consumption, and insanity.[25] If unrepressed, many believed, masturbation could
be fatal. In accounting for five deaths among the inmate population of a
New Jersey penitentiary in 1838, the resident physician reported that "one
destroyed himself by Onanism."[26] Utterly debilitating to the individual,
masturbation was also understood to be socially demoralizing, sapping
the larger community as well as the offending individual of energy, vigor,
and moral rectitude. Masturbation was also often linked with sodomy,
in a relationship that was posited sometimes as causally linked and occasionally as overlapping. A colonial New Haven law in 1646, for example,
declared that public masturbation "tends to the sin of Sodomy, if it be
not one kind of it."[27] That presumed link endured centuries later, fueling
concerns that prison life gave rise to these intertwined sins.

Early prison reports alluded to the persistent, even ineradicable problem of masturbation among male prisoners. The New Jersey prison doctor
linked the practice directly to prison and prisoners, identifying "Onanism" as "the vice of solitary confinement" and observing that prisoners so
confined almost invariably "give up to their depraved propensities."[28] The
resident physician of San Quentin's prison condemned masturbation in his
first report in 1877 as "a vice that undermines the constitution and debases
the moral instincts more than all other causes combined."[29] Officials of
Eastern State Penitentiary tried to frighten inmates out of the practice
by posting a printed notice in each cell detailing the "numerous" and "terrible" effects of "self-abuse." Habitual practitioners of "this destructive
vice" could expect to suffer "derangement of the digestion, respiration,

circulation and absorption of the secretions," followed by "derangements of the nervous system," "destruction of the intellectual faculties," and eventual insanity. "That insidious and fatal disease, pulmonary consumption, terminating in speedy death," the notice read, "is a common result." The plaque concluded by imploring prisoners who had become "addicted to this loathsome vice here described" to "*Stop, at once Stop!*"[30]

Some prison officials defended their institutions from association with masturbation, observing that its practice was limited neither to the space of the prison nor to its occupants. "Prisons are not the monopolists of these forms of vice," New York prison reformers reminded themselves, "and it cannot be expected that they shall be eradicated here, while even among persons outside of prison walls, and of respectable repute, they notoriously exercise a baleful sway."[31] But most were forced to conclude that the isolation and idleness of prison life provided the perfect conditions for a veritable culture of masturbation to take hold. In 1840, a prison physician reported with woeful resignation, "as may be expected where so many are confined, there is still much of this solitary vice."[32]

Promiscuity and Pedagogy

Known as the "solitary vice," masturbation seemed to be the inevitable result of the solitary systems of incarceration styled in the early nineteenth century. Opportunities for more sociable forms of vice, including sex between prisoners, increased during the course of the nineteenth century, as the reformers' dream of perfect isolation was eclipsed by the fact of increasingly overcrowded prisons and as rehabilitative ideals gave way to custodial and financial realities. Prisons and other carceral institutions including jails and reformatories proliferated in the course of the nineteenth century, but they failed to keep pace with the rate of incarceration. The number of prisoners rose in conjunction with the periodic economic busts endemic to that industrializing century, as well as with the disruptions and new forms of racial control following the Civil War. As the operation of prisons during most of the nineteenth century was determined more by the calculus of how to house the greatest number of inmates at the lowest cost than by philosophical commitments to solitary confinement, prison populations swelled. As early as 1828, Boston prison reformers reported that in New York City's Bellevue penitentiary, the night rooms "have remained so crowded that the convicts could not lie down upon the floor without mingling their limbs in one solid mass."[33] By the time French emissaries Alexis de Tocqueville and Gustave de Beaumont toured Auburn prison in 1831, just a little more than a decade after the founding of that model institution, they observed that inmates shared the tiny cells designed for solitary nighttime confinement, measuring only seven feet long and three and one-half feet wide. Perhaps alluding to the sexual possibilities created by overcrowding, Tocqueville and Beaumont declared the practice of double-celling "of all combinations the most unfortunate." "It would have been better to throw fifty criminals in the same room," they wrote, "than to separate them two by two."[34] By 1866, Philadelphia's Eastern State Penitentiary, the institution most famous for its solitary system, routinely confined two prisoners in cells intended for one.[35] By the turn of the twentieth century, few traces remained of the original model prisons beyond their forbidding architecture.

The number of female prisoners, always very small relative to males, rose as well during this period. Estelle Freedman notes that the conviction and imprisonment of women soared during and after the Civil War, in accordance with the rising criminalization of female moral behavior.[36] The small but growing number of women incarcerated in the nineteenth century were rarely if ever treated according to the principles of solitary confinement and isolation deemed so important by prison reformers, architects, and administrators. Even when held in the same institutions as men, as they usually were, female inmates typically lived under very different conditions. Probably due to a combination of factors—the relatively small numbers of female prisoners and the lack of faith in their redeemability— women incarcerated in the nineteenth century were typically spared the practice of isolation, the rule of silence, or convict labor—all hallmarks of the new philosophy of incarceration. Historian Nichole Hahn Rafter observes that while women were "exempted from the most extreme forms of regimentation" characteristic of many nineteenth-century men's prisons, they suffered "other forms of deprivation."[37] While men's prisons were marked by solitary confinement and often brutal corporal disciplinary punishment, women's prisons revealed "a pattern of overcrowding, harsh treatment, and sexual abuse."[38] Often confined together in close, noisy, and congested quarters, women were typically subjected to neglect rather than the strict surveillance that prevailed in the model male institutions. When New York's Auburn Prison first opened, for instance, it simply confined its twenty to thirty female prisoners together in a one-room attic.[39]

Women's prisons and jails shared one important feature with men's that especially alarmed prison reformers: the chaotic heterogeneity and indiscriminate mixing of inmate populations—criminal and innocent, young and old, and occasionally black and white. In Auburn Prison, where "the vagrant girl is lodged with the brazen prostitute," one observer noted ominously in 1870, "every thing tends lower."[40] Nineteenth-century prison investigators were horrified to find that many institutions replicated the most pernicious features of earlier prisons that they had tried so hard to eradicate, only a few decades after their founding. The Boston Prison Discipline Society referred to the "enormous evils arising from a promiscuous intercourse of villains of all ages and degrees of guilt" in its very first report in 1826.[41]

Prison reformers were especially concerned about the cohabitation of inmates convicted of minor charges, especially those held as witnesses or imprisoned for debt, with those convicted of serious offenses. Wines and Dwight cited a disturbing observation made by the inspector of the Philadelphia county prison system, who found "convicts, burglars, murderers, young and old, guilty and innocent, black and white, all having unrestricted access to each other's cells."[42] Investigators in 1869 likewise found "defects of a grave and glaring character" in New York prisons: "They found the prisoners, including the man of gray hairs and the mere child, the murderer and the vagrant, the expert and the novice in crime, all herded together, and subjected to influences the most corrupting and ruinous."[43] In the Philadelphia prison, once the site of such lofty dreams of redemptive solitude, "all ages and sexes were imprisoned together" by 1902. The cast of characters listed by a prison reformer was by then woefully familiar: "The novice in crime, the hardened criminal, the debtor, . . . the vagrant, the drunkard, and the convict."[44] Julian Hawthorne, son of Nathaniel Hawthorne and a popular author himself, wrote in 1914 of the "promiscuous herding together of prisoners" in the Atlanta Federal Penitentiary where he served a year-long sentence for mail fraud: "No effort is made to separate the old from the young, the educated from the ignorant; the hardened sinners from the impressionable youths or newcomers; or (at Atlanta, except in the cells), the negroes from the whites."[45] The effects of the latter combination were, in Hawthorne's mind, damaging to both: "The negro, being more ignorant as a rule, falls more readily into degraded vices; the white man, being as a rule the dominant element . . . , masters the will of the negro, but . . . does not erect barriers against the latter's subtle corruption."[46]

"Promiscuous" was the word used most often to characterize the combination of inmates brought together in early prisons. In its nineteenth-century usage, especially in the early decades of that century, "promiscuity" connoted any congregation of people of different sorts, the association of whom might have unruly or dangerous consequences.[47] The term captured the sense among early prison officials that the problem of prison populations lay not simply in their heterogeneity but in the troubling associations, seductive appeal, and coercive potential inherent in the intimate association of unequals—older and younger, criminal and innocent, knowing and naive. Prison reformers employed pedagogical metaphors to express deep concern about the corrupting influence that prisoners exerted on each other, and references to prisons as seminaries, schools, and reformatories of vice, as "schools of hell and hideous depravity," and as "high schools of iniquity" abounded in nineteenth-century prison records and reform writing.[48]

Behind evocations of the promiscuity of prison populations and the dangerous pedagogy practiced behind bars lay the specter of seduction and, specifically, the concern that older prisoners would seduce younger ones into a life of crime and school them in their criminal ways. Some prisoners confirmed these fears of the seductive appeal of crime and criminals. In his autobiography, *Seventeen Years in the Underworld*, Wellington Scott recalled his first jail stay: "I entered jail an amateur in crime and stayed there a little over three months. In that time I learned more of the devious methods which crooks use against society than I had ever dreamed of knowing." Scott recalled the attractions of "men grown old in the underworld," whose "tales were strong with the flavor of adventure. They fascinated me and I looked up to the old crooks as men to be envied."[49] Josiah Flynt, who would go on to produce some of the earliest ethnographic accounts of tramps and hoboes, likewise described the jail in Buffalo, New York, where he spent his first time behind bars in the late nineteenth century. There, Flynt recounted, "from morning till night the 'old hands' in crime were exchanging stories of their exploits, while the younger prisoners sat about them with open mouths and eyes of wonder, greedily taking in every syllable."[50]

Prison reformers and officials were concerned about more literal forms of seduction as well. Hierarchical differences between prisoners were imbued with both dangerous erotic potential and coercive sexual sway, and the association of unequals was understood to give rise to sexual seduction and predation as well as to criminal instruction. Like criminal pedagogy, sex between prisoners, especially male, was understood to arise from the asymmetries of power that arose in heterogeneous prison populations and was viewed as the reprehensible but predictable result of bringing together the strong and the weak, the hardened and the naive, the old and the young in dangerous intimacy. Among the most detestable ways that "the old corrupted the young," the Boston Prison Discipline Society noted in unusually candid terms in 1841, was "by practicing the sin of Sodom."[51] Sex between prisoners in these early years was seen as the consequence of the promiscuous mingling of prison populations, at once unnatural, unpardonable, and unsurprising.

Those assumptions were evident in Reverend Louis Dwight's alarmed broadside, the first detailed documentation of sex between prisoners, written in 1826. A member of the American Bible Society and founder and secretary of the Boston Prison Discipline Society, one of the nation's first prison reform organizations, Dwight visited prisons and jails on a horseback tour through New England and along the eastern seaboard states between Massachusetts and Georgia and was horrified by what he observed. Dwight's subsequent report was circulated only among "men in authority," presumably the growing cadre of prison officials and religious reformers, "with the expectation of rousing their indignation and strength." Its contents were deemed "too horrible to be exhibited more publicly," and its existence was only alluded to in published reports.[52]

Dwight documented prison conditions of squalor and brutality, in which prisoners were clothed in rags and held in chains. His report was dedicated primarily, however, to providing "melancholy testimony to establish one general fact," so demanding of attention as to require expression in capital letters, that "THE SIN OF SODOM IS THE VICE OF PRISONERS, AND BOYS ARE THE FAVORITE PROSTITUTES."[53] In recounting in detail the sexual subjection in which older convicts held younger ones, Dwight violated early-nineteenth-century standards whereby, as he acknowledged, "the mere suggestion of the subject is enough." But his observations apparently so alarmed him that he felt it necessary to break from the customary nineteenth-century language of unspeakability and to provide extensive testimony from his prison investigations and interviews with inmates. He reported asking one older convict "if he ever knew a boy [to] retain his integrity in a Penitentiary," to which the man replied, "Never."[54] Dwight documented the techniques of seduction employed by older inmates, who offered gifts and favors to younger ones: "No art was left untried, to get the boy into the same room and into the same bed." Sometimes, a relationship of intimate attachment would follow: "Meals and every dainty would be shared together, and they would, in many cases, afterwards, seem to have an undivided existence." In other cases, sex was achieved by brute force. One boy told Dwight that he had submitted to an older inmate, "Pat, an Irishman," because "he choked me! He was stronger than I!" In Dwight's account and in many that followed, sex between prisoners took place between boys and "grey-haired villains," who subjugated them through seduction, coercion, or outright violence.[55]

Far fewer women than men were incarcerated in American prisons and jails in the nineteenth century, especially in early decades, and very few accounts of female inmates in this period were published.[56] Louis Dwight appears not to have visited the few women held in prisons in his early investigation of penal institutions. Nor did Enoch Cobb Wines and Theodore Dwight provide much comment on female prisoners in their massive report on state prisons and jails commissioned by the New York Prison Association and published in 1867. Finding "very few, usually no women-convicts" in her investigation of state prisons in the Northeast, Dorothea Dix devoted only an appendix to their conditions in her 1845 survey.[57]

It was not until 1913, almost a century after Dwight's report, that the first documentation of romantic and sexual relationships between female inmates was published. Psychologist Margaret Otis's study of young women in a New Jersey reformatory reflected some shifts in register and tone that marked her distance from religiously motivated prison reformers like Dwight and identified her as a member of a new generation of scientifically trained penologists. Yet Otis proposed that attachments between female inmates, like those between the male prisoners observed by Dwight, were also sparked by difference resulting from the combinations of women found in institutional populations. Rather than age, criminal status, and physical size—the hierarchical differences between male inmates that were understood to give rise to sexual attraction, seduction, and predation—the differences most often encoded and charged with sexual possibility among female inmates were those of race.[58]

Otis offered the first in what would become a long line of accounts of the propensity of black and white women to form romantic and sexual relationships in institutions. This "form of perversion," Otis noted, had received no public attention but was "well known among workers in reform schools and institutions for delinquent girls."[59] Female inmates no doubt pursued intraracial relationships as well, but they remained largely invisible to Otis and others, who likely viewed them as natural and benign friendships. Interracial relationships between inmates, in contrast—rendered hypervisible by their racial difference—invited intense scrutiny and were viewed as nearly always and inevitably sexual. Representing the passionate attachments and "love-making between the white and colored girls" as typically overwrought and "silly," Otis allowed that some were driven by intense emotion and that "sometimes the love is very real and seems almost ennobling."[60]

Among the striking features of Otis's account was her identification of white inmates not as the passive recipients of black inmates' advances but as fully reciprocating partners who sometimes even initiated those "unfortunate attachments." To account for the attraction of white women to black women, Otis explained that relationships between them were structured by a gendered erotics of racial difference, speculating that "the difference in color, in this case, takes the place of difference in sex."[61] Otis reported that one white inmate "admitted that the colored girl she loved seemed the man, and thought it was so in the case of the others."[62] Writers followed Otis's lead for decades to come, explaining interracial lesbian attraction through racialized gender inversion.[63] These accounts reflected the denial of femininity and attribution of masculinity to black women in the broader culture.[64] They also tamed anxieties about race mixing and lesbianism by depicting interracial relations between women, and white women's desire for black women in particular, as essentially heterosexual. As historian Estelle Freedman notes, "In this interpretation, white women were not really lesbians, for they were attracted to men, for whom Black women temporarily substituted."[65]

Nineteenth- and early-twentieth-century prison investigators and officials understood sex between prisoners as an inevitable consequence of the unnatural mixing of inmates of different type and status—differences and hierarchies that were seen somehow either to naturally incline them to each other or to make them vulnerable to the other, or sometimes both. Men would be drawn to boys' vulnerability and attractiveness, and boys would be attracted to men's worldliness or be forced to submit to their assertions of power and physical strength. Less culturally explicable but equally undeniable to officials and observers in female institutions, white girls and women would be attracted to black girls and women and, presumably, vice versa (although curiously, the attraction of black to white women drew considerably less comment). Otis's analysis, and the many similar accounts that followed in its wake and echoed its logic, was remarkable for its refusal to rely on cultural stereotypes of the supposed natural libidinousness of African American women to explain interracial relationships between female inmates. In part, what appeared to be a striking departure from those assumptions may be explained by the ready attribution of sexual precocity to white inmates, invited by their status both as criminal and as working class. The fact that many female inmates were

incarcerated for crimes governed by moral and sexual codes, such as lewd-
ness, wantonness, and prostitution, would have exempted them from assumptions of sexual propriety otherwise accorded white women.[66]

The markedly gendered dangers attributed to different forms of mixing in men's and women's prisons had several likely sources. Some could
be traced to the material differences between women's and men's institutions, differences that were ultimately constitutive of the sexual practices
and dynamics that took shape in each. Because of the kinds of crimes of
impropriety and sexual transgression that women were typically incarcerated for, and because many institutions for women placed upper age limits
on those who might be sent there, female inmates were more likely than
inmates in men's institutions to be close in age, predominantly in their
teens and twenties.[67] Fewer opportunities existed, therefore, for older and
younger women to mix. Conversely, there were probably more opportunities for black and white women to mix in prison than there were for
black and white men. While African Americans were disproportionately
represented in both men's and women's prisons, Rafter finds that black
women were more heavily represented in female state prison populations than were black men within male prisoner groups, in part because
judges were often disinclined to sentence white women to penal institutions.[68] The more heavily populated men's prisons were probably also
more intensely committed to racial segregation (as well as other forms
of classification), perhaps making race mixing among male prisoners less
common.[69]

The gendered dangers recognized by Dwight and Otis also reflected the
gendered anxieties of their respective historical moments. Dwight's and
other investigators' warnings about the dangers of intergenerational mixing between male prisoners presaged a growing chorus in the nineteenth
century, continuing into the early twentieth, which cautioned against the
contaminating influence of older men on impressionable boys and young
men. Many who lamented the "boy problem" feared that male youths
were being steered away from the responsibilities of virtuous, republican
manhood and toward corruption and debauchery and urged their protection.[70] Otis's focus on women's interracial relationships in 1913, published
as the Jim Crow system was consolidating in the South and exhortations
against "race suicide" were at their height, coincided and resonated with
a larger cultural anxiety about miscegenation and the racial and sexual
purity of white girls and women.

These assumptions about the sexual dangers of mixing led to the first
efforts on the part of prison officials to classify prisoners and house like

types together. As early as 1829, the Boston Prison Discipline Society proposed that "the prospect of improvement in morals depends, in some degree, upon the construction of buildings; and that among certain classes of persons, and for certain purposes, separate sleeping rooms should be provided."[71] Classification by type was a key penological imperative, and prisons pioneered this process that would be replicated in many other types of custodial institutions, including asylums, hospitals, and schools.

In the nineteenth and early twentieth centuries, the distinctions among inmates deemed most important were those of sex, age, race, and severity of offense. Margaret Otis observed that the relationships forged between white and black female inmates led to the decision to segregate them in separate cottages and to keep them apart "both when at work and when at play."[72] This was the case as well at the Bedford Hills prison for women in upstate New York, following an investigation in 1914 that revealed "a disquieting pattern of 'unfortunate attachments' between black and white women in the reformatory."[73]

While race was freighted with sexual significance among female inmates, age was the suspect category among men. The first reformatory for juvenile boys opened in New York City in 1825, and similar efforts followed in other states, although the practice of incarcerating boys and men together continued well into the twentieth century.[74] Primary among the reasons that younger inmates were segregated from older ones were concerns about their sexual vulnerability. Donald Lowrie, sentenced to fifteen years at San Quentin prison in 1901, documented the existence of "Kid Alley" in which young inmates were segregated for their own protection.[75] Lowrie described San Quentin's "Kid Alley" as abutting "Crazy Alley" and "China Alley," suggesting that classification and segregation of inmates by mental state and by race as well as by age was practiced in this prison at the turn of the century.

Importantly, though, early prisons did not classify or segregate prisoners according to sexual type. Sex between prisoners was believed to be the dreadful but predictable result of the pairings of inmates of unequal and unlike types. While those pairings resulted in what some would begin to call "perversion" by the early twentieth century, they were, importantly, not born of it. This understanding certainly did not incline prison officials to a laissez-faire or accommodating attitude toward same-sex sexual practices, about which they were unequivocally and unanimously unforgiving. While harsh in their judgment, however, early prison observers failed to direct their ire toward any particular type of person. Dwight's alarmed charge that "THE SIN OF SODOM IS THE VICE

OF PRISONERS" reflected, in condensed form, understandings of same-sex sex shared by his early-nineteenth-century contemporaries. In representing sex between men as sinful, unnatural, and revolting, and describing those who partook as "guilty of Sodomy," Dwight wrote from a transitional moment in which same-sex sex was understood concurrently as a sin, a vice, and a crime. Yet, nothing in his report suggested that this kind of perversion illuminated anything about its practitioner's identity or essence. Sodomy was initiated by the older and "lustful," but failed to characterize a particular type of person any more specifically.

Almost a century later, Margaret Otis similarly declined to identify the "perversion" she encountered among reform school girls as the attribute of any particular type of girl. In fact, she countered the assumption, no doubt invited by new concern about the supposed sexual promiscuity of "feebleminded" girls, that these relationships might be predictably indulged in by the institution's "defective girls."[76] Proposing provocatively that "mental defect does not explain everything," Otis ventured that "the reverse might rather be said to be the truth. Some of the girls indulging in this love for the colored have, perhaps, the most highly developed intellectual ability of any girls of the school."[77] By 1913, when Otis published her observations, she might have called on an emerging science of sexology to specify the nature of the "perversion" of same-sex crushes among reform school girls. While the influence of this new field is evident in her choice of the term "perversion," however, Otis attributed the girls' attractions to a perverse sexual object choice with a longer American history: the "habit of 'nigger-loving.'" This expression was in much wider circulation in this time and place than "homosexuality" and was presumably more familiar to readers in this historical moment than same-sex desire.[78] Indeed, weighted as it was with broader cultural anxieties about racial mixing, Otis's depiction of interracial sexual relationships might have been so arresting to some readers as to eclipse altogether the aspect of homosexuality between girl inmates.

Neither, though, were expressions of same-sex sexuality among nineteenth- and early-twentieth-century prisoners understood simply as "acts," either criminal or sinful and devoid of meaning for sexual subjectivity, as some historians have interpreted Foucault's observations about a preidentitarian historical moment.[79] Nor were they contained entirely under the regimes of law and religion that many historians have identified as the defining sexual jurisdictions before the period designated as "modern." Both Dwight and Otis warned that these forms of perversion, however free-floating in the communities of prisoners they observed, might be habit-forming. And both recognized that same-sex sexual behavior in prison, if not indicative of a type of person or a sexual "orientation," could signal (or, probably more likely, produce) a sexual inclination or disposition. Dwight quoted a former prisoner who told him of "boys" in prison, "who in consequence of a criminal association with the profligate and vile, have, in less than three months, become so perfectly brutalized, as publicly to glory in every species of abomination."[80] And Otis reported that one young female inmate explained to her that, "when you have been in the habit of having a girl love, and she goes away, you have to get another; you just can't get along without thinking of one girl more than another."[81] Neither Dwight nor Otis specified the practitioners of same-sex sex as a sexual type, but both anticipated an understanding of same-sex sex as constitutive of predilection or preference, if not identity, which would come to characterize "modern" sexuality. Separated by nearly a century, their reports underline the markedly uneven trajectory of that transition.[82] They suggest as well that the prison was an unusual, perhaps singular site that made visible the habit-forming if not quite yet subject-forming effects of repeated same-sex practices.

Early Prison Narratives and "The Real Thing"

Prison officials and administrators were not alone in reflecting on and producing knowledge about the new carceral institution and its inmates. Prisoners, too, were compelled to write about the experience of confinement from their perspective behind bars, from the time of the institution's beginning. In the nineteenth century, the relatively novel and often harsh experience of incarceration generated a thriving autobiographical genre. Early prison autobiographies fed a growing American appetite for personal narratives claiming to document the real-life experiences of the oppressed and the down-and-out, and convicts and ex-convicts joined slaves, beggars, soldiers, and captives of Indians in recording their life stories.[83] Curiosity in the convict narrative grew, historian Ann Fabian argues, when "the convicted and condemned were moved to locations increasingly further from the public eye."[84] As punishment for crime moved from public spectacle to private incarceration—from the stockades and gallows of the town square to the walled penitentiary—the reading public longed for information about life concealed behind bars. First-hand accounts by prisoners, as well as by a growing number of prison chaplains, doctors, and wardens, offered to reveal the secrets of those newly private spaces and to take curious readers into the hidden world of the prison.[85] John

Reynolds's 1889 account of life in the Kansas State Prison opened with a statement of first-hand experience, effective in its directness and simplicity: "I am a penitentiary convict. . . . As I write these lines I am sitting in a felon's cell, behind prison bolts and bars."[86] Joseph Kelley prefaced his 1908 account *Thirteen Years in the Oregon Penitentiary* by offering readers this promise, implicit in all inmate autobiographies and fundamental to their appeal: "What you read will be true—no fable story. It will be the real thing."[87]

Nineteenth-century prison memoirs satisfied the curiosity of their readers by recording daily prison schedules, as well as by evoking the disorienting and disempowering experience of the loss of liberty and chronicling prison boredom, brutality, and fear. Depending on their personal proclivities, political agendas, and literary talents, inmate-authors reflected on a range of features of prison life, from the most mundane aspects of the daily and regimented routine of waking, working, and eating, to weightier quandaries about personal freedom, submission to authority, and the legitimacy of state power. Some penned vignettes introducing their fellow inmates, offering a kind of "rogues gallery" from the rogue's perspective.

While discussion of sex between prisoners would come to be obligatory to the genre of prisoner autobiography as it took shape in the twentieth century, few made direct reference to it before then. This relative silence on the part of nineteenth-century prison autobiographers, especially those who wrote in the earlier decades of the century, may be explained, in part, by there being literally less to tell. Louis Dwight's alarmed report to the contrary, sexual opportunities for inmates in early-nineteenth-century institutions, especially those in which the rules of solitude and silence were enforced, were considerably more constrained than in their successors. In prisons that held inmates in solitary confinement or restricted them to a rule of silence, there would have been few opportunities for contact of any sort.

This is not to say that those systems of separation and silence were always successfully implemented. Prisoners found ways around the rules from the beginning, and the fantasy of perfect isolation was compromised even in the institutions in which it was most rigorously implemented. In the early years of Philadelphia's famed solitary system, for instance, critics observed that prisoners communicated with each other "through the openings for fresh air, through the windows of the cells, and through the apparatus for warming the cells."[88] Beaumont and Tocqueville also discovered that defects in the construction of Pittsburgh's similarly designed Western State Penitentiary made it "very easy to hear in one cell what is going on in another; so that each prisoner found in the communication with his neighbour a daily recreation; i.e. an opportunity of inevitable corruption."[89] Seth Payne, who published an account of his brief incarceration in the Albany Penitentiary in 1873, noted that inmates there were "never allowed to communicate with one another by letter, word, or sign," nor "permitted to look at each other by their own right." Still, Payne recounted, "the tongue is an unruly creature. It can't hold still." Of his fellow inmates, Payne wrote, "we are like a secret society, a sort of Masonic-say-nothing-ku-klux, the object of which is to help each other talk." Prisoners communicated through "coughs, sneezes, tooth-aches, groans, . . . and if necessary, fits and fainting spells," Payne wrote.[90] Of his term in New York's Blackwell's Island prison, where he served a year for unlawful assembly, labor activist Frank Tannenbaum wrote that "isolation, suppression, the denial of association, of communication, of friendships, are things that men cannot accept in their completeness without resistance. . . . Sociability becomes to the prisoner the means of sustaining a semblance of normality in an abnormal environment."[91] While outside observers of the prison would have been impressed by "the sphere of isolation controlled by the administrative machine," Tannenbaum wrote,

> inside of this formal organization there exists a humming life—a life of ingenuity and association. Right under the eyes of the authorities, in spite of all the restriction imposed, in spite of the constant watchfulness, in spite of the insistence upon isolation, the men manage to find a means and a method of achieving cooperation. Anyone who has been in prison can recall a thousand ways of associating with the other prisoners. The prisoners break every rule in the prison. They talk, they communicate with each other, they exchange articles, and they even publish newspapers, in spite of all the attempts at isolation. They do it because they must. Never yet has there been a prison regime that successfully suppressed association.[92]

Yet another inmate wrote that his "heart was gladdened by the magic taps on the other side of the cell wall" in the prison where he was held in solitary confinement. Having worked as a telegraph operator in his youth, he recognized the tappings as Morse code. "That was the beginning of a series of conversations which lasted . . . during the most onerous portion of my term of imprisonment."[93] While prisoners found ways to break the imposition of rigid rules of silence and separation, however, opportunities for physical contact between prisoners in many prisons were probably slim.

The genre of the prison narrative, especially as it took shape in the early decades of the nineteenth century, may have also disinclined prisoners and former prisoners from discussing sexual relations among inmates. Genres and their conventions, by their nature, enable some stories while foreclosing others. Emerging in the early nineteenth century, the first convict narratives were driven by the transmission of the moral lesson and the story of religious conversion. Samuel Smith wrote his account of incarceration in Connecticut's Newgate Prison in 1827, "principally to prevent others from following so disgraceful and unprincipled a course of life."[94] This impulse informed some late-nineteenth-century prison memoirs as well. William Francis, an African American prisoner in the Missouri State Penitentiary, assured readers in 1896 that "it is the author's aim to write nothing that would influence the young mind in any way other than the right one."[95] Likewise Texas convict Andrew George presented his own life as an object lesson and implored the "young men who may read this book" to "shun evil associates, and thus avoid the possibility of ever crossing this terrible threshold."[96] Franklin Carr commissioned a clergyman to write the preface for his 1893 narrative *Twenty-Two Years in State Prisons*, who described the story as one of "sorrow, sin, and salvation."[97] The reflection of authors dedicated to recording their own moral slide, confession, and ultimate redemption was directed inward rather than outward, and they typically devoted little space to describing their social relations with other inmates.

Those narrative conventions would change over the course of the nineteenth century. In 1890, former inmate John Reynolds opened his account of the Kansas penitentiary where he had served eighteen months for mail fraud with this enticing warning to his readers: "The following pages treat of hell. . . . Those who desire to peruse works that tell about Heaven only, are urged to drop this book and run."[98] The titles of early prisoner autobiographies—*Hell in Nebraska*, *A Kansas Hell*, *The Twin Hells*, *A Hell on Earth*, *Five Years in Hell*, *Twenty-Nine Hundred and Forty-Four Days in Hell*, *Red Hell*, and *To Hell and Back Again* among them—make clear the reigning metaphor for inmate authors of the late nineteenth century.[99] These titles signaled a new trend in prisoner autobiographies that focused less on internal struggles and devoted themselves instead to conjuring the intensity of the particular form of misery that was penitentiary life. In so doing, they illuminated the transition in inmate narratives that Ann Fabian traces, "from spiritual document to sensational story."[100] Most striking in the late nineteenth and early twentieth centuries, that shift was already underway in earlier decades. In 1839, Coffey wrote of his account, *A Peep into the State Prison*, that although "the Reader may suspect from the title of this little work, a long catalogue of all the crimes and cruelties of which our nature can be guilty," he promised "no unnecessary gloating upon horrors, no straining to give effect, but facts told soberly."[101] As early as 1839, then, inmates were aware of the emerging generic conventions of the convict narrative and of the expectations that readers would bring to it.

As inmate-authors began more regularly to satisfy expectations of graphic depiction of prison brutalities, the physical space of the prison and relations among prisoners would come to occupy a more central place in inmate autobiographies. Authors of this increasingly sensationalistic genre recounted stories of torturous punishment, corrupt prison administrators, brutal forced labor in tanneries, mines, fields, and quarries, sadistic guards, rotten food, and dramatic escapes. J. Harrie Banka graced his 1871 account of prison life in the Southern Indiana State Prison with a long descriptive subtitle that advertised the new themes addressed in prisoner autobiographies and indulged new desires on the part of readers: "A true and detailed account of the maltreatment and cruelties formerly practiced upon prisoners; also, shame-faced criminalities with female convicts, mutinies, murders, starvings, whippings, hair-breadth escapes, sketches and incidents, narratives and pen-pictures, sunshine and shade, illustrative of prison life."[102]

This shift in conventions from spiritual confession to secular and sensationalistic exposé made the inmate autobiography of the late nineteenth and early twentieth centuries a more congenial genre for discussing sexual practices among prisoners along with other hidden truths of incarceration. Various challenges, however, practical and linguistic, still made it difficult for early prison autobiographers to document such practices. Most basic, perhaps, were the material difficulties and risks involved in writing and publishing prison narratives in this period. Prisoners in most institutions were strictly monitored in their writing, and some were forbidden from writing altogether. One prison diarist described the guile required to write behind bars. He wrote a diary with stolen pencils on wrapping paper from packages sent to him in prison, and he transcribed notes from the paper scraps onto pieces of woolen underwear. "The transcription was also stenographic, the characters being as minute as possible, so that if any sneak had got hold of the record, he could have formed no idea as to what it was."[103] Orange Pettay, who published his account of "five years in hell" in the Ohio Penitentiary in 1883, was punished when guards found his manuscript, and one guard threatened to kill him for his transgression.[104]

Prisoners who violated rules against writing assumed serious risks in doing so, and these conditions no doubt made some inmate-authors more circumspect than they may have wanted to be. "I was tempted to run into detail," Julian Hawthorne wrote, having been "made the confidant of the life stories of many of my brethren in the cells." Those stories "bleed and groan before your eyes and ears, and smell to heaven; the bluntest, simplest, most formless stuff imaginable, but terrible in every fiber," yet Hawthorne declined to include them, since "such material . . . would have been confiscated by the Warden had its existence been known, and none of it would have been permitted to get outside the walls openly."[105] Writing under these constraints, Hawthorne acknowledged that he "left out a great deal" of his experience and observations of prison.[106]

Early inmate authors, many of whom published and distributed their memoirs themselves, also confronted the practical matter of negotiating increasingly strict obscenity laws. Federal legislation familiarly known as the Comstock Law, passed in 1873, made it illegal to send through the mail material that treated sexual matters in a manner judged obscene. Authors risked legal prosecution when they wrote about sex in any detail or in terms other than proscriptive and condemnatory. In his narrative of life in a Nebraska prison, Walter Wilson struggled in his chapter on "Prostitution in the Pen" to avoid censorship and at the same time to make his meaning known to presumably naive readers. "The prostitution that exists is that which is practiced among men or by men to boys," Wilson wrote. "To make it any plainer would perhaps land me in the federal prison for many years, for it is unfit to print and transmit through the mails."[107] Jack London listed "manhandling" as among the "unprintable horrors of the Erie County pen," where he was imprisoned for vagrancy. "As regards the details of that manhandling," London wrote, "I shall say nothing."[108] Reminding readers that he was "no spring chicken in the ways of the world and the awful abysses of human degradation," London added that those details were "unthinkable" to him "until I saw them."[109]

Nineteenth-century prisoners faced material constraints in documenting same-sex sexual acts. Like their contemporaries more generally, they were also limited by the cultural and linguistic repertoire of their time to describe those acts. The Bible served as one of the most useful resources, offering the advantages of both relative specificity and safe cover. "That my reader shall understand the situation," Wilson wrote carefully, "I will say 'Get your Bible and read the first chapter of St. Paul's letter to the Romans.'" Wilson drew his readers' attention to specific verses:

> "26. For this cause God gave them up into vile affections; for even their women did change the natural use into that which is against nature. 27. And likewise also the men, leaving the natural use of the woman, burned in their lust toward another; men with men working that which is unseemly, and receiving in themselves that recompense of their error which was meet."[110]

Wilson went on to remark, "Never did I imagine that a human being could thus lower himself, and if those old steel cells at Lancaster . . . could speak, they would reveal crimes like those Saint Paul writes about, crimes almost unbelievable, practiced by the old offenders . . . upon the young inmates."[111] Wilson was not alone among convict narrators in using biblical references to speak the unspeakable. John Reynolds also resorted to the Bible to identify the "horrible and revolting practices of the mines" where convicts in the Kansas State Penitentiary were forced to work: "Men, degraded to a plane lower than the brutes, are guilty of the unmentionable crimes referred to by the Apostle Paul in his letter to the Romans, chapter 1, verse 27."[112] In the crowded and unsupervised "pandemonium" of the mines, Reynolds wrote, "every opportunity is . . . offered for this vile practice."[113] About such practices, Reynolds offered only "a hint . . . , but to the wise it will be sufficient, and but a slight exercise of the imaginative powers will be necessary to unfold to you the full meaning of this terrible state of affairs."[114] Prisoner Morgan Sipe also wrote about the Kansas penitentiary, referencing the "horrible and revolting practices" committed by inmates working in the mines who were "guilty of the unmentionable crimes referred to by Paul in his letter to the Romans (1:27)."[115]

While biblical references served some nineteenth- and early-twentieth-century prison autobiographers, others employed the language of euphemism, writing around the edges of their subject in implying sex between prisoners without confronting it directly. Some resorted to the familiar terms of the day, referring to unmentionable vices, unnamable sins, and unutterable acts. Others ventured more poetic, if not more specific, detail. Carlo de Fornaro, a radical critic indicted for criminal libel, served ten months in New York City prisons and documented his experiences in a memoir titled *Modern Purgatory*, published in 1917. About his incarceration in the newly built New York's men's detention center known as the Tombs, Fornaro wrote of the institution's "pernicious" influence and was unusual among early inmate-authors in implicating himself in the "intangible, powerful magnetism" exerted by prison life:

> Thoughts, images, desires, which I had been used from my youth and all
> through my life to consider unhealthy, degenerate, or simply unworthy of
> attention, came sneaking into my subconscious mind, in the form of disgusting, appalling, terrifying dreams. The back yard of my mind had begun to
> register and absorb all the wretched, unclean, monstrous, unmentionable
> yearnings, desires, and actions of the collective prison dreams; it was inhaling
> the moral stench which arose from a "cloaca maxima."[116]

In registering the impact of the prison on his mind and thoughts rather
than on his body (or, as was more common, the bodies of others), Fornaro
offered a rare window into his own inner life. He claimed to be strong
enough to resist the toxic and transformative influences of the prison, but
he remained worried about "all the weak, unbalanced, receptive young
minds which must have been corrupted by this intangible, powerful magnetism; and of how this unnatural, abnormal, degrading prison life began
in any absorbent or indifferent temperament a slow corrosion and led to a
complete and effective disruption and destruction of all moral and intellectual integrity."[117]

Historian Jonathan Ned Katz recites the "damning diction" available
in the nineteenth century to name and condemn sex between men: "Sodomy. Buggery. . . . Most horrid and detestable crime. Among Christians
not to be named. Against the order of nature. . . . Sodomitical, detestable,
and abominable sin."[118] Early prison autobiographers, like other contemporary writers on the prison, drew from the literary and conceptual repertoire of their day to describe sex between prisoners, employing a language
of euphemism, writing in the coded language of "unspeakability," and
citing biblical injunctions to both name and condemn same-sex sexual
acts.

The few inmate-authors who discussed sex between prisoners directly
did so with the same degree of disgust and condemnation, often expressed
in the same terms, as prison staff, administrators, and reformers. At the
same time, early prison autobiographers documented without judgment
or reticence some forms of prison homosociability yet to be tainted with
the suspicion or stigma of perversion. Like men in other single-sex communities in this period, including miners, lumbermen, and sailors, some
prisoners described physical attraction, bed-sharing, dancing, and love
between men with an utter lack of self-consciousness.[119] It was not un-

usual for adult men in the nineteenth century to sleep in the same bed, especially when exigency required it, and that practice was described by George Thompson, who served time in a Missouri penitentiary for assisting runaway slaves. Thompson wrote in his 1847 account of sleeping three to a cell measuring twelve by eight feet. The cell was originally furnished with two beds, a double and a single. But, Thompson wrote,

> After a time, James obtained permission and fixed the double bedstead wide enough for us all. In this way we fared a little better—for we could take turns getting into the middle. If an outside one was becoming frost-bitten, we only had to request the middle one to exchange places awhile; and we were ever ready to oblige and accommodate—for each knew how to sympathize with the other.[120]

Nineteenth-century narrators did not hesitate to confess to sympathy among men that could take emotional and physical, if not sexual forms. They also commented freely on the physical attractiveness of fellow inmates. In his 1873 account, Seth Payne observed easily, "We have some fine looking boys here. Some of them do not appear to be above fifteen. The twenty or thirty I have been able to see as they file past my cell each morning, noon, and night, have really prepossessing countenances."[121]

Other inmate-authors were even more expressive and expansive in their admiration for other men, writing with great feeling about relationships with fellow prisoners in the language of sentimentalism, intimacy, and even romantic love. Alexander Berkman formed an intimate friendship with a young inmate, Johnny, while he was incarcerated in Pennsylvania's Western State Penitentiary. While in solitary confinement, Berkman recalled an intimate exchange when Johnny asked him, "Am I in your thoughts, dear?" When Berkman responded, "Yes, kiddie you are," Johnny confessed, "I would like to kiss you." With this admission, Berkman declared that "an unaccountable sense of joy glows in my heart," and he told Johnny, "I feel just as you do."[122] "The springs of affection well up within me," Berkman wrote, when, "with closed eyes, I picture the boy before me, with his delicate face, and sensitive, girlish lips."[123] Berkman's characterization of his relationship with Johnny was especially notable, since in another chapter of his autobiography he discussed sex among prisoners with a frankness unusual in this period. In conversation with a fellow prisoner who was anguished by his own sexual desire and love for another man, Berkman sympathized by confessing his own love for another inmate, Russell, for whom he "felt no physical passion" but whom he "loved . . . with all my heart."[124] Katz has proposed that "romantic lovers and sodomites inhabited separate, parallel universes" in the nineteenth century. Though Berkman wrote in the early decades of the twentieth century, it remained possible for him to acknowledge his romantic love for another man, safe from stigma because of its presumably asexual nature.[125]

Other prisoners wrote of prison dances, apparently an institution in many nineteenth- and early-twentieth-century prisons loosed from the imperatives of solitude and separation, as they were in the all-male mining towns, lumber yards, and cowboy communities of the same period. John King, a Confederate soldier incarcerated in a Union military prison during the Civil War, recalled prison balls at which some men "would be selected to represent ladies." "To distinguish them from the men," he explained, they would "run strings through the center of their blankets and tie these around the waist. . . . Partners would be selected for the several dances, and their names entered on slips of paper with all the ceremony of a regular ball." Such dances, King wrote, "would enliven our spirits and give real pleasure to the participants." [126] Inmate Donald Lowrie described a dance at San Quentin as similarly uplifting: "About thirty couples—ladies conspicuous by their absence—were dancing. . . . Nearly every face that bobbed past me seemed content. There seemed to be a forgetfulness of their imprisonment, of their surroundings. . . . While it seemed strange to see men in prison dancing, nevertheless I realized that it was a good thing."[127] Eugene Block agreed, writing as late as 1924 about dances that still occurred every Sunday morning in the San Quentin yard, where "you will find a thousand men or more dancing on the concrete floor to the strains of a prison band." "Dancing is good exercise," Block wrote, "and music keeps up the morale."[128] More than two decades into the twentieth century, then, prisoners could still experience prison dances as free of the taint of sexual perversion (see plate 2).

Katz observes that King's text "implies that such balls were completely devoid of illicit, sexual innuendo" and speculates that it is "possible that nineteenth-century Americans were simply unconscious of the eros hovering over prison dances."[129] But as Katz himself suggests, perhaps that eros is produced by the retrospective reading practices of historians who are themselves inhabitants of a different sexual era. Prisoners in the nineteenth and early twentieth centuries wrote from within a culture that observed distinctions between the affectional and the sexual, the comradely and the perverse, in ways specific to their time and with considerably more fluidity than would later be allowed them. Nineteenth- and early-twentieth-century prison narrators declined to detect erotic possibility in moments that those just a few decades later would find impossible to read in any other way.

:::

The earliest visions of the prison as a place of solitude, somber and quiet self-reflection, and reformation emphasized the institution's transformative properties. From less lofty perches, observers on both sides of the bars characterized the prison as a space that transformed its occupants, although rarely along the optimistic lines envisioned by early penologists. The prison's indelible and possibly constitutive relationship to deviant sexuality, in particular, confounded the hopes of the modern prison's reformist advocates and presented new quandaries about how to comprehend, represent, and combat the phenomenon of same-sex sex behind bars. Sex was central to the reformist imaginings and anxieties of prison from the institution's beginnings and soon thereafter to the material life of prisoners. Early prison administrators, reformers, architects, and prisoners initiated what would become an increasingly polyphonous discussion of the meaning and consequences of incarceration and its apparently queer effects.

CHAPTER TWO

"Every Prison Has Its Perverts"

In 1892, anarchist Alexander Berkman made an unsuccessful attempt on the life of Henry Clay Frick, manager of the Carnegie Steel Company in Homestead, Pennsylvania, intended as a revolutionary act against what he perceived to be an exploitative capitalist system and to avenge the massacre of striking steel workers by Pinkerton guards. Berkman served fourteen years in Pennsylvania's Western State Penitentiary and published a detailed and moving account of his incarceration in 1912. He opened *Prison Memoirs of an Anarchist* with a passage written by the newly famous chronicler of prison life, Oscar Wilde:

> But this I know, that every Law
>   That men have made for Man,
> Since first Man took his brother's life,
>   And the sad world began,
> But straws the wheat and saves the chaff
>   With a most evil fan.[1]

Berkman was far from alone in calling on Wilde to convey the cruelties of prison life. In the early decades of the twentieth century, many who wrote about prison—prisoners, wardens, chaplains, physicians, and journalists, as well as a new cadre of prison professionals including psychiatrists, psychologists, and sociologists—made frequent reference to Oscar Wilde and quoted liberally from

his published writing. Thelma Roberts took the title of her 1934 book
Red Hell, written in collaboration with prisoner John Goode, from Wilde,
whom she quoted on the book's title page:

> For none can tell to what red hell
> His sightless soul may stray[2]

Chester Himes was also inspired by these lines. Himes began writing and
publishing fiction while incarcerated for burglary in the late 1920s and
1930s, and his short story "To What Red Hell," about a fire in the Ohio
penitentiary in which almost three hundred prisoners burned to death in
their cells, appeared in *Esquire* magazine in 1934 and drew its title from
Wilde's verse.[3] Nearly two decades later, inmate Joan Henry quoted a line
from Wilde's *De Profundis* in her 1952 autobiography: "For a year after
that was done to me I wept every day at the same hour for the same space
of time." "To those who are in prison," Henry confessed in her own less
writerly prose, "tears are a part of every day's experience."[4]

While many were drawn to Wilde's prison writing to conjure the experience of life behind bars, references to the famous playwright served a
more particular and layered purpose for those who wished to acknowledge sexual practices in prison. Many detected dark allusion to that subject in Wilde's final work, *The Ballad of Reading Gaol*, published in 1898
following his release from prison and shortly before his death. American
prison commentators who referenced Wilde most frequently quoted from
Reading Gaol and most often called attention to the following lines that
strung together two verses:

> The vilest deeds, like poison weeds,
>   Bloom well in prison-air;
> It is only what is good in Man
>   That wastes and withers there. . .
> And all, but Lust, is turned to dust
>   In Humanity's machine.[5]

Although Wilde's prison term was apparently spent in solitude, many read
in these lines a comment on degrading sexual practices among prisoners,
expressions of lust stripped of humanity and nurtured by the damaging
conditions of prison life. Emma Goldman used this poem of Wilde's to
illustrate her claim that in Montana, where she was a prisoner in 1918,
and "for aught we know in every State in the land, prisons continue to

be 'built of bricks of shame.'"[6] Thomas Mott Osborne likewise included verses from *Reading Gaol* in his 1916 reform treatise, *Society and Prisons*. Osborne prefaced Wilde's lines by acknowledging that "decent people do not talk nor wish to hear of such things," but he insisted that "it is time that decent people woke up to the truth."[7]

Neither Goldman nor Osborne ventured much detail about the nature of the "shame" or "truth" to which they believed Wilde referred. But for contemporary readers, Oscar Wilde's words and certainly his by-line would have sufficed to reference deviant sexuality and specifically to denote sex between men. In 1895, the famous playwright had been tried and convicted of seven counts of "acts of gross indecency with another male person" and sentenced to two years imprisonment with hard labor. During the late spring of that year, the trials of Oscar Wilde were covered extensively in the pages of almost every newspaper throughout Europe and the United States. As a result of this extraordinary publicity, argues literary critic Ed Cohen, the Wilde case "significantly altered the shape of the Victorian sexual imagination." By the time of his conviction, Cohen writes, "not only had Wilde been confirmed as *the* sexual deviant for the late nineteenth century, but he had become the paradigmatic example for an emerging public definition of a new 'type' of male sexual actor: 'the homosexual.'"[8]

Oscar Wilde's well-publicized fate—his trials, conviction, and incarceration—ensured that, at this formative moment in the public recognition of this new sexual type, "the homosexual" would become ineradicably affiliated with criminality and the prison. That confluence produced a new symbolic language with which to represent something formerly unrepresentable. Writers had long employed a representational code of noisy silence—acts and vices declared "unnamable," "unmentionable," and "unutterable"—to designate same-sex sexual practices. Those references were so ubiquitous in nineteenth-century representations of same-sex sex as to constitute less a failure of language or a demonstration of its limits than a denotative language unto itself. After the publicity surrounding Wilde's trials and conviction in 1895, prison writers could invoke Oscar Wilde's name or quote from his published writing, often unattributed but presumably so recognizable to readers that it needed no citation, to specify sex between men.[9]

This act of naming, through reference to a literal name or, one step removed, through the use of Wilde's verse, worked at once to denote homosexuality and ironically to multiply the layers of elision that surrounded same-sex sexual practices. Wilde was asked famously by the court to define "the love that dare not speak its name," a line from a poem written by his lover, Lord Alfred Douglas, and the unspeakability that surrounded same-sex practices extended to the press coverage of his trial. Cohen observes that the word "sodomy" never appeared in the newspaper articles on the Wilde scandal and that no newspaper reported the details of any sexual charge against him.[10] A coded and euphemistic language of unspeakable vice prevailed in the trial, strong enough at least for a time to withstand the glare of heated publicity.

Prison writers in the early twentieth century made frequent if cryptic use of Oscar Wilde's name and published writing. Shortly thereafter, however, Wilde was put to more clearly articulated purposes. Whereas those in the century's first decades allowed Wilde's name to stand in as a denotative proxy for same-sex sexual practices, useful in ways similar to references to biblical passages or the nineteenth century's telling euphemisms of unspeakability, prison observers in later decades pressed Wilde into more definitive and specific service. Criminologists Harry Barnes and Negley Teeters, for instance, called on the scientific language and conceptual precision supplied by the new science of sexology to diagnose Wilde as "afflicted with a constitutional sexual aberration" in their discussion of sex in prison in their 1944 textbook.[11]

By the 1920s and 1930s, "constitutional perverts," members of the "third sex," and "confirmed homosexuals" made their predictable appearance in observations of American prisons. In the words of a Maryland warden in 1923, prison officials had to "contend with the whole tribe of sexual perverts, who constitute one of the real problems of every penal institution."[12] The recognition of sexual deviants as comprising a "tribe" and the apparently disproportionate representation of this tribe among prison populations came to be widely acknowledged in this period. As Frank Tannenbaum observed matter-of-factly in 1933, "Every prison has its perverts."[13]

Comments like these signaled something importantly new. If, in the preceding century, prison observers worried that prisons were places in which sexual *perversion* was regrettably rampant, in the twentieth century, prisons began to be perceived as sites in which *perverts* could be found in abundance. Sex in prison began to appear not as the abominable practice of lustful individuals or as a disgusting habit acquired in prison but, rather, as comprising a culture unto itself. Characterized by its own rules and argot, that culture and its participants demanded explication. Accounting for the sexual life of prisoners led to some of the first efforts in the United States to understand and codify deviant sexual types and practices. Those efforts exposed the impossibilities and instabilities inherent in that taxonomical project from the outset.

The New Science of Sexology

Although not apparent in observations of American prisons until the 1920s and later, a new science, developing in Europe and England in the mid-nineteenth century and accelerating toward the century's end, rushed to fill in the discursive elisions surrounding same-sex sex. European and British doctors, scientists, and professionals from a range of disciplines and specialties theorized the origins, debated the etiology, and constructed taxonomies of deviant forms of sexuality and the nonnormative gender expression with which it was assumed to be closely tied. With the emergence of the science of sexology, the formerly unmentionable vice began to acquire an elaborate vocabulary.

German lawyer Karl Heinrich Ulrichs was among the first to develop a scientific theory of homosexuality in 1864. He was inspired to do so not by scientific or medical training but by inclinations more personally charged and activist in intent. Ten years earlier in 1854, Ulrichs had been forced to resign from practicing law when his superiors learned of his sexual activities with other men. Thereafter, he worked to redefine same-sex desire as a naturally occurring, innate, and benign human anomaly rather than as a sin or crime. Ulrichs and many others after him believed strongly in the emancipatory potential of understanding same-sex desire as inborn—the result of natural human variation rather than a sinful act or acquired vice. If homosexuality could be thus reconceived, Ulrichs imagined, it would be more difficult to justify harsh legal and social prohibitions against it. Toward that end, Ulrichs posited the natural existence of the "Urning," drawing the name from Plato's account in *The Symposium* of the motherless birth of Heavenly Aphrodite by Uranus, who inspired the noblest form of love between men. Ulrichs' theory anticipated the paradigm of "inversion," a broad diagnostic rubric within which most sexologists would come to locate same-sex sexual desire. Because sexual attraction was understood to depend naturally on sexual polarity, the concept of inversion provided a way to account for attraction between people ostensibly of the same sex.[14]

Sexologists differed widely in the methodologies they employed to study gender nonconformity and sexual deviance and in their understandings of its origins, and they promoted positions on homosexuality ranging from boldly affirming to harshly pathologizing.[15] Despite im-

portant differences and disagreements, they shared a key and overarching
assumption: that same-sex sexual desire was deeply rooted in the constitution of the individual. By "constitution," physicians and scientists
referred generally to a broad collection of human conditions and drives,
collapsing together what would later be distinguished as the somatic and
the psychic.[16]

Within this expansive understanding of the human constitution, sexologists debated the exact locus of same-sex sexual attraction. For Ulrichs, members of the "third sex" were formed by what he described
poetically as a "migration of the soul": a woman's soul in a man's body
explained a man's desire for men and vice versa.[17] Others took a more
organic approach. In 1869, Karl Westphal defined "contrary sexual feeling" as the symptom of a "neuropathic (psychopathic) condition."[18] German physician Magnus Hirschfeld proposed a theory of congenital sexual
"intermediacy," occurring naturally, akin to (and sometimes inclusive of)
physical intersexuality.[19] Havelock Ellis drew on the work of Ulrichs,
Hirschfeld, and most important, from his collaboration with John Add-
ington Symonds, a British poet, historian, and author of essays in defense
of love between men, to insist as well on the "congenital" nature of homosexuality. Casting homosexuality as a "constitutional abnormality"
analogous to color-blindness, criminality, and genius, Ellis ventured a
theory of the "abnormal" distribution of male and female "germs" that
occurred naturally, producing a person "who is organically twisted into
a shape that is more fitted for the exercise of the inverted than of the
normal sexual impulse."[20] Although he used terms such as "abnormal"
and "deviant" to characterize homosexuality, Ellis tried to strip them of
their pejorative valences, distinguishing, for example, between "anomaly" and "disease." In a more pathologizing appraisal, forensic psychiatrist
Richard von Krafft-Ebing argued in his encyclopedic survey of sexual
deviance, *Psychopathia Sexualis*, that homosexuality was evidence of constitutional degeneracy, passed from one generation to the next.[21] While
Krafft-Ebing insisted that "homo-sexual feeling" was grounded in "an
abnormal psycho-sexual constitution," he admitted that "this constitution, as far as its anatomical and functional foundation is concerned, is
absolutely unknown."[22]

Whether they described same-sex attraction as the result of benign and
inborn anomaly, organic congenital predisposition, or degenerative defect, sexologists generally agreed that such erotic inclination was inherent
in an individual's constitution. While that idea may have been inchoate
in some earlier understandings of same-sex sexuality, sexologists played

a crucial role in codifying the notion that same-sex sexual acts were indicative of a distinct type of person and in giving that idea the imprimatur of science. In the process, as Michel Foucault famously observed, "the nineteenth-century homosexual became a personage, a past, a case history, and a childhood, . . . with an indiscreet anatomy and possibly a mysterious physiology. . . . The sodomite had been a temporary aberration; the homosexual was now a species."[23] Sexologists surely did not invent this idea out of whole cloth. Whether or not they acknowledged the influence, they developed their theories in conversation with informants and patients, many of whom understood their own same-sex desires and cross-gender identities as innate and insisted, sometimes defiantly, on their recognition as "natural."[24]

Sexologists were unified in their understanding of homosexuality as rooted in the constitution; they were also dedicated to exploring its etiology and documenting its various forms of expression. Their own taxonomical thoroughness, however, sometimes undermined their confidence in homosexuality's constitutional essence. Ellis declared his intention to document the "varieties of homosexuality" when he dedicated the second volume of his massive work, *Studies of the Psychology of Sex*, to an exploration of what he termed *Sexual Inversion*.[25] Some of those varieties, however, outran and even contradicted his core theory of the constitutional basis of homosexuality. While committed to the notion that homosexuality was a congenital trait, Ellis recognized that particular spaces and circumstances seemed to encourage its practice among people "of usually normal tendency," presumably too often and too predictably to credit congenital anomaly.[26] Ellis dismissed the notion of "acquired" homosexuality as "antiquated," seeking to distinguish and distance his own theory of "congenital" homosexuality from earlier notions of "acquired vice," yet he acknowledged the prevalence of homosexual practices among men aboard ship, in prisons, and under other circumstances in which "the exercise of normal sexuality is impossible," as well as among women in boarding schools, brothels, convents, and harems. Ellis also identified certain traditionally female occupations as encouraging of lesbianism, including sewing, lace-making, and other jobs in which women are "confined for hours in close contact with one another in heated rooms."[27] Lesbianism was also disproportionately practiced among actresses, Ellis insisted. "Here, the pell-mell of the dressing-rooms, the wait of perhaps two hours between the performances, during which all the girls are cooped up, in a state of inaction and excitement, in a few crowded dressing-rooms, afford every opportunity for the growth of this particular kind of sentiment."[28]

Despite Ellis's commitment to the notion that homosexuality was congenital, he devoted considerable attention to varieties of same-sex sexual
expression that contradicted that etiology. Notably, Ellis concluded his
volume *Sexual Inversion* with two appendices that drew attention to its
"acquired" varieties, one titled "Homosexuality among Tramps," authored by the early hobo-ethnographer Josiah Flynt, and another "The
School-Friendships of Girls."[29]

Ellis was by no means alone among sexologists in acknowledging forms
of same-sex sexual desire and expression that seemed to spring from circumstance rather than constitution. Krafft-Ebing observed that "large
cities are the breeding-places of . . . degenerate sensuality" and singled
out prisons, ships, garrisons, and boarding schools as well, as spaces that
encouraged homosexuality.[30] Of these "acquired" forms, Krafft-Ebing reassured readers "there is an immediate return to normal sexual intercourse
as soon as obstacles to it are removed."[31] In a clever and probably deliberately subversive comparison, given the direction of his own sexual desires,
Magnus Hirschfeld likened circumstantial homosexuality to circumstantial or "pseudo" heterosexuality, performed by homosexuals "for private
gain, or from pity or gratitude, or because persons of the same sex are not
available." Hirschfeld quoted one male informant who told him about sex
with women, "I can only do it when I am drunk."[32]

In the writings of sexologists, observations of queer geographies—
spaces that seemed to encourage same-sex sexual expression—pulled
against their commitment to the notion of a queer constitution, rooted in
the physiology or psyche. Sexologists dedicated to understanding homosexuality as congenital were confounded by particular spaces that seemed
to encourage homosexual acts. How was it possible to contain within one
category the notion of homosexuality as an essential trait and at the same
time recognize the prevalence of homosexual behavior among presumably heterosexual people? How were sexologists to square their theories
of constitutional homosexuality with homosexual practices apparently
promoted by spaces, circumstances, or conditions? Some acknowledged
uneasily that some homosexual acts exceeded their taxonomies. As Ellis acknowledged reluctantly, "Even the most elementary groupings
become doubtful when we have definitely to fit our cases into them."[33]
The concept of homosexuality, intended to distinguish and delineate an
anomalous and distinct sexual type, in other words, was unstable from
the moment of its articulation, its boundedness called into question in its
founding texts.[34]

Another sexologist, writing in conversation with Ellis and Krafft-Ebing and, over time, in opposition to them, contributed further to confounding the category of homosexuality. In contrast to sexologists who insisted on homosexuality's congenital somatic essence, Sigmund Freud posited a dynamic model of sexual development, whereby individuals progressed through a series of stages, homosexuality among them, ideally culminating in mature heterosexuality. Homosexuality in Freud's model was more accurately understood as a form of arrested psychosexual development.[35] Though often deeply rooted and sometimes permanent, homosexuality was not the condition of an identifiable category of persons, Freud insisted, but rather was a phase that everyone passed through and to which they could conceivably return if the stresses and traumas of development stimulated regression to an earlier stage. A troubled category from the start, then, homosexuality resisted its classificatory bonds in nearly every iteration.

Faced with these apparent contradictions, sexologists struggled to find solutions to the puzzle posed by varieties of homosexuality that fell outside their understandings of it as congenital and innate. Magnus Hirschfeld proposed the concept of pseudohomosexuality, which he defined as "homosexual acts which are not determined by a consistent mentality, but are dictated by aims which are outside the sphere of the sexual impulse." In such cases, Hirschfeld wrote, though the person may participate in same-sex sex, "heterosexuality remains an essential trait of the individual's personality."[36] Hirschfeld believed pseudohomosexuality to be more prevalent in women than in men, and "most easily acquired by girls where they live or work together and association with men is for some reason rendered difficult."[37]

Havelock Ellis similarly distinguished "sexual inversion," by which he meant "sexual instinct turned by inborn constitutional abnormality toward persons of the same sex," from "homosexuality." The former, he argued, was a "narrower term"; Ellis defined homosexuality broadly enough to encompass "all sexual attractions between persons of the same sex, even when seemingly due to the accidental absence of the natural objects of sexual attraction." He added that homosexuality thus understood was "a phenomenon of wide occurrence among all human races and among most of the higher animals."[38] Ellis speculated stubbornly, however, that there were many true inverts among animals as well as among human beings.

Krafft-Ebing likewise made an effort to distinguish between homosexuality caused by inborn anomaly, which he termed "perversion," and its "acquired" forms, which he labeled "perversity." For Krafft-Ebing, a pioneer in the emerging field of forensic psychiatry, that distinction carried important legal significance: those afflicted with perversion were inclined congenitally to same-sex sexual practice and were therefore not responsible for their actions. They were degenerate and abnormal, certainly, but not criminal. Those guilty of perversity, in contrast, were neither neurologically tainted nor sexually inverted. As willful participants in perverse acts, they could therefore be held responsible for their actions. They were punishable but also potentially curable. In fact, the transmissible nature of homosexuality in its acquired form made treatment or "prophalaxis," in Krafft-Ebing's opinion, all the more imperative.[39]

Renegade forms of homosexuality, shaped by circumstance rather than by constitution, produced profound uneasiness, contradiction, and sometimes outright incoherence in sexologists' accounts. Even as sexologists recognized expressions of same-sex desire unlinked to psychic or somatic markers, they clung to their understanding of homosexuality as fundamentally congenital. Ellis speculated that certain environments might trigger a "latent predisposition" to homosexuality.[40] Focusing on prison in particular, he debated whether homosexuality was produced by the sex-segregated institution or whether there was a disproportionate "tendency" to it among criminals. "Prison life develops and fosters the homosexual tendency of criminals," Ellis acknowledged, "but there can be little doubt that that tendency . . . is a radical character of a very large number of criminals."[41] Even "acquired" cases of homosexuality, Ellis insisted, must have a congenital basis. Ellis reversed this position when he turned his attention to school girls, without comment on the apparent inconsistency. If most male prisoners who engaged in same-sex sex were constitutionally predisposed toward homosexuality, Ellis believed that the "flame," or romantic relationship among school girls, "is a *love-fiction, a play of sexual love*" that "cannot be regarded as an absolute expression of real congenital perversion of the sex-instinct."[42] Krafft-Ebing followed Ellis in clinging to his belief in the essentially congenital nature of homosexuality. Most "acquired" cases, he insisted, could be explained through "latency" or bisexuality, "which, for its manifestation, requires the influence of accidental exciting causes to rouse it from its slumber."[43] Sexologists found ways, however convoluted, to trace homosexuality back to the constitution and to attribute it to a distinctive type of person.

Sexology and American Prisons

"Homosexual practices everywhere flourish and abound in prison," Havelock Ellis wrote in his volume *Sexual Inversion*.[44] This would hardly have been news to those familiar with prisons and prisoners. In 1904, an

inmate who wrote under the pseudonym of his institutional identification, "Number 1500," declared that those prisoners who entered Sing
Sing as "Elmira graduates" (referring to former inmates of the institution for juvenile offenders in upstate New York), were "almost to a man
a missionary force of perverts working their odious influence wherever
they go." "Whatever else has been accomplished at Elmira," Number
1500 wrote, "it has created a subject for the pen of a Krafft-Ebing, if one
should arise in this country, to deal as he did with the awful subject he
studied so deeply."[45]

Number 1500 was apparently more familiar with the work of
Krafft-Ebing than many of his turn-of-the-century American contemporaries, including those with medical and scientific training. The influence
of continental sexology was slow to appear in American studies of sexuality and in prison studies in particular; indeed, some seemed almost wholly
unaware of the phenomenon of homosexuality, much less the new ways
of conceptualizing it.[46] While physician Randolph Winslow ultimately
attributed an epidemic of gonorrhea in a juvenile reformatory in 1886 to
sex between young male inmates, he was, by his own admission, initially
baffled by its route of transmission. Winslow arrived at his conclusion
through a painstaking examination of every possibility but the most obvious, detailing the practices of institutional surveillance and impediments
of architecture that would have made it impossible for the inmates to have
sexual access to women.[47] Other American doctors in the late nineteenth
and early twentieth centuries who sought to bring the topic of sex between prisoners under scientific scrutiny ultimately relied more heavily
on nineteenth-century conceptual categories of religion and law than
those of sexology, drawing attention to sinful and criminal sexual acts
rather than to perverse or deviant sexual types. In his turn-of-the-century
study, "Sodomy—Pederasty," for instance, Kentucky physician George
Monroe referred to "habits" among prisoners that were "so abominable,
so disgusting, so filthy, and worse than beastly, that the medical profession, from a sense of decency and respect, are loth [sic] to write about
them, or even to discuss them with other physicians."[48] Monroe made no
reference to the medical literature on sexual deviance, expansive by the
turn of the century, nor did he suggest that such "habits" were in any way
indicative of psychological or somatic disposition.

Soon thereafter, however, American prison writers began to turn to
the task promoted by Number 1500. The first extensive discussions of
sex in prison appeared in the late 1920s and 1930s and were part of a more
general outpouring of writing on prisons, prisoners, and sexual variance

in this period. The Depression decade witnessed a rise in popular interest in crime and criminals rooted both in concern about social disorder
and in romanticized attachments to outlaws. The 1930s reading public was
also anxious about an alleged rise in "sex crimes" and eager for information about sexual deviance.[49] At once alarmed and captivated by crime and
criminals and both troubled and titillated by the rising specter of sexual
perversion, Depression-era Americans could not help but be interested
in the convergence of those two cultural fascinations represented by sex
in prison.

That confluence of interests created a ready audience for a boom in
autobiographical and fiction writing by prisoners. When editor H. L.
Mencken solicited prisoners' writing for his magazine *American Mercury*
beginning in the late 1920s, he introduced a large American readership to
the work of convict-writers. Mencken nurtured the literary careers of several authors who began writing while they were in prison. Chester Himes
credited the beginning of his career as a writer to Mencken's patronage.
Ernest Booth and Robert Tasker, both inmates of California prisons, also
rose to considerable fame as novelists in this period. Writing by prisoners was popular enough by 1931 to support the publication of an anthology. Editor Joseph French introduced the collection of prisoner-authored
writing, *Grey Shadows*, by noting that "only of late have American cell-
men themselves become articulate" but that finally "these voices from the
awful twilight zone of broken men demand to be heard."[50] Prisoners also
published their writing in prison magazines and newspapers, which grew
in number during the 1930s.[51]

Mencken encouraged inmates to depart from earlier conventions of
prison autobiography—the confession-and-redemption narratives of
the nineteenth century as well as the antiprison polemics penned by incarcerated radicals in the early twentieth century—and urged them instead to draw on their experience of daily life behind bars. "This story
belongs to a type that I dislike," Mencken wrote to San Quentin inmate
Robert Tasker in response to a manuscript he submitted for publication.
"Why don't you write about real people—that is, people you have actually known?" Mencken urged Tasker to avoid "the question of the utility
of prisons" and write instead "an article on life in prison, a picture of
the week's round. . . . Accept the thing as it stands," Mencken instructed,
"and describe it."[52] Ernest Booth announced his own departure from the
earlier conventions of prison autobiography in his introduction to his
1929 memoir, *Stealing through Life*. "If the book starts on a plane rather
different than the usual 'prison' story, and then descends to a lower, less

pleasant plane," Booth wrote, "I attempt no excuse other than that it is so written because it was so lived."[53] Encouraged by their vogue in the American literary scene and success in the literary marketplace and no doubt inspired by the Depression-era documentary impulse that sought out and validated the authentic experience of the down-and-out, a new generation of prison writers wrote with unprecedented candor about life behind bars.

That combined set of circumstances invited accounts of prison life that included considerably less cryptic discussions of sex between inmates than those of earlier decades. In 1933, the prestigious press Little, Brown published Victor Nelson's memoir *Prison Days and Nights*, catapulting the genre of prison autobiography to new heights of popularity. Nelson went far beyond the embarrassed and oblique acknowledgment of sex between prisoners then typical of the genre, devoting a chapter titled "Men without Women" to a lengthy account and analysis of the subject. Following the success of Nelson's book, discussions of sex would become nearly obligatory in prison autobiographies and in much of the inmate-authored fiction that gained popularity beginning in the late 1920s and 1930s.

Scientific studies of prison sex began to appear in this period as well. Joseph Fishman had been "plunged into the prison world" in the 1910s and 1920s in his capacity as the nation's first (and only) federal inspector of prisons. With funding from the Guggenheim Foundation, Fishman expanded on his observations during visits to the nation's jails and prisons to write *Sex in Prison: Revealing Sex Conditions in American Prisons*, the first book devoted to the subject, published in 1934.[54] In that same year, Louis Berg drew on his experience as physician at New York's Welfare Island penitentiary to write *Revelations of a Prison Doctor*, a titillating exposé of prison life that included a long discussion of sex in prison. Psychiatrist Samuel Kahn's *Mentality and Homosexuality* followed in 1937, a study of the "psychological status" of homosexuals undertaken in the early 1920s as a master's thesis at New York University, with case studies drawn from over five hundred inmates of New York's Blackwell's Island prison and at the Women's Workhouse for female prisoners.[55]

This new generation of penologists announced their intention to bring the candid and modern approach of what Fishman called a "frank and realistic age" to a subject they believed to have been long ignored and to introduce the subject of sex behind bars "to the interested but unenlightened world."[56] Leaders in this campaign, Fishman and Berg condemned what they took to be widespread and damaging neglect of the subject of "abnormal sexuality" behind bars.[57] Fishman, in particular, criticized the "incredible timidity and evasiveness with which prison authorities approach any discussion of the subject," which seemed shrouded by a "veil of silence."[58] To introduce his book on sex in prison, he printed a selection of unforthcoming letters sent to him by prison officials "to give the reader an idea of the type of courteous but fruitless replies" he received in his request for "data" on the subject.[59]

While Fishman's remarks reflected a strategic and self-promoting posture designed to distinguish his own "modern" and scientific stance toward homosexuality from Victorian predecessors he derided as prudish and timid, his work and that of others around this time registered a genuine shift in tone and attitude toward the subject of sex between prisoners. New ways of conceptualizing prison sex began to be apparent in the outpouring of scientific and popular writing about prison that appeared in the 1920s and 1930s. The new science of sexology provided observers of the American prison with an expansive vocabulary, offering the status of science as well as the allure of modernity and frankness of attitude toward sexual matters that writers like Fishman, Berg, Nelson, and Kahn so admired.

This new generation of prison writers found the conceptual categories provided by sexologists, especially their distinctions between "true" and circumstantial forms of homosexuality, invaluable in depicting and mapping the sexual topography of the prison. In positing those distinctions, however awkwardly and contradictorily, sexologists provided a scientifically authorized account for what many had long observed in prison. Prison doctors, administrators, and other investigators were drawn to elucidate the phenomenon that sexologists unfailingly observed but tried mightily to explain away: forms of homosexuality apparently acquired rather than innate. What to sexologists were troubling inconsistencies that undermined their insistence on the congenital roots of homosexuality were, for prison observers, enabling points of departure with explanatory power.

Sexological language and concepts began to appear in American prison writing in the 1930s. Joseph Wilson and Michael Pescor distinguished the "constitutional" homosexual from the acquired type in their 1939 textbook on prison psychiatry. The latter was assumed to be "congenitally normal in his sexual inclinations, but through perverted contacts with persons of the same sex has come to prefer homosexual stimulation to heterosexual."[60] Like many sexologists, prison doctor Louis Berg pointed to spaces and circumstances that promoted homosexual behavior in those of normal sexual constitution. Berg likened same-sex sex in prison to the "sodomy and kindred abnormalities" that prevailed "in the days of sailing ships when vessels did not see a port for months."[61]

Authors of the few early studies of female inmates agreed that sexual relationships between incarcerated girls and women could be traced to circumstantial rather than constitutional causes. In a study published in 1929, psychiatrist Charles A. Ford distinguished young female inmates from the "true" homosexuals of greater interest to sexologists. Unlike the cases he observed in prison, Ford noted, those discussed by Krafft-Ebing, Ellis, and other sexologists were "truly pathological" and "usually superimposed on a neurotic constitution and represent[ing] the sexual desires of a lifetime." At the same time, Ford called on conceptual categories provided by Herbert Bloch and Krafft-Ebing, distinguishing the "temporary or pseudo inversion" he identified among institutionalized girls and women from its "pathological" forms, which were, by extension, permanent and "true."[62] Maurice Chideckel likewise failed to detect any "physical anomalies" in his 1938 discussion of female inmates involved in same-sex sex and, more specifically, none of the bodily features that many attributed to congenital homosexuality: "There was not a sign of any disturbances in their endocrine glands which could account for finding pleasure in the organs they themselves possess. The bodily contour of every one was feminine."[63] Chideckel also invoked the notion of "pseudo-homosexuality" to explain sex between female inmates. "As soon as they are let out of the institution," he reassured readers in an airy reference to prostitutes, "they resume business at the old stand."[64] In accounting for many of the romantic relationships between black and white female inmates who paired off as "honies" in correctional institutions, psychologist Lowell Selling revealed his familiarity with continental sexology when he concluded in 1931 that "most of these relationships . . . could be looked upon as pseudohomosexuality, according to Hirshfeld's [sic] terminology."[65]

Of course, the notion of "acquired" homosexuality depended on a belief in "true" homosexuality, permanent rather than fleeting and lodged in the constitution rather than motivated by circumstance. Discussions of sex behind bars reflected the influence of the emerging medicoscientific discourse that defined homosexuality, however unstably, as a congenital trait with somatic causes. They also followed from observations of gender inversion assumed to be constitutively linked to sexual deviance. In prisons and on city streets, those referred to variously as queers, fairies, and pansies were understood to be constitutionally different from other men not in their sexual object choice but in their gender inversion. As historian George Chauncey has argued, "The determinative criterion in the identification of men as fairies was not the extent of their same-sex desire or activity . . . , but rather the gender persona and status they assumed."[66] Before the mid-twentieth century, Chauncey argues, men understood themselves and were understood as homosexuals "only if they displayed a much broader inversion of their ascribed gender status by assuming the social and other cultural roles ascribed to women."[67]

Almost without exception, the status of "true" homosexual was applied, in prison and out, to gender deviants or "inverts": effeminate men and masculine women. The effeminate man who played the "passive," penetrated role in sex, known variously as fag, fairy, gal-boy, queer, pansy, and queen, and the masculine woman who was the "active" sexual partner, known as butch, daddy, husband, or stud, were understood to be motivated by constitutional disposition rather than by the abnormal conditions of incarceration. "Sissies" were familiar figures to Carlo de Fornaro in 1917, who catalogued their presence as prison types alongside others including "aristocrats of crime," con men, and tramps.[68] Perry Lichtenstein, physician at the Men's House of Detention in New York City known as the Tombs, referred to these presumably congenital types in the title of his 1921 article, "The 'Fairy' and the Lady Lover." Most early-twentieth-century reports focused on male inverts, but Lichtenstein singled out for closer attention the "class of females who abhors the company of men and gains sexual satisfaction from association with other females," some of whom "show distinct male characteristics. They wear strictly tailor-made clothing, low shoes, and they seldom wear corsets." Although gender inversion in women was not always detectable by outward appearance, Lichtenstein joined many others in this period in proposing that "a physical examination of such people will in practically every instance disclose an abnormally prominent clitoris."[69]

Fishman similarly underlined the gender inversion of members of the "third sex" incarcerated at Welfare Island: "The inexperienced person finds it difficult to distinguish them as males. They rouge their face and lips, walk with mincing steps, usually have high pitched voices, and wear feminine ornaments such as earrings, bracelets, and other trinkets."[70] Prison fairies went to great lengths to maintain their feminine gender expression, making rouge by soaking the labels of tomato cans in water and producing face powder from chalk stolen from the prison school.[71] Louis Berg was also struck by the brazenness of the fairies at Welfare Island and by the verisimilitude of their feminine gender presentation: "At first glance, they appear like women with their long hair and painted cheeks and mincing gait. But as they come quite close, you recoil; this can't be true! It is. These are men like women."[72] Berg boasted of his familiarity with what he called euphemistically "the facts of life," gleaned from excursions into Berlin's gay nightlife and American "Bohemian affairs," and of his familiarity with homosexuals—"I even numbered some among my acquaintances."[73] But nothing in those experiences apparently prepared him for his first sight of "the fairies at home," housed together in Welfare Island's "South Annex." "The first sight of perverted humanity in mass" was for Berg "one that I can never forget."[74] What impressed Berg most strongly about the "chattering 'ladies' of the 'South'" was what he characterized as "the absolute freedom from self-consciousness and the completeness with which these men like women accepted themselves in the feminine role they had chosen."[75] After observing them, Berg came to a sympathetic conclusion similar to that of many sexologists: "I soon found that in the main these were not maladjusted individuals suffering from soul-rending conflicts. . . . All they asked of the world was to let them be true to themselves."[76]

Occasional sympathy for "true" homosexuals, however, did not prevent Berg from blaming "fairies" for being "a constant stimulus to sexual abnormality" in prison.[77] "Such individuals," Berg wrote, "with their rouged faces, mincing gait and coquetting manner, are a constant reminder of unsatisfied desire and a ready source for pollution to a soil eager for the seed of abnormality."[78] Fishman agreed, writing that "the actual presence of so many 'fairies' with their feminine carriage, gestures, and mannerisms, in itself tends to keep aglow the fire of sex in even the most heterosexual of the prisoners."[79] The recognition of the "constitutional homosexual" provided a new way to understand sex between prisoners as well as a scapegoat on which to blame it. Those who had searched for explanations for prison sex in the overcrowded and "abnormal" conditions of sex-segregated institutions would come to focus anew on the seduction of normal prisoners by congenital perverts.

The expectation that otherwise "normal" men would be tempted by "fairies" underlay the decision on the part of officials in nearly every large men's penitentiary to classify and segregate homosexuals, typically identified as such by their effeminacy, from the general prison population.[80] As early as 1916, the New York Prison Association recommended a classification scheme that would segregate "perverts" as well as the feebleminded, psychotics, the tubercular, and "cardiacs." "By weeding out such confirmed perverts and making contact impossible between them and the uncontaminated," the association predicted, the institutional problem of "homosexualism" would be largely solved.[81] The ninety-six "perverts" identified among the 4,804 New York prison inmates of Auburn, Clinton, Great Meadow, and Sing Sing were assigned to the penitentiary at Clinton, the association reported, "because they usually require a rigid form of discipline and close supervision."[82] In his 1920 report "Sex Perversion and Crime," psychiatrist Harry Hoffman commented that the "self-confessed perverts" sentenced to Chicago's House of Correction were "of such pronounced types that the attendants in the receiving room can pick them out." "The large majority," he explained, "are of the inverted type."[83] In New York City's jail on Welfare Island, authorities placed any man convicted of homosexual solicitation or cross-dressing, as well as those whose dress or mannerisms were in any way effeminate, in the South Annex, where they joined "other specially classified inmates under observation, such as psychotics, mental defectives, scabies cases, syphilitics, etc."[84] Homosexuals in the South Annex were also segregated by occupation, working in the laundry (an occupation understood to be "women's work" and reserved for male homosexuals in many prisons). "The object in view," Kahn wrote of the practice of segregation, "is that there shall be no chance for the homosexuals to mingle with the nonhomosexuals."[85] The understanding implicit in these policies was that those types comprised two distinct and discrete groups and that homosexuals could be effectively identified by their gender inversion and separated from heterosexuals.

Inside and Outside: Wolves and Punks

Early-twentieth-century observations of sex between prisoners were shaped by a burgeoning sexological literature whose conceptual categories proved useful in understanding and mapping prison sexual culture. But heightened attention to prison sex in the 1920s and 1930s, on the part of penologists, prison administrators, and prisoners themselves, is not explained simply by the availability of a new conceptual template. While sexologists puzzled over the etiology of same-sex practices performed by apparently "normal" people, those practices would have been more easily and readily comprehended in urban working-class communities of the period. George Chauncey has documented the visibility of queer life in early-twentieth-century New York City and its integration in working-class and immigrant communities. In that world, Chauncey writes, "the fundamental division of male sexual actors . . . was not between 'heterosexual' and 'homosexual' *men*, but between conventionally masculine males, who were regarded as men, and effeminate males, known as fairies or pansies, who were regarded as virtual women, or, more precisely, as members of a 'third sex' that combined elements of the male and female."[86]

Prisons were enclosed communities that gave rise to and perpetuated their own distinctive cultures, but they were far from hermetically sealed. The attribution of sexual deviance or "queerness" to the gender transgression of "fairies" and the possibility of conventionally masculine men having sex with them without compromising their status as "normal" found an echo in men's prison populations.[87] Prison vernacular, especially the terms used to denote participants in prison sex, overlapped closely with working-class vernacular and the roles and expectations it delineated, no doubt reflecting its importation into prisons by a disproportionately working-class inmate population and perhaps its exportation into working-class communities as well.[88]

Prison sexual vernacular was part of a prison argot that attracted considerable attention more generally, from both prison insiders and outsiders. Industrial Workers of the World (IWW) organizer and prisoner Hi Simons was fascinated by prison language that seemed to him "full of swagger and laughter, because of the vivid if often violent and vile poetry that streaked through it. . . . To use it," Simons wrote, "made us feel bold and free."[89] Simons acknowledged that "except for a few terms from the I.W.W. vocabulary," incarcerated labor organizers "added nothing" to the specialized vocabulary of prisoners, but he worked to compile a dictionary of "prison lingo" he learned while an inmate of the U.S. Disciplinary Barracks at Fort Leavenworth and published it in 1933.[90] Others in this period published glossaries of prison terms as well, testifying to the emergence of a collective consciousness and shared culture among prisoners.[91]

Central to prison argot were the coded terms that delineated sexual types and declared expectations about sexual acts and roles, offering a vernacular analog to sexological taxonomies. Noel Ersine included eighteen terms referring to same-sex sex among the fifteen hundred entries in *Underworld and Prison Slang*, published in 1933.[92] Simons imagined that "a complete prison dictionary" would constitute "an encyclopedia of all imaginable sexual deviations," rivaling the sexologists' ambitions in cataloging sexual variance.[93]

Prison constituted a unique transfer point between expert and vernacular sexual discourses, the terms of one often inflecting the other. Those typed by sexologists as "pseudo-homosexuals" or "semi homosexuals" were known to male prisoners as "wolves" and "punks." These were men whose participation in same-sex sex was presumed to spring not from their nature but from the exigencies of circumstance. Wolves, sometimes also referred to as "jockers," were typically represented as conventionally, often aggressively masculine men who preserved (and according to some accounts, enhanced) that status by assuming the "active," penetrative role in sex with other men. As Victor Nelson made clear, "The wolf (active sodomist) . . . is not considered by the average inmate to be 'queer' in the sense that the oral copulist . . . is so considered."[94] In contrast to many accounts by penologists and some prison officials who blamed fairies for prison seduction, those most familiar with prison life typically credited wolves with initiating sex behind bars. That initiation was often aggressive. As their name suggested, wolves were understood to be sexual predators, wooing, bribing, and sometimes forcing other men to have sex with them. Wolves were "always on the lookout for a handsome boy with a weak mind, who had nobody to send them in some food and money," sociologist Clifford Shaw wrote in his 1931 case study of a young juvenile delinquent.[95] Berg described the process by which the wolf secured a sexual partner as "a campaign in which all the luxuries of prison—candy, tobacco, sweets, and choice foods—are pressed upon the newcomer."[96] Once the object of the wolf's affection accepted the goods offered, "he is quickly given to understand that he must repay the favor in kind."[97] Sometimes seduction by wolves was described as a deliberate and cold-hearted maneuver of engaging a younger inmate in a relationship of indebtedness, which could be repaid only by sex. Others offered examples of more heartfelt and romantic courtship. Nelson recalled "Dreegan," the "champion 'wolf' at Auburn Prison," who "outrageously flattered the objects of his lust; he gave them cigarettes, candy, money, or whatever else he possessed which might serve to break down their powers of resistance; and otherwise 'courted' them exactly as a normal man 'courts' a woman. Once the boy had been seduced, if he proved satisfactory, Dreegan would go the whole hog, like a Wall Street broker with a Broadway chorus-girl mistress, and squander all of his possessions on the boy of the moment."[98]

Wolves may not have been motivated by "true" homosexuality, in the understanding of contemporaries, but the relationships they forged in prison were often far from casual. Jealous rivalries and violent confrontations among inmates were credited to the passionate feelings of some wolves for their partners. Inmate-author Goat Laven described "brutal fights," some fatal, that arose from sexual jealousies: "It means a knife in the back to steal another man's kid."[99] Louis Berg seconded Laven's account. "The unwritten law of the prison forbids any 'wolf' to make approaches to another's 'boy friend' once he is wooed and won," Berg observed. "But it is not to be expected that men who break the laws for lesser urges will hesitate when they are driven by passions that rock them to the roots of their being. Fights occur between 'wolves' over some boy which are sanguinary and even end in murder."[100] Berg went on to recount the murder of "Mildred," an inmate at Welfare Island, by her partner. "From all accounts," Berg observed, "'Mildred' was the victim of jealousy caused by 'her' unfaithfulness. That 'she' paid with 'her' life shows the seriousness with which such 'prison marriages' are regarded." To some, the jealous violence that prison relationships could spark testified not only to depth of feeling but also to their similarity to heterosexual relationships. In a disturbing comparison, Berg concluded that Mildred's murder "proves how completely such relationships are identified with the normal ones between men and women."[101] Charles Ford described jealousies among female inmates that resulted in fist fights, "hair pullings," and "every other conceivable type of trouble making activity" and that were "even more real than husband-wife jealousies."[102]

One theory explaining the existence of prison wolves, enshrined in inmate lore by the early twentieth century, proposed that "a 'wolf' . . . is an ex-punk looking for revenge!"[103] The object of wolves' and jockers' attentions were known as "punks" and "kids," often identified as younger inmates, unfamiliar with life behind bars and unable or unwilling to defend themselves physically. A type recognized in prison argot since at least the early twentieth century, punks were understood to be "normal" men, vulnerable to sexual coercion by other inmates because of some combination of small physical stature, youth, boyish attractiveness, and lack of institutional savvy. A few accounts suggested that punks were "potential homosexuals" whose latent desires were nurtured and realized in the prison context, but most saw them simply as the unfortunate victims of wolves.

The punk's fate was often attributed to naïveté and, especially, his ignorance of the inmate code and the consequences of indebtedness and obligation to other prisoners. Charles Wharton wrote in his 1932 prison account of a fellow inmate, "a mere boy" who "seemed to have come direct from a farm" and who had "all the bewilderment of a child thrust into strange, frightening surroundings." The youth soon became the object of "pretended interest and sympathy" from other convicts, who showered him with presents—"silk hose, fancy underwear, food stolen from the kitchen, and best of all, cigarets [sic], the gold standard of prison barter." In the process, Wharton wrote, the boy "became a wretched victim of the most vicious circle in Leavenworth's convict population."[104] Punks also suffered as a result of their youthful good looks. Jim Tully, author of many books on his experiences on the road as a hobo and time in prison, recalled Eddie, a young inmate "with yellow hair and wondering hazel eyes" who was "too beautiful to be a boy." Eddie's life in prison as a result "was made a constant hardship by sex-starved men."[105] Berg wrote that prison populations always include "boys at that uncertain age where they have a good deal of the feminine in them." Such boys, Berg wrote, "are as much prized in jails and prisons as virgins."[106] Berg also attributed the fate of punks to "biologic inadequacy (another name for lack of guts)."[107]

Whether understood to be the victims of their own attractiveness, their youth and small stature, or their cowardice, punks were never depicted as wholly willing participants in sex with other men. Although there was little attention to overt sexual violence in early-twentieth-century prison writing, many acknowledged that some form of coercion was often involved in sex in prison, in men's prisons especially. Like wolves, punks were also understood under the rubric of "acquired" homosexuality— they participated in sex with other men not because of a constitutional condition but because of the unusual circumstances of prison life. "Had they never gone to prison," Berg wrote ruefully, "most of them would today be normal men."[108]

Prison sexual vernacular and the culture it delineated overlapped particularly closely with that of itinerant laborers, tramps, and hoboes who traveled the country's highways, rural byways, and railroad arteries in the early decades of the twentieth century. The association between tramping and homosexuality was strong enough by 1939 for a textbook on prison psychiatry to warn of "the possibility of homosexuality in prisoners of the vagabond type," since "this tendency . . . appears to be very widespread among them."[109] In his 1923 study *The Hobo*, sociologist Nels Anderson characterized homosexual practices among homeless men as "widespread" and described relationships between older men, known as wolves or jockers, with younger men, referred to as punks, kids, or "prushuns."[110] In transient communities, young men partnered with older, more experienced men who promised to protect them and teach them how to survive life on the road in return for domestic and sometimes sexual favors. Judging from many accounts, those relationships were often predatory and abusive. Jim Tully, whose experiences as a "road-kid," hobo, circus worker, prisoner, and professional prize-fighter provided the material for his twenty-six books, characterized the jocker as "a hobo who took a weak boy and made him a sort of slave to beg and run errands and steal for him." Punks, he reported, "were loaned, traded, and even sold to other tramps."[111] John Good recalled that the "criminal tramps or yeggs" who were his companions on the road in turn-of-the-century Denver "needed a boy to beg and steal for them, and to listen around for information." "These boys are degraded to unnatural uses," Good reported, "as well as trained in the arts of pickpocketing and sneak-thieving."[112] Josiah Flynt, an early participant-observer of transient life, also described relationships between boys and their jockers, in which "abnormally masculine" men take "uncommonly feminine" boys as partners.[113] Those attachments sometimes lasted for years, and boys remained with their jockers until they were "emancipated."[114]

Men who lived on the road and on the economic margins were vulnerable to arrest, and incarceration in jails and prisons was a nearly inevitable experience for hobos, tramps, and transient workers.[115] It is not surprising, then, that the vocabulary of prisoners would borrow closely from that of hobo culture, another nearly uniformly single-sex world populated by working-class men. Some prison terms revealed a direct etymology between hobo and prison terminology. When Jack London was arrested for vagrancy in Niagara Falls in 1894, he was locked up in the "Hobo." "The 'Hobo,'" he explained, "is that part of a prison where the minor offenders are confined together in a large iron cage. Since hoboes constitute the principle division of the minor offenders, the aforesaid iron cage is called the 'Hobo.'"[116] Hi Simons defined the term "Bo" as both a "hobo" and a "boy, catamite" in his dictionary of prison argot.[117] The direction of influence was probably two-way, and some prison terms were no doubt exported into hobo and working-class vernacular as well.

The importation of sexual vernacular, customs, and assumptions about same-sex practices from transient men as well as from a larger urban working-class world meant that some prisoners were familiar with the sexual culture they found behind bars. Fiction writer Chester Himes, who was sentenced to the Ohio State Penitentiary in 1928, claimed that "nothing happened in prison that I had not already encountered in outside life."[118] Himes grew up in a middle-class African American neighborhood in Cleveland, but youthful desire for excitement drew him to the city's rougher side. In prison, he wrote, "all sex gratification derived from sodomy, and I had encountered homosexuals galore around the Majestic Hotel and the environs of Fifty-Fifth Street and Central Avenue in Cleveland."[119] The many incarcerated men with transient pasts would have been similarly familiar with wolf-punk relationships in prison, which mirrored man-kid relationships on the road.

But while prisons, then as now, were disproportionately populated by working-class inmates, they drew prisoners from other demographic groups as well, some of whom were unfamiliar with prison sexual terminology and the roles and assumptions it described. The persecution of political radicals under the Espionage and Sedition Acts passed during the First World War and in the wake of the Palmer raids of 1919 resulted in the incarceration of activists in the 1920s, many of whom became vocal and articulate critics of the American prison system while behind bars.[120] These spokespeople for the working class often betrayed their own distance from and naïveté about working-class sexual life in their prison writing, and many were shocked by the sexual life they witnessed behind bars.

Alexander Berkman, for example, was candid in detailing his own prison sexual education in a chapter on an encounter with another prisoner, "Red," a hobo who worked alongside Berkman. When Red announced to Berkman, "you're my kid now, see?" Berkman claimed not to understand him and asked him to explain. Bewildered by Berkman's naïveté, Red exclaimed, "You're twenty-two and don't know what a kid is! Green? Well, sir, it would be hard to find an adequate analogy to your inconsistent maturity of mind."[121] When Red explained to him the practice he termed "moonology," which he defined as "the truly Christian science of loving your neighbor, provided he be a nice little boy," Berkman professed not to "believe in this kid love," and was deeply shocked, protesting that "the panegyrics of boy-love are deeply offensive to my instincts. The very thought of the unnatural practice revolts and disgusts me."[122]

The pedagogical question-and-answer structure of this chapter allowed Berkman to tutor his readers in "moonology" while maintaining claims to his own sexual innocence. He may also have intended to contrast Red's perverse sexuality with his own presumably platonic love for another inmate that he described later in the memoir. But Berkman was far from alone among early-twentieth-century inmate narrators in professing innocence of same-sex sexuality before life behind bars. When attorney and former Illinois state congressman Charles S. Wharton was sentenced to two years in Leavenworth penitentiary in 1928 for conspiracy in armed mail robbery, he acknowledged his own pre-prison innocence. Prefacing his discussion of "the worst of all phases of prison life," which he attempted to describe "as delicately as possible," Wharton wrote that, "looking back, I felt that I had been everywhere, seen everything, and done about all which the average man-about-town is expected to do, and I held that impression until Leavenworth made me feel like a country yokel staring slack-jawed at his first sight of urban sin."[123] Socialist and antiwar activist Kate Richards O'Hare was similarly shocked and appalled by the homosexuality she witnessed as an inmate of the Missouri state penitentiary in Jefferson City in 1919–20. Scoffing at O'Hare's estimate that 75 percent of her fellow inmates were "abnormal" as "entirely too high," Fishman speculated that she was "naturally led into such an exaggeration because, having no previous personal knowledge of prisons, she was swept off her feet to find that such things existed. She was utterly amazed when I told her that homo-sexuality was a real problem in every prison."[124] Eugene Debs, who was convicted of violating the Espionage Law in 1918 and sentenced to ten years in prison, lamented that "every prison of which I have any knowledge . . . reeks with sodomy" and wrote with dismay about "this abominable vice to which many young men fall victims soon after they enter the prison."[125] "I shrink from the loathesome [sic] and repellant task of bringing this hidden horror to light," Debs wrote. "It is a subject so incredibly shocking to me that, but for the charge of recreance that might be brought against me were I to omit it, I would prefer to make no reference to it at all."[126] Debs wrote in near-apocalyptic language about the fate of the boy "schooled in nameless forms of perversions of mind and soul" and prison sexual practices that "wreck the lives of countless thousands and send their wretched victims to premature and dishonored graves."[127]

Whether shocked or inured, prisoners of all stripes acknowledged sex in both men's and women's prison as nearly ubiquitous and its roles and customs elaborated to the point that it constituted a culture unto itself. That culture occupied a curious status in early-twentieth-century prisons. Officially, sex between prisoners was unequivocally forbidden. Prisoners who were found engaging in sex were punished, often by placement in solitary confinement and extension of their sentences. Some prisons took harsh and sometimes draconian measures to distinguish homosexual prisoners from the general population in order to humiliate them and punish their behavior. In the federal penitentiary at Leavenworth, inmates were reportedly forced to wear a large yellow letter *D* (designating them as "degenerate") if they were discovered having sex.[128] The superintendent of the Ohio prison at Chillicothe boasted to the director of the Bureau of Prisons, in response to a question about how he handled the problem of "sex perversion" at the institution, that he had found a way to deter such practices through the use of humiliation. "By this I mean that all known perpetrators or anyone anyway connected with sexual perversions have been compelled to sit at a certain table at the mess hall."[129] A report from Kentucky noted that inmates convicted of sexual offenses had one side of their heads shaved to identify them.[130] These practices of marking prisoners as homosexual were forms of punishment for sexual transgression; they also suggested the need for the production of a legible marker of homosexuality that ran counter to the notion that homosexuals, inside and out, were easily identifiable by their gender transgression.

Homosexual prisoners were also dealt physical punishments. A photograph from a Colorado prison depicted two African American prisoners wearing loose dresses, perhaps as another form of stigmatizing marker of sexual deviance, and pushing wheelbarrows filled with heavy rocks as a form of punishment for same-sex sex (plate 6). Kentucky physician F. E. Wylie proposed sterilization and "emasculation" that would "make it impossible for degenerates to commit sex crimes," adding that "surgery might even be used as a punishment" for homosexuality.[131] The authors of an investigation of the Oregon state penitentiary in 1917 moved further to argue that "in cases of congenital homo-sexuality in the penitentiary," the more radical surgery of castration was necessary, to deprive offenders not only of the ability to procreate but of their libido as well.[132] By the 1920s, more than half of the United States had adopted sterilization laws, and some targeted "moral degenerates and perverts" specifically.[133] Those laws were most easily and readily applied to people in prisons, mental asylums, and other carceral institutions.

Sex in prison was officially prohibited and sometimes harshly punished. But because of the difficulty of detection and the belief in its inevitability, prison officers often seemed to take it in stride. Joseph Wilson and Michael Pescor criticized prison officers who "regard homosexual practices as only another kind of dirty joke" and wrote that it was "essential" that "this question shall always be considered gravely—never with smiles, smirks, and a shrug of the shoulder" in their 1939 text on prison psychiatry, suggesting that this was often precisely how it was treated.[134] Berg confirmed that to officials at Welfare Island, "the 'fairies' were, for the most part, simply the butt for lewd jokes. When they spoke of perverts it was with the kind of indulgence that one uses toward children whose peccadillos are amusing rather than serious."[135] He added that "sex indiscretions" were "rarely detected and still less frequently punished."[136]

If prison guards could not be relied on to maintain a properly vigilant and condemnatory attitude regarding prison homosexuality, then, some hoped, prisoners themselves would rise to this role. "Only the cooperation of the decent element will ultimately weed them out," Sing Sing warden Lewis Lawes speculated in 1938.[137] Wilson and Pescor went so far as to suggest that if homosexuals "received a reasonable dose of violence" at the hands of prisoners "known to be aggressively heterosexual," it would "help build up a correct prison community attitude towards this question."[138] But the community attitude in men's prisons, to the extent that it is possible to generalize, seemed often to be characterized by a rough tolerance, even by those who presumably did not participate in same-sex sex. Samuel Roth, who spent several years in prison for publishing what was considered obscene material, noted that "one thing happened immediately," on his incarceration; "I lost my horrors of [homosexuality] as a vice."[139] He was far from alone. Recalling his experience on a Georgia chain gang in the 1930s, George Harsh had "too many other things to think about to care what two consenting adults do between them." "Under the conditions," Harsh wrote, "I think such a situation was inevitable, and I could understand it—and condone it."[140] Indeed, the institutional culture of some prisons recognized the established place of prison fairies. Though fairies were segregated in Welfare Island's South Annex, they were allowed to stage a bawdy Christmas show called the "Fag Follies."[141] In later decades, prisons would sponsor football and baseball games that pitted queens against jockers.

Progressive-Era Prisons and the Emergence of Prison Sexual Culture

"Fag Follies" and football games would seem to be worlds away from the systems of solitude and enforced silence held as carceral ideals just a few decades before. Changes in prison administration and prison architecture and penology aimed at enhancing inmate sociability in the 1910s and 1920s combined to create new sexual possibilities among prisoners. Material changes in prison architecture and administration that made possible new forms of contact between inmates made sexual contact more likely as well, creating new sexual geographies behind bars. Prison writers probably devoted more attention to prison sex in the early twentieth century, at least in part, because there was more sex in prison to attend to.

Beginning in the 1910s, Progressive reformers undertook an ambitious agenda to transform the prison. While few prisons if any had achieved the utopian nineteenth-century goal of perfect carceral solitude, a new generation of prison reformers and administrators judged those earlier visions at once inhumane and impractical. Armed with progressive ideas about criminality that emphasized environmental and psychological causes over congenital and moral ones, reformers repudiated nineteenth-century religious strategies of solitary penitential reflection as well as the disciplinary practices of lockstep marching, the rule of silence, the humiliation of striped uniforms, and corporal punishments such as flogging, water torture, and the shackling of inmates to cell walls still practiced in many prisons.[142] Embracing a new commitment to correction and rehabilitation, they encouraged inmate sociability, collective labor, exercise, and recreation that, they hoped, might approximate the normal society to which the reformed criminal would return. The federal penitentiary in Lewisburg, Pennsylvania, opened in 1932, was built with six dormitories rather than cells, with the notion that "the openness 'promotes rehabilitation by teaching men how to get along with each other.'"[143] (See plate 7.) Some prisons built baseball diamonds and exercise yards and organized football leagues and prison bands, and prisoners in many institutions began to enjoy weekly movie nights. Some reform-minded prison administrators went so far as to give prisoners a role in the government of their own community. A pioneer in the concept of inmate self-government, reformer and warden Thomas Mott Osborne established the Mutual Welfare League in the New York state prisons at Auburn and Sing Sing. Designed to train prisoners in the exercise of democracy, the league was composed of a committee of prisoners elected by their peers and responsible for overseeing prison disciplinary procedures.[144]

Changes in prison architecture and its uses, reflected most centrally in the yard, accompanied and reinforced new ideas about prison life. An iconic feature of the "Big Houses" of the day—Sing Sing, San Quentin, Stateville, and Jackson foremost among them—"the yard" referred typically to an open expanse in the middle of the prison. Often surrounded by imposing and fortified walls and towers, its barbed-wire (and later electrified) borders were closely patrolled by armed guards. The activities within, however, were often considerably less strictly monitored than its perimeters. As "freedom of the yard" was gradually extended, prisoners spent less time by themselves in their cells and more time mingling with each other. The resulting prison sociability ran directly counter to the Benthamite vision of strict surveillance and perfect discipline, and was captured in the writing of many prisoners. On admission to Utah's state penitentiary, Jack Black explained that he was "turned loose in the yard where there were about one hundred prisoners." There, the prisoners "played poker all day in the yard on blankets, and occasionally a game of baseball, when they could get up enough ambition."[145] Inmate George Wright described the federal penitentiary at Leavenworth in 1915 as "a little city": "All the prisoners are allowed to roam anywhere inside the walls, you can sing, run foot races, or anything you like."[146] Edward Bunker told of living "two lives" as an inmate at San Quentin a few decades later in the early 1950s, "one in the cell from 4:30 p.m. to 8:00 a.m., the other in the Big Yard." "In those days," Bunker explained, "convicts had the run of the inside of the prison. Each morning when the cell gate opened, I sallied forth to find adventure."[147]

The yard was a place of exercise, organized athletics, and casual congregation. Reformers and administrators hoped that these changes would promote a healthier, more "natural" environment that would help prepare prisoners for life after release. But inmates in early-twentieth-century prisons took advantage of the new blind spots in prison surveillance to engage in a range of illicit as well as licit activities, including drug dealing and consuming, fighting, and sex. "Every day at nine o'clock the cells were opened by the turnkeys, and the men circulated freely in the entire prison block for the rest of the day," African American Communist organizer Angelo Herndon recalled in his 1937 autobiography. "This made it possible for the prisoners with homosexual inclinations to go prowling around for their private pleasures."[148] Prisoner Malcolm Braly recalled a time, before the segregation of homosexuals at San Quentin initiated at the beginning of warden Clinton Duffy's regime in 1941, when "the queens had been free to swish around the yard and carry on open love affairs."[149] The "corner of the yard" was the site of a wedding ceremony between male inmates observed by Piri Thomas, as well as for the wedding ceremonies of inmates of the women's penitentiary at Bedford Hills years later.[150]

The new uses of the yard opened up a place of sexual display and opportunity in many prisons. But a loosely supervised yard could also be a place of sexual vulnerability and danger. "Vast and forbidding when empty," the yard, in prison chaplain Julius Leibert's description, was "a monster when packed. Five thousand heads, . . . and a million pent-up hungers aching to burst forth—that's the yard. Perverts on the prowl—'jockers' ganging up on a fish, 'queens' reveling in fights between rivals for their favors, homos pairing off for an affair or quarreling like obscene lovers."[151]

The early twentieth century also witnessed the expansion of profit-making prison industries, bringing together prisoners to work in laundries, woodshops, metal shops, forges, mines, quarries, and farms. Collective workshops were much less closely monitored than cellblocks, and the movement of prisoners there, as on the yard, was less carefully regulated. These changes also produced new opportunities, settings, and spaces for encounters between prisoners, some of them sexual. Inmate John Reynolds had earlier warned of the "horrible and revolting practices of the mines" where prisoners labored together at the penitentiary in Leavenworth, Kansas.[152] There, "far removed from light and even from the influences of their officers," prisoners were free to "mistreat themselves and sometimes the younger ones that are associated with them in their work."[153] Years later, Ted Ditsworth described his first day working in a coal mine as a prisoner in Missouri in the 1920s: "I had many propositions where these miners would dig my task for me if I would be their kid—what they meant was that they wanted to use me in a homosexual way."[154]

Some of this new inmate sociability and relative freedom from scrutiny was the result of progressive planning, and some was simply the inevitable consequence of the overcrowding of prisons that had vexed nineteenth-century prison administrators and intensified in the twentieth century. The prison population in the United States more than doubled between 1890 and 1925 and grew even more rapidly from 1920 until World War II, swelling with the rise in unemployment during the Depression.[155] Despite a new commitment to identifying and classifying homosexual, mentally ill, and "hardened" prisoners in order to segregate them from the general population, not all prisons could afford to employ trained psychiatrists or had the physical space to put those plans fully in place.

Overcrowded prisons carried associations of sexual impropriety for early-twentieth-century observers, as they had for their predecessors a century earlier. Louis Berg cited overcrowding as a serious factor contributing to prison homosexuality, writing that "when two or more men are confined in one cell and sex starvation has existed for some time, 'doubling up' becomes more than a mere expression to denote cell occupancy."[156] One prisoner described life in the military disciplinary barracks in 1919 as a place where "a man of refined sensibilities is often quartered in the same double-decked bunk with a degenerate or a moral pervert."[157] Investigator Dean Harno wrote to sociologist Ernest W. Burgess in 1927 about the reformatory at Pontiac, Michigan: "All cells have two inmates and quite a number have three. This brings a very acute matter in connection with the morals of the institution."[158] A prisoner of that institution called Pontiac "a 'deformatory,'" noting of sexual perverts: "They ought to take them fellows and separate them in a separate building so they don't have to mix with the other fellows."[159] Unevenly instituted in prisons for men, the practice of segregating homosexuals was virtually unheard of in institutions for women. Kahn noted that, at the Women's Workhouse on Welfare Island, "the homosexuals have been unclassified and are not segregated . . . , so that they all mingle freely with the other inmates."[160]

Prisons varied dramatically by geographical region, and certainly not all prisons put progressive reforms into practice. Many Western state penitentiaries in the early decades of the twentieth century, some resembling hastily built stockades, allowed for little if any classification and segregation of prisoners by offense, sexual disposition, or any other taxonomy.[161] Prisons were peripheral to the criminal justice system that emerged in the South after the Civil War, and some Southern states lacked them altogether.[162] Instead, convict-lease systems flourished in the postbellum South, drawing heavily on a newly criminalized population of black men and essentially replacing the labor system of slavery.[163] Prisoners in that system were contracted out by the state to work on sugar and cotton plantations, in coal and phosphate mines, turpentine farms, brickyards, quarries, and sawmills, and on levee and railroad construction, where they were exposed to harsh conditions and often brutal treatment. Later in the 1930s, prisoners in the South worked on chain gangs, moving about in labor camps rather than housed in permanent prisons. Mississippi's notorious Parchman penal farm, with its sprawling cotton acreage, predominantly African American field hands, and armed white overseers, resembled an antebellum plantation more closely than it did a modern prison. Constructed in 1904, Parchman served the postbellum imperatives of racial subordination and control and provided as well a cheap and steady labor supply for the rapidly industrializing New South.

Even those prisons furthest removed from Progressive ideals, however, allowed for considerable interaction among prisoners. Convicts leased by railroad companies "slept side by side, shackled together" in mobile iron cells.[164] Collective work and living conditions on prison plantations, in which men worked together by day and slept together in stacked bunks in barracks known as "cages" by night, also allowed for considerable unsupervised contact among inmates, albeit under horrific conditions.

With this increase in inmate interaction and sociability emerged a distinctive and broad-based prison culture that expanded and flourished in the early twentieth century. Prison accounts in this period recognized the development of a prisoners' code of behavior and ethics, the establishment of a tradition of prison tattooing, prison songs and work chants, and the emergence of a comprehensive prison argot. Prison sexual culture was part of this efflorescence of inmate cultural life and increasingly expansive communal life among prisoners.

: : :

If, in the nineteenth century, observers identified sexual perversion as a problem inherent in the abnormal conditions of prison life, in the early twentieth century, the prison began to be perceived as a refuge of perverts. Indeed, in Louis Berg's Welfare Island account, prison was their natural "home." It may not be an exaggeration to claim that the prison played a part in the solidification of the notion of sexual identity—distinguished by its nature as congenital and innate. At the same time, observations about sex in prison exposed the instabilities and incoherence in the category "homosexual," present from its inception.

But while early-twentieth-century prison administrators were concerned about the problems that homosexuality posed to morality and prison discipline, few distinguished the forms it took behind prison walls from those beyond them. As the modern practice of classifying individuals primarily according to sexual object choice grew in influence, however, prison homosexuality would look stranger and its threat to emerging notions of sexuality would loom larger.

CHAPTER THREE

The Problem of Prison Sex in Mid-Twentieth-Century America

In the early twentieth century, the phenomenon of sex in prison was discussed behind closed doors among prison officers and administrators, documented in relatively arcane medical and scientific journals, and usually only alluded to in prison autobiographies. In January of 1934, newspaper coverage of a prison scandal in the wake of a dramatic raid of a New York City penitentiary brought sex in prison into broad public view for the first time. Located in the middle of the East River, the Welfare Island prison had a long-standing and well-earned reputation as a badly managed institution that housed inmates in wretched conditions. The island institution first drew attention in 1887, when undercover investigative journalist Elizabeth Cochrane (writing under the pseudonym Nellie Bly) wandered the streets of New York feigning insanity until she was picked up and sent to the asylum on what was then known as Blackwell's Island. Her exposure of the abuses and deprivations suffered by inmates there sparked a grand jury investigation.[1] In 1924, the city's commissioner of correction urged that the institution be closed after yet another investigation declared it an "unsanitary, overcrowded fire trap."[2] The long list of deficiencies detailed in that report included a lack of classification and segregation among prisoners that "made it possible for sex perversion to become rampant."[3]

Conditions at Welfare Island did not improve in the decade that followed. And with the election of anti-Tammany mayor Fiorello

La Guardia in 1934, there was political capital to be gained from addressing the prison's long history of corruption and cronyism. Within his first
weeks of taking office, La Guardia appointed former prison superintendent Austin MacCormick to the position of commissioner of corrections
and charged him with the task of cleaning up New York City's prisons.
Just a few days later, at dawn on January 24, 1934, MacCormick led a team
of wardens, detectives, and journalists on a spectacular surprise raid of the
Welfare Island prison. Their expressed aim was to strip the warden of his
powers and to recapture the prison from the control of gangster-convicts
who ruled over other prisoners. The raid made front-page news for days
afterward, intriguing readers with stories of the "nether depths of prison
life" that resonated with the popular currency of pulp detective novels.[4]
Reporters wrote of battles between prisoners affiliated with the "Irish
mob" and the "Italian mob," of drug-dealing inmates who used homing
pigeons as couriers, and of dogs trained to attack prison guards. They also
drew scandalized attention to the outrageous privileges and luxuries that
some prisoners had accorded themselves. Welfare Island was exposed as a
"gangsters' paradise," where powerful prison leaders "had valets to press
their clothing, shine their shoes, cook their food, and wait upon them
hand and foot as if they were feudal barons."[5]

Alongside drugs, weapons, and expensive cigars, the cellblock search
produced what one reporter termed "an altogether different line of contraband."[6] Inside one section of the jail was found "every conceivable article of women's apparel," the *New York Herald Tribune* reported. Raiders
found "dozens of compacts, powder puffs, and various types of perfume,"
as well as "silk step-ins, nightgowns, and other bits of negligee," which
were reportedly "strewn about the cells." "One man even boasted a blond
wig," the reporter added in near disbelief, "while another clung desperately to a set of false eyelashes."[7]

Alan Sinfield and other historians have argued for the indeterminacy of
male effeminacy in an earlier period, noting in particular its failure to align
neatly with sexual deviance through most of the nineteenth century. By
the 1930s, however, it had come to be the sexual deviant's primary refer-
ent.[8] Some journalists were reticent in relating these particular details of
the raid; for others, the meaning of cosmetics in men's prison cells was
self-evident. Some resorted to the time-honored practice of referencing
same-sex sexuality by refusing to name it, at the same time drawing on
the telling language of elision by hinting at "horrible depravity" among
prisoners "too dreadful to be mentioned."[9] Others, however, broke from
that long-standing rhetorical practice to offer more detailed descriptions

of Welfare Island's "sexual perverts." Identified as such by their gender inversion, those perverts were recognized as "fairies." Housed in the prison's South Annex, the fairies were scandalous and bold in their effeminacy, "some of them heavily rouged, their eyebrows painted, their lips red, hair in some instances hanging to the shoulder and in most cases hips swinging and hands fluttering" and going by campy theatrical names like Broadway Rose, Greta Garbo, and Lillian Russell.[10] Journalists denounced the liberties granted the fairies, who were reportedly allowed to "parade along the tiers in high heels as showoffs," flaunting their femininity in front of other prisoners.[11] Among MacCormick's first prison "reforms" was to impose stricter segregation of prison fairies and to force them to submit to "military haircuts," an edict that reportedly caused them "considerable indignation."[12]

Marked as perverts by their gender inversion, prison fairies would have been titillating but not wholly unfamiliar figures to many New Yorkers and perhaps to other urbanites. Historian George Chauncey has documented a public gay culture in early-twentieth-century New York City, made visible largely by the presence of self-identified and identifiable "fairies" and "pansies."[13] And the late 1920s and early 1930s had witnessed a "pansy craze," in which flamboyantly cross-dressing actors appeared on the Broadway stage and on the pre–Motion Picture Production Code screen. Indeed, many of the Welfare Island fairies may have had direct links to that cultural scene, some of them as performers. Louis Berg, the prison's physician, attributed their theatrical "*noms de plume*" to the fact that "any number . . . had worked as chorus men at one time or another."[14] The powerful backlash against sexual excess and crackdown on urban vice that followed in the late 1920s and 1930s, reflected in the forced closings of Broadway shows with gay and lesbian content, the high-profile obscenity trial that resulted in the banning of Radclyffe Hall's *Well of Loneliness* in 1929, and police raids on gay commercial establishments had the ironic effect of making homosexuality more visible still.[15] In drawing attention to "inverts" of both sexes, early-twentieth-century queer visibility and the hostile response to it strengthened the association between gender transgression and sexual deviance.

In its more risqué coverage of the Welfare Island raid, however, the New York scandal sheet *Brevities* introduced readers to a less familiar and potentially more distressing sexual type. A *Brevities* cartoon featured a wolf wearing tight pants, fists clenched, who asks, "Where the hell's my lipstick?" The cartoon was titled "Just a Pansy" (plate 10).[16] *Brevities* was not alone in this period in casting suspicion on the otherwise normatively mas-

culine wolf or in marking the wolf as a kind of homosexual. "A 'wolf,'"
psychiatrists George Henry and Alfred Gross stated plainly in 1941, "is
a homosexual of masculine appearance and behavior."[17] Observing that
"all homosexuals. . . . are not obviously 'fairies,'" Henry and Gross noted
that "many, whose appearance, gait, speech, and manner are those of
coal-heavers assume a feminine role in sex play."[18] Clinton Duffy, warden of California's San Quentin prison through the 1940s and early 1950s,
agreed. Among "overt homosexuals," Duffy wrote, "some look the part,
some don't." But while "some play the male role, some the female . . . all
have one thing in common," Duffy insisted: "They are deviates."[19]

Henry and Gross, Duffy, and others in this period who identified the
gender normative partners of gender transgressive queers as themselves
homosexual (typically labeled "active" or, in the case of men, "aggressive" homosexuals), registered a fundamental shift in the understanding
of sexual identity, newly if still very unevenly defined by sexual object
choice rather than gender style.[20] They did so even when confronted by
prisoners who resisted that identification. Henry and Gross introduced
the case of Jimmy, whom they described as a "drug-addict hoodlum homosexual" who had "convinced himself that he is not a homosexual because he enjoys the masculine role in homosexual intercourse." Insisting
to "any one who will listen" that he was "no G—d d—n fag," Jimmy
referred to himself, when pressed, as a hustler or as straight "trade" who
had sex with gay men for pay.[21] An unfailingly masculine gender presentation and an "active" or penetrative role in sex, crucial to Jimmy's sexual
self-identification, however, was to Henry and Gross a deluded distinction without a difference that kept him from acknowledging the truth of
his homosexuality.

While the presence of wolves and jockers had been observed in prison
populations for decades, the possibility of their comprising a sexual type,
different from normal men and no less implicated in perversion than the
more frequently regarded fairies, provoked anxious questions about the
potentially transformative experience of incarceration. Fears that the sexual perversions long associated with prison life were not just habit-forming
but subject-forming challenged notions of sexual identity and fixity at the
time of their supposed solidification.

Ultimately and more broadly, the new classification of the prison wolf
as homosexual raised questions about the boundaries of homosexuality
and heterosexuality and, consequently, about the stability and essence of
sexual identity itself. Nineteenth- and early-twentieth-century prison
officials had treated sex between prisoners as a problem of morality and

discipline and had concerned themselves primarily with its physical management and control. Those problems continued to plague prison administrators, many of whom believed that the wolf, driven by an aggressive pursuit of sex, posed a grave threat to institutional order. But beginning in the 1930s and accelerating in later decades, those committed to a belief in the homo-heterosexual binary were faced with an epistemological problem as well: How to understand the same-sex desires and practices of those, previously ignored, who identified as heterosexual? Just as the prison was coming to be identified and exploited as a site for the production of knowledge about deviant sexuality, it came to pose troubling questions about the nature of normal sexuality.

Midcentury Anxieties

Understanding the prison wolf as a kind of homosexual ran counter to the long-standing association between gender inversion and sexual perversion. Most immediately for prison administrators, that new understanding posed important practical problems with regard to detection and classification. Since the early twentieth century, prison administrators had relied on gender cues to identify homosexuals in order to segregate them from the general prison population. Welfare Island's South Annex, known popularly as the "fairy wing" or "fag annex," represented one such effort. Samuel Roth, a New York publisher indicted and incarcerated several times for publishing literature deemed obscene, described the Welfare Island fairies who "wore the uniform of male prisoners" but who went by female names, "rouge and powder themselves," and "imitate in their walk all the seductive and shameless graces of women."[22] The Welfare Island fairies had counterparts in many if not most other men's prisons. James Blake described a "notorious den" in the Florida State Penitentiary at Raiford, where he was a prisoner in the 1950s: "Here the overt homosexuals lived in perfumed, screaming lurid celebrity, wearing earrings, their faces garishly painted. A line hung across the cell was draped mysteriously with feminine undergarments." The inmates housed there "were known as pussyboys, galboys, fuckboys, and all had taken girls' names like Betty, Fifi, Dotty, etc., and were universally referred to as 'she' and 'her.'"[23] Roth's and Blake's descriptions and many others like them highlighted the close association between male homosexuality and gender nonconformity that had long guided prison classification and segregation policies.

Few women's prisons appear to have made the effort to segregate lesbians before the 1960s and 1970s (and very few did so even then).[24] This was probably the case in part because there were relatively few female inmates in earlier decades and also because prison lesbianism was more easily dismissed and trivialized as akin to harmless schoolgirl crushes. Before the postwar period, too, lesbians were believed to be more subtle than gay men in their cross-gender expression, making their identification more difficult. Problems of distinction among female inmates were exacerbated, however, by what some investigators identified as a problem of numbers. Some researchers judged "a homosexual orientation" to be so common in institutions for women that "no attempt can be made to separate these individuals from the seemingly heterosexual group."[25]

Making that distinction proved difficult in men's prisons as well. "If all [male] homosexuals were 'fairies,'" psychiatrists Joseph Wilson and Michael Pescor observed in 1939, "aping the mannerisms of women and applying perfume to their bosoms and necks, it would not be difficult to recognize them."[26] But since by all accounts wolves were indistinguishable from normal men, total segregation of every male inmate who participated in same-sex sex was impossible. Joseph Ragen, the powerful warden of Illinois's Stateville prison, acknowledged the difficulty of identifying "certain types of homosexuals." While "the known deviates" could be easily singled out, those Ragen referred to as "the 'x' quantity, or unknown perverts" were "not as easy to restrain from practicing their peculiarities."[27] "Fairies" and "queens" betrayed themselves as "sex perverts" by "a peculiar twist to the hips, a sly smirk, and other . . . mannerisms," wrote a prison physician in 1940, but wolves were largely invisible in the general population.[28] Prison administrators were increasingly aware of the limitations of relying on "dress, mannerisms, and the stereotyped manner of speech" to detect homosexuals among prison populations.[29]

Purportedly more scientific diagnostic tools to detect homosexuality became available in the late 1930s, notably developed using prisoners as subjects. But since they continued to rely on assumptions based on a presumed link between gender inversion and sexual deviance, they failed to help prison administrators identify inmates likely to engage in same-sex sex with any greater degree of accuracy. Some prison administrators had high hopes for a test developed by Stanford psychologist Lewis Terman and his associate Catherine Cox Miles in 1936. Popularly known as the M-F test, it aimed to measure differences in what its authors termed "mental masculinity and femininity" and to chart the significance of what would come to be called gender to various characteristics and traits, including sexuality.[30] Like investigators before them, Terman and Miles turned to inmates of jails, prisons, and reform schools for accessible and identifiably homosexual subjects for their study, captive in the most literal sense. "Because homosexual persons in the general population live in constant fear of public exposure and consequent social ostracism," Terman and Miles acknowledged, "they are not easily accessible for study."[31] They selected prisoners identified by prison administrators as homosexual, many of whom were serving sentences for sodomy, solicitation, or "lewd and lascivious conduct" with other men. Their definition of a homosexual—"a person who out of preference has sexual relationships with persons of the same rather than of the opposite sex"—followed new understandings of sexual identity defined by sexual object choice rather than gender expression. Terman and Miles included both participants in same-sex sex in their definition of homosexuality, explaining pedagogically that "he is said to be an *active* homosexual if he plays the male role in the copulatory act, and a *passive* homosexual if he plays the role of the female."[32]

The M-F test consisted of a series of questions about knowledge of terms, preferences and inclinations, and hypothetical choices, the responses to which Terman and Miles scored on a continuum with extreme masculinity at one pole and extreme femininity at the other. They found that the "passive" male homosexual inmates of Alcatraz typically scored high on the feminine scale, indeed "more feminine than that of 38 college women athletes." The fact that none of the "passive" subjects associated "Yale" with "lock" signaled to the investigators a "lack of interest by inverts in things mechanical." Their familiarity with the concept of a "buffet" betrayed their "housewifely interests," and their ability to define "charades" was predictable, given that "charades is a feminine indoor game that probably holds more interest for inverts than for the norm group."[33] About their "greater liking for movie love scenes, poetry, and dramatics," Terman and Miles wrote drolly, "comment is hardly necessary."[34] The small number of lesbians "of the active type" that they tested also confirmed their predictions by earning "high masculine scores."[35]

Terman and Miles also tested the "active" partners of "passive" male homosexuals. Although Terman and Miles considered the masculine participants in same-sex sex to be homosexuals, however, their test of "mental gender" failed utterly to identify them as such. In fact, they found that the "active male homosexual" subjects "not only test[ed] much more masculine than the passive homosexuals, but also significantly more masculine" than subjects drawn from the armed forces of similar age, education, and social status.[36]

That distinctive flaw in the M-F test hindered its application at the Indiana State Prison in 1941. Investigator Edward Walker hoped that the test might make possible "an objective segregation" of homosexual prisoners, and he reported on the results of an experiment in which the test was administered to all new inmates.[37] While it was successful in identifying many known "sodomists," Walker recognized, however, that the test failed to identify "the aggressive type, or wolf," who "would be indistinguishable from other males as far as masculine and feminine characteristics are concerned." Since the test "will in no way point out the active homosexuals in the prison population," Walker concluded, it "is of little practical value as a diagnostic tool" that might aid prison administrators in identifying and segregating homosexuals.[38] Psychiatrist Charles E. Smith described a similar test designed to diagnose homosexuality two decades later, in 1956, in which prisoners who participated in same-sex sex were asked to evaluate themselves according to masculinity and femininity. Smith found that the group was about equally divided, "25 regarding themselves as predominantly masculine and 22 as predominantly effeminate." These findings, he concluded, "offer further corroboration of the concept that [male] homosexuality cannot be diagnosed with any degree of accuracy on the basis of presence or absence of effeminate traits alone."[39] Terman and Miles were ultimately forced to scale back their claims and to admit that the M-F test "does not measure homosexuality." They were reluctant, however, to abandon completely the equation of gender inversion and homosexuality, insisting that their test "does measure, roughly, degree of inversion of the sex temperament, and it is probably from inverts in this sense that homosexuals are chiefly recruited."[40]

Another problem with the M-F test was that it was easily subverted by those who took it. Since the test relied wholly on responses generated by the subject, Terman and Miles understood that the "faking of scores" would be easy. They promised, however, that since "subjects almost never suspect the purpose of the test," active subterfuge was rarely a problem.[41] The test's formal name, the Attitude Interest Analysis Survey, was designed to be vague enough to conceal its aims.[42] "The danger is present only when the subject has a definite motive in appearing other than he is," Terman and Miles wrote.[43] But given the wide range of penalties incurred by homosexuals in prison—including segregation from the general population, the possibility of long-term institutional commitment, and forfeiture of parole, as well as stigmatization, routine harassment, and vulnerability to sexual assault—they often had a great deal at stake in appearing to be other than what they were. Prisoners as a group were also considerably more knowing than the test's authors gave them credit for. Prison inmates in the 1940s and 1950s had more contact with psychiatrists and psychologists, when the rehabilitative optimism and enthusiasm for psychological treatment for prisoners in those decades granted those professionals new presence and authority in many prisons.[44] They were consequently increasingly sensitive to being "bugged," or classified in any way that might result in a diagnosis that would lead to their indefinite institutionalization or segregation.

Convict-novelist Malcolm Braly betrayed some of those sensitivities in his recollection of being administered the M-F test while an inmate at San Quentin in the 1950s. Serving time for burglary and armed robbery, Braly had been suspected by the prison's psychologist of "latent homosexuality," a diagnosis he found "one of those impossible charges to defend against, like the nutbusters Joe McCarthy was beginning to invent." (As he explained, "If you said, and how already damning to even have to say it, 'I don't suck dicks,' the response was, 'Yes, but how do you know you don't want to?'")[45] A long-term inmate with prior experience in several prisons, Braly was also keenly aware of the costs of such a diagnosis:

> At the time I was threatened with their lot . . . the life of a homosexual prisoner was even drearier than a mainliner's. They were strictly segregated and celled by themselves in the Old Spanish Prison, the first block constructed on the site, without toilets or running water, and they were marched everywhere, isolated in a strutting and giggling squad, and the only work to which they were assigned was in the prison laundry.[46]

Given the stakes of the outcome, Braly approached the M-F questionnaire "with some apprehension" and with strategic intent. He explained that he found the statement, *I would like to be a flower arranger* "easy to answer No." The next one, *If I were a reporter, I would like to cover the ballet*, struck Braly as "on the edge," but he also answered "No." In response to the statement, *If I were a reporter, I would like to cover sporting events*, Braly wrote, "[I] told my first outright lie and said Yes." He decided that he could both safely and truthfully say that he would *enjoy the work of a forest ranger*, but lied again when he said that he would not like to write poetry. His scores, he wrote, placed him "firmly in the safe male zone of the M/F index, but not so firmly as to open the suggestion of overreaction."[47] Based on the results, his damning diagnosis of latent homosexuality was revoked, he was allowed to remain with the general inmate population, and he was assigned to the print shop instead of the prison laundry, stigmatized as "women's" work.

Terman and Miles and the many prison administrators who hoped the M-F test would help them detect homosexuals in order to remove them from the general prison population had no difficulty discerning those they understood to be "true" homosexuals among male prisoners whose scores placed them on the feminine end of the gender spectrum. Prison officials rued the presence of queens and fairies like those at Welfare Island who made no secret of their femininity. And they were far from alone in clinging to the equation of gender deviance and sexual perversion proposed by sexologists in the nineteenth and early twentieth centuries. As late as 1940, sociologist Donald Clemmer still relied on late-nineteenth-century concepts of congenital abnormality and gender inversion in his description of the male homosexual, in prison and out, as "an individual who presents some feminine characteristics in the bone formation, the deposits of fat, the high voice, absence of beard, or other physical traits common to the female."[48] But what to make of the man who had sex with him? This question was newly troubling. Writers in earlier periods had cultural means at their disposal that equipped them to understand the ways in which otherwise "normal" people might be tempted by same-sex acts. Nineteenth-century observers might attribute that phenomenon to the sin of lust or the acquired habit of vice; a few decades later, it could be dismissed as the reprehensible but predictable attraction of "normal" men to fairies. The changes of just a few short decades, ushering in the practice, especially among psychiatrists and psychologists, of classifying individuals primarily according to sexual object choice rather than gender style, would render prison sexual culture stranger and more unsettling.

Apprehension about the meaning of sex behind bars, evident in the explosion in criminological, sociological, reform, and popular writing on prison homosexuality in this period, reflected a new sense of urgency about homosexuality in the culture at large. In addition to confounding distinctions between homo- and heterosexuality, sex in prison and warnings about its prevalence contributed to the specter of a rising incidence of sexual perversion more generally. Homosexuality was becoming more troubling in this period, in part because there appeared to be more of it. In the 1940s and 1950s, the newly manifest presence of gay men and lesbians in American cities, together with Alfred Kinsey's revelation in 1948 that "perhaps the major portion of the male population has had at least some homosexual experience," fueled a growing concern about the pervasiveness of perversion.[49]

The threat of what seemed to be the rising incidence of homosexuality was especially dire when linked to warnings about sex psychopaths that emerged in the sex crime panics of the 1930s and resurfaced in the late 1940s and 1950s. George Chauncey and others have cautioned against imagining gay history as a steadily progressive tale of growing visibility and acceptance, since gay life, at least in major urban centers like New York and Chicago, was more open and tolerated in the 1920s than it would be in the more repressive climate ushered in by the Depression and the cold war. Those decades witnessed a series of sex crime panics that depicted homosexuals as threats to the nation's security and to children. Collapsing and conflating sex psychopathy, violent crime, and male homosexuality, widely publicized sex psychopath scares lent urgency to warnings about the rising incidence of sexual deviance.[50]

The perception that homosexuality was on the rise was expressed in metaphors of disease and contagion that writers in this period began to employ to describe the pernicious effect of homosexuality, and of prison homosexuality in particular. Clemmer, for instance, identified "homosexual psychopaths" as "infectious foci . . . who spread perversion throughout the community."[51] Other accounts traced the etiology of prison homosexuality to the space of the prison and the experience of incarceration more generally. In 1937, for instance, one physician stated that prisons provided "the culture medium in which the *bacillus homosexualis* . . . flourishes."[52]

Implicit in these diagnoses, of course, was the notion that homosexuality was catching. That threat, hardly limited to the prison, resonated loudly for Americans anxious about the links between sexual and political contagions that threatened to weaken the national body. Fear of contagion was the structuring phobia in the 1950 U.S. Senate investigation of homosexuality in the federal government, which concluded that "one homosexual can pollute a Government office" and which resulted in mass purges of homosexuals from employment in the federal government.[53] And given the convergences understood to exist between the homosexual and the communist—in the subversive ability of both to pass undetected, their tendency to form underground subcultures, and the allegedly contagious and seductive quality of both communism and homosexuality— that threat was dire and destabilizing.[54] In the outside world, however, the fantasy prevailed that homosexuals, like communists, comprised relatively small minorities that might be effectively identified and cordoned off. In prison, in contrast, as one journalist wrote ominously in 1951, "homosexuality creates an atmosphere of rottenness and depravity that becomes part of the air all inmates breathe."[55]

The close association of prisons with sexual deviance, of course, was not new. The prison had a long-standing reputation as a space that collected more than its share of perverts. As Joseph Fishman declared matter-of-factly in 1934, "there are more lesbians in women's institutions than on the outside, just as there are more 'fairies' in male prisons."[56] But that relationship was understood, in most cases, to be circumstantial rather than causal. To many, the overrepresentation of homosexuals in prison was understandable, given prisons' tendency (and indeed their purpose) to siphon off society's dregs. The Welfare Island prison, for instance, was characterized in a 1934 journalistic exposé as a sieve for "the sweepings from New York City streets," collecting together the "petty thieves, drug users, vagrants, homosexuals, drunkards, and rowdies."[57] Homosexuals, in that understanding, were simply one among many forms of social detritus bound to land in prison.

Others explained the allegedly disproportionate presence of homosexuals in prison by positing a more direct link between sexual perversion and criminality. Clinton Duffy and Al Hirshberg essentially equated the two, writing in their 1965 textbook on sex and crime that "all convicts are potential homosexuals. And most homosexuals are potential convicts."[58] Because of the close connections between criminality and sexual deviance forged in the criminological imagination, the fact that the population of criminals and homosexuals substantially overlapped was utterly predictable. Of course, the criminalization of same-sex behavior made this equation between criminality and homosexuality a self-fulfilling prophecy. Historian Estelle Freedman has documented the disproportionate arrest and prosecution of gay men under new sex psychopath laws.[59] Many men were swept up in the surveillance of cruising spots and gay bars that intensified at midcentury.[60]

Increasingly in the mid-twentieth century, however, there was a growing fear that prison, rather than simply collecting perverts, played an active part in producing them. A heightened concern about the role of prisons in making homosexuals ran through writing about prison in this period, as investigators began to explore the formative place of the prison itself in the still-confounding etiology of homosexuality.

Seized by these new concerns, prison writers began to speculate about the sexual fate of inmates after release. A question that had generated no previous interest consumed sociologists, psychologists, and prison administrators as well as popular writers beginning in the mid-twentieth century. While a few offered reassurances that the practice of homosexuality would be shed along with prison garb at the gates on release, most were less sanguine. Psychoanalyst Benjamin Karpman warned in 1948 that homosexual practices in prison "'grow' or get so fixed in the individual that even on discharge from confinement he often finds himself unable to return to normal sex activities." Karpman cited the case of "young boys, of whose heterosexuality there was no previous doubt, who after a confinement of several years, have become confirmed homosexuals."[61] Duffy and Hirschberg considered the "not infrequent transformation from heterosexual to homosexual preferences" to be "one of the worst tragedies of long-term prison life."[62] "When they start they're certain it will last only until they get out," they wrote, "but many of these men become so used to a male sex partner that they can't resume a normal relationship when the time comes."[63]

Although there were far fewer studies of female prisoners in this period than of male prisoners, observers at midcentury worried about the transforming effects of prison life on women as well. To social worker Katherine Sullivan, writing in 1956, "the most tragic inmates are the ones who lived normal lives before being sent to prison and who after 'doing time' have not the slightest interest in leading normal lives again."[64] Psychiatrist Frank Caprio declared in his 1954 study of lesbianism that "most women inmates are never the same sexually speaking by reason of their prison experience."[65] And in her sensationalist 1967 exposé of New York City's Women's House of Detention, sociologist Sara Harris worried that women in prison "may be ruined for a life of heterosexuality" because prison butches "have a fascination that drab women, like the majority of those who land in the House of Detention, find hard to resist."[66] Others worried that women whose pre-prison experience with men had been disillusioning or traumatizing were especially vulnerable to lesbianism behind bars. Radical activist and labor organizer Elizabeth Gurley Flynn, who served a two-year sentence at the Federal Women's Reformatory in Alderson, Virginia, in the early 1950s, speculated that "incestuous fathers and brutal husbands had contributed to a hatred of sex as practiced by men" among many of her fellow inmates.[67] In Flynn's estimation, those women turned understandably to other women for comfort and sexual satisfaction absent in their relationships with abusive men.

Fears of the sexually warping experience of incarceration were buttressed by the new popularity and authority of psychoanalytic theories of sexuality. Psychologists and psychiatrists rose in influence at midcentury, both in prisons and in the larger culture. In opposition to sexologists' primary claims—in particular their insistence on the constitutional, congenital nature of homosexuality—Freud and other psychoanalysts

proposed that homosexuality could result from an interference in an individuals' psychosexual maturation, perverting the sex drive away from the
heterosexual object of desire.[68] Many drew on these theories to explain
prison homosexuality as the consequence of the psychologically regressive effects of incarceration. Prison, psychoanalyst and popular author
Robert Lindner wrote evocatively, transports the prisoner "back through
a sexual landscape he has already passed." Lindner went on to describe
"the peculiar liability of imprisonment to move back the clock and to
foster a slow but progressive return to the psychic stages of childhood
and infancy."[69] Benjamin Karpman agreed that prison tended to bring
neuroses to the surface "by constantly forcing regression to lower levels
of sexual adaptation."[70] In these and other psychoanalytic accounts, the
considerable stresses of prison life exerted a regressive pull to more primitive and immature stages of human development, homosexuality primary
among them. Prisoners were particularly vulnerable to sexual regression,
many argued, because the fact of their criminality betrayed their stunted
development more generally. "Convicts, in many ways, are like children,"
Louis Berg wrote; "indeed, it is their adolescence and emotional infantil-
ism which is often their undoing."[71]

While criminals were understood by many to be figurative adolescents,
others worried about the effects of prison life on literal young people, a
concern that was heightened by the midcentury panic about rising rates
of juvenile delinquency as well as the new prominence of psychoanalytic
theories of adolescence. Psychoanalysts who identified adolescence as a
defining moment in psychosexual development pointed to the increasing numbers of inmates in juvenile institutions as especially vulnerable to
the apparently sexually swaying effects of carceral life.[72] Confinement in
a single-sex institution at this crucial juncture, many speculated, would
almost certainly impede progress toward the goal of mature heterosexuality. Promoted by psychiatrists and echoed by prison administrators, this
view was reflected as well in the convict slang that referred to inmates
whose long histories in juvenile institutions denied them the possibility
of forming heterosexual relationships as "state-raised" or "prison-made"
homosexuals. Even Alfred Kinsey, who strongly opposed the normative
assumptions and stigmatizing consequences of psychoanalytic understandings of sexuality, believed that "lifetime patterns of sexual behavior are greatly affected by the experiences of adolescence," a life stage,
Kinsey noted, "in which the boy's abilities to . . . solve the issues of a
heterosexual-homosexual balance, are most involved." If these adolescent
years were spent in a single-sex institution, "where there is little or no

opportunity for the boy to develop his individuality, . . . and where all his companions are other males," Kinsey proposed, "his sexual life is very likely to become permanently stamped with the institutional pattern."[73]

Some inmates writing at the time confirmed these speculations about the sexually transforming power of prison life with stories of fellow inmates (and, much less often, themselves). Victor Nelson recalled his friend Barton, whom he first met at a juvenile reformatory. "At that time," Nelson wrote, "Barton was a pretty rough, tough boy" and "perfectly normal" sexually. When Nelson met up with Barton at the Massachusetts state penitentiary at Charlestown ten years later, however, he noticed a "vast difference" in him: "Gone was the rowdyish toughness, the coarse language, the rebellious spirit." After years in prison, Barton had become "a very well-behaved, gentle, almost effeminate creature." Nelson learned that Barton had "gone homosexual," and doubted that he would "ever go back to normal sexual intercourse."[74] Long-term prisoner Lou Torok wrote similarly about his first cellmate, Jim, with whom he often bantered about sex and women and who insisted "he would never allow any of the prison 'queers' to get near him." Torok was shocked several years later to find Jim to be "one of the most notorious and promiscuous homosexuals in prison," wearing the ring of another man he had married in a prison ceremony.[75] Virginia McManus, who served time in the Women's House of Detention for prostitution in 1959, wrote of "J.," a teenager arrested for promiscuity, who seduced "one of the favorite 'bull dikes' on the floor." "What J. actually wanted was love and fondling from her man," McManus speculated. "But, like so many girls when they are faced with long periods of separation from their men, she was ready to settle for the nearest substitute." When "the bull dike gave J. what she was asking for," McManus observed, "the transformation . . . was remarkable. From a teenager whose chief interest had been men, she became a convert to homosexuality."[76]

While prisoners were typically more forthcoming about their fellow inmates than they were about themselves, a few spoke to the ways in which the experience of incarceration altered their own sexual desires and occasionally their identities. Haywood Patterson, one of the five Scottsboro defendants who spent sixteen years in Alabama prisons after being falsely accused of rape in 1931, believed that "the Northern cities have so many gal-boys in the streets today" because "Southern prisons breed them."[77] Patterson went on to describe his own participation in prison sexual life, ultimately taking a "gal-boy" for himself. While at first, "it went against all my nature," Patterson confessed, "I was drawn more and more into this life."[78] Another prisoner, Paul Warren, recalled his affair with a young inmate known as "Janet" in the Illinois state penitentiary. Warren worried that other inmates would find out, even though the norms of prison culture dictated that "it was okay for a con to have a kid." "If the affair had meant nothing," Warren added, "I wouldn't have worried." But "it meant more to me than I dared admit. . . . Suppose I grew to like it more than any other way? . . . No matter how I tried to rationalize, I had to admit that Janet was a boy and according to the books, I was as much a homosexual as he was."[79] Former inmate Donald Lee finessed the question of his own participation in prison sex but referred to Pennsylvania's Western State Penitentiary where he served a three-year sentence as a "faggot factory."[80]

Midcentury anxieties about the seemingly contagious quality of sexual perversion, the apparently blurred and permeable line between homo- and heterosexuality, and the inability to reliably identify "true" homosexuals through gender cues were distilled in the prison context but were certainly not confined to that setting. The explosive findings of Kinsey's study, *Sexual Behavior in the Human Male*, published in 1948, contributed perhaps more than anything else to erode confidence in a sexual binary and in the stability of sexual identity as a fundamental reality, just as those ideas were rising in prominence.[81] Uncertainty, then, was structured into the sexual binary from its alleged beginning. Kinsey's most shocking revelation to postwar readers was how many American men—nearly 40 percent—had engaged in homosexual sex as adults. "This is more than one male in three of persons that one may meet as he passes along a city street," Kinsey added for emphasis.[82] His figures for women, published a few years later, at around 13 percent, were lower but still surprising and troubling to many.[83] Against the grain of a growing belief in a homo-/heterosexual binary, Kinsey insisted that human sexuality be understood on a continuum, and he criticized the dominant understanding of sexuality for its "failure to recognize the endless gradations that actually exist."[84]

An immediate bestseller, Kinsey's report on male sexuality was greeted with a mixture of fascination, controversy, and criticism. Shocked especially by the extent of homosexual practice Kinsey revealed among American men, some critics blamed his inclusion of the sexual histories of prisoners in his study for overrepresenting the incidence of sexual perversion, especially homosexuality. The relatively large representation of prisoners in Kinsey's data set was the consequence of the convergence of several of his interests and commitments. The disproportionate representation among prisoners of men from poor and working-class backgrounds offered Kinsey an opportunity to diversify his sample along socioeconomic lines. Kinsey was also interested in understanding the process of adjustment to sexual deprivation in institutions and in readjustment on release. He was interested in the histories of sex offenders in particular because of his strong criticism of laws that criminalized a range of sexual practices he considered common and benign, including homosexuality, premarital sex, and oral sex. Beginning in 1940, then, Kinsey collected sexual histories from inmates at the Indiana State Penal Farm and the Indiana State Women's Prison and, later, conducted interviews with California prisoners at San Quentin, Folsom, Soledad, and Chino. Kinsey's colleagues attributed his success in winning the confidence and trust of prisoners to "the attitude of total objectivity he conveyed to them, the familiar, nonjudgmental approach," and to their faith in his promise to keep their responses confidential.[85] "The cons were receptive to Kinsey," one warden at San Quentin believed, "because they saw in him that rarity, a man who made no judgments about them."[86]

Critics blasted Kinsey for including the sexual histories of convicts, outcasts, and deviants, and especially those of imprisoned sex offenders in a data set that he presented as a representative sample of American men.[87] Including convicted criminals in the data, many argued, skewed the results and exaggerated the extent of sexual perversion. Kinsey responded to this criticism by removing prisoners from the sample and recalculating his results, reportedly taking pleasure in pointing out that their omission made little difference.[88] However, he decided to exclude the sexual histories of women who had served prison sentences in his study of female sexuality at the urging of his associates, after acknowledging reluctantly that they "differ[ed] as a group from the histories of the females who have not become involved with the law" and would distort the calculations of the total sample.[89] This criticism haunted Kinsey's studies long after their publication, and Paul Gebhard and Alan B. Johnson's subsequent publication, The Kinsey Data, published in 1979, attempted to compensate further for the "contamination" believed to result from the overrepresentation of prisoners in the original Kinsey studies.[90]

A Single Swallow Does Not Make the Summer

Criticism of Kinsey's inclusion of the sexual histories of prisoners in his study of American sexual behavior, Pomeroy observed, "was based on the old fallacy that criminals are made of different stuff from the rest of the population."[91] Writing to novelist Nelson Algren in 1962, prisoner and fellow writer James Blake noted bemusedly that "some people have the idea that jailhouse sex is arcane, esoteric and incredibly exotic."[92] The depiction of the prison as a strange world unto itself, implicit in the criticism of the Kinsey study, was one of several strategies that midcentury writers called on to tame the newly unsettling implications of prison homosexuality. Louis Berg wrote of his own disorientation on witnessing the prison fairies segregated in Welfare Island's South Annex: "Looking back now, it seems as if when the outer gate slammed to behind me . . . I left behind all the world that I knew and could understand, and entered into a strange land whose symbols and language I had difficulty in comprehending."[93] Robert Lindner likewise insisted that the sexual world of prisoners differed in fundamental ways from the one occupied by ordinary people, emphasizing in 1951 "how truly *terra incognita* is that land beyond the ken of the average citizen, how exotic and strange its geography."[94] Employing anthropological conventions usually reserved for the study of foreign tribes, prison writers titillated readers with stories of life behind bars at the same time that they deflected their implications for the larger culture.

Prisons were understood to stand apart from the broader culture and indeed to comprise cultures unto themselves. This was the powerful consensus forged by new sociological studies of prisons that began to appear in the 1940s, which, in contrast to psychoanalytic accounts, located the causes of sex among prisoners in community norms rather than in the psychic processes of individuals. The understanding of inmate culture promoted by sociologists at midcentury was expressed in newly intensive efforts to taxonomize prison sexual roles and to decode prison sexual argot. Prison writers in this period, both professional and popular, shared an impulse to discern the intricacies of prison sexual norms and practices and a passion for classification. Sociologists Donald Clemmer, Gresham Sykes, Rose Giallombardo, and others brought ethnographic techniques to their studies of inmate life, mapping the geography of prison sexual culture and delineating its sexual types and roles. Investigators positioned themselves as guides with privileged access to the foreign world of the prison and as translators of inmate vernacular; indeed, many made a point of including glossaries in their published work.[95] The language of lesbians in prison, the author of the 1958 pulp novel *My Name Is Rusty* explained, "is one which cannot be understood without special translation." Accordingly, the book opened with a glossary of terms, titled "The Language of the Down People," "down" defined by the author as a "term identifying lesbians in prison."[96] The implication, of course, was that prison sexual culture existed in a world apart, one that required maps, dictionaries, and guides for the uninitiated, safely thrilling to contemplate from a distance and reassuringly without correlative in the outside world.

The belief that prison sexual culture was the nearly unique creation of what Erving Goffman would come to term "the total institution" was promoted in the most influential analysis of prison life of the day.[97] In the 1930s, Donald Clemmer took advantage of his position as staff sociologist at the Menard branch of the Illinois state penitentiary to conduct a comprehensive study of the inmate community there. Published in 1940, Clemmer's *The Prison Community* argued that the prison cultivated a culture of its own, shaped by the totality of the experience of incarceration and giving rise to a "code" among prisoners that encouraged disdain for and noncooperation with prison officials and mandated loyalty to fellow inmates. Strongly influenced by the Chicago school of sociology's interest in the distinctive cultures of marginalized groups, and following models presented in ethnographic studies of hoboes, prostitutes, taxi drivers, and gang members, Clemmer and other sociologists proposed that prisons were unique spaces that produced unique cultures among inmates. To capture this transformative phenomenon, Clemmer coined the term "prisonization." Prison life exerted a disorienting, "prisonizing" effect on inmates, Clemmer argued, stripping them of their prior status and identity and socializing them in a criminal culture and code of conduct, folkways, and identities.[98]

Among the distinguishing features of the prison community was its sexual life, marked by many midcentury observers as different in fundamental ways from that which prevailed in the outside world, in which participation in homosexual sex was nearly the rule rather than the exception and whose participants included many who maintained identities as heterosexual. With the rising prominence of those understandings came the first references to sex in prison as comprising a culture, with its own norms, rules, and expectations. "Certainly the prison atmosphere creates a 'miasma of homosexuality,'" criminologist Herbert Block wrote in 1955, "through inmate tradition, gossip, culture, and example, to which some latent and marginally disposed individuals will inevitably yield."[99] "The degree to which a man becomes 'prisonized,'" Block wrote, "provides a crucial factor as to whether the road toward sexual aberration is facilitated or not."[100] In outlining this process, Clemmer shifted in tone from the ethnographic to the colloquial and near-pornographic, adopting an imagined first-person voice in describing the internal feelings of an inmate who was tempted by same-sex sex: "Funny he hadn't noticed what a lovely, soft-looking body that kid had. Wonder how it would feel to snuggle against such a soft-looking body. The sensation couldn't be very different from that of lying close to the body of a woman, rubbin' against her, feelin' her soft, warm body pulsatin' against his."[101] Sociologist Arthur Huffman offered a less heated example of how this process of sexual defamiliarization and reacculturation worked in practice. In his 1960 study of homosexuality in prison, Huffman detailed the "jocker's strategy," whereby the jocker would work to convince a prospective partner "that a homosexual relationship was, of itself, a 'common occurrence'; 'nothing to be ashamed of'; 'everyone did it.' . . . He would then seek by every means to destroy every preconceived distaste or revulsion" for homosexuality and would assure the new inmate "that he was in a situation where this sort of thing was ordinary, normal, and necessary."[102]

Prisoners from a diverse range of backgrounds offered support for these arguments, linking the process that Clemmer termed "prisonization" with tolerance for and sometimes participation in same-sex sex. Percy Parnell, a long-timer in the Oklahoma state penitentiary at McAlester, considered participation in homosexuality "the first step toward becoming a true convict."[103] Illinois inmate Thomas Green marked "the complete absence of the female sex" as "the initial and most important aspect in the process which molds an inmate into a member of another culture."[104] Sylvan Scolnick, also known as "Big Cherry" or "Cherry Hill Fats," a renowned swindler sentenced to five years in the Federal Penitentiary at Lewisburg, Pennsylvania, wrote about the "lop-sided thinking" promoted by life in the "lop-sided society" of prison. "The place is full of homosexuals," Scolnick wrote, "and you start to think that homosexuality is normal. A guy would call himself 'Susie' and I start calling him 'her' or 'she' when I made reference to him to somebody else. You aren't surprised any more about men sleeping with men, or involving themselves in oral sex."[105]

Former prisoner Donald Lee confirmed this concept of the disorienting and reacculturating effects of prison: "Put a sane person in an insane asylum for a long period of time and he will begin to doubt his sanity. His standard of reference is the society he lives in. . . . The same thing happens in prison. The newcomer may be shocked and repelled at the propositions and the talk and the sexual acts, but the unremitting daily exposure soon conditions him and rubs off the taint of abnormality. Homosexuality suddenly begins to sound normal."[106] Recalling her experience as an inmate at the federal women's prison in Alderson, West Virginia, following her House Un-American Activities Committee indictment in 1950, Helen Bryan wrote, "I think all of us felt our life was so abnormal, isolated and remote that [lesbianism] did not appear as irregular to us here as it would have on the outside."[107] "You're in these surroundings and you look at it every day—kissing and petting and anything else they care to do," another young female prisoner commented. "You look upon it as an everyday thing. You don't think anything about it."[108] Piri Thomas, a prisoner in the New York prisons at Sing Sing, Comstock, and the Tombs in the 1950s, cast his own temptation toward sex with men in prison as an aspect of prisonization that he had to work hard to resist. Believing that if he gave in just one time he would be "screwing faggots as fast as I can get them," he promised himself that he was "not gonna get institutionalized."[109]

The trajectory implicit in the notion of "prisonization" also structured much prison fiction of the time. Prisoner-authored novels often opened with the naive narrator's shock of entry and moved from there to chart the lessons and rites of passage experienced by the new prisoner. Learning to think about gender and sexuality in new ways was often marked as key to that process. "I'd had trouble, during my first years in stir, getting accustomed to referring to these males as 'she' but it soon came quite naturally," the narrator of former inmate Christopher Teale's 1957 autobiographical novel, *Behind These Walls*, explained. "The feminine pronunciation was a part of their language, and it soon became a part of mine."[110]

The ideas in Clemmer's study of the prison community were quickly taken up by others, who expanded on the notion of prisons as nurturing distinctive cultures among inmates. Strongly influenced by Clemmer's notion of prisonization, sociologist Gresham Sykes proposed in his 1958 study of the New Jersey State prison that the "pains of imprisonment" combined to create a "society of captives."[111] Inmate society, in Sykes's analysis, was formed by the adaptation of prisoners to the fundamental deprivations of incarceration, key among which was the deprivation of heterosexual sex. "The lack of heterosexual intercourse is a frustrating experience for the imprisoned criminal," Sykes wrote, "and that is a frustration which weighs heavily and painfully on his mind during his prolonged confinement."[112]

Sykes's argument that prison sex was an understandable response to the deprivation of a fundamental human need invited another explanation of prison homosexuality, increasingly popular in the mid-twentieth century, which also helped to ease the trouble it made for the notion of sexual identity as fixed in the individual and of homosexuality as constituting a discrete sexual type. Many called on Sykes's observations about deprivation to explain sex behind bars as a wholly understandable adaptation to the unnatural conditions of imprisonment. Some presented same-sex sex in prison as so commonsensical as to render any further explanation or analysis almost unnecessary. In 1962, psychologist Fred Cutter simply stated the "obvious fact that separation of the sexes induces some people to seek homosexual gratification. This is a rational or logical reason for homosexuality."[113]

Sometimes, the same writers who depicted prisoners as inhabitants of foreign worlds and practitioners of bizarre sexual customs, at other points underlined how comprehensible, banal, and even how normal homosexuality in prison was, given the abnormal conditions of prison life. The same Louis Berg who claimed to find the prison sexual culture of Welfare Island so mystifyingly alien acknowledged, without noting the contradiction, that "in the end, all normal men . . . will find themselves torn by this natural hunger where satisfaction is denied for any length of time."[114] To Robert Lindner, the inmate who engaged in homosexuality simply responded to "the agonizing call of his biology."[115] "Let's face it," Frederick Baldi wrote plainly in his 1959 memoir on his experience as medical director and superintendent of the Philadelphia County Prison, "life in prison is an unnatural existence. It curbs the inmate's everyday routine, thwarts his smallest desires, habits, and instincts—and, most important of all, diverts those innermost drives which are too powerful to be halted or cut off."[116] The "sex urge" was "too great and vital to be tampered with," Baldi wrote. "Yet tamper with it we do when a man or woman is confined and isolated for too long a time from members of the opposite sex."[117] "Prison inmates are individuals with the same biological drives as their fellow-citizens in the free world," psychologist Richard Stiller agreed in 1960. "Prison may alter the direction of the sexual drive; but the sexual drive goes on."[118]

The explanation of prison sex as an understandable and compensatory response to the deprivations of incarceration, in some versions, construed sex behind bars as a poignantly human and almost salutary adaptation to prison life. Anthropologists George Deveureux and Malcolm Moss, for example, judged "the sex act in prison" to be "a forceful affirmation of the self":

> It is a sociable gesture, a powerful gesture of spontaneity and an affirmation of the undiminished integrity of the self. It should be noted that other opportunities to manifest these psychic states and needs are conspicuously lacking in prison, as are opportunities of finding pleasure of any kind. In brief, sex behavior in prison is a substitute for baseball and marriage and movies and bragging and friendship and success, a substitute for anything and everything that makes life worthwhile.[119]

Sociologist Sara Harris likewise proposed that the voluntary relationships between women in prison, drawn together "out of their own needs, loneliness, disappointment with the men in their lives, any one of a hundred reasons . . . cannot be condemned wholesale. In some cases," she added, "they may even be therapeutic."[120] Together, these accounts worked to deexoticize and depathologize same-sex sex in prison, presenting it as inevitable, understandable, and fundamentally human.

The explanation of prison sex as a compensatory response to heterosexual deprivation was cited as well by many prisoners. Some framed the desire for sexual relationships as ways of alleviating the general deprivations and pains of prison life, large and small. Helen Bryan attributed lesbianism in prison to "the need for recognition, the pressing demand for something out of the ordinary, something exciting to break the monotonous routine, plus the overwhelming desire for the total affection of one person."[121] Others focused more specifically on the irreducible and irrepressible nature of the human (and especially male) sex drive. Donald Lee wrote of himself and his fellow prisoners (using the oddly distancing "they" to refer to a prison community of which he was a member): "These are men in their physical prime. They have the same drives that young men on the outside do, but they don't have the same opportunities for satisfaction. They crave sex, but there are no girls. So, of necessity, prisoners turn to each other."[122] "The natural sex drive becomes almost unbearable as months grow into years," Piri Thomas agreed, "and the absence of a woman to love becomes the greatest sense of lonely pain next to the agonized yearning for freedom."[123] "Deprived of socially accepted relations," George Sylvester Viereck observed in his 1952 prison memoir, "men may become involved in things that they would shun ordinarily. They are not 'inverts,' but merely sex opportunists who, when their normal outlets are blocked, accept any available substitute."[124] Or, as Iowa State Prison inmate Robert Neese noted plainly, "salt thirteen hundred men away where they can't get to women and some of them are going to find substitutes."[125]

To many at midcentury, prison sex was simply the natural and inevitable expression of a normal sex drive, temporarily and understandably rerouted. In their defensive insistence on drives, nature, and biology over psychology, personality, or identity, these writers worked to sever the connection between perverse desire and individual identity. More ambitiously, they endeavored to unburden sexual object choice, at least as manifested behind bars, from the weighty significance it was coming to assume. "This type of sexual experience seems to have little real meaning" to the "situational or transitory homosexual," psychiatrists Russell Dinnerstein and Bernard Glueck wrote.[126] By extension, they suggested, it need not have much meaning to or for the larger culture.

Understanding same-sex sex behind bars as the simple and instinctual expression of the human sex drive, by necessity shunted from normal to perverse channels, led some in this period to press for conjugal visits for prisoners as a way to ease the sexual tension and need that they believed led to homosexuality.[127] "When sexual intercourse is allowed," physician Joseph Wilson wrote in 1953, "the odd or aberrant practices so frequent in our prisons and reformatories seldom occur."[128] "There is nothing new or daring in this suggestion," Barnes and Teeters wrote reassuringly, noting that Mexico and many Latin American, Scandinavian, and European countries had long sanctioned conjugal visits, overnight home visits, and furloughs for prisoners.[129]

Few were aware that one U.S. prison, quietly and without fanfare, had sanctioned conjugal visits as well. Since the turn of the twentieth century, African American inmates of the Mississippi State Penitentiary at Parchman were allowed to visit with their families on prison grounds and to meet privately with their wives in cottages on the prison plantation, known as "red houses" and designated for that purpose.[130] The discretion surrounding Parchman's pioneering role in conjugal visitation in American prisons probably had a few sources. For one, the practice of permitting Parchman inmates to "visit" with women derived at least in part from the racist notion that African American prisoners, assumed to be more driven by sexual needs than whites, would be more tractable and productive workers in Parchman's plantation-style labor system if allowed regular access to heterosexual sex. As historian David Oshinsky observes, "The motivating forces behind this system were the same ones that dominated all other aspects of the Parchman operation: profit and race."[131] In addition, at least in its early years, Parchman's practice was not strictly conjugal. The prison reportedly had a long history of allowing prisoners access not only to their wives but to prostitutes, who arrived at the prison on Sundays on flatbed trucks from neighboring Mississippi Delta towns.

Beginning in the postwar period, some ventured arguments, often tentatively, for extending the practice of conjugal visits. "It's time for us to stop burying our heads in the sand and acknowledge the facts of prison life," Clinton Duffy and Al Hirshberg wrote in 1965. "Even normal, well-adjusted men find it difficult to get along without women."[132] Conjugal visits, they speculated, "would cut homosexuality appreciably."[133] Most acknowledged, however, that conjugal visits would be difficult for most

Americans to accept, given strong sentiments against "coddling" prisoners, as well as what many identified as a peculiarly American sexual reticence. "Because of the mores and prudishness of our own society," Arizona prison guard Daniel Moore wrote in 1969, "I am sure that we would never sanction such measures."[134] A 1951 survey found "little favorable attitude" among prison administrators toward conjugal visits, observing that, "in the United States, sexual relationships . . . are usually thought of in a context of marital companionship rather than as a limited physical relationship."[135] Sociologist Columbus Hopper confirmed that, in the United States, "the chief objection is that such visits would be incompatible with existing mores, since the visits seem to emphasize only the physical satisfactions of sex."[136] It was not until 1968, with the loosening of some of the moral objections to conjugal visits and a briefly renewed faith in prison's rehabilitative role, that some California penitentiaries began an experimental program that allowed a few married male inmates nearing the end of their sentences and with records of good behavior to spend a weekend with their wives in apartments on prison grounds.

The weight of American moralism fell more heavily on women than men, in this regard as in most others, and recommendations for conjugal visits to curb prison homosexuality were restricted to male prisoners. But the "pains of imprisonment" were also believed to be heavily gendered, and women prisoners were believed to suffer the loss of human affection, love, and warmth more than sex. While men's prisons were often depicted as anarchic spaces seething with sexual tension, in which "the sight and smell of naked bodies" and the natural male sex drive combined to make homosexuality inevitable, women's prisons, as rendered by a range of observers, assumed a distinctly domestic and asexual cast.[137] In a lecture given at the Conference of Women Superintendents of Girls' and Women's Correction Institutions in 1944, for instance, Margaret Mead pronounced relationships among female prisoners to be "much less dangerous" than those between male prisoners because the former consisted primarily of "one person look[ing] after the welfare of the other, mak[ing] them silk underwear, etc."[138] Because of the widespread belief that women "tolerate the absence of overt sexual activity far better than do men," many attributed the sexual relationships between women prisoners to a desire for companionship, emotional connection, and a misplaced maternalism.[139]

To those who understood homosexuality in prison as a temporary response to unnatural circumstances, it was reasonable to expect that when those circumstances changed, so would sexual object choice. The concept of situational homosexuality came into use in the 1940s and 1950s, coined by sociologists to describe participation in same-sex sex by those who otherwise identified as "straight," "heterosexual," or "normal." The word "situational" connoted an encouraging superficiality; it also communicated an implicit reassurance that when the situation changed, so would the behavior. In so doing, the concept of situational homosexuality worked to allay the anxieties of those who feared that the experience of incarceration would have permanent sexual effects. For most prisoners, John Bartlow Martin wrote in his 1952 prison memoir, "it's only a temporary fixation," assuring readers that "the minute they step out of the front doors they forget about it." Those who engaged in homosexuality because of circumstance were different from the "fruits," who, Martin wrote, were "born like that."[140] Rather than a neutral description of sexual acts produced by the presumably ahistorical forces of circumstance and environment, the articulation of the category of situational homosexuality was a rhetorical maneuver by which midcentury social scientists sought to contain the disruptive meanings of sexual acts apparently unlinked to, and therefore unsettling of, sexual identity.

As prison writers negotiated the anxieties provoked by sex in prison, they adopted positions that were inherently unstable. The tension that literary critic and theorist Eve Sedgwick draws between minoritizing and universalizing understandings of homosexuality is useful in understanding the seemingly incongruent explanations of prison sex offered at midcentury. Sedgwick draws attention to the ways in which homosexuality has been understood as attributable to a small class of deviant individuals and has been presented alternately as "an issue of continuing, determinative importance in the lives of people across the spectrum of sexualities."[141] Sedgwick makes clear that those two rival claims, while contradictory, do not form a binary but rather coexist, however uneasily and incoherently. Both concepts were proposed in midcentury discussions of prison sexual culture, sometimes by the same person, to contain the disruptions posed by prison sex. Prison writers aimed to hold steady a coherent and definitive sexual identity—a minoritizing understanding—and at the same time promoted a universalizing view by acknowledging that heterosexual men could participate in and even initiate same-sex sex. Indeed, in some accounts, such participation, driven by the universal need for sex, confirmed their normality. Prison sex, in these accounts, was alternately exotic and banal, alarming and uninteresting.

Attempts to contain and resolve the contradictions presented by prison sex, in this period and others, were invariably fragile and contradictory. Investigations of prison sex forced midcentury social scientists into accepting and even promoting convoluted explanations that were, quite literally, difficult to keep straight. Not surprisingly, the seams of those strained constructions sometimes showed. "It is an anomaly to speak of 'normal sex perversions,'" prison historian Negley Teeters wrote uneasily in 1937, "but that is a fairly good descriptive term to apply to what occurs when persons of the same sex are deprived, for long periods of time, of normal relationships with members of the opposite sex."[142] Tom Runyon, drawing on his experience at the Iowa State Penitentiary, agreed, writing in 1953 that "in his unnatural way, the homosexual remains a natural part of the modern prison."[143] Another prisoner distinguished between those he termed "normal homosexual[s]" from the "abnormal" variety, the former being "the average guy" who only participated in homosexuality in prison.[144]

The midcentury imperative to distinguish between "true" homosexuality and forms that came to be defined as situational, circumstantial, or acquired led investigators to insist that prison homosexuality was altogether different from its manifestations in the outside world. Robert Lindner deliberately confounded the expectations of his readers when he prefaced a 1951 article devoted to the problems of sex in prison with the breezy claim that "homosexuality is not an outstanding problem in prison." Lindner went on to explain that "the adventitious and transient sex exchange between members of one sex do not constitute homosexuality any more than the single swallow makes the summer."[145] Rather, Lindner wrote, "the whole thing is a matter of definition."[146] Observers consequently did what they could to distinguish prison homosexuality from its presumably "truer" form.

Prison Sex in Popular Culture

Precisely at the moment that social scientists sought to evacuate prison sex of meaning or consequence for the outside world, the outside world became newly, pruriently fascinated by it. As homosexuality in prison became increasingly dissonant with dominant understandings of sexuality, its representation in popular culture became ironically more ubiquitous. Beginning in the late 1940s and accelerating in the 1950s and 1960s, prison sex—often implied, sometimes explicit—was featured in virtually every popular genre of the day, in pulp novels and other mass-

market fiction, in B movies, and in more "highbrow" literary, stage, and
screen productions. This was not the first time that popular audiences had been drawn to
depictions of prison life. Filmmakers in the 1930s had catered to the widespread interest of Depression-era Americans in criminal transgression, and
prison films joined gangster movies, Westerns, and horror films as among
the period's most popular cinematic genres. Prison films continued to enjoy huge popularity in the 1940s and 1950s. Stories of prison life were
also featured on the radio, and the program "I Was a Convict" ran from
1945 to 1949. Prison was a popular subject as well for authors of the thriving pulp fiction and popular-scientific nonfiction of this period. Featuring
provocative covers, these genres traded heavily in sexual subjects, prison
sexual experience among them.[147]

The borders among social scientific writing, journalism, and popular
culture were permeable and porous, and representations and understandings of sex in prison circulated freely between and among them. Barnes
and Teeters quoted from Felice Swados's 1941 novel *House of Fury*, as well
as from works by Oscar Wilde, Havelock Ellis, and the prison memoirs
of Victor Nelson and Alexander Berkman, in their 1944 criminology
textbook. Haywood Patterson's account of taking a "gal-boy" in his 1950
memoir, *Scottsboro Boy*, was reprinted alongside ethnographic prison studies written by academics in the 1962 textbook *The Sociology of Punishment
and Correction*. James J. Proferes referenced Philadelphia district attorney
Alan Davis's investigation of sexual violence in the Philadelphia jail system in the foreword to his 1969 work of pornographic paperback fiction,
Prison Punk.[148]

Social-scientific and popular depictions of prison sexual culture often
shared broad concerns and conventions, but tensions implicit and quickly
eased in the sociological literature were given freer rein in popular domains. Sexual fluidity and instability posed as threatening in some scholarly and scientific accounts were sources of profound fascination as well
as phobia in more popular genres. While social scientists' efforts to shore
up the differences between the "real" and the "situational" homosexual
constantly threatened to crumble under the weight of their own contradictions, popular culture exploited those contradictions for their titillating appeal.

Those dynamics were on dizzying display in the 1954 *True Confessions*
story, "I Lived in a Hell behind Bars."[149] The story is narrated by Lola, sentenced to a year in prison for forging checks. Lola confronts "the strange
and evil code of the prisoners" on her first day, when she is forced to fend

off the advances of the most predatory prison butch, Faye, who tells Lola "you've got a lot to learn, and I'm just the guy to teach you."[150] Lola manages to fend off Faye's advances, but when Faye's lecherous attentions turn to attractive and naive new inmate Julie, the only way Lola can think of protecting her is by posing as her girlfriend. Faye is left to believe that her mistake was not in assuming that Lola would be a willing sexual participant but in misreading her as femme.

Once committed to this plan, Lola realizes that "I had to make the act look good." Over time, she assumes the prison nickname "Tex" and becomes increasingly comfortable with the ruse. At first embarrassed, Lola grows adept at "pretend[ing] a relationship with her which did not exist": "It had been necessary to caress her for others to see so as to establish my claim to her as against Faye's. Now, unconsciously, my hands would touch her hair when she would lean her head on my shoulder. My arms were tighter around her at night, without my being aware of it."[151] The martial art of jujitsu had earlier served Lola well in defending herself against Faye, and one day on a prison outing, she decides to teach Julie a few fundamentals so she can protect herself. But the lesson gets out of hand; Lola flips Julie to the ground, and, overwhelmed by "an amazing flood of tenderness," kisses her on the mouth. She explains, "I could no more have stopped that kiss than I could have halted the outgoing tide of the ocean. That was how my love flowed to her then, and the second kiss was long and rich with feeling. Julie's amazing response was warm."[152]

Lola's actions and feelings compel her to question her true nature. "What of me?" she asks. "Was I, I asked myself fiercely, in the same category as Faye?"[153] Her excessive defensiveness betrays her doubts: "I was a normal, healthy woman with a normal woman's impulses. I had always found men desirable. I had never before had even close friendships with women." But by the next day, Lola is able to place her relationship with Julie in what she calls "its proper perspective." Shaped by what she describes as "remarkable circumstances," the relationship was "tender" but not "evil," "unless I chose to make it so, which I certainly did not."[154] Like temporary insanity, situational homosexuality, or at least Lola's brush with it, could be explained by dint of circumstance, not nature.

The story might have ended there, narrating in spicier language and juicer detail an account that echoed social-scientific accounts: Lola's desires were pulled in unnatural directions by unnatural circumstances. Her feelings for Julie were rooted not in sexual desire but in feminine sympathy and maternal instinct. But pulp conventions led *True Confessions* readers to expect loopier twists and turns, and the story continues. After some awkwardness, Lola and Julie resume their performance as lovers, and the night before Julie's release, a matron catches them in bed together. Lola absolves Julie of all responsibility, and her sentence is extended. Julie is released from prison, falls in love with Lola's brother Pete, and marries him.

Despite Lola's emphatic assertion that the kiss was never repeated, its meaning and the questions it compels continue to reverberate throughout her life after her release from prison. While she professes to be pleased by Julie's marriage to Pete, Lola worries about her brother's reaction to the "strong feelings" she has for his new wife, tellingly posed in the present tense. But Pete apparently knows about the kiss, and in a queer moment of brother-sister bonding, Pete taps Lola lightly on the chin with his fist and tells her, "It must have been good, considering [Julie's] reaction to it."[155]

"I Lived in a Hell behind Bars" played with the slippages between heterosexuality and homosexuality and then went to some lengths to restore the boundary between the two. Lola takes solace in her brother's assurance that her relationship with Julie was "normal" and, in a final paragraph, announces that she is engaged to marry Julie's uncle. But the attempt at heteronormative closure, hasty, half-hearted, and utterly lacking in narrative attention and detail, fails to recoup Lola's suspect sexuality. Their marriage to each other's relatives suggests their continuing bond and unwillingness to let each other go. And by the end, it is difficult not to read Lola's obsessively repetitive self-reassurances about the normality of her love for Julie as protesting too much. Most important, her prison experience has permanently stigmatizing consequences: While Julie is identified in the police report as an "unwilling victim of homosexual attack," Lola's record classifies her as a "self-admitted pervert."[156]

The 1958 lesbian pulp novel *My Name Is Rusty*, in a more direct way, detailed the apparently inevitable process by which heterosexual women were recruited into homosexuality in prison. To that end, the novel invoked what would become an overworked metaphor of perverse reproduction, describing lesbians as "created much the same way as vampires, who were once victims of vampires themselves—a perpetually vicious circle."[157] The novel told the story of that seduction in the first-person narrative voice of the protagonist Rusty, identified as a "stud" serving a five-year sentence for second-degree manslaughter. Rusty tells of her successful seduction of new inmate Marcia in torrid and sexually explicit detail. Initially, Marcia resists Rusty's advances, stuttering in protest, "I—I'm a normal woman."[158] But Rusty's coercive charms and sexual

skills, which she credits in part to her "knowledge of the female erog-
enous zones," soon win Marcia over. "I played her entire being as a master
violinist plays a fine old Stradivarius," Rusty boasted. "A clever *stud* is
much better than a stupid lover of the other sex," she explained. "That is
why a lesbian can take so many women away from men."[159]

The novel confirmed every midcentury fear about the seductive appeal
of homosexuality and its degrading and damaging effects. Like "I Lived
in a Hell behind Bars," *My Name Is Rusty* attempted to recuperate the narrator's heterosexuality in a surprise ending. When Rusty is released from
prison, she shocks everyone, not least the reader, by donning a dress and
putting lesbianism and gender transgression behind her: "The morning I
walked through those gates, I knew that the *stud* part of my life lay behind
me."[160] She goes home to live with her mother, falls "head over heels in
love" with a man, and marries him. But Marcia does not escape her sexual
fate so easily. The novel ends on a homophobically didactic note, consistent with the tone and message of many social scientific studies of the day.
That message was delivered at the novel's conclusion by Rusty herself. "I
am writing our story," Rusty narrated, "to reveal the insidiousness of a
way of life imposed in prison upon helpless young girls who are forcibly
segregated from men for long periods of time."[161] In the process, however,
the novel unsettled readers' assumptions about their ability to identify the
"real" lesbian, as well as about the essence and stability of heterosexuality.
In the end, former prison stud Rusty is happily married and pregnant.
Marcia is admitted to a sanitarium for drug addiction after being released
from prison and later commits suicide when she "came to feel the hope-
lessness of being queer when she thought that nothing could be done to
cure her."[162]

Prison lesbianism received considerably more attention in popular than
in social scientific writing, at least before the early 1960s. Men's prisons
were also exploited for popular storylines that often featured same-sex
sex. Christopher Teale's 1957 novel, *Behind These Walls*, in many ways
echoed "I Lived in a Hell behind Bars" and *My Name Is Rusty*. The novel
is narrated by Tex, a hardened ex-con who, at the story's opening, is re-
turning to prison. When he encounters the naive and young new inmate
Red, Tex protects him by making other prisoners think he's his "kid," or
submissive partner. "There's guys out there who'd crawl over a dozen vo-
luptuous women just to get next to you," Tex explains to Red. "There's
jockers, queens, queers, punks, fairies, faggots—everything here—we've
got 'em all."[163] Explaining to Red that the other prisoners are attracted to

his "youth" and "pretty face," Tex surprises himself by admitting, "If I ever decided to become a jocker, I'd want someone just like you, Red." He is shocked when Red responds, "Yeah, Tex, and if I ever wanted to be punked, I'd want someone just like you to punk me."[164]

Tex is disconcerted by this exchange and by his own feelings, having earlier expressed his disdain for older prisoners who "turn kids out." He subsequently tries to suppress his desires and maintain a fatherly relationship to Red. Tex tutors Red in the rules of the prison and ways to stay "clean" and schools him in what he casts as the ugly truth of prison homosexuality by taking him on a tour of fellow inmate "Barbara's" cell, decorated with a pink crocheted bedspread and matching pillow and ruffled curtains and strewn with "feminine articles—perfume bottles, combs and brushes in elaborate, matched sets, innumerable jars of expensive looking creams, compacts, jewelry box, everything."[165] When Red is speechless in response, Tex congratulates himself on having imparted an important cautionary lesson. "Without seeing Barbara's cell," Tex noted, "he'd never know prison."[166] At the same time, Tex acknowledges that "there were times when I looked into [Red's] eyes or felt his hand on my shoulder as we headed for the mess hall when my feelings were not paternal."[167] Despite their mutual attraction, their relationship remains platonic, and when Red is released from prison, he marries a woman. "Red's life was normal, happy and his future looked bright," but Tex wonders, "When a future looks bright, can the past somehow, some way, return to blight it?"[168] That concern drives Tex's anguished decision to cut his ties to Red. When Red writes to Tex, signing his letter "Your kid, Red," Tex instructs the prison mail clerk to stamp the letter "Deceased" and to return it.

The stories told in these fictional accounts—featuring the transformation of heterosexuals to homosexual desire and sometimes homosexual practice and identity under the pressure and deprivations of prison life— echoed those in social scientific reports. Together, they communicated the message that incarceration undermined and sometimes undid heterosexuality. But they did so with a notable difference: each of these stories put the reader in the vicarious place of a protagonist who found pleasure, however ambivalent, in same-sex sex. Perhaps inadvertently, "I Lived in a Hell behind Bars," *My Name Is Rusty*, and other popular cultural representations of prison sexual culture revealed and sometimes seem to glory in conclusions that social scientists tried their best to repress. Concern about homosexuality in prison masked a deeper fear about the fragility and instability of heterosexuality.

: : :

Sexual practices observed in prison unsettled convictions about true homosexuality; inevitably, and more troublingly, they called true heterosexuality into question as well. Revealing the border between homosexuality and heterosexuality to be blurred and permeable, sex in prison suggested that desire and even sexual subject positions were unfixed and unstable, produced at certain moments and in certain circumstances, rather than inhering in the psyche or body.

CHAPTER FOUR

"The Deviants Are the Heterosexuals"

In the 1940s and 1950s, the first wave of sociological studies of men's prisons raised and worked mightily to resolve questions about the meaning of sex in prison for notions of fixed and stable sexual identity. Soon after that period of intense interest in men's prisons, women's prisons and female prisoners became the subject of close attention and investigation for the first time. The first book-length studies to be published on women's prisons appeared, in a nearly simultaneous rush, in the mid- to late 1960s. David Ward and Gene Kassebaum's study of the inmates of Frontera, a state prison for women in California, was published in 1965, followed closely in 1966 by Rose Giallombardo's investigation of the Federal Reformatory for Women in Alderson, West Virginia. Sara Harris's more popular exposé of the New York Women's House of Detention, the sensationalistic tone of which was announced in the book's title, *Hellhole*, appeared in 1967. And Esther Heffernan's analysis of the rich and varied inmate subculture at the District of Columbia's Women's Reformatory in Occoquan, Virginia, was published a few years later in 1972. These pioneering works inspired more attention to women's prisons and women prisoners—social scientific and popular—in the years that followed.[1]

The surge in interest in women's prisons did not respond to an increase in the number of women behind bars, nor did it reflect a widespread fear that female criminality was spiraling out of control. The publishing boom in women's prison studies preceded by more than a decade the increasingly harsh and mandatory sentencing laws, zero-tolerance policies, stiff penalties for drug offenses, and feminization of poverty that would result in the massive influx of women into American prisons beginning in the 1980s, producing a rise so sharp that the rate of growth in the imprisonment of women would outpace that of men. In 1970, there were under 6,000 women incarcerated in state and federal prisons, comprising a mere 3 percent of all prisoners held in the United States.[2]

In turning their attention to women's prisons, sociologists aimed to fill an obvious gap in the scholarly literature, taking the models offered by classic prison ethnographies such as Donald Clemmer's *The Prison Community* and Gresham Sykes's *The Society of Captives* to an understudied if numerically small segment of the prison population. "Compared to the sociological literature on men's prisons," Ward and Kassebaum pointed out, "little is known about the social organization of the women's prison."[3] "The female prison community has been overlooked," Giallombardo agreed, insisting that it merited study, "as does any other complex organization, in order to add to the growing body of theory on group behavior."[4]

Investigations of women's prisons, however, were driven by more than the scholarly duty or opportunity suggested in these dry rationales. The high incidence of lesbianism among women in prison, represented as reaching "epidemic proportions" in some accounts, was the subject of primary interest.[5] In a period marked by heightened awareness of, prurient interest in, and anxiety about lesbianism generally, the women's prison provided what these researchers, like many who came before them, considered a "laboratory"—one in which they might test sociological theories of carceral communities and cultures, certainly, but which also allowed them to search for the cause of lesbianism reportedly rampant in women's prisons, to examine the dynamics of same-sex attachments between women behind bars, and to consider the meaning and consequences of the participation in same-sex sex by otherwise heterosexual women.

At the same time that sociologists worked to garner academic legitimacy for the study of prison lesbianism, the subject was also exploited for its popular appeal. Representations of prison lesbianism that flourished in the popular realm in the 1960s and 1970s, especially in offbeat and exploitation cinema, worked both within and against the grain of the sociological accounts of women's prisons. While sociological studies tended to domesticate prison lesbianism, taming its subversive implications by locating it in the most normative feminine needs and desires, popular cultural depictions mined the subject's transgressive appeal. In addressing the phenomenon of lesbianism behind bars, both professionals and purveyors of popular culture entered into larger cultural debates about female sexuality and gender roles in flux in this period. Read together, sociological and filmic depictions of prison lesbianism chart the contradictions and complexities, the threat and the thrill, posed by lesbianism more generally in a period witnessing the waning of cold war domesticity and the flourishing of sexual liberalism.

"The Deviants Are the Heterosexuals"

Donald Clemmer's recognition of prison sexual culture as an important aspect of inmate community life marked a turning point in prison studies and granted the imprimatur of scholarly legitimacy to the examination of prison sex. Following Clemmer, sociological studies of men's prisons typically included a more than cursory discussion of sexuality. Still, same-sex sex was usually cast as only one aspect, and a subterranean and usually shameful one, of men's prison culture. Jockers, punks, kids, and queens took their place among a much larger cast of characters in men's prisons cataloged in the classic midcentury ethnographies, which also included right guys, politicians, merchants, snitches, and gorillas—prison types defined by their relationship to prison authorities, prison politics, and the prison economy rather than to its sexual culture. Lesbianism, by contrast, was characterized by sociologists, prisoners, and in popular culture in the 1960s and 1970s as the single most salient feature of the life of women behind bars, central to the culture they made there and occupying its mainstream rather than its margins.

The observation of the predominance of lesbianism among women prisoners was heralded as a "discovery" by some investigators, but it was not altogether new. The few studies of female incarceration earlier in the century had all documented a culture of romantic relationships among girls and young women in reform schools and other juvenile correctional facilities, a phenomenon readily if overanxiously attributed to the emotional excesses of immaturity and teenage sentimentalism. Charles Ford dismissed the letters passed between "friends" in the institution he observed in 1929 as "the slushy love note type of thing, filled with adolescent terms of endearment."[6] The euphemisms that incarcerated girls and young women used to refer to their own culture of same-sex attachments—"the sillies," "chick business," "girl stuff," "playing," "housekeeping," and "friends"—invited investigators to take them less than seriously and were perhaps designed to deflect the scrutiny of prison administrators.

Investigators characterized relationships between female inmates as a particularly benign form of situational homosexuality, shaped by and limited to the sex-segregated institution, more romantic than sexual, and akin to crushes long observed between girls at boarding schools.[7] While 69 percent of the inmates of the Wisconsin School for Girls surveyed by psychologists Seymour Halleck and Melvin Hersko in 1962 admitted to having engaged in "girl stuff" during their incarceration, for example, the investigators characterized their relationships as short-lived and superficial and found "nothing to suggest that more than a few . . . are emotionally disturbed in the sense of being sexually perverted."[8] Girl stuff "assumed many forms," Halleck and Hersko reported, and was usually expressed by kissing, embracing, and fondling and only rarely by "direct genital contact."[9] "You can't explain chick business just by calling it homosexuality," another researcher insisted in 1953, since "it's normal for them to have crushes on other girls at that age."[10] Psychiatrist Joseph Wilson observed similarly that while notes passed between inmates at the State Home for Girls in Trenton, New Jersey, "speak of love affairs, jealousies, and hates of the writer," those sentiments did not represent "truly homosexual urges."[11] Instead, Wilson characterized relations among young female inmates as "comparatively innocent and harmless play," unlikely to be "converted into actual homosexual practice."[12] While social worker Abraham Novick acknowledged in 1960 that such behavior on the part of the adolescent boy "would immediately be constructed as homosexual," he judged the development of "youthful 'crushes' on members of the same sex during latency and early adolescence" among girls to be "characteristic of normal female psychological development."[13] Temporally located in adolescence, same-sex attachments between incarcerated girls were judged to be normal, unsurprising, and reassuringly temporary.[14]

The new sociological studies of women's prisons, however, in documenting the predominance of romantic and sexual relationships among adult women behind bars, called into question the reassuring vision that likened the attachments of delinquent girls to harmless schoolgirl crushes. Virtually all of the sociologists studying women's prisons in the 1960s and 1970s focused on lesbianism as an important and often primary aspect of their investigation, even when they did not begin their research intending to foreground questions of sexuality. Ward and Kassebaum approached their study of Frontera with a broad interest in comparing women's prison culture to men's in order to discern "whether there were female prisoner types consistent with the reported characteristics of male prisoners."[15] When they discovered early in their research, however, that "the most salient distinction to be made among the female inmates was between those who were and those who were not engaged in homosexual behavior in prison, and further, of those who were so involved, between the incumbents of 'masculine' and 'feminine' roles," Ward and Kassebaum reoriented their study to focus on the sexual aspects of women's prison life.[16] Giallombardo likewise began her study of Alderson with an interest in examining the prison "as a system of roles and functions and to make comparisons with the literature on the male prison."[17] But when she found that the argot in women's prisons, unlike that in men's prisons, referred almost exclusively to sexual types, customs, and norms, she revised her study as well to focus almost exclusively on the structure and dynamics of the sexual culture of women's prisons.

While investigators were struck by the predominance of lesbianism in women's prisons, they struggled with challenges in assessing it empirically. Some researchers admitted the difficulty of obtaining reliable and accurate information on illicit and punishable behavior, which typically took place as privately as could be accomplished in the surveyed space of the prison. Sex among women prisoners was policed and punished to greater or lesser degrees depending on the institution, but, as in men's prisons, it was officially prohibited in all. Getting caught in a sexual act with another prisoner or, in some institutions, in any act that could possibly be perceived as sexual, often carried serious punitive sanctions. Violation of the rule against hugging or any other bodily contact with another inmate at one state prison for women in Indiana, for instance, was punished by solitary confinement.[18] At California's Terminal Island Prison, one prisoner reported, "just touching another woman could get you a D.R. (Disciplinary Report). If you were caught getting down with a woman you could land in the Hole."[19] One Oregon prisoner reported that "you can't even touch somebody, let alone hold their hand or put your arm around them. That's homosexual activity."[20] Prisoners who were discovered having sex were sometimes required to appear before a disciplinary committee and could receive a letter in their file. This was known as "having an *H* in your jacket," marking a prisoner as homosexual and placed in her permanent record.[21] Sometimes a letter was sent to the prisoner's home as well, informing her family of her sexual "degeneracy." Prison lovers were often separated and moved into different housing complexes and sometimes re-

ceived punitive work assignments. More seriously, their chance for parole could be revoked.[22] As the inmates' manual at the State Correctional
Institution for Women Offenders in Muncie, Pennsylvania, explained,
"indulgence in sex play, when detected, will slow up your chance for parole because such acts will indicate that you are not ready to be trusted to
mingle with others in your community."[23]

Given the disciplinary responses to prison lesbianism, it is not surprising that investigators of women's prisons found it a challenge to obtain
candid responses to their questions about sex.[24] Some were stymied as
well by uncertainty about what counted when counting lesbians. "The
ambiguous definition of homosexuality among staff and inmates," sociologist Catherine Nelson observed, "produces a conceptual phenomenon
having amorphous parameters."[25] Investigators debated over whether to
include hand holding, love-note writing, kissing, and embracing among
women—practices that some identified as "homosexually tinged" but
that others argued were innocent of sexual desire—or whether to restrict
their definition to behavior more commonly and unanimously accepted
as sexual.[26]

Despite the practical and epistemological difficulties involved in quan-
tifying prison lesbianism and no matter the measure used, most investigators in the 1960s judged its incidence to be strikingly high. Using a
strict definition of unequivocal sexual behavior, Ward and Kassebaum
estimated that at least 50 percent of the women at Frontera had engaged
in some overt sexual act during their sentence.[27] Psychologist Kenneth
Dimick ventured a considerably less conservative estimate that "probably
ninety-five percent of all women who are imprisoned for longer than one
year have participated in homosexual relationships while in prison," a figure that more closely matched the estimate of Alderson inmates as well
as prisoners in other women's institutions who judged that "almost all"
inmates engaged in homosexuality.[28]

Regardless of the exact number, inmates and their observers would
have agreed with Nelson's startling proposition that in women's prisons,
"the deviants are the heterosexuals."[29] That view was reflected in the argot
unique to women's prisons, which labeled those prisoners committed to
heterosexuality "squares" and considered them "truly the pariahs of the inmate community."[30] Those who declined to become involved in same-sex
relationships in prison, Ward and Kassebaum noted, "must learn to live in a
society dominated by homosexual ideology and behavior."[31] One woman
confirmed that, at the Women's House of Detention, "if you're not in the
racket, . . . you're like an outcast."[32] Not only were squares "excluded and

ostracized" by other inmates, Giallombardo observed, "squares are pitied."[33] Squares who refrained from homosexual behavior themselves but tolerated it in others were recognized at Alderson as hip squares, enjoying only slightly higher status than their judgmental, squarer peers.[34] Women prisoners who disdained the same-sex involvement of other inmates and adopted a "'holier-than-thou' attitude" toward prison lesbianism were strongly resented. As Giallombardo explained, "The behavior expected of inmates who do not engage in homosexuality is contained in the expression: 'If you don't dig "playing"—solid, but don't rank it!'"[35]

Same-sex sexuality in women's prisons as observed by sociologists was both more ubiquitous than in men's prisons and more constitutive of their dominant culture. The sexual organization and dynamics of women's prisons were observed to diverge from those in men's prisons as well. While men's prisons at midcentury were typically represented as pressure cookers of sexual frustration, tension, and need that could boil over into sexual coercion and sometimes overt violence, women's prisons were characterized as distinctly domestic spaces populated by consensually partnered couples and in many cases organized into elaborate kinship networks.

The organizing structure of women's prison culture, as observed by many sociologists, was the surrogate family. "Family" was a long-standing keyword of women's penology, defining and distinguishing women's institutions from their beginning and expressing the ideology and aims of their founders. Indeed, among the primary goals of early women's prisons was to reclaim deviant women for normative domesticity, and their architecture and administration reflected a belief in the rehabilitative power of family life. Intended to be more "home-like" than men's prisons, many women's institutions were designed according to a plan known as the "cottage system," in which women lived together in groups housed in small buildings, often with private bedrooms, rather than in tiered cells or dormitories. The cottage plan, historian Nicole Hahn Rafter observes, was "an architectural embodiment of the notion that criminal women could be reformed through domestic training" and had its origins in the women's reformatory movement of the 1870s.[36] Since their founding, women's institutions had also encouraged incarcerated girls and women to think of each other and their supervisors in familial terms. In some institutions, cottages were supervised by matrons known as "house mothers." At the first reform school for girls, in Lancaster, Massachusetts, groups of inmates were referred to as "families" and were composed of girls of varying ages. These groupings were designed deliberately with familial relation in mind, as historian Barbara Brenzel points out, so that the younger might be "gentling influences on the older, who in turn were to act as big sisters."[37] Investigators who viewed family formations among women and girls as regrettably abnormal if understandable adjustments to the unnatural conditions of single-sex institutional life failed to note the irony in the ways in which women prisoners turned the institutionally sanctioned model of the rehabilitative family into alternative and often transgressive kinship forms. One women's prison family at California's Terminal Island Prison, for example, proudly named themselves "hippies, hypes, whores, and homosexuals."[38]

Surrogate families were apparently a long-standing and durable feature of women's institutions, first observed among incarcerated girls and young women in the early twentieth century. In 1931, sociologist Lowell Selling documented mother and daughter relationships in addition to "numerous family ramifications" among the girls he observed in correctional institutions.[39] "Here, a girl had a mother who was another inmate," Selling explained, "and this mother might have a mother of her own who would be called 'grannie' by the first girl to complete the picture."[40] In 1953, a journalist commented on the elaborate family structure forged by inmates at Los Guilucos School for Girls in California: "One girl is another's 'daddy,' 'grampa,' 'brother,' or 'cousin.' Each girl has a 'twin,' with whom she dresses exactly alike, and with whom she walks about arm in arm."[41]

Some investigators attributed the impulse on the part of incarcerated girls and young women to form surrogate families to an understandable desire to compensate for their own "broken" family histories. Prison families, as represented in many of these accounts, fulfilled the needs of young women who had been deprived of affection and stability in their own families before prison. "Most of these girls come from disrupted homes where the family and marital relations are most unstable and hectic," Sidney Kosofsky and Albert Ellis wrote in 1958 of the delinquent girls they studied. "In consequence, they may well prefer to build their own 'family' units and to try to derive from them the kind of love and security which they often miserably failed to achieve in their actual families."[42] Others represented institutional families as "simply a continuation into the age of puberty of the ordinary house-playing of little girls."[43]

Family formation among female prisoners, however, was not restricted to juveniles. Giallombardo and others documented the continued presence of surrogate families in many adult women's prisons.[44] Organized around a couple recognized as husband and wife, women's prison families often incorporated grandparents and children and sometimes included extended networks of aunts and uncles, nieces and nephews, and in-law relationships so elaborate that investigators resorted to charts and diagrams to track their complexities.[45] In institutions that were desegregated, which was the case in most women's prisons outside the South by the mid-1960s, prisons families were sometimes formed across lines of race.[46]

While investigators treated women's prison families as a situational form of kinship, dubbing them "play," "make-believe," "surrogate," and "pseudo" families, prisoners took their family roles and responsibilities very seriously. Prison families fulfilled a variety of important functions. Some sociologists likened them to gangs formed in men's prisons for self-defense, but women's prison families served primarily affectional, social, and economic roles rather than protective ones. As one inmate of California's Terminal Island prison in the 1970s recalled simply, "we took care of each other."[47] Families offered women prisoners the companionability of group membership and identification, and kinship groups typically spent their recreational time together and attended prison events such as movies, dances, and ball games as a group.[48] Being in a family "is better than not belonging to anything," one prisoner noted. "It gives you a small feeling of security" and "makes you feel a part."[49] Families socialized new inmates, typically cast in the roles of children, in the norms and etiquette of prison life. Families were also the primary economic unit in women's prisons, sharing among their members prized commissary goods such as cigarettes, candy, and toiletries. They cooperated as well in the theft, smuggling, and manufacture of illicit goods, primarily alcohol and narcotics, in the underground prison economy.[50]

Family members served the important practical function of facilitating a range of activities among members that transgressed prison rules and regulations, including sexual rendezvous. Since sex between prisoners was prohibited, it required cooperation and organization among inmates. Prisoners often made use of a lookout, known as a "pinner," who would keep the staff occupied and warn lovers of their presence. "If you're makin' it with someone," one Frontera inmate observed, "you need a pinner." "Maybe I've got two friends who are involved with each other," she explained. "O.K., well I'll go into the office and keep the officer busy for an hour talking about a problem I have or make one up. She can't be in two places at one time, so usually this is a safe procedure."[51]

Another important function of women's prison families was their role in regulating same-sex relations through gender norms and incest prohibitions that identified some women as acceptable sexual partners and declared others off limits. Sexual competition among women prisoners, by

all accounts, was fierce; without some means of regulating the selection
of partners, Giallombardo explained, "the Alderson community would be
characterized as a 'war of all against all.'"[52] Because sex role differentiation was considered crucial to partnerships and family formation among
women prisoners, an inmate's adoption of a gendered and familial role
foreclosed some romantic and sexual possibilities while opening others.
Women's prison partnerships, as depicted by both sociologists and prisoners, were almost always organized by gender, pairing prisoners who
assumed male roles, known as butches and studs, with femmes, who assumed female roles.[53] While women inmates were occasionally observed
to change gender roles, usually to take advantage of a sexual opportunity,
gender role-switching was frowned on. As one prisoner noted of those
known derisively at Alderson as turnabouts, "if you keep switching from
one sex role to another . . . you don't know what you've got. Once, you
think you got a mother, or a sister, and then the next thing you know,
it's a father or a brother."[54] "One week they're my brother," one Frontera butch complained about the inexperienced "kids" in prison who "just
play a role," "and the next week they're hitting on me."[55]

In addition to maintaining gendered distinctions among inmates, family relations imposed an incest taboo that worked to regulate sexual relations. Husband-wife relationships were sometimes observed to transmute
into platonic brother-sister pairings when partners separated, but prison
norms dictated strongly against prison siblings becoming romantically or
sexually involved, as well as against prison parents forming partnerships
with their "children." "Homosexual relations between inmates who stand
in kinship relationship are considered misconduct and are classified as incestuous behavior," Giallombardo recorded, adding that she was aware of
only one instance of incest during her fieldwork with the community of
women prisoners at Alderson. "Kinship thus becomes a device for openly
declaring one or more persons sexually . . . out of bounds."[56] "With the
exception of the husband-wife relationship cast into the form of a homosexual alliance," Giallombardo observed, "the other roles defined in kinship terms are rendered neutralized of sexual content."[57]

Investigators in decades past had made an effort to cleanse the family
relations forged among incarcerated girls of the taint of homosexuality.
Selling, for instance, had identified the families formed by incarcerated delinquent girls and young women in his 1931 study as a "non-pathological
example" of same-sex relationships clearly distinguished from "lesbianism
and pseudohomosexuality," and he estimated that only ten in one hundred
girls "definitely find each other in an overt homosexual existence."[58] That

proved a more difficult distinction to make among adult women, however. The relationship between prisoners committed to each other as husband and wife—the basic nucleus around which women's prison families were formed—was recognized as a marriage, romantic and sexual by definition. "Acting as man and wife, they will do everything married couples do," Williams and Fish wrote, adding that "ordinarily there is an element of romance in the marriage."[59] Organized in a gendered partnership, the couple served as the core relationship around which the inmate family structure evolved. Marriages were sometimes formalized by a wedding officiated by another prisoner, marked by an exchange of rings or other tokens, and sealed with a marriage certificate (plate 12). (Communion at church services was discontinued at one young women's Midwestern state training school in the 1960s because some inmates were taking advantage of time at the altar to perform marriage ceremonies there.[60]) Prison marriages were observed to last anywhere from weeks to years, and according to the unwritten rules of some institutions, their dissolution required an equally formal divorce.[61] In other institutions, marriage and divorce were initiated simply by a decision and declaration of the couple.

While family formation among inmates was common to many but not all women's prisons, the gendered organization of women's prison partnerships was nearly ubiquitous.[62] Investigators had long turned to prisons to provide a lens onto deviant sexuality that was less easily observed in the outside world. For sociologists, prisons provided a window onto a butch-femme lesbian world usually visible only to its participants. Historians Elizabeth Lapovsky Kennedy and Madeline Davis have noted the increasing dominance of butch-femme sensibility, signification, and erotic dynamics in organizing lesbian social life and relationships beginning in the 1940s, and have documented the vibrant butch-femme community life forged by working-class lesbians in particular.[63] Populations of women's as well as men's prisons were drawn disproportionately from the working class, and the increasing importance of butch-femme dynamics and gender signification began to be apparent in women's prisons beginning in this period as well. Prison superintendent and reformer Florence Monahan tracked this change, observing that the inmates at the Minnesota state reformatory at Shakopee "did not flaunt their abnormality" in the 1920s as they did by the early 1940s. "I do not recall one woman at Shakopee who dressed like a man" in the earlier period, Monahan wrote, "nor one who arrived without a single feminine article of clothing." But that was hardly the case in later decades, when, she wrote, "professors of homosexuality are brazen about it."[64]

"Profession" of homosexuality, to Monahan and others, was rendered visible by gender transgression. At a time when gender nonconformity was being called into question as a reliable signpost for male homosexuality, investigators continued to assume a link between female masculinity and lesbianism. Sociologists thus carefully, even obsessively, scrutinized the gender signifying practices of butch prisoners. They betrayed a special fascination with the earnestness and verisimilitude of butches' masculine gender presentation and with the ingenuity they exhibited in crafting and maintaining their masculinity, constrained by the limitations of prison uniforms and often in violation of prison regulations.

The most important butch signifier undoubtedly involved hair. Butches typically cut their hair short, "ranging from a practical crew to the popular 'Duck's Ass,'" and some further flouted prison rules by sporting sideburns.[65] The effect could be disarming to the uninitiated. Male members of the California Department of Corrections were reportedly scandalized by the sharp gender differentiation that made butch-femme couples so visible and overtly sexualized during a visit to Frontera and ordered that the butches have their "mannishly short hair" set and curled, the feminizing results of which were described as "grotesque" by one sympathetic staff member.[66] In institutions that refused to give butches the short hair cuts they desired, inmates cut their hair themselves with pilfered razors or with the glass from broken light bulbs.[67] Despite a prohibition at Alderson against mannishly cut and styled short hair, Elizabeth Gurley Flynn recalled that "there were plenty of shorn heads . . . and even some sidelocks, to look like Elvis Presley."[68] Because the young women in one institution for juveniles were not allowed to cut their hair short, they found other ways to signify masculinity through hair style, parting their hair on the left side, "brushed back and slightly elevated in front" into a kind of pompadour.[69]

Butches also communicated masculinity through clothing, often in violation of institutional rules. One institution for young women revived a previously lax regulation prohibiting inmates from wearing denim jeans in the early 1960s after visitors' reactions to Levi-wearing butches embarrassed prison staff members.[70] And some women prisoners, later in the 1970s, reported being held to increasingly stringent and feminine dress codes. One attributed the "crack-downs on homosexuality" at the California prison at Pleasanton, manifested in part by a mandate banning the receipt of men's clothing in the mail, "to an increasing backlash against gay visibility" and the "Briggs/Bryant right wing onslaught" of that period.[71]

Where institutional regulations allowed it, butches favored pants with loosely fitted legs, "styled like men's trousers," and shirts "cut in a mannish style," and they sometimes sported ties fashioned from neckerchiefs.[72] Butches commissioned femmes to sew for them or made use of prison sewing shops themselves to convert institution-issued blouses into men's-style shirts, starching and ironing the collars "to look like the starched collar of a man's shirt."[73] Butches at Frontera stole men's underwear from laundry done at the prison for men's institutions, and boxers and men's t-shirts were especially prized (and strongly prohibited) contraband. In institutions that forbade the wearing of pants, butches chose longer, looser black skirts than those worn by femmes and paired them with black vests. Giallombardo noted that "during a period when Parisian designers were inching women's skirts above the knee" and prison femmes were following suit, Alderson studs wore their skirts long, at about eight inches below the knee.[74] Since "differential dress for studs is intended to disguise externally the curves of the female and to achieve a flattened look," Giallombardo observed, "the shape of their skirts can best be described as 'baggy,'" and they wore their shirts loose over their skirts rather than tucked in.[75] Butches forced to wear skirts also sometimes left the side zipper unzipped, "making it possible for the inmate to place her hand through the opening as if it were a pocket."[76]

Masculinity, Giallombardo noted with a combination of ethnographic distance and commitment to detail, was "also communicated by head-gear" and other, more nuanced, sartorial codes. Butches at Alderson wore caps with the brim worn down over their ears, knitted caps with visors, or fedora-style hats.[77] Whereas femmes folded their socks at the ankle, butches pulled them up. Some butches made an effort to flatten their chests, taking in the cups of their bras or fashioning binding material from knit undershirts. Butches also often assumed male names—"Barbara becomes Bob; Rachel, Ray; Katherine, Kelly; Mary, Marty; Lucile, Lou, and so on"—and many preferred to be referred to with male pronouns.[78]

Butch identity was established through gesture, behavior, and affect as well as through outward appearance and dress. "You can show what you are by the way you stand and sit and smoke your cigarette," Harris observed.[79] Some traced butch prison style to "the hip-walking, cool-talking" model of black masculinity.[80] Butches adopted a masculine stride, described by Ward and Kassebaum as "a swaggering, hunching carriage and gait," and sat with knees spread apart or with one leg drawn up to the chin or slung over the arm of a chair.[81] Some made a habit of hitching up their pants "as if there were a penis which had to be tucked in place."[82] Butches held cigarettes between thumb and forefinger. They also displayed the courtesies that men were expected to perform for women, opening their doors, helping them with their coats, lighting their cigarettes, and fetching refreshments.[83] Butches were expected as well to adopt the reserve of midcentury masculinity, "to be discreet in their talk and not indulge in wanton gossip," and "to incorporate the traits of reliability and emotional control in their character."[84] Drawing on the range of cultural conventions of American masculinity, butch behavior was often appreciated by femmes, but it could also be experienced as a form of bullying dominance. "They act like a boy," reported one young woman. "Bullying a girl, pick on you like a man. They act tough."[85] As one Frontera butch told Ward and Kassebaum about her femme partner: "I don't like her showing any independence—when I tell her to do something I expect her to do it," amending boastfully, "it's almost exactly the way a man feels toward a woman."[86]

There are a few references in earlier accounts to prisoners in women's institutions who identified unambiguously as male and lived as men before their incarceration. Prison superintendent Florence Monahan told the story of Leslie, who arrived at Minnesota's Shakopee prison in the late 1930s "dressed exactly like a man." Leslie had apparently "always lived as a boy or a man," had been a member of the Boy Scouts, and "explained to the psychiatrists who examined her that her mother regarded her as a son." A few years earlier, in 1935, Leslie had married a woman. Leslie's wife, Monahan reported, "did not know she was not a male until the publicity broke," presumably after his arrest.[87] On arrival at prison, Monahan insisted that Leslie "adhere to our rules." Prison staff members were ordered to use female pronouns to refer to the new prisoner, who was forced to wear dresses in the dining room and dormitory. Prisoners, however, failed to enlist in Monahan's disciplining of Leslie's gender. "We called her Leslie," Monahan reported, "but the inmates called her Bud."[88] On release, Monahan noted, Leslie went back to living as a man.

Monahan implicitly distinguished Leslie from other prison butches in his wholesale male identification (although butch signification would not have been as elaborated or codified in the late 1930s as it would come to be in later decades). But the practices and preferences of prison butches in the 1950s, 1960s, and 1970s suggest that the boundary between butch identity and what would later come to be called transgender identity was fluid. While many prison butches in this period identified as "gay" or as being "in the life," few referred to themselves (or were referred to by femmes) as women or as lesbians. Some clearly identified strongly as "guys," "fellows," or simply as men.[89]

Comments by heterosexually identified prisoners testified to the success of butch gender presentation and sometimes to the attractions of butch charm. Butches at Bedford Hills, inmate Jean Harris noted, "are all muscular, strong, work out with weights at the gym and can often look more like men than women."[90] Florrie Fisher, in and out of prison through the 1950s and 1960s for drug and prostitution convictions, described her first prison lover, Jean, whom she met at the Women's House of Detention, as "boyish in a girlish kind of way, or girlish in a boyish sort of way."[91] Tamsin Fitzgerald, sentenced to Alderson in 1969 for attempting to hijack a plane to Cuba with her draft-evading boyfriend, described one prison butch, Noel, who "looks like a boy hippie. She wears high-top sneakers too big for her and baggy sweatshirts." Fitzgerald was especially impressed by Noel's courageous commitment to a consistently masculine identity. While other butches "masquerade for the Parole Board," by wearing dresses, Noel was, in Fitzgerald's admiring estimation, "a true rebel" for insisting on wearing pants.[92] Linda, a prisoner at the Women's House of Detention, recalled her attraction to a butch named Topper, who "looked like a man and a hell of a good-looking one too."[93] Weatherman activist Susan Stern described her crush on a butch named Johni, incarcerated in the Seattle jail with her in 1971: "She is handsome and beautiful at the same time. From the back she looks like a man, from the front, a masculine woman. She wears her hair like the Elvis greasers of the late fifties; a cigarette hangs perpetually from the corner of her mouth." "She has a way of looking at me that makes my heart beat," Stern wrote. "I always get flustered when she enters my cell."[94]

Investigators, too, sometimes seemed to submit unwittingly to the erotic attraction of prison butches. Sara Harris described inmate Rusty Bricker, identified by Harris as the "official king" of the Women's House of Detention, in attentive and sensory detail. "Every time you see Rusty," Harris wrote, "she just got a haircut. Her mannish-cut red hair is constantly slicked down as tight as she can get it, and she smells of barbershop perfume." Adorned in "new, resplendently bright men's shoes" and "men's jeans that button in front," Rusty was, in Harris's estimation, "a handsome woman, and would be even handsomer as a man."[95]

Femmes merited considerably less description in sociologists' accounts, in large part because they were understood simply to perform their "natural" role as women. Ward and Kassebaum, for instance, found it "less difficult to describe and to understand the role played by the femme because she often does in the homosexual affair what she did in a heterosexual one." While butches transgressed gender and sexual norms, they wrote, "the femme changes only the love object."[96] Inmates agreed, one telling Giallombardo, "it's easier to be a fem," since "the way she acts and dresses are natural, as if straight."[97]

However natural many perceived the role to be, some detected a degree of performativity in femme signification as well as butch. Young reform school femmes, Carter observed, "affect in an exaggerated fashion behavioral patterns culturally associated with femininity," although she added that "most girls perceive this as just acting 'natural.'"[98] Sociologists and inmates alike emphasized the submissiveness expected of femmes, a stance that some by the 1970s depicted as anachronistic in its deference to butches. The femme, Williams and Fish observed, "plays the stereotyped role of the woman: that is to say, she is submissive and does the housekeeping. She does the cleaning, the sewing, the bed making, and frequently the commissary shopping. She performs the functions of a nonliberated housewife."[99] "The femme is expected to be submissive," Carter observed, "or, as the girls say, 'to do what the butch tells her.'"[100] One femme in the Women's House of Detention found her butch lover "different at first" from her boyfriend on the outside, but "once me and her got to be a thing, she was just like a pimp." It "went without saying," she noted, "that I had to do all her dirty work around the jail, wash her underwear and keep her cell clean."[101] Femmes were also expected to take pride in their appearance and to make an effort to maintain their attractiveness under the constraints of prison life in order to reflect well on their butch partners. Adding to the incentive was the competition born of an imbalance in prison gender ratios: femmes were observed to outnumber butches in every prison by as many as two to one.

Explaining Women's Prison Sexual Culture

A world populated by female husbands, brothers, and uncles, in which otherwise heterosexual women competed for the attention of butches and married them in prison ceremonies and where by all accounts "the deviants are the heterosexuals," was a world that upended the period's orthodoxies in a number of ways. The apparent ubiquity of prison lesbianism and the troubling questions it posed for notions of sexual fixity and gender normativity demanded analysis and explanation.

Efforts to locate the phenomenon of homosexuality in women's prisons in a distinctive psychic or somatic type were as futile as they had been in studies of male prisoners. One study published in 1963, for instance, searched for psychological, cognitive, and behavioral differences between women prisoners who became homosexually involved while in prison and those who abstained. Investigators collected detailed biographical case histories and submitted inmates to a battery of tests, including the Minnesota Multiphasic Personality Inventory, the Kuder Preference Record, the Wide Range Achievement Test, and the Otis Quick-Scoring Mental Ability Test, but they ultimately failed to find any evidence of factors common to either group. Women who participated in same-sex sex, this study and others found, were indistinguishable from those who refrained.[102] Ward and Kassebaum reported that although many butches at Frontera "appear masculine . . . in terms of body structure and physiognomy," prison physicians assured them that they found no constitutional differences between butches and other inmates "in terms of distribution and abundance of body hair, size of clitoris, muscle distribution or any other factor."[103]

In their efforts to explain the sexual culture of women's prisons, sociologists continued to rely heavily on the paradigms supplied by the classic midcentury studies of men's prisons that characterized prison homosexuality as one of a complex of adaptations to what Gresham Sykes termed the "pains of imprisonment." Those pains, classified by Sykes into five basic categories, were produced by the deprivations of liberty, goods and services, heterosexual relations, autonomy, and security. While both men and women behind bars were understood to suffer those pains, cast as fundamentally and universally human, incarcerated women were believed to undergo additional deprivations. Sociologists pointed to the distinctly female anguish resulting from the dispossession of their roles as mothers, wives, and daughters, which made their prison experience uniquely difficult and by some accounts, more painful than for men.[104] The deprivations felt most keenly by women prisoners, investigators argued, were those of human connection, family relation, warmth, and love.

While some attributed the purportedly different response of men and women to incarceration to essential and natural differences between men and women, most drew on relatively new theories of sex role socialization to explain gender differences.[105] Women suffered the pains of prison differently from men, sociologists proposed, because they were socialized differently prior to incarceration. While male prisoners—socialized to prioritize occupational identity—might be expected to suffer the loss of employment and their status as "breadwinners" more painfully than women,

Giallombardo argued, "the female is oriented inward to the home, and it is in the role of wife and mother that she derives prestige and status."[106] As such, she wrote, the women's prison family and the prison marriage were "singularly suited to meet the inmates' internalized cultural expectations of the female role."[107] In other words, since women found their primary identity and esteem in the roles of wife and mother, they understandably attempted to replicate those roles in prison.

To make this argument, investigators of women's prisons combined older arguments that posited inmate culture as a response to the pains of imprisonment with newer paradigms that explained it as the consequence of the importation into prison life of pre-prison roles, norms, and values. Beginning in the early 1960s, some sociologists proposed that inmate culture, rather than produced entirely by the disorientating prison experience, was imported by inmates, who brought identities, expectations, needs, and habits from their lives in the outside world with them into prison.[108] Building on those ideas, investigators of women's prisons argued that women imported their "latent cultural identity" as mother, wife, and daughter into prison and attempted within the harsh constraints of prison life to replicate and sustain those traditional female roles behind bars.[109]

Investigators used these understandings of sex role socialization and the importation of gender roles to explain the discomfiting phenomenon of women's prison families and the troublingly high incidence of prison lesbianism. "Given a proper understanding of the family role orientation of female prisoners," Williams and Fish wrote reassuringly, "it is less difficult to understand the social significance of female homosexuality in prison."[110] The families and romantic partnerships women forged in prison were uniformly understood by sociologists as efforts to fulfill traditional female roles and to ameliorate the gendered pains of imprisonment. Kinship and marriage ties made it possible for female inmates to "ascribe and achieve social statuses and personalities in the prison other than that of inmate which are consistent with the cultural expectations of the female role in American society," Giallombardo argued.[111] Women entered into partnerships and family relations in prison in an effort "to make their society as much like the outside world as possible."[112] Giallombardo thus characterized women's prison culture as a "substitute universe" and as an "'as if' world," whereby women sought to preserve identities "relevant to life outside the prison."[113] In pairing with other women and building prison families, Williams and Fish agreed, women prisoners "are attempting to make their society as much like the outside world as possible."[114]

In framing these arguments, sociologists arrived at a stunningly anodyne interpretation of the predominance of lesbianism in women's prisons. According to the sociological consensus, women's prison life mirrored rather than subverted traditional gender and sexual norms. Rather than signaling a rejection of dominant notions of femininity and heterosexuality, prison lesbianism constituted a comforting confirmation of their most normative expression. Relying on sex role socialization to explain women's prison relationships, investigators represented women's prisons not as strange and perverse worlds unto themselves, as confirmation of the dangerous allure of homosexuality, or as evidence of the fragility of heterosexuality (theories proposed at various historical moments to account for same-sex sex in men's prisons) but, rather, as a mirror image of the most traditional form of heterosexual femininity. Prison homosexuality and family formations were, in Giallombardo's estimation, "consistent with the cultural expectations of the female role in American society."[115] Aspects of women's prison life that could easily have been construed as a dangerous antithesis of prescribed norms—culturally sanctioned lesbianism, all-female kinship groups, masculine-presenting and male-identifying women—were cast as a reassuring mirror of gender normativity and an assertion of dominant gender norms under difficult conditions.

Sociological accounts that underlined the traditional gender roles of women prisoners worked to ease the subversive implications of the high incidence of prison lesbianism, then, through the most reassuringly conservative of narratives. It is worth noting that sociologists attributed to women prisoners the most traditional notions of femininity, precisely at a moment when those sex roles were being debated and challenged in the larger world. Studies of women's prisons were published at a time of intense national debate over the proper roles of women, articulated most famously in 1963 by Betty Friedan in *The Feminine Mystique*.[116] Friedan joined and catalyzed a larger debate over how natural gender roles were and how satisfied women were in them, and about the meaning of women's paid employment and participation in public life for traditional femininity and family life. At the same time that Friedan argued that middle-class American housewives experienced their prescribed destiny of mother and housewife as stifling, repressive, and even dehumanizing, sociologists underlined the durability of those roles and the longing for them by women prisoners. Sociologists surely did not understand themselves as conservative champions of postwar domesticity, and they did not cast their work in this way. But it is difficult not to read their studies collectively as offering support for the most normative understandings of femininity precisely as those values were being questioned.[117]

Among the factors that may have led sociologists to such interpretations was the larger context of postwar sexual ideology that continued to
cast a shadow into the 1960s. Postwar prescriptive literature had vilified
women who defied sexual convention, among them unmarried mothers, prostitutes, and women seeking abortions as well as lesbians. Many
women prisoners would have occupied one or more of those stigmatized
categories. The dedication to "objective" and nonjudgmental explorations of the lives of women prisoners may have inclined sociologists to
propose prison lesbianism as a confirmation rather than transgression of
normative femininity.[118]

Explaining women's prison sexual culture as a confirmation rather
than subversion of the dominant heteronormative ideals of midcentury
American life allowed investigators to offer reassuring speculations about
the direction of women's desire after release from prison. While butches
in prison endorsed the boastful maxim that "Once you've had a woman
you never want a man again," sociologists insisted that the vast majority
of women returned to heterosexuality after their release from prison.[119]
The "adaptation" to prison sexual norms, Ward and Kassebaum wrote,
"is most frequently seen as temporary and prompted only by the prison
experience."[120] They explained the tendency of women to revert to heterosexuality on release, in part, to the pressures of homophobia: "The
implications of continuing to play a homosexual role outside of prison are
so serious and socially stigmatizing," Ward and Kassebaum wrote, "that
most women appear to return immediately upon release to their roles as
mothers, wives, and girlfriends."[121] The fact that they had maintained
those roles in proxy in lesbian relationships and surrogate families while
in prison, in the minds of sociologists, facilitated rather than undermined
that transition.

Investigators who attributed the formation of women's prison families
and butch-femme relationships to the importation of traditional gender
roles failed to consider the possibility of a more literal form of importation. Several studies conducted slightly later in the 1970s—mostly in the
form of dissertations few of which found their way into print—found
evidence that a large percentage of women prisoners acknowledged pre-
prison lesbian experience. Catherine Nelson found in 1974, for instance,
that almost half of the inmates she studied in New Jersey and Pennsylvania
prisons "admit to sexual relations with another woman before prison."[122]
African American women entered prison with more experience with homosexuality than white women, according to Nelson, but white women
reported far more experience with lesbianism than expected as well.[123]

Prison staff members "believe that much of the homosexuality is indigenous to prison," Nelson concluded, "and in fact, it is not."[124] Alice Propper also found that "a fairly substantial proportion" of young women reported having had a homosexual experience prior to their incarceration, in her 1976 study.[125] William Fitzgerald found similar results in his study of black female prisoners, and he criticized the major sociological studies of women's prisons for their lack of attention to the pre-prison sexual experience of inmates.[126]

The best predictor of women's participation in homosexuality during incarceration, these investigators found, was previous homosexual experience. Conducted primarily by graduate students and circulating much less widely than the major sociological studies of the day, these studies located the sources of prison lesbianism not within the peculiar confines of prison life but in the broader culture of working-class and African American women. Their efforts to understand the pre-prison homosexual experience of imprisoned women sometimes contributed to a long tradition of mapping masculinity onto black women. Nelson attributed what she found to be the disproportionate number of black studs to the socialization of black women to be more aggressive and to assume greater economic responsibilities: "Because of greater aggressiveness and domination in the general socialization process, lower class black females appear more likely to take on a male homosexual role than her white lower class counterpart."[127] Fitzgerald likewise attributed the homosexual behavior among black women prisoners to "lower-class black survival and coping mechanisms which economic pressures often bring them to apply."[128] In reading black women as masculine and aggressive, Nelson and Fitzgerald borrowed from a long-standing convention of women's prison representation and an overdetermined trope of black female masculinity in the culture more generally. But in noting the presence of women of color in prison populations and in considering the importance of race and pre-prison experience, they grappled with issues completely elided by the major sociologists of women's prisons.

There were other striking features of the sociological consensus, emerging in the mid-1960s, which attributed prison lesbianism and family formation to the efforts on the part of women prisoners to preserve their feminine identity and normative sex role expectations as wives and mothers while behind bars. Perhaps the most curious was its seemingly unconscious erasure and virtually wholesale disinterest in the meaning of prison sexual culture to women prisoners who assumed male sex roles. An odd dissonance between sociologists' ethnographic fascination with prison butches and their apparent blindness to their presence when it came to explaining women's prison sexual culture marked their accounts. Explaining the participation of women in prison families and lesbian relationships as evidence of the importation of feminine sex roles and expectations required willful inattention to its meaning for prisoners who fulfilled the roles of husbands, grandfathers, uncles, and brothers and entered into romantic and sexual partnerships with femmes. This remarkable incuriosity on the part of sociologists required ignoring the meaning of prison sexual culture for a sizable minority of women prisoners. Investigators and prisoners alike noted a sex-role imbalance in most women's prisons, where femmes were always observed to outnumber butches, but butches still comprised a significant portion of women's prison populations. Ward and Kassebaum, for instance, estimated that about one-third of the four hundred inmates at Frontera identified as butch.[129] While prison femmes were understood to assume naturalized roles as wives and mothers, prison butches occupied an almost wholly untheorized (if highly scrutinized) place in women's prison culture.

In part, this analytical neglect on the part of investigators can be explained by their common attribution of "true homosexuality" to prison butches. Like the participation of fairies, queens, and fags in male prison sexual culture, the same-sex sexual activity of butches was understood to be a natural (and therefore unremarkable) expression of their essential nature. Homosexual before they arrived, they would understandably seek sex with women while in prison and return to "gay life" on their release.[130] While butches were typically identified as "real" or "true" lesbians, their femme partners were often identified, somewhat dismissively, as jailhouse turn-outs: women who were heterosexual before their prison sentence and who preferred sex with men, but who "turned" to homosexuality as a way of adjusting to prison life and who would presumably return to heterosexual relationships when they left prison.

The distinction between "true homosexual" and "turnout" was a meaningful one to women prisoners as well as to the sociologists who studied them, especially in a culture that granted considerable prestige to the "real" butch and sometimes viewed the phenomenon of "turning out" with a suspicious and jaundiced eye. The young female inmates studied by Giallombardo distinguished between "gay people" and "game players," the former referring to those who came to the institutions with prior experience of homosexuality in the outside world and the latter suspected of "playing 'institutions games.'"[131] Many butches and some femmes looked down on women understood to be "jailhouse turnouts." "True homosexuals," Ward and Kassebaum reported, using the terminology used by women prisoners, "are disturbed over the *chippying* (promiscuity) of the *gutter-snipes* and *dogs* (women who will *turn a trick* or have sexual relations with any other inmate)."[132] Ward and Kassebaum quoted one "disgusted true homosexual" on the "superficial and opportunistic character of the jailhouse turnouts": "They're playing a game, and to me it's no game. It's something I do on the streets."[133]

While prison "turn-outs" were usually understood to be femme, women prisoners reserved special disdain for the prisoner who represented herself as butch but revealed herself as straight or femme when it might work to her advantage—at a parole hearing, during visiting hours with family members or a boyfriend, or upon release. One butch told Ward and Kassebaum about "the ones that come in here with long hair and all of a sudden they're big, romp-stomping butches." But "they don't feel any of this inside, they don't go through any of the emotions that a butch goes through, they're not involved in this and they're gonna forget it as soon as they're out of the institution."[134] "There are those who play the 'hot-shot stud' in here," another prisoner wrote, "then, the day they parole, it's all about the High Heels, a Dress, Make-up, and their 'Old man.'"[135] Butches who turned femme were held up for particular derision by other prisoners and were often ridiculed for their inauthentic, partial, or insincere commitment to masculinity. As one Frontera inmate remarked caustically about prison butches who were revealed to have boyfriends and husbands on the outside, "there's something hypocritical about a pregnant butch."[136] Alderson inmates mocked butches who switched roles with taunts such as "How pretty you look with your earrings on today," "Your makeup is crooked," and "You got a run in your stocking."[137]

At the same time, some aspects of sociological investigations of women's prisons ran counter to the representation of prison butches as simply "true" homosexuals. Some acknowledged that at least some prisoners adopted a butch identity and male gender presentation only after incarceration. That transformation was sometimes understood as the result of a prisoner coming to terms with her "true" identity but was more often dismissed as an opportunistic play for economic gain or femme attention. The butch turn-out, Giallombardo reported, was understood by inmates to be a "commissary hustler," who, "in the free community . . . would tend to exploit men, but since there are no men at the prison, she exploits women."[138] Economic need could indeed compel some prisoners to become butch. New prisoners who entered prison with few resources were sometimes advised by others to turn butch in order to take advantage of the sex-role imbalance and femme generosity. "If you don't have any money coming in, cut your hair and drop your belt and wear high socks and you've got it made," one Frontera inmate explained. Women who affected butch gender presentation, according to this prisoner, "got all kinds of girls chasing them, buying them coffee, cigarettes, knitting them sweaters . . . you name it, they've got it."[139] Others identified prison butches simply as unsuccessful femmes—less attractive, on average, than other women, and those whose "plainness" or "homeliness" resulted in "little success in developing the kinds of affectional relationships with men that the traditional female role calls for."[140] Prison butches, sexologist Leonard Gross observed, "tend to be less pretty and feminine than the other women" and were often "less happy in the female role to begin with."[141]

The simple equation of butchness with "natural" homosexuality was also complicated by the recognition of butchness, by sociologists and prisoners alike, as a carefully crafted performance. Young inmates were observed by Giallombardo, for instance, to be "in various stages of perfecting their maleness."[142] "To be a butch," one young woman told Giallombardo, "you have to learn how to walk, how to talk, how to act and how to dress."[143] The understanding of butchness as comprised not of an ineffable and essential masculinity bespeaking "true" homosexuality but, rather, of a series of signifying practices, troubled the easy attribution of true homosexuality to them.

The understanding of women's prison sexual culture as the consequence of female sex-role socialization not only conveniently overlooked the presence of butches, it also worked to erase sexual desire as a driving force behind women's prison relationships. An important effect of the sociological reliance on sex role socialization to explain women's prison sexual culture, and no doubt one of its great appeals, was its striking desexualization of women's prison families and prison relationships, elaborating on a pattern apparent in earlier writing on women prisoners. That desexualization was effected in part rhetorically. Investigators used the sterile language of social science to describe women's prison families and partnerships in the driest possible of terms. Giallombardo's definition of the "role refinement" of butches and femmes in prison as "an organizing principle of social organization," for example, dampened the erotics of butch-femme coupling.[144] The desexualization of women's prison sexual culture was underlined by sociologists in more overt ways as well. Some characterized women's prison relationships as primarily economic in nature, sexual only in service to their more fundamental resource-garnering purpose. "A femme often enters into a love relationship," Williams and Fish wrote, "because the butch supplies the items she cannot get in any other way."[145] One inmate confirmed the economic underpinnings of some prison relationships, explaining that "when the system is such that you have to fend entirely for yourself, you learn to play the game. . . . You pay a price." She went on to lay bare the economic calculus behind some expressions of same-sex affection in women's prisons: "Perhaps holding hands on line to eat will earn you a pack of cigarettes, or rubbing knees in the TV room will buy you a bar of soap, or listening closely to someone's problems will buy you a cup of coffee."[146]

Others emphasized the emotional character of women's prison relationships, which, according to many, overshadowed their sexual character. Researchers typically insisted that women tolerated sexual deprivation more easily than did men.[147] "Men in prison," Ward and Kassebaum wrote, "more often represent the significance of the homosexual relationship in terms of physical satisfaction. The women are more concerned with sexual relationships which are seen as symbolic of affectional ties."[148] Leonard Gross likewise contrasted men, for whom the "sex drive" was "prime motive for homosexual behavior," with women, who, he argued, turned to same-sex sex in a search for "human warmth." "This is probably attributable to a difference between men and women in general," Gross wrote, "in that men primarily want sex, while the foremost interest of women is affectionate bonds."[149] As a consequence, women's prison relationships fulfilled women's needs for "companionship and a feeling of belonging" and for "love and affection" but were rarely understood as motivated by sexual desire or attraction.[150] Buffum proposed in 1972 that since "women are socialized in the language of love before they learn about sex, . . . men are socialized in the language of sex before they learn about love," women "show considerably fewer problems managing sexual deprivation than do men."[151] Women therefore entered into relationships, Buffum suggested, "as part of a search for affection and stability in personal relationships," clarifying that "physical homosexual contacts" were "less sought for the physical release that they afford than for the validation of emotionally binding and significant relationships."[152] Investigators brushed awkwardly past (and often denied outright) the romantic and sexual nature of husband-wife pairings, emphasizing instead the range of emotional resources they offered women prisoners. Even when those relationships were overtly sexualized, many investigators stressed their familial underpinnings, which helped women compensate for deprivations of incarceration. The distinctly female desire for human warmth, emotional connection, and kinship, not sexual desire, was cited again and again as the motivating force behind women's prison relationships.

Some women inmates concurred with these desexualizing accounts. About sex with other women, for instance, one prisoner told an investigator, "it's not really a sex thing, even when it's sex."[153] "When a girl makes love to you," one woman explained, "there's a little bit of a mother in it." When a young women enters prison, she is scared and "needs somebody's shoulder to cry on." "So naturally the first person that's going to come and put her arm around her . . . and make like a little mother, that's the person she's going to end up going gay for."[154] But representing prison lesbianism as the consequence of women's desire to fulfill their roles of wife and mother rather than their sexual desire required eliding considerable evidence to the contrary. Prison observers' insistence on the essentially asexual nature of women's prison relationships was sometimes sharply contradicted by women's own assertions of sexual desire. Elizabeth Gurley Flynn recalled that one woman in prison explained to her, "I had all the sex I wanted outside and I'm going to get all I want in here."[155] Former prisoner Fran O'Leary reported that loneliness and the need for protection could incline an otherwise heterosexual woman to enter into a homosexual relationship in prison but that, "among the emotional strains on your system, the most outstanding lies in your sexual frustrations."[156]

Sociologists' cultivation of objectivity and their commitment to ethnographic techniques that required listening to their subjects gave voice to incarcerated women and girls, even when they contradicted the assumptions and interpretations of the investigators. Notes passed between prisoners, known in prison argot as "kites" for the tightly folded triangular shape that made them easy to conceal, often communicated the sexual desire underlying prison relationships. "Mild and wild passion surges through my body aching for your touch," one Frontera prison femme wrote to her lover "Duke." "Never before has every nerve tissue in my entire being been ever so on fire with desire."[157] "I want you to hold me and run your fingers through my hair and kiss me sweet and tenderly," one Alderson prisoner wrote another whom she addressed as "Mi amor." "I dream about making love to you and it is violent and at the same time it's sweet and gentle." She signed her letter "Chiquita Diablo."[158] Women described sexual desire for other women in less heated terms as well. One "jailhouse turnout" interviewed by Ward and Kassebaum found sex with women more satisfying than with men, so much so that she divorced her husband and planned to live with a woman after her release: "I find the physical relationship much more satisfying than with men. A woman can't tell a man she wants to be kissed or touched in a certain way and women start slowly."[159] Another woman marveled over the fact that "the sudden complete absence of males" in prison was "rarely brought up" when people asked about the things she missed most while incarcerated. Once she was released from the Ohio Reformatory for Women in Marysville, friends would ask "whether I ever got to eat ice-cream, could I watch any television, could I get newspapers," she wrote, "but no one asks me— did you have any sex." She was clear in attributing her same-sex activity behind bars to sexual deprivation: "Being taken away from sex like that for a said period of time is a heavy reason why I had relations with women."[160]

Sociologists committed to representing prison lesbianism as the result of an effort on the part of female inmates to reproduce normative femininity behind bars also ignored evidence of sexual coercion in women's prisons and of violence between women prisoners more generally. Indeed, one of the principal differences between men's and women's prisons, as described by investigators, was the relative absence of sexual coercion, intimidation, and violence among female prisoners. Sex among women prisoners was represented as almost uniformly consensual. Ward and Kassebaum found evidence at Frontera neither of any inmate using physical force to achieve sexual access to another nor of inmates being coerced into paying off debts with sexual favors, phenomena common in men's prisons but apparently very rare in women's.[161] Giallombardo similarly found that homosexual relations at Alderson were typically "established voluntarily between the principals involved, with no physical coercion applied."[162] Jealousy between inmates could occasionally precipitate violent confrontation, but violence was reportedly not used by women prisoners to obtain sex.

The weight of evidence from other sources, however, suggests that sexual violence, while rare in most women's prisons, was not unheard of. Criminologist Lee Bowker observed that violence in prisons for women was "considerably lower" than in men's prisons but cited examples that countered the insistence on the part of sociologists that it was virtually nonexistent. One woman reported that soon after her entry into prison, another inmate approached her "with a goddamn tonic bottle" and demanded that she undress.[163] Alice Propper was told of incidents of rape in girls' training schools.[164] Charges of sexual assault and threat of assault in a women's prison were levied in the precedent-setting 1974 California appellate case, *People v. Lovercamp*. In that case, Marsha Lovercamp and a codefendant successfully appealed their conviction of escape from the California Rehabilitation Center on the grounds that they had been continuously threatened with sexual assault by a gang of lesbian inmates—in the text of the legal decision, given the alternatives to "fuck or fight"—and feared for their lives.[165] In 1968, Dorothy West reported being brutally beaten and raped in Chicago's Cook County Jail when other inmates blamed her for a shakedown and search of the women's tier.[166]

The leading sociologists of women's prisons themselves sometimes offered evidence that contradicted their own arguments. Kassebaum reported the case of a "quiet girl" who was "severely kicked in the stomach and the breast by five other inmates, evidently because, after first encouraging them, she would not submit to homosexual threats."[167] Harris recounted stories of sexual violence among inmates at the Women's House of Detention, as well. "They come in," one woman told Harris of prison butches, "and you have to fight your way out like a tiger." When she refused sexual advances, "two dykes had me against the wall and the third burned me with a cigarette."[168]

While sociologists found little evidence of sexual violence among women, they documented cases of violence more generally that fit awkwardly within their larger story of normative femininity and domestic quiescence. Giallombardo attributed "the generally passive orientation of the female" to the infrequency of violence among women prisoners but noted the violence "in connection with a homosexual triangle" that occasionally erupted among Alderson inmates, where "the great fear is not so much fear for one's life as a fear of disfigurement," as some inmates used razors or scissors "to disfigure the other's face."[169]

Caged Heat: Prison Lesbianism and Popular Culture

"Rape (by women inmates) in prison is not nearly so prevalent as the public is led to believe," lesbian prisoner Ruby Leah Richardson claimed in 1982, "notwithstanding movies such as *Women in Chains* and *Glass House*."[170] While sexual violence was rarely represented in accounts of women's prisons by sociologists or by prisoners themselves, sexualized menace and sometimes violence occupied the center of the popular genre of women's prison films that flourished in the 1970s. Largely as a result of its representation in popular culture, and in direct contrast with sociological studies, the women's prison became virtually synonymous with lesbianism of an overtly sexualized and threatening sort.

Filmic representations of women in prison preceded the period of sociological interest in the subject of women prisoners in the 1960s. Women's prison movies comprised a small subset of a larger popular genre, the vast majority of which featured men's prisons, which had attracted audiences since the 1930s. Because of restrictions against sexually explicit representation and against any direct reference to "sex perversion" upheld after 1930 by the Motion Picture Production Code, however, these early films were usually restrained and coded in their depiction of prison lesbianism.[171] The critically acclaimed film *Caged*, for instance, released in 1950 and the prototype for the women-in-prison genre as it evolved in the 1970s, only hinted at the subject.

While lesbianism in *Caged*, as film critic Judith Mayne observes, was necessarily "mediated through ambiguity and displacement," the innuendos would have been readily comprehended by canny viewers.[172] Lesbianism in *Caged* was connoted in part through the not-so-veiled metaphor of recruitment, ostensibly to a life of crime but carrying clear sexual valances as well. When the hardened, masculine, and bullying prisoner Kitty Stark lies alongside first-time offender Marie in her bunk and tries to convince her to join her shoplifting ring with the promise of finagling her early parole, she warns Marie pointedly, "if you stay in here too long you don't think of guys at all. You just get out of the habit." In a later scene, Kitty's rival, the ascot-wearing, close-cropped, and sternly glamorous Elvira Powell, eyes Marie leeringly and asks her name. But by this time a more seasoned Marie senses that more is being asked of her, and responds, "I'm a big girl and this isn't my first year away from home. If I said no to Kitty, I'm sure not going to say yes to you." "She's a cute trick," Elvira tells her sidekick, and ultimately succeeds in recruiting Marie to a criminal career, implicitly as a prostitute. Marie communicates her acquiescence in a sexually charged scene toward the end of the film in which she saunters over to Elvira's bunk and boldly uses her compact to apply her lipstick.

In another midcentury film, *Girls in Prison* (1956), a prison dance seems an occasion of spirited fun. But looking on with disgust, new inmate Anne Carson identifies it as the site of sexual perversion when she confesses sneeringly to the prison chaplain, "You know what I'm afraid of most? That I'll become like them. It's contagious." The advertising poster for *Girls in Prison* posed the ominous question, "What Happens to Women without Men?" Both *Caged* and *Girls in Prison* echoed midcentury anxieties about the contagion of homosexuality and the vulnerability and instability of heterosexuality and femininity under the pressures and deprivations of prison life. Another film of the same period, *Women's Prison* (1955) concluded with the heterosexual redemption of the lead character, a young housewife incarcerated for accidentally hitting a child with her car, who is met by her husband at the prison gates on her release. But *Caged* refused that happy ending. Embittered by the denial of her parole and the seeming impossibility of leading an independent and respectable life as a single woman with a criminal record, Marie ultimately accepts Elvira's offer and her parole is approved. On her release from prison, she scornfully tosses the wedding ring that she had tearfully relinquished on her arrival into the lap of the prison officer.

Midcentury women's prison melodramas like *Caged*, *Girls in Prison*, and *Women's Prison* attempted to depict and treat seriously the problems of the prison system and to capture the gritty verisimilitude of men's prison films. Virginia Kellogg researched four women's prisons while writing the screenplay for *Caged* in an effort to make the film as authentic a portrayal of women's prison experience as possible.[173] Finely acted, often by identifiable stars (both Hope Emerson and Eleanor Parker received Oscar nominations for their performances in *Caged*), and shot in noirish black and white, these films evoked the period's social-problem genre in their critique of prison brutality and corruption as well as through their aesthetic. They also referenced the iconography of men's prison movies in their depictions of bleak tiered cells, hard labor, and the dreary monotony and tension of cellblock life that had long been staples of the genre. One scene from *Girls in Prison*, in which inmates watch a prison movie, shows one guard telling another, "they never get things right in prison pictures." Knowingly self-referential, the ironic comment also intended to distinguish the film's treatment of prison life as more realistic than other popular representations.

These midcentury films offered models for later women-in-prison films that would care not at all about authenticity and would flourish in the straight-to-drive-in sexploitation genre that exploded in the 1970s with the rise of independent films and the demise of the Production Code.[174] These films referenced their predecessors in some of their basic character development and plotlines. Most followed the formula, long since established in prison films more generally, that depicted the arrival of a naive and frightened new inmate to prison, often incarcerated by mistake or because of a crime committed on behalf of a boyfriend or husband, and charted her fall from innocence after harsh encounters with the brutality of prison life and hardened convicts, at least one of whom dedicates herself to making the new "fish's" life miserable. But the later women-in-prison films differed markedly from the earlier prototypes in tone and intended audience. Produced quickly and cheaply and associated with soft-core pornographic appeal, camp sleaze, over-the-top acting, and lurid spectacle, the women-in-prison films of the 1970s departed from the earlier films' aspirations to cinematic respectability in nearly every way.[175] "These films—so clearly beyond the realm of 'art' and 'high culture,'" Mayne asserts, "are thus given free rein to unleash the perverse, the hybrid, the grotesque."[176]

The 1970s films departed most notably from the earlier films in their depictions of sex. The women-in-prison movies of the seventies sexualized the very fact of women's prisons, exaggerating themes implicit in their predecessors and running directly counter to sociological efforts to desexualize and domesticate women's prison experience. In so doing, they mapped the outer reaches of a larger cultural movement toward sexual liberalism and away from the postwar containment of female sexuality, and they highlighted the sexualization of culture more generally in a period of sexual revolution. The characters in women-in-prison films were often marked as defiantly, even ravenously, heterosexual. When one prisoner is brought back to the women's dormitory, traumatized and shackled after being forced to submit sexually to the male warden in *The Big Bird Cage*, another prisoner complains, "she's the only one around here who ever gets any, and she won't even tell us about it." "If only I could get laid by a real man," one prisoner tells another wistfully in *The Big Bird Cage*, "I think I could stand it." Another scene in that film depicts the gang rape of a male prison guard by heterosexually starved women prisoners. In *The Big Doll House* (1971), an inmate rapes a delivery man at knifepoint, ordering him, "get it up or I'll cut it off."

Unhampered by the restrictions of the Production Code, which had begun to dissolve in the early 1960s and was replaced by the Motion Picture Rating System in 1968, women-in-prison films of the 1970s also made lesbianism central to their depictions. Nearly invisible in mainstream cinematic representation, lesbians were a staple in women-in-prison films. While explicit depictions of lesbian sex remained rare, the subject was not handled cryptically or communicated through innuendo as it had been in the past. Indeed, women-in-prison films were, in Mayne's analysis, "one of the few established genres where lesbianism is not an afterthought or an anomaly."[177]

In her reading of women-in-prison films, Judith Halberstam argues that the prison came to occupy a privileged place within what she terms the "homophobic imaginary."[178] Central to that imaginary was the association of prison lesbianism with the overlapping and linked phenomena of female masculinity, sexual predation, and sadistic psychosis. Newly overt in its depictions in women's prison films of the 1970s, lesbianism was typically associated with sexual aggression. *The Big Bird Cage* initially identifies the inmate Karen as a lesbian by her veiled come-on to a new inmate. Telling her, "you know, you've got a very pretty face," Karen echoed the codes of implicit lesbianism of the earlier films, communicated in the overly solicitous and overlong gaze. Karen is later identified and mocked by another inmate as a "big dyke" and a "sex maniac." "You can tell what they're thinking just to look at them," she tells a newcomer to the prison. "Like this big dyke here. . . . You can tell how she'd love to put those big horny hands on my skin. And put that big ugly body down on top of me." *The Big Doll House* (1971) was unusual among women-in-prison films in featuring a lesbian as a main character. In this film, Pam Grier plays butch con Helen Grear, domineering "old man" to her junkie cellmate, who greets a new inmate with the menacing welcome, "green, scared, and pretty. Boy are we gonna have fun."

The themes of female masculinity, sexual predation, sadism, and psychosis often came together in these films in the figure of the warden. The model for this character can be traced to several midcentury women's prison films. In *Caged*, Hope Emerson played the brutal warden Evelyn Harper, whose sadism is contrasted with the kindness of her reform-minded counterpart, Mrs. Benton, played by Agnes Moorehead.[179] Harper's sexual orientation is alluded to by the power she holds over prisoners she refers to as "my girls," from whom she demands gifts in exchange for narcotics, communication from the outside, and easy work assignments. Harper's masculinity is expressed, paradoxically, through a burlesque of exaggerated femininity, exposed as artificial and strained through its contrast with her coarseness and swagger as well as with Emerson's physical size, which she deployed in this film to hulking effect (a large woman at six foot two and over two hundred pounds, Emerson had earlier played the circus strongwoman who held Spencer Tracy aloft in his chair in the courtroom scene in *Adam's Rib* [1949]). Gorging on caramels, reading romance novels propped up on pillows in her overdecorated room, and dressing in garish outfits for dates with an unseen boyfriend, Harper's hyperfemininity seems staged primarily to taunt the inmates. As Halberstam observes, "Femininity, in prison, is simply a luxury the women cannot afford, and the butch warden Evelyn Harper . . . indulges herself in 'feminine comforts' such as romance novels and dressing up not, one feels, for the pleasure that she gains from femininity but because femininity is what is denied to the inmates."[180] That claim is underlined by an unforgettably brutal scene in the film, shot in extreme close-up, in which Harper disciplines Marie by shaving her head.

Harper was joined by other sadistic women's prison superintendents in midcentury prison films. In *Women's Prison* (1955), Ida Lupino plays the unfeeling warden Amelia Van Zant, dedicated overzealously to her career and diagnosed by the prison's kind-hearted male psychologist as a "psychopath" unable to find love with a man. "You're feminine, attractive— you must have had opportunities to marry," he tells her. "Maybe you even cared for someone once in your cold way. But he turned to somebody who could give him what he *really* wanted. Warmth. Understanding. Love." Van Zant exacts retribution on her charges by sending them to solitary confinement in straitjackets. Her beating of one pregnant prisoner leads to her miscarriage and death and provokes a rebellion among the inmates.

Caged Heat (1974), Jonathan Demme's directorial debut, took the model of the sadistic warden offered by these earlier films and elevated it into a camp icon. Barbara Steele plays wheelchair-bound and psychotic Warden McQueen, in league with an equally insane male doctor who treats recalcitrant inmates with electroshock torture and lobotomies. Lesbianism was often coded, in the 1970s as in the 1940s and 1950s, as sexual repression and prudishness. Scandalized by a bawdy vaudevillian drag act performed by two mustachioed inmates to an appreciative audience at the prison play, McQueen shuts down the performance and later releases her repression (and her tightly bound hair) in wild sexual fantasies in which she trades her tweed suit for leather fetish wear. The wardens in other women-in-prison films also played to type. In *Women in Cages* (1971), Pam Grier appears as the lesbian prison matron "Alabama," who punishes prisoners in a torture chamber she calls her "playpen." In *Black Mama, White Mama* (1972), prison matron Densmore masturbates while watching prisoners shower through a peephole. "If she digs you," one prisoner tells a newcomer about Densmore, "things in here can be a hell of a lot easier." When the new prisoner refuses Densmore's advances, Densmore dons a long black leather glove and slaps her. In the *Big Doll House* (1974), the warden's baroque torture of prisoners, involving electroshock, whipping, and a cobra, is overseen by an ominous leather-clad and masked figure in the corner later revealed to be the female prison superintendent.

Charges of sexual perversion among female wardens, prison superintendents, and occasionally female guards were no doubt linked to the assumption of authority and power on the part of women in nontraditional professions. Insinuations about the sexual proclivities of male wardens

and guards were rare but not unheard of. Progressive era prison reformer
Thomas Mott Osborne was accused of engaging in sexual relations with
male inmates at Sing Sing Prison, where he served for a brief time as warden.[181] And male prisoners occasionally charged prison staff with sexual
abuse. But the superintendents and wardens of women's prisons became so
closely linked with lesbianism as to render the lesbian prison warden a stereotype. Historian Estelle Freedman has charted the travails of Miriam van
Waters, superintendent of the Massachusetts Reformatory for Women in
Framingham, who battled charges that she was soft on lesbianism among
prisoners as well as insinuations about homosexuality among reformatory
staff and her own sexual inclinations, in a public hearing in 1948.[182] Sexual
intimations about female wardens and superintendents occasionally sur-
faced in the sociological literature as well. Halleck and Hersko alluded to
the "unhealthy attitudes on the part of the staff" that contributed to the
culture of "girl stuff" at a state institution for delinquent girls in Wisconsin.[183] And one Frontera prisoner identified a matron as a lesbian—"my
friend had seen her at parties on the outside"—who allegedly turned a
blind eye to sex between prisoners at that institution.[184]

The lesbian of women-in-prison films, then—perverse, predatory, sadistic, often psychotic, and typically represented by a warden or superintendent who exploited her position of power—stood at a far remove
from the domesticated prisoner depicted in sociologists' accounts, whose
situational lesbianism expressed a fundamentally conservative desire for
normative femininity and heterosexuality. Some 1970s women-in-prison
films set the women's prison and the lesbianism with which it was coming
to be synonymous at a distant geographic remove from domestic American national borders as well. Many films of this era were shot and set in
unnamed "third world" countries, further exoticizing the women's prison
and its inhabitants. This setting allowed plotlines that focused on corruption and miscarriages of justice attributed to third world nations (and
implicitly spared the U.S. prison system from similar indictments). New
inmate Collier tells her cellmates that her trial was "a joke" and condemns
the "banana republic cops," for example, in *The Big Doll House*, filmed
in the Philippines.[185] Third-world settings also facilitated revolutionary
plotlines, however ludicrous and tangential to the prison story. In *The
Big Bird Cage* (1972), for instance, Pam Grier plays a rebel who is planted
inside the prison by her revolutionary boyfriend Django to help orches-
trate a prison break and "steal some women for the revolution." Tropical
climates also served the interest of this sexploitation genre by demanding

the wearing of short shorts and skirts by the prisoners and sometimes by their keepers.

While women-in-prison films of the 1970s, unlike their predecessors, were almost wholly unconcerned with creating an authentic depiction of the experience of women's prisons, they did render visible some features that were erased in sociological accounts. Among the striking erasures of those accounts was the racial composition of women's prison populations and the meaning of race for women prisoners' relationships. While investigators earlier in the century had maintained a fascination with interracial attraction between female inmates first articulated by Margaret Otis in 1913—a preoccupation that continued to shape many mid-twentieth-century accounts—race largely disappeared from the scholarly agenda and from the ethnographic gaze of investigators of women's prisons by the 1960s. In their unacknowledged but evident commitment to color blindness, authors of the major sociological studies of women's prisons in this period echoed the inattention to race by midcentury sociologists of men's prisons like Clemmer and Sykes, whose studies they took as models. Their reluctance to engage the issue of race in women's prison was no doubt prompted as well by an investment in racial liberalism—a racial ideology unto itself, of course, that led to their implicit representation of female prisoners as white.

Racial diversity among women prisoners, virtually absent in sociological accounts, was almost always present in women-in-prison films. Unlike sociological studies, of course, the visual medium of film created new possibilities for the representation of racial difference in women's prisons. Films of the 1940s and 1950s sometimes depicted racially segregated cellblocks and often a gospel-singing, floor-scrubbing, and deferential black prisoner. Later women-in-prison films were always peopled by women of color, otherwise marginalized or excluded entirely from mainstream Hollywood cinema as well as in sociological accounts of women's prisons. Black women, and sometimes Asian women and Latinas, were always among the inmate populations represented in women's prison films, their presence remarkable only for being unremarked on. Suzanna Walters distinguishes (and lauds) the representation of interracial prison friendship in *Caged Heat* for "its refusal to problematize the 'difference'" between women prisoners. "These two prison buddies live and die for each other, without narrating their racial difference at all."[186] The interracial female buddy plot structures *Black Mama, White Mama* (1972) as well, in which a white, blonde rich-girl-turned revolutionary and a black prostitute escape from prison shackled together and spend the rest of the film on the run, literally bonded by a chain. As a consequence, Walters argues that *Caged Heat* and other women-in-prison films present a utopian and feminist vision of "multicultural sisterhood."[187] Many of these films conclude with a scene of unity among prisoners, always across lines of race and in opposition to the cruelties and corruption of the administration.[188]

Female criminality, curiously muted in sociological accounts of women's prisons, was also on vivid display in women-in-prison films. Giallombardo, Ward and Kassebaum, and Harris rarely commented on the reasons for women being in prison, and remarkably, women prisoners' status as criminals was rarely if ever even noted, much less analyzed, in the major sociological studies. Overemphasis on the criminality of women prisoners presumably would have compromised their claims to femininity and undermined the primary claim of sociologists that women prisoners were driven by normative female desires for marriage and family. Women's prison films, by way of contrast, from their beginning, foregrounded and often gloried in female criminality. Indeed, criminality was central to formulaic plotlines that tracked the new inmate's fall from innocence through her contact with prostitutes, thieves, and murderers. The opening scenes of both midcentury films *Caged* and *Girls in Prison* depicted their innocent heroines arriving at prison alongside jaded repeat offenders, some identified as prostitutes through their fancy dress, heartily welcomed back as regulars by prison staff and other inmates. That iconic opening was repeated in almost every women-in-prison film of the 1970s.

Lesbianism was implicitly part of the underworld culture depicted in these films, linked with criminality and transgression rather than domesticity and femininity. Women-in-prison films participated in homophobic representations of prison lesbianism, coded as predatory and contagious. But the reading of women-in-prison films of the 1970s as simply homophobic is overly reductive, ignoring the many other valences—the carnivalesque excesses, anarchic incoherence, and ineffable weirdness—that these films shared with other low-budget sexploitation, blaxploitation, and horror films of the same period. These films featured jokes about lesbians and lesbianism, plotlines revolving around lesbian relationships, and lesbian characters that often exceeded the codes of homophobia. At the same time that lesbianism was equated with predation and sexual perversion, especially in the midcentury films, by the 1970s, it was also part of their tongue-in-cheek camp appeal. It is often difficult to take too seriously the dangers of lesbianism as represented in these later films, and many signs within the films themselves suggest that it was not meant to be. Homophobia was certainly marshaled in these films' representations of lesbianism, especially in wardens whose sexual repression was unleashed in sadistic torture, but its excesses suggested a knowing citation of the codes of homophobia rather than a genuine condemnation of homosexuality. The excesses of homophobia itself were sometimes ridiculed in these films. It is hard to truly believe in the menace represented by lesbian inmate Karen in *The Big Bird Cage*, for instance, when she slathers her naked body with chicken fat to elude the grasp of the prison guards and attack her homophobic nemesis. Later, she earns the audience's sympathy when she stands up in sisterly defense of an abused fellow prisoner and is killed by a guard for her insubordination.

Lesbianism also lost its threat when exploited for pornographic appeal and recuperated for presumably male heterosexual pleasure, as it often was in these films. Although these films presumably attracted a diverse audience of men and women, their depiction of lesbianism can be understood to be performed for an implied male gaze. The films' obligatory group shower scenes and catfights referenced formulaic lesbian scenes in heterosexual pornography, although often with a knowing sense of self-referentiality and even self-mocking.

Like popular genres more generally, the ideological meanings of women-in-prison films were unstable and often incoherent. As Walters writes, "Alternately hilariously funny . . . and nauseatingly violent, these films switch codes instantaneously, forcing the viewer to concede the illusory nature of image making. Realist narrative is not simply dethroned but is, rather, effectively deconstructed."[189] In the process as well, these films deconstructed the sociologists' vision of prison lesbianism as a confirmation of the most normative version of femininity.

In their depiction of violence, criminality, and sexuality, women-in-prison films of the 1970s gave voice to subjects submerged or elided entirely in sociological accounts of women's prisons. Sexual violence and sexual desire, negated and tamed in sociological accounts of women's prisons, were the common currency of women-in-prison films. Read together, the sociological analyses of women prisoners that focused on women's family and domestic roles and women-in-prison films that gloried in sexual psychosis and predation mapped dichotomous ways in which academic and cultural producers grappled with prison lesbianism. Sociologists at once highlighted, domesticated, and contained it, shoring up and affirming the period's gender orthodoxies at a moment when they were being questioned in the broader culture and transgressed in the most flagrant ways behind bars. Women-in-prison films, in contrast, exoticized and eroticized prison lesbianism, exploiting it for sensationalistic appeal. While the multiplicity of stories that emerge in these very different representational forms attested to the impossibility of a unified, coherent, or finally authoritative version of prison lesbianism, both forms succeeded, in very different ways, in trivializing and containing it. They also illuminated the distinctly gendered anxieties posed by the sexual culture of women's prisons and the distinctly gendered resolution of those anxieties. Those distinctions would be sharper still when contrasted with the representations of men's prisons that emerged in the same period.

CHAPTER FIVE

Rape, Race, and the Violent Prison

In September of 1968, an investigation in Philadelphia culminated in a report that announced an "epidemic" of sexual assaults in the city's jails and in the sheriffs' vans in which prisoners were transported between courts and jails.[1] The report's author, District Attorney Alan J. Davis, singled out young white men with slight builds as especially vulnerable. Typically approached sexually within days of their admission and often before their trial and sentence, they were sometimes raped repeatedly by gangs of inmates. The investigation documented 156 assaults reported by 3,034 inmates interviewed over the course of a little over a year. Since the findings were based on a small sample of the total number of men that passed through the Philadelphia jail system and because Davis recognized that male prisoners were especially reluctant to report sexual assault—due to embarrassment, threat of retaliation, fear of being labeled a homosexual, or belief in the futility of reporting to prison officials—he believed that number to be the "tip of the iceberg."[2] Davis placed what he considered a conservative estimate of the total number of assaults in the Philadelphia jails during this period at "about 2,000."[3] Accompanying the report's alarming statistics were graphic first-person accounts of sexual violence. "In an early draft," Davis wrote, "an attempt was made to couch this illustrative material in sociological, medical, and legal terminology," but he abandoned that distanced ap-

149

proach in the interest of fully representing the "raw, ugly language used by the witness and victims."[4]

Davis's report provided one touchstone for a new concern about sexual violence in men's prisons that emerged in the late 1960s and 1970s. Activist Stephen Donaldson's searing and widely publicized account of his experience of gang rape in a Washington, D.C., jail provided another. A participant in a protest against the bombing of Cambodia held in front of the White House in the summer of 1973, Donaldson was among a group of activists arrested for criminal trespassing. Originally placed with his fellow protestors in a "gentle tier" for first offenders, recently incarcerated Watergate conspirator G. Gordon Liddy among them, Donaldson was transferred after several days to a cellblock for violent offenders. Donaldson believed strongly that the warden, knowing that Donaldson had worked as a newspaper reporter and fearing that he would write an exposé of the jail's treatment of political protesters, deliberately exposed him to violence to punish and silence him. Donaldson concluded that he was "deliberately set up by the Department of Corrections for a mass rape on the assumption that such an assault would quickly force me out of the jail and that I would, as all male rape victims had done for as far as memory stretches, remain silent about the experience."[5]

But Donaldson was far from quiet. After his release from jail and following surgery to repair his lacerated rectum, he called a press conference and later spoke publicly about his experience at a Washington, D.C., city council hearing, estimating that he was raped more than sixty times by an estimated forty-five men over a two-day period and charging the prison administration with responsibility for his assault.[6] Donaldson went on to help found and direct the organization Stop Prisoner Rape and achieved national prominence as an antirape activist who could testify from first-hand experience about the terror and trauma of sexual victimization in men's prisons.

Although prison today is closely associated in the public mind with male sexual violence, that association was forged remarkably recently. Despite sporadic references to rape in prison earlier in the century, the subject did not receive significant attention until the late 1960s and 1970s. Beginning in this period, however, a new surge of writing about prison life, inspired in part by a wave of highly publicized prison riots, often seemed to focus on little else. Davis's report announcing an "epidemic" of sexual violence in men's prisons launched, in turn, an epidemic of investigations, sensationalistic journalistic exposés, prisoner autobiographies, and film and fictional representations of American prisons and jails, the primary focus of which was the alarming frequency and horror of rape among male inmates.[7]

New in intensity and number in this period, representations of prison sexual violence also featured new narrative elements that distinguished them from earlier depictions. The most striking change was the near-unanimous insistence on race as the most important structuring aspect of rape in prison. According to virtually every report in this period, prison victims were disproportionately white and assailants disproportionately African American. This was the case in Davis's study, in which 85 percent of the assaults he documented were committed by black men. Davis acknowledged that these statistics in part reflected the fact that a majority of Philadelphia inmates were African American, yet even in prisons in which black men did not constitute a majority they were identified as comprising the majority of sexual aggressors.[8] From an analysis of prison disciplinary records and interviews with informants in a study of a maximum security prison in Rhode Island conducted in 1970 and 1971, sociologist Leo Carroll was struck by the frequency with which sexual attacks were interracial and estimated that "75 percent or more of the sexual assaults involved black aggressors and white victims"—a ratio that, unlike that in Davis's study, approximately reversed the racial composition of a prison population in which black men comprised a minority.[9] The phenomenon of interracial sexual violence behind bars, perpetrated by black prisoners on white, was supported by anecdotal evidence from prisoners. All of Stephen Donaldson's assailants, he reported with some ambivalence, were black. Inmate Jim Johnson had fewer qualms in attributing his "almost savage, irrational hatred for Negroes in general" to the overrepresentation of black men "as the masculine aggressor" in cases of sexual assault in the many penitentiaries in which he had served time.[10]

Depictions of the racialized nature of sexual violence in men's prisons corresponded to material changes in those prisons and in the larger political culture, the histories of which I trace here. But they did more than simply document those changes. They contributed as well to a larger debate about black politicization and citizenship in the aftermath of the civil rights movement and embattled expressions of black power, and at a time in which black men were incarcerated at increasingly disproportionate rates. Heightened attention to the racialized aspects of prison sexual violence took part in a much broader and deeply contested national conversation about race. Less directly and less obviously, it offered a new way to explain same-sex sex in prison and to reassert the notion of stable sexual identities.

Rape as the Defining Sexual Practice in Men's Prisons

While representations of sex in prison have changed in important ways over time, one rhetorical convention has remained strikingly constant, evident from the early nineteenth century and continuing through the early twenty-first. Those who documented sex in prison across this long expanse of time often wrote about the subject as if they were exposing it for the first time. From Louis Dwight in 1826, to Joseph Fishman in 1934, to Alan Davis in 1968, to the U.S. Department of Justice's first statistical report on prison rape in 2005 mandated by the Prison Rape Elimination Act of 2003, prison investigators wrote as though they were the first to dare document a subject that had, until that time, received little attention.

As generations of prison observers had done before them, then, writers in the 1960s and 1970s announced their exposés as the first glimpse into the shadowy truth of life behind bars. "Sex is prison's hidden agenda," journalist and gay prison activist David Rothenberg wrote in 1977, and is "rarely discussed by prisoners or their keepers."[11] By the late 1960s, the subject highest on that agenda was sexual violence in men's prisons. To Carl Weiss and David Friar, authors of the sensationalistic book *Terror in the Prisons: Homosexual Rape and Why Society Condones It*, published in 1974, rape was "the most closely guarded secret of American prisons." "No library, no bookstore," they wrote, "contains a single . . . book that concerns itself with the rape that is rampant in our prisons."[12] "Our knowledge of prison rape and its context, prison sexuality," Stephen Donaldson agreed, "is pitifully small." Donaldson insisted that "the academics— researchers, armchair theorists, and others who have written on prison rape"—had "a good deal to learn" from talking to prisoners themselves about their "experiences in the field," since "the culture of confinement is strange, forbidding, secretive, and resistant to standard research techniques."[13] Investigations followed, using ethnographic research, participant observation, surveys, and interviews to study the phenomenon of rape behind bars from the perspective of victims and witnesses, wardens and guards, and occasionally assailants. If before this period it was difficult to find any substantive discussion of the subject of sexual violence in men's prisons, after the mid-1970s that subject virtually drowned out discussion of anything else.

To recognize sexual violence as the privileged subject of representations of prison life beginning in the late 1960s does not mean that it was never mentioned before this time and certainly does not mean that it was never experienced by prisoners in earlier periods. Sexual manipulation, coercion, and sometimes lethal violence were recognized as features of the male prison scene from the time of its earliest renderings. While focus on rape in prison was rare before the late 1960s, considerable attention was paid to the sexual manipulation, intimidation, and extortion reportedly common in men's prisons and constituting a continuum of coercion that sometimes ended in violence. Accounts of the jocker's strategy of manipulating another inmate, usually someone new to prison and naive to its customs and codes, into a relationship of indebtedness that would then have to be paid off with sexual submission had appeared in representations of prison life since the early twentieth century. Wolves initiated a "campaign," Louis Berg observed in 1934, in which "all the luxuries of prison—candy, tobacco, sweets and choice foods—are pressed upon the newcomer." Once the targeted inmate accepted any favor, typically commissary items or the promise of protection against more aggressive inmates, "he is quickly given to understand that he must repay the favor in kind."[14] Haywood Patterson recounted a similar version of the wolf's strategy that he observed (and later practiced) in Southern prisons in the 1940s, in which the wolf promised protection to the fearful newcomer, followed by a proposition: "First the wolf . . . gave the new guy money and bought him what he wanted from the commissary. He told the boy . . . he would protect him from the tough guys. He would fight for him. . . . After he spent four or five dollars on the boy, he propositioned him."[15] Propositions were sometimes accepted and sometimes not, but the prison wolf, Robert Lindner noted in 1951, was "unable to brook denial." If nonviolent methods were unsuccessful, the jocker would resort to other "tools for obtaining his wants": "The 'shiv' against back, the kick in the groin, the razor blades between his fingers, the homemade 'billie,' the ragged edge of a medicine bottle."[16]

The recognition of sexual coercion and violence behind bars, then, was far from new in the 1960s and 1970s. But writers in this period drew attention to the subject in an increasingly urgent and unrelenting way. Their accounts were newly ubiquitous, newly graphic, and newly univocal in depicting sexual violence and brutality, so much so, in fact, that rape would come to be understood as the defining practice of sex in men's prisons.

Among the many signs of the privileged place that sexual violence came to hold in accounts of the world behind bars was its new prominence in popular representations of prison life. Prison films, which in the past had often culminated in a rebellion against a sadistic warden or in a

climactic escape, began to foreground violence between and among prisoners as central to the drama. And with the relaxation of obscenity laws
and the erosion of the restrictive Motion Picture Production Code, the
depiction of sexual violence grew more explicit and was often represented
as an inevitable and definitive aspect of men's incarceration. Unlike the
campy women-in-prison film genre of the time, men's prison films were
distinguished by their claims to an almost documentary realism and their
stark depiction of violence and brutality.

The popular representation of prison most widely referenced in this
period was John Herbert's 1967 play *Fortune and Men's Eyes*, staged off
Broadway at the Actors' Playhouse in New York City and developed into
a critically acclaimed feature film in 1971. Structured around the damaging and self-perpetuating effects of sexual violence, the play represented
the brutality in a Canadian reformatory that transformed its protagonist, Smitty, from a good-hearted if naive young man incarcerated for
a minor drug offense into the kind of callous and brutalizing prisoner
he had so feared on his arrival. Reluctantly submitting to his bullying
cellmate Rocky's sexual advances in exchange for protection against gang
rape, Smitty ultimately finds the courage to overthrow Rocky's sexual
ownership. But his experience of sexual subjugation proves to be tragi-
cally transformative, and the play concludes with Smitty's attempted rape
of his gentle and abused young cellmate, Jan.[17] Herbert was not alone in
charting this trajectory. Miguel Piñero's award-winning 1975 play *Short
Eyes*, written while Piñero was a prisoner at Sing Sing and performed in a
prison theater workshop with an all-inmate cast before appearing at New
York City's Lincoln Center and later produced as a film, concluded with
the near-rape and brutal murder of an accused child molester.[18]

As in earlier periods, prison genres mixed, blurred, and borrowed from
one another, extending the long history of the intertextual circulation of
the production of knowledge around the subject of prison sex. Newly
sexually explicit fiction and nonfiction paperbacks of the period often
courted the imprimatur of social science, some including forewords, appendices, and back-page blurbs by alleged experts to bolster their claims
to authority and perhaps in an effort to gain the cover of First Amendment protection against obscenity charges by demonstrating "redeeming
social value."[19] At the same time, mainstream journalism and social science
sometimes exploited the appeal of popular culture. Sociologist James R.
Rudolph cited Herbert's play, *Fortune and Men's Eyes* as one among several
"sources of evidence" that "sexual assault in jails is a problem" in his application for a grant from the U.S. Department of Health, Education, and

Welfare to fund a study on sexual assault in the San Francisco men's jails.[20] And in the words of a *Time* magazine reporter, Alan Davis's report of the near-ubiquitous sexual violence in Philadelphia jails read "like a scene from last year's off-Broadway prison exposé, *Fortune and Men's Eyes*."[21]

Reaching a broad and diverse audience, novels, plays, and films that represented violence as a constitutive feature of prison life also inevitably shaped the expectations of those sentenced to prison. The first-time inmate entering prison with knowledge gleaned from popular culture, investigators found in a 1989 study, was "afraid of being hurt. He is afraid of dying. And, perhaps more than anything else, he is afraid of being sexually assaulted."[22] One prisoner commented that at the time of his sentence, "all I knew was what I'd seen on TV or in the movies," and as a consequence, "I don't think I'd ever been that scared before."[23] Ken Carpenter reported that his own fears about prison years earlier were "formed partly by news articles of attacks on young draft resisters . . . , and by seeing the powerful prison play, *Fortune and Men's Eyes* and reading the grim prison scenes in Daniel Curzon's novel, *Something You Do in the Dark*."[24]

Both social scientific and popular domains registered another new feature of representations of prison sexual violence in their close and sympathetic attention to the trauma suffered by the rape victim. Observers in earlier periods often seemed to share prisoners' contempt for inmates labeled punks, who, some suggested, got what they deserved as a consequence of their naïveté, physical weakness, cowardice, and their apparent willingness to submit sexually in exchange for protection and the promise of an easier life in prison. Many framed that contempt in gendered terms, accepting the notion that submission to sexual assault was inherently feminizing in its effects and sometimes communicating a suspicion that it betrayed an internal and shameful effeminacy that existed before the fact. "Most individuals who succumb either to pressure or to 'courtship' are weaklings," Louis Berg wrote plainly in 1934.[25] Gresham Sykes characterized the punk in 1958 as having "an inner softness or weakness" and failed to distance his own feelings from those he attributed to prisoners, that the punk's "sacrifice of manhood is perhaps more contemptible than that of the fag because he acts from fear or for the sake of quick advantage rather than personal inclination."[26]

Investigators from the late 1960s through the 1980s, in contrast, were much more likely to sympathize with the victims of prison rape and to attend to the psychological as well as physical trauma of sexual assault. In so doing, they drew on feminist writing that insisted on recognizing sexual violence as a uniquely traumatizing experience. Sociologists Ed-

ward Peeples and Anthony M. Scacco, Jr., wrote of the "turmoil" suffered by the male victim of rape, an experience that "unleash[es] a tide
of inner disturbances" that produce "a state of chronic stress" and result
in a range of sometimes incapacitating stress-related problems.[27] Rape is
"the ultimate shame," journalist David Rothenberg wrote in 1976, resulting in "maimed bodies, disturbed psyches, and bitter recriminations."[28]
Those men who "experience this horror" and resist "retreating into madness," sociologist Inez Cardozo-Freeman wrote, "never recover from the
psychic damage done to them."[29] Unlike earlier observers who implicitly
and sometimes explicitly called into question the sexuality as well as the
masculinity of the victim of sexual assault, this generation of writers also
typically assumed their heterosexuality. They did so against the grain of
prisoners' identification of punks as "made homosexuals," countering as
well an older attribution of homosexuality to the "passive," penetrated
participant in same-sex sex. Davis went so far as to distinguish those he
termed the "innocent victims" of prison rape from "homosexuals, known
as 'sissys,' 'freaks,' or 'girls.'"[30] The victim's heterosexuality, in his and
others' view, made sexual assault all the more traumatizing.

Sympathy for the victims of sexual assault in prison was also evidenced
in a new willingness on part of the courts, albeit tentative and limited,
to offer some legal recourse to inmates threatened with or victimized by
rape. Courts were traditionally reluctant to intervene in the internal operation of prisons, a stance premised on their acceptance of the doctrine
established in 1871 in the case *Ruffin v. Commonwealth*, which defined the
prisoner as civilly dead, literally (and evocatively, given the proximity
of the decision to the conclusion of the Civil War) "a slave of the state
with no rights."[31] To justify this hands-off judicial doctrine, courts cited
the limits of their jurisdiction over the internal management of prisons,
a lack of judicial expertise in penology, a reluctance to believe in the legitimacy of complaints made by prisoners, and concern that judicial intervention would undermine prison discipline. The disinclination on the
part of courts to intervene in prison matters left inmates with virtually
no recognized rights and with little recourse beyond appeals to prison administrators. As historian Edgardo Rotman points out, this judicial policy
"virtually abandoned penal institutions to the unchecked power of their
administrators, who were entitled to pursue whatever punitive or des-
potic methods they chose to apply."[32]

Beginning in the early 1960s, however, prisoners argued for the recognition of their rights, and with help from outside advocates as well as
through their own aggressive jailhouse lawyering they pressed the courts

for redress. The first significant victory was won by Muslim prisoners on the issue of freedom of religion. The Nation of Islam had recruited prisoners as members since the 1950s, and from the beginning they had clashed with prison administrators. Muslim prisoners fought for the right to receive outside publications, to be served pork-free meals, and to be allowed to meet together to worship. While they defended their demands as basic constitutional rights to assembly and freedom of religion, they were part of a broad and radical critique of the prison system, and Muslim prisoners were perceived by prison administrators as issuing a wholesale challenge to their authority.[33] When prison officials refused these demands and moved to suppress the Nation of Islam and punish its members, Muslim prisoners took their case to court, issuing thousands of habeas corpus petitions beginning in the late 1950s challenging the legality of the conditions of their incarceration. In the landmark 1964 decision *Cooper v. Pate*, the U.S. Supreme Court ruled in their favor, overturning an appeal from a lower court upholding the right of prison officials to refuse Muslim prisoners access to the Quran and opportunities to worship and granting prisoners' standing to seek redress under federal law.[34]

Emboldened by this victory and inspired by the momentum of a growing prisoners' rights movement in the 1960s, prisoners turned to the courts to challenge a wide array of correctional practices, including the use of corporal punishment by guards, overcrowded housing, lack of recreational and exercise opportunities, racial segregation, inadequate medical care, restrictive mail policies, arbitrary classification, and insensitivity to religiously mandated diets. For the first time, prisoners who were threatened with sexual assault in prison began to seek redress from the courts as well. Arguing that exposure to sexual violence violated their rights under the Eighth Amendment prohibiting cruel and unusual punishment, they received mixed results. Some courts held firmly to the traditional stance of nonintervention in prison affairs. When two inmates who had been sexually assaulted in a Milwaukee jail sued the county sheriff in 1971, for instance, the court held in *Kish v. County of Milwaukee* that the sheriff was not liable because "the assaults were a result of the physical layout and overcrowding of the jail, both matters beyond the control of the defendant."[35]

But beginning in the late 1960s, some state courts proved willing to hear cases about prison sexual violence and occasionally if cautiously to rule in prisoners' favor. The most successful and far-reaching of these cases presented the issue of prison sexual assault in the context of the crime of escape. Courts had previously justified escape by inmates who were faced with life-threatening circumstances, the classic example of which was the right to escape from prison to avoid death in a fire. Prisoners made analogous arguments about sexual violence. In *People v. Lovercamp*, a California appellate court held in 1974 that an escape from prison in response to the threat of sexual assault could be justified, provided the inmate prove that the threat was specific and imminent and that he or she had exhausted all judicial and administrative remedies, had not resorted to violence against prison personnel during the escape, and had immediately contacted prison authorities on successfully escaping.[36]

Lovercamp set an almost prohibitively high bar for judicial consideration of justifiable escape in the case of rape or the threat of sexual assault. But the decision established an important symbolic precedent, and an avalanche of civil damage suits against correctional officials followed. In 1974, a Michigan appellate court judge expressed the belief that "the time has come when we can no longer close our eyes to the growing problem of institutional gang rapes in our prison system." Although a person sentenced to prison gave up certain rights, the court held, that person was not "entirely bereft of all of his civil rights" nor did he or she "forfeit every protection of the law."[37] In 1979 a federal jury awarded $130,000, the largest damages paid to a prisoner plaintiff in a civil rights case up to that time, to an inmate of the Michigan prison at Jackson who argued that the state's failure to supervise the prison hospital ward led to his rape, constituting a violation of his civil rights under the Eighth Amendment. In a few spectacular cases in the 1970s, courts responded to inmates' charges that incarceration subjected them to a range of abuses including sexual assault by declaring entire prison systems unconstitutional.[38] These decisions and others offered some encouragement to inmates threatened with rape to press charges. And as one legal critic pointed out, the logic embedded in the *Lovercamp* decision suggested implicitly that "confinement wherein the inmate is afforded no protection from homosexual assault" was itself unlawful.[39] This suggestion raised the possibility that inmates might protest the unlawful conditions of their confinement and might even require proactive effort on the part of prison officials to alleviate those conditions.[40]

Prisoners' judicial victories in this period were markedly circumscribed in their language and limited in their effects. Only a very small number of prisoners who were sexually threatened or assaulted gained a hearing in court and many fewer gained redress. But while no court held specifically that inmates had a constitutional right to be free from sexual violence, some judicial decisions suggested a trend on the part of some state courts to consider seriously the sexual plight of prisoners. It was very difficult (and remains so) for inmates to receive legal remedy for sexual assault in prison. But in recognizing sexual violence behind bars as a serious issue for the first time, these decisions constituted a striking and symbolically important turn.

The Violent Prison

There is considerable evidence that the tenor and tone of writing on men's prisons in the late 1960s and 1970s and the willingness of the courts in this period to intervene in prison affairs, distinguished by a newly intense concern about sexual violence, shifted in correspondence to material changes in prison life. Writers focused on prison violence, sexual and otherwise, with greater urgency in this period, at least in part for the simple reason that prisons were becoming increasingly, alarmingly violent.

That was certainly the inescapable impression of the American public, as a series of highly publicized episodes shone a spotlight on prisons riven with tension and out of control. In January of 1970, a guard at California's Soledad prison fired several shots into a group of prisoners allegedly fighting in the yard, killing three black inmates, one of whom had brought suit against the Soledad warden for provoking racist divisions in the prison the year before. Ruled "justifiable homicide," that event ignited a period of extreme violence between prisoners and guards at Soledad and led to the escalation of hostilities in other prisons as well. Prison activist George Jackson was among a group of prisoners indicted for the murder of a guard, allegedly in retaliation for the Soledad shooting. Jackson was later gunned down in what was reported to be an escape attempt from San Quentin where he had been transferred, three days before he was to go on trial.

Nineteen days later in September of 1971, after participating in a day of silent protest in response to Jackson's murder, thirteen hundred prisoners took control of New York's Attica prison and held forty guards hostage. The insurrection was broken when state police and National Guardsmen opened fire on the prison yard. Forty-three people were killed in the Attica takeover, thirty-two of them prisoners. Far from an isolated event, the Attica rebellion was part of a national wave of prison strikes and riots, preceded by major uprisings at California's Folsom prison in 1968 and again in 1970, the latter a massive strike in which over two thousand inmates issued a slate of demands and refused to leave their cells for nineteen days. Within several weeks of the bloody conclusion at Attica, riots broke out in prisons and jails across the country. Prison uprisings, like urban riots of the same time, heightened public awareness of the deplorable conditions inside many prisons at the same time that they contributed to the growing sense of prisons as volatile and violent.

These dramatic events pitted prisoners, sometimes organized together to demand better conditions and respect for their rights, against prison authorities. Emboldened by a new prisoners' rights movement, prisoners defied and even physically attacked guards in significantly greater numbers than ever before. While in past eras, violence against guards and other staff members was extremely rare, defiance became "open and bold" by the late 1960s and 1970s.[41] Six guards were killed by prisoners at Soledad between 1970 and 1972. Sociologist James Jacobs documented a "substantial increase" in inmate attacks on guards at Illinois's Stateville prison, combining with other instances of violence and collective rebellion to constitute "a crisis in control" at that institution between 1970 and 1975.[42] Guards responded with brutal and often deadly force to violence and the threat of violence posed by newly politicized prisoners who challenged their authority in increasingly overt ways. Sociologist and former prisoner John Irwin blamed the violent retaliation of guards and the punitive response of prison administrators to the organized prison movement—in particular their abandonment of all pretense to a commitment to rehabilitation in exchange for an overtly repressive ethos of punishment—for ushering in "the violent prison" of the last decades of the twentieth century.[43]

Prison violence was not confined to battles between prisoners and guards. The reverberations of the dramatic prison uprisings of the early 1970s, Irwin observed, "left most men's prisons fragmented, tense and often extremely violent," and the 1960s and 1970s witnessed a marked rise in violence between prisoners as well as between prisoners and authorities.[44] While prisoner-on-prisoner violence had always existed, this period witnessed its profound escalation. In earlier periods, prisoners had complained of numbing monotony, arbitrary rules, the weight of time, claustrophobia, loneliness, the dullness of institutionalism, the loss of liberty, bad food, and the myriad humiliations, deprivations, and irritations large and small that comprised the pains of imprisonment, much more frequently than they did violence, real or threatened. Irwin identified the "major characteristics" of the "Big House," the iconic penitentiary that predominated at midcentury, as "isolation, routine, and monotony."[45] Texas prisoner Billy McCune evoked the spirit of that earlier prison life as well as a canny understanding of the conventions of the prison memoir and audience expectations of that genre as they had evolved by the 1970s when he recalled his experience in the 1950s: "I can't write about intra-prison clashes and riots, breaks, killings, inmate suicides, hostages, struggling, battling for power, bloodthirsty cut throats, dog eat dog, 'cause really Texas inmates, so far as I have known, are fully domesticated and adjusted. They live an animal-plus-robot existence."[46] Irwin described Soledad prison as "a very peaceful and orderly institution," in which "the general mood among prisoners was tolerance and relative friendliness" when he was a prisoner there in the 1950s. Despite "somewhat hostile" interracial relations among prisoners, Irwin reported, "there was commingling between all races and many prisoners maintained close friendships with members of other racial groups."[47] When prisoners referenced violence earlier in the century, they more often cited the abuse of inmates by prison guards than they did violence between prisoners.

But beginning in the 1960s and increasing in the 1970s and 1980s, prisoners began to write extensively and evocatively about living with violence and with the stress of the constant threat of violence that occurred between inmates, often identifying it as one of the most salient features of prison life. San Quentin prisoner Bill Sands described that threat as constituting the very atmosphere of prison: "Everywhere, every minute—like the air you breathe—there is the threat of violence lurking beneath the surface. Unlike the air, it is heavy, massive and as oppressive as molasses. It permeates every second of everyone's existence—the potential threat of sudden, ferocious annihilation. It is as grey and swift and unpredictable as a shark and just as unvocal. There is no let-up from it—ever."[48] The intensity of violence at Louisiana's Angola prison in the early 1970s, inmate Billy Wayne Sinclair wrote, "shocked even hardcore convicts." When Sinclair joined Angola's general prison population after his death sentence was commuted to a life term in 1972, it "eclipse[d] any horror I had seen on the Row." Living up to its reputation as "the bloodiest prison in the nation," Angola was "a fierce dog-eat-dog world where the law of violence prevailed."[49] As a consequence, Sinclair wrote, Angola inmates "walked on the edge of paranoia." Each day, he estimated, "an inmate was stabbed, killed, raped, or brutalized."[50] One prisoner remarked that by the 1960s, Soledad prison "had earned the label of 'Gladiator School,'" and he described the day-to-day existence there as "composed of terror," where "murder, insanity and the destruction of men is accepted as a daily way of life."[51] Some prisoners who served long sentences charted the rise in prison violence. One commented on the evolution over time from sexual manipulation to sexual violence, noting that the wolf's technique

in "wooing a kid," once "masterful" in its subtlety, finesse, and "insight
into human psychology," had devolved into "caveman shit" as prison life
"[got] a little crazy."[52]

Prisoners in this period described adopting performances of intimidating masculinity and bravado in an effort to make themselves less vulnerable to assault. Richard Shoblad, who lived his term as a prisoner "with my
gut always tensed," assumed "a variety of defensive postures to frighten
troublemakers away," exchanging his "urbane, courteous speech" for
"tough hipster argot" and shaving his head to appear more intimidating.[53]
Another prisoner noted that "if anything about your walk is feminine,
you are in for trouble. You got to strut around, puff out your chest, and
act like you own the place."[54] David Miller likewise "acquired all of the
affectations and attitudes necessary" to deflect attention from himself during a year in prison for resisting the draft in the early 1970s. Miller learned
"how to side-step those inmates who were dangerous . . . how to give and
take and roll with the jokes about who was going to suck whose dick and
who was going to put his foot up whose ass," as well as "which inmates
not to joke with."[55]

Some attributed the rise of violence among prisoners to the tensions
produced by overcrowding, a problem lamented almost since the birth of
the modern American prison in the early nineteenth century but emerging as especially severe in some prisons by the mid-1970s. While this period preceded the massive expansion of the U.S. prison population in
the 1980s and 1990s, and a short-lived deinstitutionalization movement
reduced the number of inmates in some prisons, there were harbingers
in the 1970s of what was to come. In 1973, two years after crushing the
Attica rebellion and eager to strengthen his political hand by appealing to
white middle-class voters, New York Governor Nelson Rockefeller recommended mandatory prison sentences of life without parole for drug
offenders. The drug laws passed by the New York State legislature established slightly less severe but still draconian mandatory minimum prison
terms of fifteen years to life, punishing even minor drug offenses with
long sentences. The revolutionary wave of harsh mandatory sentencing
laws in other states that followed in the wake of the Rockefeller drug
laws, as well as the move to deny parole for many offenses, heralded an
aggressive new "war on crime" that would dominate the American political agenda for the next three decades and produce a massive increase in
the number of people incarcerated in the United States.[56] From approximately 200,000 prisoners in 1972, representing an incarceration rate that
had held roughly steady for about fifty years, the U.S. prison population

ballooned to 1 million by 1990 and surpassed 2 million for the first time shortly before 2000.[57]

Not surprisingly, overcrowded conditions exacerbated tensions among prisoners in the already tense environment of the prison. Overcrowding was high among the sources of resentment among Attica prisoners, housed in a facility where the maximum capacity had been exceeded by nearly 40 percent. Attica was far from alone in this regard. A *New York Times* reporter attributed the 1970 riots at the Manhattan Men's House of Detention known as the Tombs to overcrowding as well. While the official capacity of the Tombs was 932, the jail housed more than 1,400 inmates at the time of the riot, who slept three and sometimes four to cells designed for single occupancy.[58] Inmates in other prisons also double- and triple-bunked in single-person cells, slept in tightly packed dormitories converted from warehouses, trailers, and tents, and in some prisons slept on mattresses on the floor.[59] Prisoner Thomas Green described Chicago's Cook County Jail as "a mad house," where over 140 inmates were placed in a cell block intended for eighty-four: "Inmates slept on every inch of floor space available, and fighting was an hourly occurrence."[60] The indignities engendered by overcrowded prison conditions led Jack Abbott to declare that "it's the prison system in America that drives us to outrages on one another. We're not animals," he insisted, "but we are herded like animals."[61]

In addition to exacerbating tension among prisoners, overcrowding made supervision less effective and consequently made prisons less safe. Crowded conditions meant that workshops, cellblocks, yards, and showers—prison sites identified earlier in the century as places of sexual opportunity—could be much less effectively surveyed and were sometimes wholly unsupervised. Incarcerated antiwar activist Philip Berrigan singled out "the jungle"—a huge dormitory complex housing seventy men at the federal penitentiary at Lewisburg, Pennsylvania—as the place where inmates were "subject to sexual assault."[62] At Lewisburg, journalist Ben Bagdikian explained, one guard was responsible for watching six dormitory wings on three different floors. "As the guard leaves his desk for another floor there is a quiet scuffling in the newly unwatched wing as the rape gang moves to the victims, stuffs a sock in his mouth and beats him until he is terrified and unconscious."[63] A guard at Pennsylvania's Bucks County Prison explained that guards "can't be all over the jail." "I know it's goin on," he added. "But . . . it's impossible for you to catch a guy in the act, cause the guys are wise."[64] Boxer Rubin "Hurricane" Carter identified the fifty-stall shower room at the Trenton State Prison where he served time as a young man, housed in "an old, dilapidated shack that had once been used as a barn," as "a rape artist's happy hunting grounds—and a monument to the living hell the young kids in the joint had to suffer." "Everyday," Carter wrote, "some poor unsuspecting fool would get ripped off in the dense clouds of concealing steam."[65]

The level and intensity of prison violence varied significantly among different types of institutions. Stephen Donaldson requested that he be transferred from a medium-security prison in Danbury, Connecticut, where inmates served shorter sentences, to a maximum-security institution, claiming that the latter offered greater protection from gang assault. Explaining the fatalistic logic of prison life to his attorney, Donaldson wrote, "I am a punk. The way a punk gets protection is to link up with a 'Man.' The higher the security level, the more long-term the prisoners. The more long-term the prisoners, the more they are likely to appreciate the presence of a punk, claim him and protect him. So the higher I go in security level, the safer I'll be."[66]

Many studies confirmed Donaldson's counterintuitive claim that minimum-security institutions were among the most dangerous. Federal and state prisons, however violent, were often judged less dangerous than city and county jails.[67] Housing inmates between arrest and trial, those sentenced to short terms for minor offenses, and those awaiting transfer to prisons, jails were often chaotic places. Recalling early-nineteenth-century warnings of the dangers of the "promiscuous" mixing of prisoners of different ages and criminal experience, many blamed the violence in jails on their volatile and heterogeneous combination of minor offenders and inmates convicted of serious crimes, "green novices" and hardened convicts.[68] In jail, as one inmate observed, "any young boy is easy prey for an experienced con who may be in jail waiting trial for his fourth felony."[69] Jails were also characterized by greater anonymity than prisons because of the transience of their inmates, who were therefore less accountable to community norms.[70] Often drastically overcrowded, understaffed, and undersupervised, with dormitory-style sleeping arrangements, jails offered more opportunities for sexual assault. Conditions in Chicago's Cook County Jail erupted into public view in 1967 when a grand jury investigation into several murders and sexual assaults produced "a stomach-turning catalogue of depravity."[71] An inmate there for two months, Thomas Green reported that "no officer ever came inside the cell block." In that unsupervised space, he reported, "only the strong survive as men—the weak are used for the sexual expressions of the strong."[72]

Some blamed sexual violence in prison on the deliberate indifference of guards. By some accounts, guards retreated to prisons' perimeters in the wake of the violence attending the prisoners' rights movement, responding to overt challenges to authority with massive force but declining to intervene in outbreaks of violence among prisoners. In institutions of the 1970s, sociologist Donald Cressey observed, guards "have withdrawn to the walls, leaving inmates to intimidate, rape, maim, and kill each other with alarming frequency."[73] As one prisoner boasted to another on his arrival at Louisiana's Angola prison in 1972, "we run the joint. The screws just put in their eight hours and stay out of our business. If there's a killing on the Yard, they just come to collect the body."[74]

Others attributed to guards a more active and deliberate role in perpetrating violence among prisoners, and some went so far as to charge them with fomenting violence among prisoners, especially sexual violence, in a conscious strategy of divide-and-conquer designed to undermine inmate solidarity or as a calculated system of punishments and rewards. "They use gays in the same way they use heroin trafficking in the joint," gay prisoner Jon Wildes charged in 1978, "to pacify and subdue the most dangerous inmates."[75] Howard Levy and David Miller agreed that prison administrators "profit by the perverted and poisonous atmosphere which they themselves maintain," asserting that they "consciously use the exploitable homosexual atmosphere to their own ends."[76] The sexual fear and frustration of inmates manipulated by guards, they added, "plays havoc with inmate solidarity," which was no doubt part of the point.[77] Jack Abbott claimed to have been told by the police who transferred him to prison that he was being sent there "to be reduced to a punk, to be shorn of my manhood. They felt I would be less arrogant once I had been turned into a cocksucker." "To the authorities," Abbott charged, "there is nothing seriously wrong with anyone getting raped in prison. On the contrary, the idea excites them; they *enjoy* it."[78]

The densely populated prisons of the 1970s also housed an increasingly heterogeneous community of prisoners, and one in which racial divisions and hostilities were newly and powerfully prominent. People of color, and African Americans in particular, had always been overrepresented in the disproportionately working-class and poor populations of American prisons. As early as 1833, French investigators Gustave de Beaumont and Alexis de Tocqueville observed that "in those states in which there exists one Negro to thirty whites, the prisons contain one Negro to four white persons."[79] After the Civil War, the use of vagrancy laws and Black Codes to police the movement and labor of freedpeople meant that Southern prison populations were overwhelmingly dominated by African Americans, a pattern that persisted in that region through the twentieth century. But the increase in the number of prisoners in the 1970s shifted the racial composition of many prisons in other parts of the country, in some cases strikingly.

As prisoners of color increased numerically in this period, in large part because of their disproportionate prosecution under the new drug laws and mandatory minimum sentencing laws as well the racial bias that continued to inform police surveillance, arrest rates, prosecution, verdicts, and sentencing more generally, white prisoners in some institutions outside the South were outnumbered by black and Latino prisoners for the first time.[80] At Illinois' Stateville prison, for instance, the percentage of black inmates increased from 47 percent in 1953, already a dramatic over-representation of their numbers in the state's population generally, to 75 percent in 1974.[81] In that year, close to half of the nation's prisoners were African American.[82] At the same time, the desegregation of prisons in this period introduced racial mixing among prisoners in housing, recreation, work, dining, and everyday encounters, in some institutions for the first time, producing resentment among some white prisoners and contributing to heightening racial tensions.[83]

While the proportion of black prisoners grew in this period, an influx of war resisters and other activists into prisons in the late 1960s and early 1970s, mostly white, middle-class, and unfamiliar with prisons, added a new group of prisoners to an increasingly diverse inmate population. The resulting heterogeneity could occasionally result in a productive cross-pollination of ideas, ideologies, and outlooks among prisoners. Inmate Ronald Phillips described his transformative friendship with another prisoner, forged through conversations over the course of their cross-country transfer from a California jail to the federal penitentiary at Lewisburg, Pennsylvania. A convicted burglar who "identified with the 'regulars'—the hip and tough guys" and "completely apolitical at the time," Phillips initially distanced himself from his draft-resisting companion. But the forced intimacy of the conditions of their travel led to conversation: "We were shackled, legs and wrists to the waist, for two months in the back seats of some U.S. marshal's car, going across the country, stopping every night at some county jail, then waiting for some marshal who was headed to the next stop," Phillips explained. During the course of the trip, "we argued and talked and argued," and in the process, "we became real friends." "He was the first person I knew well who was educated, had real conversations about society and was totally nonviolent."[84] Antiwar activist Philip Berrigan remarked that "there weren't many resisters" in the federal penitentiary at Lewisburg, Pennsylvania, but he noted, perhaps idealistically, that since "almost everyone there is anti-federal government," there was a sense of connection among prisoners: "You have immediate sympathy, because even though you're there for different reasons than they are, at the same time you're there for the same reasons."[85] One African American man observed that he "met people with sophistication, people from different races" for the first time while in a Maryland prison. When he was on the street, he would "only associate with criminal elements. . . . All I dealt with was young inner-city black folks, and you know, that's real narrow." Since coming to prison, he noted, "my horizons have expanded."[86] Interracial unity occasionally found expression in prison politics as well as personal friendships. At San Quentin, white, black, and Latino prisoners engaged in multiracial activism and staged a Unity Day strike in 1968, coming together across racial and ethnic lines, if only briefly, to protest their shared conditions as prisoners.[87]

Cross-class and interracial mixing in prisons, however, did not always result in such gratifying scenarios. Countering the stories of personal and political alliances formed across lines of class and race was considerably more evidence of heightened racial tension, hostility, and conflict in prisons beginning in the late 1960s. Bunker declared that "the racial turmoil of the streets was magnified in San Quentin's sardine can world," where he was a prisoner through the 1960s.[88] By 1970, sociologist James Jacobs observed, "racial avoidance and conflict had become the most salient aspect of the prisoner subculture."[89] Of Angola prison, still racially segregated in the early 1970s, one inmate wrote that "a razor could not have sliced through the tension circulating at both ends of the Yard."[90]

Fragmentation among prisoners along race lines hastened the demise of what was known as the convict code, observed by Donald Clemmer in 1940 and sociologists after him, which mandated solidarity among prisoners and supported their group consciousness in opposition to prison officials. One inmate commented on the prisoner code that prevailed at New Hampshire's Concord prison in the 1950s, where there was a "very palpable atmosphere of solidarity" among inmates and "a very clear line of demarcation" between prisoners and guards.[91] The culture of the Big House, John Irwin claimed, was one in which "individuals and groups persistently, defiantly pursued plans opposing the rules or wishes of the staff," and prisoners "carried on rackets, brewed alcoholic beverages, and planned escapes."[92]

That old prison social order, which Irwin characterized as one of "cohesion and monotonous tranquility," was disrupted by new forms of fragmentation and polarization among prisoners in the 1960s and 1970s.[93] Some questioned whether the convict code had ever extended across lines of race, since the sociologists who studied the prisons of the 1930s, 1940s, and 1950s failed to consider race relations among inmates as a structural feature of prison communities. "Loyalty . . . was probably always coterminous with primary group cohesion," Carroll remarked later, "and the inmate code has probably always been more fiction than fact."[94] Nostalgia for the convict code, in some cases, could have concealed a nostalgia for the racially segregated prison or an era in which white supremacy was less often challenged. Piri Thomas was impressed less by the unity of prisoners than "the controlled atmosphere of racism," in which white guards actively encouraged white prisoners "to feel superior to nonwhites," in the New York prisons at Sing Sing, Comstock, and the Tombs when he was a prisoner there in the 1950s at the supposed height of the era of the convict code.[95] Thomas bonded most closely with a small group of fellow Puerto Rican prisoners, who celebrated the anniversary of Thomas's fourth year at Comstock with a cake and drawing of El Morro Castle in San Juan. Thomas was moved to identify with prisoners as a group against the prison administration through his experience of the 1955 riot at Comstock, provoked when guards responded to a peaceful protest with tear gas and water hoses.[96]

Prisoners and sociologists noticed a change in patterns of loyalty among prisoners in the increasingly heterogeneous prisons of the 1970s. Billy Sinclair distinguished between "the traditional convict code," an ethic marked by an "anarchic hatred of authority" and "honor among thieves," from "a new standard of inmate behavior" that prevailed at Angola in the early 1970s, which sanctioned "violence as a means to an end."[97] By the 1970s, Jacobs observed that prisoners at Stateville "no longer identify themselves primarily in terms of their inmate status, but according to their organizational allegiance." This change had the effect of undermining "whatever unifying effect the inmate code may once have had and balkanized the inmate social system."[98] Carroll noted as well the corrosive effects of racial and ethnic hostility on inmate cohesiveness during his observation of a Northeastern state prison. There, prisoners formed associations organized primarily along racial lines, creating stronger bonds among groups of prisoners and divisiveness between those groups.

The most striking evidence of the reconfiguration of prisoner solidarity, and an important factor in the rise of prison violence and racial polarization, was the emergence and spread of prison gangs in the 1970s. Gang membership constituted a direct violation of a time-honored mantra of prison survival that counseled inmates to "do your own time." Existing somewhat paradoxically alongside the credo of inmate solidarity, that long-standing shibboleth advised prisoners who wanted to stay out of trouble to avoid prison cliques, remain uninvolved in prison politics, keep their head down, and mind their own business. Gangs, by contrast, whose organization along racial and ethnic lines was advertised in names such as the Mexican Mafia, the Black Gangster Disciples, the Latin Kings, the Black Guerrilla Family, and the Aryan Brotherhood, demanded group loyalty. Gangs began to appear in California prisons in the early 1960s and spread nationwide in the years that followed. When white supremacist inmates formed gangs such as the Aryan Circle, the Aryan Brotherhood, and the White Knights, racial divisions among prisoners escalated in intensity.[99] A prisoner at Stateville during this time, Malcolm Little observed that gangs "actually wrested most of the power from the prison administration."[100] Defiant and sometimes violent toward prison authorities, gangs also perpetrated violence against other prisoners. Between 1974 and 1975 there were 268 stabbings and 56 deaths in California prisons alone, most of them attributed to four major gangs.[101]

The Jungle

The new attention to prison sexual violence in social scientific studies, popular accounts, fiction and film, and autobiographies, which signaled a striking shift in the representation of prison life in the late 1960s, 1970s, and 1980s, corresponded to a likely empirical rise in the incidence of sexual violence and heightened racial tension in men's prisons in those decades. But attention to the rhetorical excesses evident in many of those representations suggests that their cultural work went beyond the merely documentary and descriptive. Writers who characterized the "dominance" of black men in prison as a form of "Negro Rule," for instance, betrayed deep anxiety about what they saw as the subversion of a racial hierarchy in prison that had elicited no comment when reversed. And the many references to black men as "beasts," as well as the new depiction of the prison as a "jungle," evoked a racialized narrative, deeply embedded in American history, of black degeneracy and specifically of the predatory black male rapist. An overdetermined story readily available for any depiction of interracial sexual violence, that narrative took on distinctive and telling contours and meanings when used to account for same-sex assault in prison.

To many, the world of the late-twentieth-century prison, one in which black men dominated white men sexually and otherwise, was a world turned upside down. Anthony Scacco described prison society as "a definite reversal of the majority and minority roles that are the natural order in free society."[102] Home to a social order in which black prisoners were allegedly "on top," whether or not they constituted a numerical majority, prisons unsettled the "natural order" of white supremacy. One white prisoner described the disorientation of being "immediately slapped in the face with the knowledge of the Negro 'king'" and with the recognition of prisons as a place of "Negro Rule."[103] Comments like these suggest that prison writers were captured not simply by the statistics marking a rise in the incidence of sexual violence but also by the story of black aggression and white victimization in which they were embedded that resonated in the larger cultural context of this period, in the wake of the civil rights and black power movements.

Some attributed the alleged physical dominance of black prisoners to their numerical dominance. Because "the Negro inmate is, for the first time of his life in the majority," one inmate claimed, he "completely monopolizes on his advantage."[104] Others argued that the superior physical condition of black prisoners, often represented as a natural racial advantage that black men cultivated behind bars, reinforced their supremacy. Black men tended to be sexual aggressors, a prison officer speculated, in part because of their "physical size and power": "Most of them work out and are big, and as a group they appear to be more threatening and intimidating."[105] Black male prisoners, Scacco agreed, "are usually physically more powerful than the average white" and "tended to be well versed in the art of self-defense."[106] Their commitment to physical dominance, Scacco argued, was reinforced by the ideology of "black militant groups," who were "bent on making the black man aware of his individuality through physical strength and self-assertion."[107] Still others cited the importance of racial solidarity among black prisoners, buttressed by new ideological commitments to black power, which strengthened their prison "rule."

Interracial rape emerged in these accounts as the most potent expression of racial dominance in prison. While writers in earlier periods had understood prison rape as an act driven by the frustration of sexual deprivation, observers in the 1970s and 1980s represented it as an expression of dominance and control, consciously employed by black prisoners to send a message to white prisoners, white prison officials, and sometimes to white America. "In raping a white inmate," Carroll wrote, "the black aggressor may in some measure be assaulting the white guard on the catwalk."[108] Sexual assault, Scacco argued, "lets the white inmates, as well as the staff, know that they consider themselves as the dominant, not the dominated, in spite of the fact that they are locked up."[109]

Some pushed that argument further, representing interracial sexual violence as a conscious and deliberate tool of racial retaliation. "The motive force" behind prison sexual assaults, Carroll wrote, "has its roots deep within the sociocultural context of race relations in this country." Given that context, Carroll proposed, the prison "is an arena within which the rage of black males at their social and psychological oppression is vented against white males."[110] "Rape of 'whitey,'" Weiss and Friar agreed, "helps appease the black rage at white racism."[111] Carroll quoted one black prisoner who supported this analysis of sexual assault as racial score-settling, explaining, "You guys (whites) have been cutting our balls off ever since we been in this country. Punking whites is just one way of getting even."[112] One white inmate likened the sexual pressure from African American prisoners as "like white slavery," infused with "this hostile 'get Whitey' attitude that they all vented through sex with me and others like me."[113]

It was all the more poignant to prison observers that those reportedly most vulnerable to this form of retribution were incarcerated white activists, whose attempts at solidarity with black prisoners could be misread in a prison context. Howard Levy and David Miller, authors of a handbook on prison for incarcerated activists, devoted considerable attention to "the various factors that conspire to make many political prisoners potential targets for homosexual advances," including their youth, long hair, and naïveté about prison life.[114] Political prisoners, Levy and Miller wrote, tend to be "polite, intelligent, articulate, and usually pleased to explain their position and actions to anyone who will listen," and they urged activists to repress their affability and candor, which might be misconstrued as a "come-on by aggressive homosexuals."[115] (Levy and Miller failed to note that the affect they characterized as politeness and candor might have been interpreted by other prisoners as condescension and privilege.) Another factor that contributed to the vulnerability of white activists, they noted delicately, was "the manner by which white political prisoners relate to the black-liberation struggle." Levy and Miller warned white activists not to allow their sympathy for black prisoners to be mistaken for "an inroad to a homosexual relationship" and counseled them to refrain from making friends with black prisoners, since their efforts at racial solidarity might be misinterpreted. Miller wrote of his own experience as a prisoner at Lewisburg, where he "made several mistakes," including being "too friendly with black inmates."[116] "If one flaunts his pretentious liberal attitudes and eats and talks with black inmates," Levy and Miller wrote, "he will only get himself in trouble."[117] One white war resister who reported that black prisoners "hound[ed] the hell out of me" during his two-week incarceration judged in retrospect, "I think I let myself in for it. I had decided before I came in that I was going to contribute a lot—be friendly, open, helpful." But he found that "you can't be that way in prison. They get the wrong idea. Then they assume you'd be easy to force into something."[118] These observations were supported by an African American prisoner, who identified "a definite weakness" in incarcerated war resisters that, in his view, connoted effeminacy and invited sexual aggression: "They are seen as meek pacifists, as not being aggressive. In an institution of this nature, because of their mannerisms, because of their more comfortable backgrounds, this is going to be interpreted as not being too masculine."[119]

To support the argument that prison sexual violence was driven by a desire to establish dominance, writers called on new conceptions of rape formulated by feminist theorists writing at the same time. The most influential text for prison writers, Susan Brownmiller's *Against Our Will: Men, Women and Rape* countered the long-standing understanding of rape as motivated by sexual lust, stressing instead the male desire for power and domination over women. Identifying sexual violence as the linchpin in an overarching system of patriarchal control, Brownmiller proclaimed famously that rape was "a conscious process of intimidation by which *all* men keep *all* women in a state of fear."[120] While primarily concerned with sexual violence perpetrated by men against women, Brownmiller incorporated observations about male sexual victimization into her analysis, including a discussion of prison rape that referenced its most prominent representations, by district attorney Alan Davis, prison activist Stephen Donaldson, and playwright John Herbert.[121] Like sexual violence perpetrated by men against women, Brownmiller claimed, male rape in prison was motivated by a desire for control and a drive for dominance. While the problem of prison rape had previously been understood as "symptomatic of the deranged brutality of a few prison guards or an 'infection' spread throughout a cellblock by a certain number of avowed homosexuals," Brownmiller argued instead that it was the result of "an acting out of power roles within an all-male, authoritarian environment in which the younger, weaker inmate, usually a first offender, is forced to play the role that in the outside world is assigned to women."[122]

Brownmiller's analysis of sexual violence offered an apt frame through which to understand the gendering intent and effect of same-sex rape, establishing a hierarchy among men that confirmed the masculinity of the aggressor and the femininity of the victim. This conception was ratified in the common prison understanding of the effect of rape as "making a woman" out of the victim. It spoke as well to the subjective experience of many men who experienced rape as an assault on their manhood. As inmate Jack Abbott wrote, "The normal attitude among men . . . is that it is a great shame and dishonor to have experienced what it feels like to be a woman," and many prisoners cited the gendering effects of rape as central to the trauma of sexual violence.[123]

Brownmiller's argument that rape was essentially political rather than sexual in nature, motivated by a desire for dominance rather than sexual gratification, was a tremendously generative claim for prison writers in this period. Social scientists, journalists, and prison administrators called on Brownmiller's and other feminists' insights to dismiss earlier arguments about sex in prison that focused on the irrepressibility of the male sex drive in exchange for a focus on the assertion of masculinity and power. Alan Davis noted that "the need for sexual release is not the primary motive for sexual aggression" in the cases he documented, and other writers echoed his argument. Some disarticulated the act of rape from sexual drive almost entirely.[124] Sexual assaults in prison were simply "not very sexual," Bowker declared, drawing on the work of feminist theorists to compare them to "heterosexual rapes on the street," which "have only a very limited sexual component."[125] "The prison rapist does not rape primarily to appease a sexual hunger or to satisfy a burning passion for his victim," Weiss and Friar agreed, moving further still to propose that rapists experienced "no sexual pleasure" whatsoever. Instead, the prisoner "rapes to prove he has power—power to dominate his prey."[126] Wilbert Rideau and Billy Sinclair, two inmates who formed a friendship and writing partnership across lines of race in Louisiana's Angola prison, confirmed from their point of view as prisoners that rape in prison was "rarely a sexual act, but one of violence, politics, and an acting out of power roles."[127]

The insistence on rape as a political rather than sexual act distinguished this version of the story of black male rape from earlier mythic associations of black men with sexual predation that had emphasized black men's purported hypersexuality, even as it sustained a representation of black men as sexually dangerous. It departed as well from studies just a decade or so earlier, in which observers had struggled to accommodate the recognition of same-sex sexuality behind bars with understandings of homosexuality and heterosexuality as distinct, stable, and immutable identities. Newly understood, prison rape in this period, as summarized by one reviewer, had "little or nothing to do with homosexuality" and "everything

to do with institutionalized violence and racism."[128] New representations
of sexual violence in men's prisons engaged in almost no psychic scrutiny
of what it meant for black men to engage in same-sex sex behind bars,
reversing the impulses of the preceding decades and participating in a long
history of denying psychological depth or complexity to African Americans. Instead, they engaged in a deeply political scrutiny that focused on
race resentment and race rage. Sexual violence was newly understood to
be about anger, aggression, and power, and not about sexual desire, drive,
or identity. Scacco distinguished white from black sexual aggressors in
this regard. While the white aggressor, in Scacco's view, selected a victim
with affective and sexual needs in mind, "both as a person he can relate
to as well as for sexual release," he wrote, "the black jock looks upon his
white victim purely from the standpoint of validating his masculinity or
dominance."[129]

While Brownmiller and other feminist theorists were frequently cited
by prison writers to support the depiction of rape as an act of dominance,
another body of literature was at least as formative to new understandings
of racialized sexual violence among prisoners but exerted a more shadowy influence in their accounts. The many explanations of rape as an aggressive and compensatory assertion of power on the part of black men
implicitly referenced a growing body of social scientific studies that tal-
lied the social costs of damaged black masculinity. Foremost among those
works was Daniel Patrick Moynihan's *The Negro Family: The Case for National Action*.[130] Published in 1965, Moynihan's report blamed the supposed
disintegration of the black family on the weakened role of black men,
emasculated by the legacy of slavery and a long history of racism as well
as by the usurpation of control by black women in female-headed households. Levy's and Miller's depiction of prison rape as "a means by which
a poorly constructed masculine image can puff itself up," Carroll's representation of rape as an expression of "the rage of black males at their psychological emasculation," along with many others who attributed prison
sexual aggression to the inadequate masculinity of black men, testified to
the powerful influence of Moynihan's argument and its rapid dissemina-
tion into the larger cultural common sense.[131]

The story of prison rape as an act of dominance and racial retaliation
could have different political valences depending on its teller. Most sociologists writing at this time worked to shield their analyses of interracial
rape from the possibility of racist readings. Scacco was careful to identify
racism, not race, as being "at the very root of the sexual assaults perpe-

trated by black men on white victims in prison and in jail." Since black men faced widespread discrimination and persecution under the criminal justice system, Scacco proposed, they understandably sought to "even the score against [their] white oppressors once behind the walls."[132] Framed within the terms of racial liberalism of the day, interracial rape was cast as a compensatory act born of the diminished opportunities for black men to express and affirm their masculinity through culturally acceptable means. Alan Davis noted that most of the sexual aggressors in his investigation were "members of a subculture that has found most nonsexual avenues of asserting their masculinity closed to them."[133] Because most black prisoners "belong to a class of men who rarely have meaningful work, successful families, or opportunities for constructive emotional expression and individual creativity," Davis wrote, they were deprived of the ability to affirm their masculinity through avenues other than physical aggression and sex.[134] "Once inside the walls," Scacco agreed, the black prisoner was deprived of sex with women, around which "he has centered his claim to virility." "Eventually the overly aggressive (and probably more threatened and frightened concerning his masculine image) inmate will enter into homosexual activity in which he can conceive of himself as fulfilling his masculine prowess."[135]

Alert to ways that their accounts could be put to racist purposes, these writers and others were careful to distinguish their claims from arguments that black men were inherently more violent or more sexually driven than white men.[136] Lee Bowker made clear that he "explicitly reject[ed] any attempt to link the current racial imbalance in violent crime and rape rates with inherent racial differences."[137] Leo Carroll went further to connect the racialized sexual violence in prison to larger systems of racism, insisting that "the problem of sexual assaults in prison is not likely to be eliminated until . . . the more encompassing problem of racial inequality and oppression is resolved."[138]

As historian Daryl Michael Scott notes, however, the liberal strategy of garnering white sympathy by locating the social problems of race in the psychological "damage" of black people could quickly turn to contempt and fuel conservative reaction.[139] While African American male prison autobiographers typically framed an insistence on self-respect, pride, and humanity in the gendered terms of manhood and masculinity, drawing on a long-standing representational strategy with origins in male slave narratives, social scientists saw in those claims evidence of dangerous and compensatory hypermasculinity.[140] Depictions of black men as sadistic rapists, even those that located the cause of rape in racial oppression, inevitably resurrected an older discourse of black savagery and a newer one of black cultural pathology.

In this instance, the rapist's passions were ignited not by white women, or even by white men, but by black nationalism. Representing interracial rape as motivated by a desire for racial retribution and dominance, prison writers simplified and caricatured a critique of American racism, and of the prison as among the most potent institutional sites of that racism, which emerged in this period as part of the prisoners' rights movement. African American prisoners had grown more assertive during this period, some politicized through participation in the civil rights and black power movements before their incarceration and some while prisoners. By the late 1960s, some black prisoner activists had achieved extraordinary celebrity, most prominently, of course, Malcolm X, and also including Eldridge Cleaver, George Jackson, and Huey Newton. Many blamed black separatist and black power politics for fomenting race hatred and violence behind bars. The reductionist analysis that characterized interracial prison rape as a cruel and perverse form of reverse racism was easily marshaled as ammunition in a growing arsenal of arguments in the 1970s about the excesses of black militancy and the declension of a civil rights movement into nihilistic rage and antiwhite race hatred. Representations of interracial prison sexual violence also heightened fears about black men's purportedly unregulated and dangerous masculinity, fueling the intensely racialized anti-crime politics in the late 1960s and 1970s that would drive the mass incarceration of the decades that followed.

The racialized story of prison sexual violence was also abetted by a new sociological paradigm that came into prominence in this period. Challenging the functionalist model of prisonization promoted by Donald Clemmer, Gresham Sykes, Erving Goffman, and other midcentury sociologists, which portrayed inmate culture as a collective adaptation to the distinctive deprivations of the total institution, sociologists in the 1960s and 1970s argued that the values and customs associated with prison culture were imported from the outside. Leaders in developing this new theoretical framework of importation, sociologists John Irwin and Donald Cressey made the important claim that prisons were not separate societies hermetically sealed off from the outside world but, rather, were permeable to the communities and cultures from which prisoners came, shaped in particular by the importation of a "criminal subculture."[141] Prisoners were not "made" in prison, Donald Cressey insisted, but "carry a great deal of behavioral baggage" in with them, "and retain it during their stay."[142]

Irwin and Cressey did not mention race in arguing that convict culture was nurtured first on the street rather than formed out of whole cloth in the unique circumstances of prison life. But many called on this new theoretical model to attribute the rise in prison sexual violence to the importation into the prison of a ghetto-bred culture of violence and compensatory hypermasculinity characteristic of urban street gangs. Mindful that this argument could be "misinterpreted to support racist notions," Lockwood specified that "it is not black culture that is behind prison sexual aggression; rather, it is a criminal, male, youthful, black subculture of violence."[143] But in an era in which black men were coming to be synonymous in the public mind with criminality, an argument about the importation into prison of a culture that was expressed in the rape of young white men could not help but buttress that association.

Others attributed interracial sexual violence to distinctive ways of understanding sex and sexuality that black prisoners imported into the prison. In so doing, they participated in a long history of pathologizing African Americans through the deployment of normative ideas about gender and sexuality.[144] There would be "no such phenomenon as male rape behind prison walls," Scacco proposed in the most literal reading of the new sociological theory of importation, "if it did not first exist on the streets."[145] Prison sex in this new iteration was no longer conceived as "situational" but was attributed instead to a distinctive and pathological African American sexual culture. Confinement did not cause what Scacco referred to vaguely as "the differing modes of expression" observed in prison sexual life; instead, he claimed, "they were inherent and in many instances practiced by the inmate before he was sentenced."[146]

Some drew support for their arguments from Alfred Kinsey's 1948 study of male sexuality, the findings of which were later amplified in a study of sex offenders in prison undertaken by Kinsey's associates, which suggested that "lower social level males" had a "simpler" understanding of sex than did their upper- and middle-class counterparts and a more casual and instrumental relationship to homosexuality in particular.[147] "The lower level Negroes," Pomeroy summarized in a lecture to prison wardens, "appear to be much more relaxed about sexual behavior," including homosexuality, than whites, and they approached sex in general with "less emotional involvement than whites."[148] In part, researchers attributed what they viewed as a casual, "emotionally detached" attitude on the

part of African American men to a pre-prison familiarity with homosexuality.[149] The "lower-level male," Scacco wrote, echoing Kinsey's language,
"appears to be well versed in the homosexual culture of his neighborhood, if not taking part in it directly."[150] Because of that familiarity, many
argued, African American men were less burdened by feelings either of
repugnance or of strong emotional connection with regard to same-sex
sex. That "lack of positive or negative affect," to many, signaled a more
primitive relationship to sex and sexuality governed by instinct rather
than affect. To Huffman, "Negroes appear to practice homosexuality in
a primitive way, according to stimulus and response."[151] Alan Davis also
commented on the "startlingly primitive view of sexual relationships"
shared by African American sexual aggressors, "one that defines as male
whichever partner is aggressive and as homosexual whichever partner is
passive" and that allowed sexual aggressors to consider themselves heterosexual, even after engaging in homosexual acts.[152]

   In repudiating the modern association of sexual acts and identity by
maintaining identities as heterosexual, sociologists suggested, African
American men revealed themselves as sexually atavistic, not yet fully
aligned with the precepts of sexual modernity. Midcentury sociologists
had eased anxieties by representing prison as a strange sexual world unto
itself, out of sync with (and therefore reassuringly having no bearing on)
the modern sexual regime that defined sexual acts as reflective and constitutive of sexual identity. A new generation of prison writers represented
their studies as spotlights on the fugitive and primitive sexual cultures of
a dangerous racial underclass.

   Sociologists often marshaled testimony from prisoners to support their
argument that sexual violence was the product of racial animosity and
black dominance and was motivated by a desire for power and domination
rather than sex. But the unpublished results of one study in which over
three hundred prisoners in San Francisco jails were interviewed in 1977
and 1978 suggested that inmates entertained a much wider range of opin-
ions about the causes of sexual violence behind bars than that represented
in the professional literature.[153] Some prisoners interviewed for the Sexual
Assault and Violence Evaluation Project (SAVE), to be sure, confirmed sociological theories in their responses to the question, "What do you think
causes inmates to sexually assault other inmates?" One white prisoner
called rape the "ultimate power trip you can run on someone."[154] "It gives
them an edge over the person assaulted . . . e.g. I've fucked you, you're
less than me," another white prisoner responded.[155] "Sex is secondary,"

another white prisoner insisted; "it is a power trip more than it is sex."[156] One white prisoner echoed the sociologists in attributing prison rape to "mostly racism," adding that "blacks like to fuck white women and white boys are a substitute."[157] But only a tiny percentage—five white prisoners and one black prisoner out of 314 respondents—mentioned race as in any way relevant to the question of sexual violence or to the dynamics of power in prison rape. The sole black prisoner who cited "the race thing" as responsible for sexual violence added that "of course, a good many Black men aren't like that, they see right through that hatred bullshit and just try to be cool, to get along."[158]

The responses of some prisoners to the SAVE interview testified to the persistence of older understandings of sexual assault, uninflected by either criminological theories of importation or by feminist analysis, as driven by sexual deprivation and desire and provoked by its victims. Nearly half of the respondents (152 of 314) identified sexual frustration as the primary cause of sexual violence in prison. "Sex is a big thing to the human body," one black prisoner noted. "There is a lot of tension that needs to be released."[159] Men rape other men in prison, another black prisoner reported, because "they can't have sex with their wives or girlfriends."[160] "No pussy," a white prisoner stated plainly. "Lack of sex leads to frustration."[161] Twenty-two respondents located the cause of sexual violence in the behavior, appearance, or sexual identity of its victims. "Young feminine looking dudes cause assaults," one white prisoner reported.[162] "The other dude may give off vibes of wanting to be fucked," a black prisoner responded in agreement.[163] "Someone comes in weak showin' homosexual overtones," another commented.[164]

Countering the long-standing prison sexual code that upheld the heterosexuality of the "active" participant, however, several prisoners attributed prison sexual violence to the sexual orientation of the assailant. Some proposed that assailants were "sick." "A male who wants to have sexual relations with another male," in the opinion of one white prisoner, "has mental problems."[165] Another white prisoner attributed sexual violence to "something within them . . . some kind of tendency."[166] "They are freaks, perverts," one black prisoner said of sexual assailants.[167] "They have some kind of homosexual tendencies," another stated, "and no moral about themself."[168] "Some just dig buddys," one black prisoner stated less judgmentally.[169] Still others, however, indicted the dehumanizing conditions of prison itself. A Chicano prisoner cited "oppression of the jail system" as responsible for sexual violence.[170] A black prisoner reported that sexual assaults occurred in prison "because the institution needs more men to act like animals."[171] "They treat us like animals," a white prisoner agreed. "Pretty soon we act like that."[172]

Erasures

Sociologists, journalists, and many prison insiders writing in the 1970s, in the substance of their writing on sexual violence as well as the sheer number of pages they devoted to the subject, often gave the impression that sex in men's prisons was essentially reducible to rape. Sex was inarguably a domain for consolidating masculinity, for constructing and maintaining hierarchies among men, and for asserting authority and dominance. But sexual assault and victimization did not make up the whole of men's prison sexual experience, even in this period of heightened violence. The overwhelming volume of representations of prison sexual violence deafened observers to other dynamics in men's relationships in prison that would have unsettled the increasingly dominant story of interracial rape and would have kept alive questions about the stability of sexual identity and the stability of heterosexuality in particular. Attention to the ellipses in the dominant representations of interracial prison sexual violence exposes the shifting boundaries of acceptable representation of men's same-sex relationships, as well as the evolving anxieties about the nature of what had come to be understood as "situational homosexuality."

Most simply, the intense focus on black sexual predation and white victimhood in men's prisons erased the existence of white assailants and black victims of sexual assault. Both figures appeared in descriptions of men's prisons, their presence noted but generally unremarked on. A lone dissenter from the consensus that emerged around the most prominent explanation for prison rape in this period, sociologist Daniel Lockwood asserted that the understanding of sexual violence as a form of racial retaliation failed to account for the significant number of African American prisoners who were the victims of sexual aggressors, both white and black.[173] Alan Davis suggested a possible cause for the scarcity of black men among the documented victims of sexual assault in his investigation of the Philadelphia prison system, observing that "Negro victims seemed more reluctant than white victims to disclose assaults by Negro aggressors."[174] Researchers' assumption that near-insoluble race solidarity prevailed among prisoners may also explain how little attention they paid to intraracial sexual violence, coercion, and exploitation. Carroll suggested, almost in passing, that white prisoners failed to respond collectively to the rape of other white prisoners by black inmates because they ultimately benefited from the "class of 'punks' and 'kids'" produced by those sexual assaults, implicating at least some white men in a culture of sexual aggression that was otherwise almost uniformly attributed to black prisoners.[175]

The deafening story of male sexual violence in prison, organized so intensely around interracial hostility, rendered interracial attraction and desire virtually invisible. Interracial desire between male prisoners was squelched materially as well as discursively, as prisoners and prison staff often condemned consensual interracial sex and harassed participants in on-going interracial relationships. Leo Carroll observed that black prisoners who were involved with white partners were ostracized and taunted by other black inmates and ousted from the prison's Afro-American club. White participants in interracial relationships were also "the object of verbal taunts from other whites, ostracized, and occasionally assaulted sexually."[176] According to Donaldson, "it's rather like a white girl dating black guys, the whites would like to tar and feather them both."[177] When a black prisoner known as "Pretty Boy," identified by a fellow inmate as an "unabashed homosexual," and his white partner Sammy were forbidden by the deputy warden of Pennsylvania's Western State Penitentiary from speaking with each other and threatened with solitary confinement if they were caught having any contact, Pretty Boy wrote letters of protest to the NAACP and to the governor, "complaining that he was being forbidden to associate with a white man."[178] Terry Dobson, a white gay prisoner, reported that "white inmates shun other whites who have sex with blacks." He decided to ignore their contempt, however, since his relationship with a black lover in a North Carolina prison "really made me feel good," adding, "for once I was happy and I was doing what I wanted to do."[179]

The hardening script of interracial sexual violence in this period left little room for expressions of consent, like Dobson's, much less intimations of happiness. Granted, it was sometimes difficult to distinguish consensual from coercive sex behind bars, since much of it took place in the context of what Alan Davis called a "fear-charged atmosphere."[180] One factor complicating any neat distinction of violent from consensual sexual expression was the tendency of prison sexual violence, or perhaps at least as often the threat of violence, to generate relationships that appeared to be consensual but were born of intimidation and fear. Prisoners would often agree only under duress to a committed sexual relationship to avoid further violence or to obtain protection from gang rape. Donaldson encouraged new inmates to enter into "protective pairing," submitting to a relationship with one protector in order to spare themselves the likelihood of gang assault. As one inmate counsels another in the film *Fortune and Men's Eyes*, "one is a lot better than eight"; a committed relationship with one man, Donaldson and others advised, could spare prisoners the trauma of gang rape. The "senior partner, or 'man' in prisoner slang," Donaldson explained, "is most often not a rapist himself, though he may take advantage of the consequences of a rape by offering protection to a new punk." Once publicly paired, Donaldson noted, "everyone else will back off and stop hassling you."[181] But Donaldson termed these relationships "survival-driven," reminding readers that "from the typical punk's point of view, none of his passive sexual activities are truly voluntary, since if he had his own way, he would not need to engage in them."[182]

In these ongoing and sometimes contractual relationships, the man or jocker obligated himself to provide complete protection for his partner, known as a punk or kid, at the cost of his life if necessary, and often provided commissary items as well. In exchange, he expected obedience, sexual service, and "wifely" domestic labor such as doing the laundry, making the bunk, cleaning the cell, and making and serving coffee. Man-kid relationships varied enormously in character, "from virtual slavery and complete exploitation at one end," Donaldson wrote, "to a mutually supportive, tender and human exchange of affection at the other."[183] Illuminating one end of that continuum, Jack Abbott explained that

> if I take a punk, *she is mine*. He is like a slave, a chattel slave. It is the custom that no one addresses her directly. He cleans my cell, my clothing and runs errands for me. Anything I tell him to do, he must do—exactly the way a wife is perceived in some marriages even today. But I can sell her or lend her out or give her away at any time. Another prisoner can take her from me if he can dominate me.[184]

Abbott's use of alternating pronouns underlined the gendered hierarchy established by prison sexual ownership and the power of the man to determine the gender identity of the punk, often against the grain of the punk's own self-identification. Sexual ownership was understood to be total, and some men lent or rented punks and kids out to have sex with other prisoners or sold them to another inmate when they were released from prison, in need of money, or simply bored.

Given the conditions under which prison partnerships were formed, it is difficult to imagine that they could nurture anything but fear and resentment in their subordinate participants. But as one Missouri inmate noted of the different types of relationships that developed in prison, "there are probably as many as there are out on the street."[185] Prison relationships could take many forms, some defined by the dynamics of power, dominance, and fear stressed in the sociological literature of the time, but some involving tenderness, trust, romance, and comfort. Few were more attuned to the horror of sexual violence in prison and the context of intimidation that so often structured men's prison relationships than Stephen Donaldson, yet Donaldson attributed prison sex generally to "a need for touch, intimacy, otherness, for the interruption of isolation, for warmth, for relationship" that he experienced even in the context of otherwise coercive relationships while in prison.[186] Donaldson described the possibilities of jocker-punk pairings, in which, under some circumstances, "you have a good chance at developing a human relationship where each of you really cares about the other."[187]

Under the protection of one of his several pseudonyms, Donaldson wrote provocatively about this phenomenon when he expressed "nostalgia" for prison relationships in which he served as punk to a man: "When I am feeling lonely, I think of how I used to belong to someone, be with him at every meal, talk to him every day, sleep together, sharing a cell, get high together, relax together, plot together and in that relationship I felt secure, protected."[188] Donaldson recalled a relationship with Dan, one of four marines he submitted to in a county jail in 1976, who along with his cellmates "demanded blow-jobs" from Donaldson but also "liked to read—usually Westerns—sitting on his bunk, with . . . my head in his lap," stroking Donaldson's hair. Donaldson described this surprising prison experience of "real affection" as "a critical turning point in my life. . . . I was guarded and protected night and day by four strong marines—greater physical security than I had ever known in my life."[189] In retrospect, Donaldson acknowledged, "it is fair to say I fell in love, especially with Dan."[190] After his first arrest and experience of gang rape in 1973, Donaldson was reincarcerated several times—for possession of marijuana, for violating his parole, for threatening workers at a Veterans Hospital with a gun—and he suggested in his private correspondence and pseudonymous writing that he deliberately sought out arrest in order to return to relationships he found compelling, both emotionally and sexually.[191]

Donaldson was unusually forthcoming when writing about the unexpected dynamics and emotional complexities of prison sex and his own deeply ambivalent relationship to it. Few expressed themselves as freely outside the bounds of the script of sexual violence. "Accounts written by prisoners or exprisoners," Donaldson observed, "tend to draw veils over areas which might reflect unfavorably on the writer." Heterosexual prisoners in particular, he noted, "tend to remain silent concerning their sexual experiences in confinement."[192] Sociologist Edward Sagarin likewise detected "deliberate dissembling" among the former inmates he interviewed, whose initiation into homosexuality occurred during prison, in an effort to "project an image of self as heterosexual."[193] As the "masculine" or "active" partner in prison sexual exchanges, jockers maintained a sexual identity as heterosexual and typically understood the sex they had in prison as heterosexual as well. Many outsiders viewed the heterosexual identification of prison jockers as a form of delusional and self-serving thinking. Feminizing one's partner, sociologists Wayne Wooden and Jay Parker wrote, "sets the homosexual at a psychologically safe distance from the 'macho' image the heterosexual convict is so desperately trying to project."[194] Inmate Jack Abbott explained this aspect of prison sexual culture from an insiders' point of view, writing to Norman Mailer from the state penitentiary where he was incarcerated about his relations in prison,

> It really was years, many years, before I began to actually realize that the women in my life—the prostitutes as well as the soft, pretty girls who giggled and teased me so much, my several wives and those of my friends—it was years before I realized that they were not women, but men.[195]

"I do not mean to say I never knew the physical difference," Abbott clarified; "no one but an imbecile could make such a claim." But he understood those prisoners who partnered with men like him as "a natural sex that emerged within the society of men, with attributes that naturally complimented masculine attributes." It was only on painful reflection that Abbott recognized that "many of my 'women' had merely the appearance of handsome, extremely neat, and polite young men."[196] "It's a hell of a thing to say," another prisoner noted, "but . . . before long another man begins to look like a woman to you."[197] Inmate Donald Lee recalled that "the teen-agers and young men with smooth, firm skin and a trace of baby fat merged with our memories of girl friends and wives. The ready smile of a young man, his puppy playfulness, his high-pitched but pleasant voice, . . . in time made the rest of us equate all youth with women."[198]

The feminization of the partners of prison jockers could be coercive. Donaldson explained that "for these guys to be turned on and horny doesn't really require any kind of feminine qualities in you, though the jockers usually prefer to imagine such qualities so they won't have to think of their attraction as homosexual. That's why they'll try to tell you have feminine qualities even if it's not true."[199] Some prison jockers made their partners shave their legs, grow their hair, and assume female names.[200]

For prisoners who identified as queens, ladies, and girls, by contrast, femininity was chosen and carefully cultivated under very difficult circumstances. In prisons where normative gender was policed, queens had to be creative in cultivating and accentuating their femininity, tearing the back pockets off their pants and tightening them, fashioning makeshift cosmetics or smuggling it in from the outside, growing their fingernails and plucking their eyebrows. Prisoners often commented on how compellingly feminine queens could be. "I swear to God," one Walla Walla inmate noted, "sometimes you see a broad walkin in the wing with panty hose and a short skirt . . . it's a helluva sight, . . . , and she has better legs than those goddam women caseworkers that was walkin around here."[201] Inmate Andreas Schroeder admitted that he was "thoroughly taken aback" at his first view of prison queens, some with "remarkably full breasts, graceful figures and a thoroughly feminine bearing" who were "astonishingly beautiful and they knew it."[202]

The maintenance of a public heterosexual image and internal sense of heterosexual selfhood demanded that prison sexual relationships be organized along strictly hierarchical and often gendered lines. Since jockers' heterosexuality was premised on assuming the penetrative sexual role culturally ascribed as masculine, prisoners typically adhered to distinct and gendered sexual roles, and jockers' sexual desires and sexual expressions were legitimated by strictly dichotomous and hierarchical gender codes that defined their partners as feminine. While sex with other men did not compromise jockers' heterosexuality, any hint of sexual reciprocity threatened to undermine it.

In 1962, however, psychologist Wardell Pomeroy told prison wardens that the Kinsey research team had found "much more mutuality in homosexual relationships than the literature might lead one to believe," including a surprising degree of sexual reciprocity.[203] And some prisoners acknowledged such reciprocity, especially as relationships evolved over time. San Quentin inmate and novelist Edward Bunker cited a "jocular credo" that "after one year behind walls it was permissible to kiss a kid or a queen. After five years it was okay to jerk them off. . . . After ten years, 'making tortillas' or 'flip-flopping' was acceptable, and after twenty years anything was fine."[204] Inmates' acknowledgment of sexual reciprocity was often undercut with anxiety about the potential instability of the sexual dichotomies on which prison sex depended, expressed in the prison truisms, "today's pitcher is tomorrow's catcher," "if you flip, you'll flop," and "when you make the team, you agree to play any position."[205] In some prisons, jockers who partnered with queens rather than punks were "believed by other inmates to 'flip-flop,' that is, sometimes play a passive role," since such a relationship was believed to resemble heterosexual relationships more closely and therefore be more likely to include "emotional elements" that might lead to sexual reciprocity.[206]

Emotional reciprocity was at least as taboo as sexual reciprocity to those identifying as men in prison relationships. Prison orthodoxy, long observed and repeated by sociologists, dictated that the jocker could not exhibit any "softness" with his partner. "To be engaged in a pseudo-marriage and at the same time to preserve his image of masculinity," Carroll claimed, "he must at least publicly demonstrate some degree of disaffection from the relationship."[207] Carroll represented prison relationships as a purely "contractual exchange of sexual services for protection and material reward," wholly "devoid of emotion and intimacy."[208] But as one prisoner observed, "People have to be close to other people, even if it's another man. . . . You've got to have that physical warmth with another individual. If you don't, you become so stagnated and dead-headed."[209] Although almost every aspect of the conditions in men's prisons and their sexual norms conspired against genuine human connection and affection, Pomoroy observed that "a great deal of mutual affection which sometimes spills over into overt homosexual relationships in prison without any concern as to who is playing a masculine or feminine role," and some inmates concurred.[210] The most prominent and influential representations of prison sexual culture in this period were resoundingly silent on the emotional range and complexities of men's relationships behind bars, which could involve warmth, intimacy, and even love.

While few prisoners spoke candidly about sexual experiences with other men, either in their own autobiographical writing or in interviews with social scientists, they sometimes were more willing to do so in anonymous interviews in which their confidentiality could be ensured and especially in private writing unintended for public view. A remarkable collection of inmates' letters and diaries from years slightly preceding this period, confiscated by wardens and submitted to Kinsey and his associates in the 1950s and 1960s, offer a rare window onto the sexual subjectivity of prison jockers and men.[211] It was perhaps not surprising that one male prisoner, who preferred to be referred to as "Dorothy," wrote letters addressed to "my sweet man," full of expressions of love and desire, to let him know that "I am thinking of my sweet little darling."[212] But "men" penned similarly devoted if less flowery missives to their prison lovers. "I have known a lot of queers," Johnny wrote to Billy, "but I never fell in love with them as I have you."[213] Another inmate, Eddie, signed his letter to the prisoner he considered his wife, "I love you with all my Heart."[214] "After awhile," one inmate admitted, "you fall in love . . . just like he would with a real woman," adding, "I don't think you got to be a fruit or anything like that."[215]

Sociologists emphasized the exploitive dynamics of men's prison relationships. But other dynamics were at work as well. In the course of her ethnographic work with prisoners at Walla Walla in the late 1970s, Inez Cardozo-Freeman observed relationships in which "couples are devoted to each other and tend to keep to themselves, living like conventional married people in the free world."[216] Prisoners occasionally marked those relationships with marriage ceremonies, attended by other invited prisoners and confirmed with a certificate. As one jocker observed, "It's just like with a woman except you don't go through the whole matrimony bit in a church, but it's the same thing. What's yours is hers and what's hers is yours. You help each other and you look out for each other and things like that." As a result, "you don't feel lonely. You feel like you've got a little more freedom. . . . You don't worry about nobody else and what people think."[217] Sometimes devoted marriage relationships between prisoners were not even sexual. One prison queen reported that "my husband and I have never had sex together" but that a marriage helped make time in prison "easier": "You've got two people doing your time instead of one. You've got someone to tell your problems to, you're not by yourself."[218]

One Missouri inmate observed that some prison relationships "are very satisfying and last for a long time—even extending past the period of incarceration."[219] Male prisoners sometimes imagined continuing their relationships beyond prison walls after their release. "Some day I want to own one of the largest and beautifulest colored hotels in California," San Quentin prisoner Mickey wrote to his prison lover Pauline. "Baby I know that you and I can do it together," Mickey wrote reassuringly, asking, "what do you think about it. Do you think we can do it?"[220] Gil, another San Quentin inmate, also wrote to his "darling," expressing his hope to "have your love for many years if you'll have me outside." "A lot of guys in here fall in love with other persons because they have nothing else to love but there [sic] love stays here in the joint when they leave," Gil wrote. "That is not the way it is with me."[221] Gil promised that he would "be willing to wait until I got outside with you with out laying a finger on you just to prove to you that my love for you went much deeper than wanting your body."[222] Johnny wrote to his prison wife Tina that hearing from her made him "the happiest guy in the joint," signing his letter, "I love you with *all* of my heart."[223] Wardell, a man with whom Stephen Donaldson had partnered during one of his prison terms, struggled to describe (and perhaps to comprehend himself) the nature of his love for Donaldson in a letter he wrote after Donaldson's release: "My love for you is not like the love I have for my woman or my children," he insisted. "It's different, but the same. You understand?"[224] "I am now 7 months short of being with you," Wardell wrote in a later letter in which he urged Donaldson to wait for him. "If you happen to fall in love with somebody between that time, just remember . . . that my desire is to experience out *there,* what I've experienced with you in here."[225] Gus, another inmate who identified as the man in his prison partnership, explained the motivation for prison relationships as essentially the same as that in any relationship—"to be wanted in here, the same as out there." Gus planned to continue his relationship with the man he had married in prison after they were released, "and we're gonna go to California and live."[226]

The popular and professional reduction of sex between male prisoners to the nearly invariably violent assertion of racial animosity had no way to account for expressions like these. Erased in the sociological accounts of the time, these accounts also elude historical understandings of sexual subjectivity. Written against the grain of the most degrading social conditions and debasing cultural discourses, such expressions of human longing and connection fall outside the frameworks of either "acts" or "identities." Historians have argued that homosexuality was increasingly aligned with same-sex object choice in the course of the twentieth century, but people's desires did not necessarily align with that new order. Expressions like these encourage us to expand our sexual and emotional lexicon as historians, as well as our frame of vision and classificatory frameworks, in order to come close to capturing desires, practices, and identifications that failed to map neatly according to modern identity categories.

: : :

The core of prison sexual violence, Scacco stated categorically, "is not homosexuality but heterosexual brutality."[227] Reducing sex in prison to rape and conceiving of it as motivated by a drive for dominance rather than desire, the story of prison sexual violence as it emerged in the 1970s effectively disaggregated prison sexual expression from its troubling relationship to sexual identity. The intensely racialized template adopted by those representations, locating the cause of prison sexual violence in black degeneracy and cultural pathology, worked further to cordon it off, effectively isolating its implications from the larger culture. Representing interracial rape either as an expression of pathological rage enflamed by black nationalism or as evidence of the primitive relationship to sexuality nurtured in black communities, these arguments fixed the responsibility for prison sex in black men. Within the space of just a few short decades, then, anxieties about rape, black rage, and the sexual violation of vulnerable white men replaced anxieties about the instabilities and uncertainties of sexual identity that had preoccupied earlier observers. However alarmed the reports of prison sexual violence were in this period, and however much they stoked fears and resentments about race, they worked paradoxically to ease concerns about the instability of sexual identity. The discomfiting fact of the participation of heterosexual men in homosexual sex was explained away by discourses of race. The unsettling possibility of love between men was elided altogether.

1. Tiered solitary cells designed to ensure separation of prisoners, at Auburn Prison, New York, 1934 (Correctional Photo Archives, Eastern Kentucky University Archives, Richmond, KY)

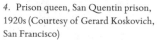

4. Prison queen, San Quentin prison, 1920s (Courtesy of Gerard Koskovich, San Francisco)

opposite top

2. Dance at New York's Auburn Prison sponsored by the Mutual Welfare League, 1914 (Correctional Photo Archives, Eastern Kentucky University Archives, Richmond, KY)

opposite bottom

3. Women at San Quentin in costume for prison show, 1930s (Leo Stanley and Evelyn Wells, *Men at Their Worst* [New York: D. Appleton-Century Company, 1940])

5. Prison queen posing with staff member at the 20th Annual Olympic Club Track & Field Meet, San Quentin Prison, 1920s (Courtesy of Gerard Koskovich, San Francisco)

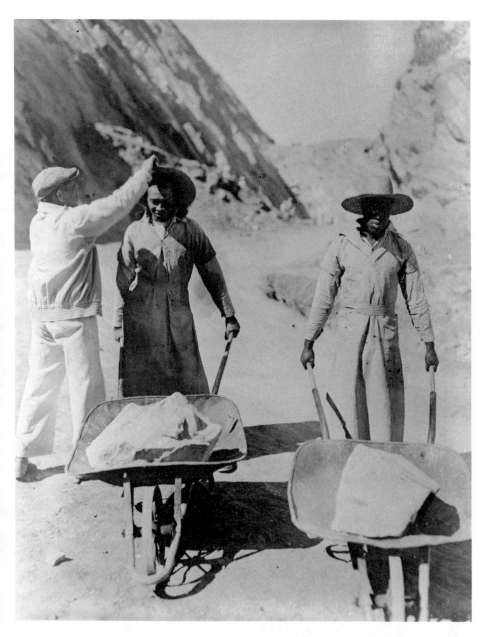

6. Male prisoners punished for homosexuality, pushing wheelbarrows of rocks, unidentified western prison, 1920s? (Courtesy Denver Public Library)

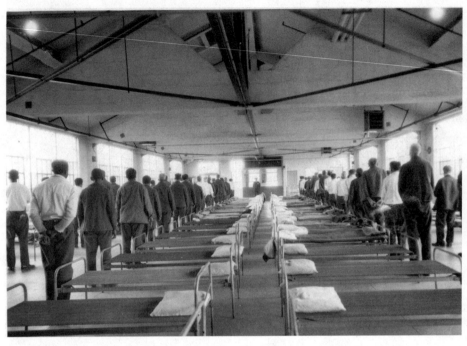

7. Dormitory-style sleeping arrangements in many men's jails and prisons were blamed for promoting homosexuality. Riker's Island prison, New York. (Correctional Photo Archives, Eastern Kentucky University Archives, Richmond, KY)

8. Black and white women prisoners were assumed to be sexually drawn to each other and racial difference in women's prisons was invariably sexualized over the course of the twentieth century. (Maurice Chideckel, *Female Sex Perversion: The Sexually Aberrated Woman as She Is* [New York: Eugenics Publishing Company, 1938])

JUST A PANSY

Joe Werner
WITH
SINCERE
APOLOGIES
TO WALT
DISNEY

"Where the hell's my lipstick?"

9. Prisoners marching in lockstep required a physical intimacy among prisoners that was later credited with contributing to same-sex sex. (Courtesy Denver Public Library)

10. Claims of the prison wolf to normal masculine heterosexuality began to be called into question. (*Brevities* [Feb. 12, 1934])

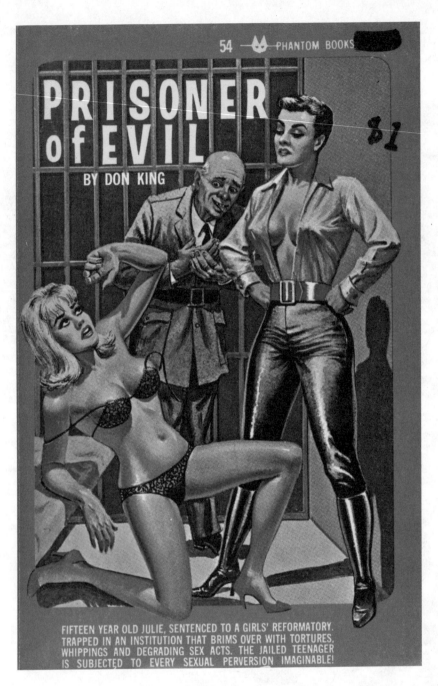

11. Prison lesbianism was a popular subject for pulp novels.
(Don King, *Prisoner of Evil* [Detroit: Foremost Publishers, 1965])

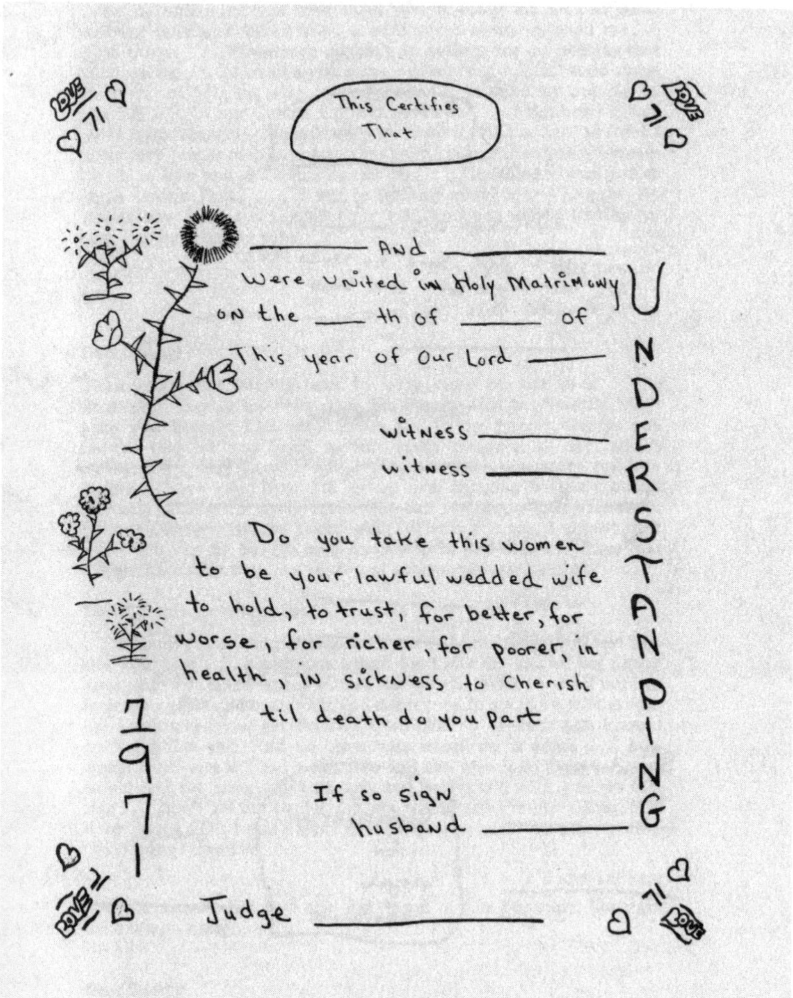

This Certifies That

——— And ———
Were United in Holy Matrimony
on the ___ th of ___ of
This year of Our Lord ———

witness ———
witness ———

Do you take this women
to be your lawful wedded wife
to hold, to trust, for better, for
worse, for richer, for poorer, in
health, in sickness to cherish
til death do you part

If so sign
husband ———

Judge ———

UNDERSTANDING

1971

12. Marriage certificate from women's prison (Alice Propper, *Prison Homosexuality: Myth and Reality* [Lexington, MA: Lexington Books, D.C. Heath and Co., 1981])

13. Ed Mead and his lover, Washington State Penitentiary
at Walla Walla (Ethan Hoffman; courtesy Robert Hoffman;
from John McCoy, *Concrete Mama: Prison Profiles from Walla
Walla* [Columbia, MO: University of Missouri Press, 1981])

opposite top

14. Prisoners in the yard, Washington State
Penitentiary at Walla Walla (Ethan Hoffman;
courtesy Robert Hoffman; from John
McCoy, *Concrete Mama: Prison Profiles from
Walla Walla* [Columbia, MO: University of
Missouri Press, 1981])

opposite bottom

15. Gay college students teach Atascadero
prisoners to dance and cruise in therapeutic
role-play scenario. (Rob Cole, "Behind Bars,
Lessons on Being Gay." *The Advocate* [June
20, 1973]: 1-2)

16. Gay liberationists proclaimed unity with "brothers" and "sisters" behind bars.
Collage by "Read," "We are All Fugitives" appeared on the cover of *Gay Sunshine* newspaper
14 (1972). (Published with permission of the publisher, Winston Leyland)

CHAPTER SIX

"Lessons in Being Gay"

On June 28, 1970, the first gay march in New York City com-
memorating the Stonewall rebellion of the preceding year passed
the Women's House of Detention. The march's route was not an
accident. The jail was symbolically important, having held many
renowned activists in the distant and more recent past. Catholic
radical Dorothy Day, labor organizer Elizabeth Gurley Flynn, and
accused Communist spy Ethel Rosenberg all had been imprisoned
there in earlier decades. A Bennington College freshman in 1965,
Andrea Dworkin spent five days in the House of Detention following her arrest in a peace demonstration outside the United
Nations. Dworkin's outraged revelations about the conditions of
the jail and her own rough treatment during her brief incarceration prompted a grand jury investigation. Radical feminist Valerie
Solanas was held at the House of Detention after shooting Andy
Warhol in 1968, as were Angela Davis and Weather Underground
member Jane Alpert in that same year. At the time of the 1970
demonstration, two members of the "Panther 21" arrested on
bomb conspiracy charges in a COINTELPRO (Counter Intelligence
Program) frame-up—Joan Bird and Afeni Shakur—were incarcerated inside.[1]

The geographical location of the Women's House of Detention would also have been meaningful to gay and lesbian marchers.
Boasting what Elizabeth Gurley Flynn called "a swanky-sounding
address" near Sheridan Square, situated on a triangular block at the

busy intersection of Sixth Avenue, Eighth Street, and Christopher Street, the women's jail lay in the heart of Greenwich Village and its flamboyant and newly politicized queer scene.[2] Sheridan Square was a popular gay cruising spot and home to several gay bars, including the Stonewall Inn. The jail's downtown location had long invited a boisterous exchange between women behind bars and their friends and relations on the street. An inmate there in the early 1950s, Flynn recalled that "there was a constant flow of traffic—buses, cars, trucks, people passing on all sides at all hours. . . . Whistles came up from the street to attract the attention of a particular inmate. . . . Families, friends, sweethearts, pimps, all arranged such contacts with the women on visiting days."[3] Two decades later, lesbian-feminist activist Karla Jay recalled a similar scene from outside the jail: "There was no time of day or night when one could not hear the shouts of friends, lovers, children, husbands, mothers, sisters, and even pimps calling up advice, messages, words of comfort, and questions to the women within."[4] Joan Nestle remembered the "House of D" as "a shrine for separated lovers," where lesbians would call up to their incarcerated girlfriends late at night after the bars closed.[5]

The permeability between street and urban jail that gave rise to that social and sexualized scene facilitated political connections as well, connections in evidence at that first gay march in June of 1970. As the demonstrators passed the Women's House of Detention, Gay Liberation Front members chanted, "Free our Sisters! Free ourselves!"[6] Expressions of solidarity between gay activists and prisoners grew bolder and more reciprocal later that summer. On August 29, a march protesting police harassment began on Forty-Second Street and proceeded downtown, concluding with "a battle cry" in front of the women's jail. Protestors on the street called up, "Power to the sisters!" and prisoners yelled back to the crowd, "Power to the gay people!"[7] When demonstrators happened upon a police raid taking place under the guise of a fire inspection at The Haven, a popular neighborhood gay club, they responded with rage, hurling bottles at police, overturning cars, looting stores, and setting fires. The riot spread upward to the Women's House of Detention, where prisoners threw burning paper from their barred windows to the cheering crowd on the street below.[8]

The Women's House of Detention was shut down the following year and demolished soon after. But political connections between lesbian and gay activists and prison inmates persisted as an important and underrecognized feature of the gay liberation movement of the 1970s. Many marches and demonstrations of the movement's early years chose jails and prisons as rallying sites. In February of 1971, representatives from several New York gay liberation groups picketed outside the Men's House of Detention in lower Manhattan to protest allegations of the "routine brutality" faced by gay prisoners there.[9] During Boston's Gay Pride Week in 1972, activists led a candlelight march to the Charles Street Jail, where they chanted and sang "to let the prisoners know they were there."[10] And in 1973, gay activists in Chicago sponsored a demonstration in support of gay prisoners at the Cook County Jail.[11]

Those demonstrations were part of a much broader commitment to prison activism and advocacy on the part of gay men and lesbians. Beginning in the early 1970s, gay activists initiated a wide range of projects on behalf of prisoners they called "brothers" and "sisters," publishing newsletters, investigating and publicizing prison conditions, offering legal counseling, organizing prison ministries, sponsoring pen pal and outreach projects, and assisting parolees. At the same time, prisoners who identified as gay began organizing on their own behalf against discrimination, harassment, and violence. The unity evoked in the chants of solidarity exchanged between prisoners and activists in the summer of 1970 masked much more complicated and at times fraught connections between newly politicized gay men and lesbians and prisoners who inhabited a sexual world permeable to but different in marked ways from the one taking shape outside.

"What's Outside Is Inside Too"

It was perhaps not surprising that gay men and lesbians working to forge a politics of liberation—from the suffocating strictures of the closet, from persecution under discriminatory laws, and from the shame of pathology as well as from stigmatizing and stifling sexual and gender norms—would turn their attention and energies to those literally imprisoned.[12] Gay activists joined others on the radical left in this period in allying with prisoners and in theorizing connections between the worlds behind and beyond bars.[13] Indeed, leftist credibility seemed to depend on radical prison activism. Many gay men and lesbians came to promote activism on behalf of gay prisoners after participating in the prisoners' rights movement more broadly. At a 1975 rally in support of the San Quentin Six, Bay Area gay liberation activist Karen Turner pledged her movement's support for the struggles of all prisoners, "because we understand that the system that has created and maintained prisons as a method of social control is the same system that oppresses us on the outside who have the least vested interest in this social system."[14] As African American, Chicano and Chicana, and Puerto Rican militants embraced prisoners as a revolutionary vanguard and formulated a radical critique of the prison in the early 1970s, participants in the gay liberation movement, too, came to see gay prisoners as "victims of a vicious system." "Whether the charge emerges from their homosexuality (sodomy, solicitation, 'lewd conduct'), or indirectly (burglary, prostitution, shoplifting)," gay liberationist Allen Young insisted, "all gay prisoners are political prisoners."[15]

Intervention in the judicial and correctional systems around issues of sexuality and advocacy on behalf of incarcerated gay people preceded the liberationist efforts of the 1970s. Soon after its founding in the early 1950s and into the 1960s, the Mattachine Society, the first organization to argue on behalf of "homophile" rights in the United States, recognized that heightened police surveillance of gay cruising spots, routine raids on gay bars, and the felonious status of same-sex sex in many states more generally made it likely that gay men would at some point run afoul of the law.[16] That persecution hit close to home for Mattachine activists in 1952, when Dale Jennings, one of the organization's original members, was charged with "lewd and dissolute behavior" after being entrapped by a plainclothes member of the Los Angeles vice squad. In response, Mattachine mobilized to expose and protest the then-common use of police entrapment against gay men. Mattachine also printed wallet cards with practical instructions for gay men titled "What to Do in Case of Arrest" and notifying them of their rights.[17]

Gay men's criminalized status and vulnerability to arrest continued to inspire gay prison activism into the 1970s. Almost twenty-five years after Mattachine's campaign against entrapment, the editors of *RFD*, a quarterly newsletter aimed at rural gay men that drew its title from the U.S. Postal Service acronym for "rural free delivery" (and was variously interpreted as standing for *Rural Fag Delivery* and *Radical Fairy Digest*), justified devoting a section called "Brothers behind Bars" to prison issues by reminding readers of their own vulnerability to arrest. "One of the few ways rural gay men have to meet each other is at the tea rooms in parks and along highways," the editors noted, where they risked entrapment and arrest.[18] Since "anti-gay laws are most often enforced in small towns and rural areas, away from the group power of organized gayness," *RFD* editors argued, gay men in those areas were "likely to be scapegoated for a crime" and sent to prison. The editors of *RFD* envisioned "Brothers behind Bars" as a way to bring together "victims of this injustice" and "potential victims" in common cause.[19]

The politics of gay liberation and the larger context of radical ferment in the early 1970s produced analyses that envisioned connections between gay activists and gay prisoners in newly intense, if often more analogized, terms. Mike Riegle, founder of *Gay Community News*'s Prisoner Project in 1975, declared that "what's outside is inside too" and proposed that the multiple oppressions faced by gay prisoners were simply exaggerated versions of those experienced by all gay men and lesbians. Riegle extended the comparison of conditions for gays behind and beyond bars by inverting it, asserting that "what's going on inside is only an exaggeration and a distortion of what's happening right out here, in what some of my prisoner friends call 'minimum custody.'"[20] Incarceration, Riegle claimed, could be understood as an "intensified version of what we *all* have gone through. . . . *All* of our lives are profoundly affected by the pressure of a legal code and a justice system and social attitudes that push us hard in the direction of conformity, in sexual things especially."[21] By supporting lesbian and gay prisoners, he wrote, "we help our community understand that the same system that puts people in prison also organizes the oppression in their lives."[22] Insisting on the connections between a "politics of 'crime'" and "the general politics of social control, control of bodies, and even control of desires," Riegle asked, by way of instructive provocation, "kissed your lover in public lately?"[23] The organization Black and White Men Together offered a similar analysis in their call to members to support prison work as an act of solidarity rather than philanthropy: "This is not just an appeal for 'charity' for the unfortunate. *All* of us have to live with this threat of being caged if we don't 'behave' ourselves. The quality of all our lives is affected by the 'lock-em-up' attitude."[24]

Prison activism was "not just about giving prisoners a 'hand out,'" a group of Illinois gay activists insisted, "it's about building a new kind of community."[25] From these powerfully imagined connections emerged a rhetoric and politics of unity based on an assumed kinship between gay prisoners and gay activists. The language of brotherhood and sisterhood infused the rhetoric and ideology of gay prison advocacy and inspired strong commitment to a range of activist efforts on behalf of prisoners.

Confronting Representations of Prison Rape

Among the battles taken up by gay and lesbian prison activists was a discursive one, presented by heightened media attention to what was typically referred to as "homosexual rape" in men's prisons. The emergence of the gay liberation movement coincided almost exactly with the newly urgent concern over sexual violence in men's prisons and its extensive coverage in scholarly and popular writing. In the many alarmed reports on rape in men's prisons that appeared in the late 1960s and 1970s, most writers attempted to make clear that prisoners who identified as heterosexual, not homosexual, were responsible for sexual violence behind bars. Sociologists attributed rape in prison to a desire for dominance rather than sexual desire, often motivated by racial animosity. But the nuances of that argument were often lost in the common use of the term "homosexual rape." Anthony Scacco, for instance, stated "categorically" in his 1975 book, *Prison Rape*, that the issue of prison rape was "not homosexuality but heterosexual brutality."[26] But the confusing formulations sometimes used to make that point, as well as Scacco's and others' routine references to "homosexual rape" committed by "aggressive homosexuals," inevitably contributed to the belief in the rapacious, predatory, and corrupting nature of homosexuality.[27]

The association between homosexuality and prison rape was also abetted by the increasingly hegemonic equation between sexual object choice and sexual identity. The notion that "normal" people could participate in and even initiate same-sex sexual acts was hardly new in the 1970s— prison writers had made this point for decades—but it was an increasingly disquieting and disorienting one. If prison sexual violence was indeed epidemic, as Scacco and others insisted it was, "the rational man" must conclude that "even heterosexually-oriented males are partaking in this conduct."[28] But reason was easily trumped by the commonsense association between homosex and homosexuality, as well as by Scacco's own odd use of the word "even," which seemed to suggest that heterosexually identified assailants were the exception rather than the rule. Scacco's insistence that sexual violence was "not the act of homosexual perverts" ironically reinforced that association, even while purporting to absolve "perverts" from responsibility for prison rape.[29] That linguistic pairing, of course, conjured images of the predatory and dangerous homosexual that had circulated with damaging repercussions during the postwar sex crime panic and continued to reverberate decades later.

Representations of prison sexual violence characterized sexual aggressors in ways that could easily be misconstrued to blame homosexuals, even if their authors insisted otherwise. Characterizations of the victims of assault as almost invariably heterosexual abetted those misreadings. While some reports noted dutifully that self-identified (and especially identifiable) gay men were very often the victims and rarely if ever the perpetrators of sexual assaults in prison, many accounts in this period—by journalists, sociologists, prisoners, and novelists—paid more attention and granted considerably greater sympathy to the victim status of presumptively heterosexual prisoners who were subjected to sexual coercion and sometimes assault, known in prison parlance as punks. A time-honored prison aphorism declared that "Queens are born. Punks are made."[30] Punks were distinguished from queens and fags (understood to be "born" or "true" homosexuals) by their pre-prison heterosexual identity and their unwilling, coerced participation in prison sex, and many writers in this period lamented the possibly irreparable damage done to their (hetero)sexual identity.[31] "Repeated homosexual rape causes the inmate victims to develop a new sexual identity," wrote Carl Weiss and David James Friar in their popular 1974 book, *Terror in the Prisons: Homosexual Rape and Why Society Condones It*.[32] "It is fair to guess," sociologist Lee Bowker agreed, "that the heterosexual life of prison rape victims may be damaged by their experiences . . . they may find it easier to continue homosexual behavior after their release from prison than to attempt to switch to heterosexuality."[33]

Observations like these reinforced phobias of homosexual reproduction through the seduction and forced recruitment of vulnerable heterosexuals. A *Playboy* letter-to-the-editor series that ran six issues in the late 1960s, titled "Sodomy Factories," published letters from ex-convicts who denounced prisons as "breeding grounds for homosexuality."[34] Lou Torok, a self-identified "convict writer," referred to prisons as "state-operated perversion mills" in his popular 1973 memoir.[35] Torok was joined by many other prisoner-autobiographers in this period who reinforced the equation between sexual violence and homosexuality. Rubin "Hurricane" Carter recalled Trenton State Prison as "plagued by faggotry."[36] "Vicious, gutter-sniping he-shes," in Carter's estimation, were "ten thousand times more deadly to the men in the jail than sickle cell anemia was to the entire black population on the streets." In prison, Carter wrote, "the fags would strip the masculinity from their victims and turn them into whores. To sisters!"[37] Prisoner-authored autobiographies and fiction enjoyed a tremendous boom in this period, and the narrator's violent refusal of sexual advances, usually made by an inmate identified as a "sissy" or "old pervert," became one of the genre's defining tropes.[38]

Prison writers sometimes went so far as to distinguish the "innocent victims" of sexual assault, whose heterosexual identity might be damaged as a result, from gay men, who, it was sometimes implied, invited the attention, had it coming, or even enjoyed it. Since gay men's sexual identity was presumably fixed and unalterable, their experience of prison sex, however violent, was assumed to be less traumatizing.[39] Jules Burstein speculated that gay men in prison "need not suffer the anguish of the heterosexual prisoner . . . wracked . . . by overwhelming feelings of homosexual guilt."[40] Sociologist Wayne Wooden, who teamed up with prisoner Jay Parker to write an important study of sex between male prisoners that was often sensitive to the plight of gay men in prison, agreed that sexual assault "may be far more damaging to those men whose basic sexual orientation is heterosexual, because the victims feel a sense of loss of their 'manhood.'"[41] Philadelphia district attorney Alan Davis, author of one of the first and most influential investigations of prison sexual violence in 1968, distinguished prisoners he termed "innocent victims of homosexual rape" from homosexuals, whom Davis identified by their prison terms as "sissys, freaks, or girls."[42] It is telling that Stephen Donaldson, who first drew sympathetic media attention to prison sexual violence by speaking publicly about having been raped repeatedly over a period of two days in a Washington, D.C., jail in 1971 and who went on to help found the national organization Stop Prisoner Rape, declined to acknowledge his own long history of participation in gay activism or his bisexual identity.[43] In private correspondence, Donaldson explained that he ultimately decided not to press charges against the jail administration "because they would have claimed consent and tried to undermine the case by showing that I was homosexual."[44] In some of his published writing, Donaldson went so far as to suggest that he was heterosexual, distinguishing his status as punk from that of other gay inmates, presumably as a way to escape the trivialization of prison sexual violence when suffered by gay men.[45]

Gay activists struggled to disaggregate the terms "homosexual" and "rape," the fusing of which made possible such disingenuous renderings of prison life and damaging representations of homosexuality. Donaldson termed the expression "homosexual rape" a "verbal atrocity" owing to "middle-class concepts of homosexuality" that attributed a homosexual identity to anyone who participated in same-sex acts and that led writers who "ought to know better" to designate men who raped men as "aggressive homosexuals."[46] "One would have to look long and hard . . . to find a case of a *genuine* gay raping some straight dude," one gay prison activist stated plainly. "It just doesn't happen."[47] Gay men, activists pointed out, were often victims of rape in prison, not perpetrators.

Others analyzed more deeply the cultural and political effects of the association of prison rape and homosexuality. "One of the most vicious slurs upon us," Carl Wittman wrote in his 1970 "Gay Manifesto," "is the blame for prison 'gang rapes.' These rapes are invariably done by people who consider themselves straight." Wittman attributed conscious and hostile motive to that association: "The press campaign to link prison rapes with homosexuality is an attempt to make straights fear and despise us, so they can oppress us more."[48] Allen Young agreed that in the contemporary political climate, "linking up the word 'homosexual' and the word 'jail' conjures up images of sex perverts attacking 'normal' men." "The gay liberation movement," Young added, "is beginning to break through the distortions, lies, half-truths and ignorance on this topic."[49] Ken Carpenter, who distinguished popular representations of prison rape from the complicated realities of sexual coercion behind bars that he witnessed during his prison term for draft resistance, agreed: "The view of prison sex as violent, sadistic and perverted has been seized on by all kinds of commentators, from law-and-order hard-liners to reform-minded liberals. . . . All of them see homosexuality (i.e. rape) as a major sickness besetting prisons."[50]

In an effort to disarticulate homosexuality from prison rape, some gay liberationists went further to indict the dynamics of heterosexuality. Young, for instance, attributed prison rape to the sexist conventions of heterosexuality rather than to homosexual predation: "To the extent that there are violent homosexual acts in any jail," Young wrote, "this is due exclusively to the aggressive behavior of straight men. . . . Such sex is a form of bogus homosexuality which is nothing but an under-the-circumstances parody of heterosexuality."[51] Wittman agreed: "It's typical of the fucked-up straight mind to think that homosexual sex involves tying a guy down and fucking him. That's aggression, not sex. If that's what sex is for a lot of straight people, that's a problem they have to solve, not us."[52]

Efforts on the part of gay men and lesbians to intervene in this popular discourse of prison sexual violence met with some limited success. As a consequence of pressure from gay organizations, the Federal Bureau of Prisons announced publicly in 1978 that "through the use of such terms [as 'homosexual rape'], the public is led to believe that these assaults are committed by persons who are homosexual. While homosexuals are frequently the victims, the vast majority of rapes and assaults are committed by persons who are not homosexuals."[53] While activists could claim credit for that official pronouncement, references to "homosexual rape" in prison continued to circulate widely.

Gay activists who contested the assumptions about predatory homosexuality implicit in representations of prison sexual violence were notably silent regarding the intensely racialized nature of many of these rep-

resentations. Sociological studies of prison sexual violence highlighted
the disproportionate participation of African American men as assailants
in cases of prison rape, but gay activists' commitment to radical politics no
doubt attuned them to the racist overtones of those representations and
may have inclined them to ignore them. Their fragile alliances with black
activists may also have contributed to keep them from noticing, much less
engaging, the issue of race when rebutting attributions of "homosexual
rape." The only exception to this strategy of seemingly willful disengagement around the question of race and prison rape was Ken Carpenter,
who included the depiction of "white men raped by darkskinned men" as
part of what he termed the "prison rape scenario" that gratified tabooed
sexual fantasies, underwrote homophobic narratives of predatory homosexuality, and served as a means of social control warning "would-be mis-
creants" of the horrors of prison.[54]

Gay liberation politics provided the ideological tools and activist bravado required to challenge the terms of the national preoccupation with
prison sexual violence and to contest the damaging consequences of the
discourse of "homosexual rape" that circulated so widely in the late 1960s
and 1970s. Conversations with prisoners supplied activists with crucial
behind-the-bars information and the authority to challenge homophobic narratives of prison life. Against the grain of these images, prisoners
and their activist allies insisted that prison was "no sissies' paradise."[55] In
so doing, they confronted an idea with a long history. In 1930, Samuel
Roth, a publisher and bookseller who served a two-month prison term
for selling copies of James Joyce's Ulysses, described Welfare Island as a
"Fairies' Paradise," adding that "if it were generally known how well
they live on Welfare Island, there would be no keeping the fairies on
Broadway."[56] That opinion was reiterated, sometimes almost word for
word, throughout the twentieth century. Prison superintendent Florence Monahan described the State Prison for Women at Tehachapi, California, as "a happy hunting ground" for lesbians.[57] Psychoanalyst Robert
Lindner likewise insisted in 1946 that "prison is often a relatively happy
place for [the homosexual] to be, since therein he has less competition
from females (or from males in the institutions for women), his services
are in greater demand and his worth is immeasurably increased.[58] Because
"the 'girls'" were in such high demand among male prisoners, journalist
John Bartlow Martin reported in 1951, "prison is a rather happy place"
for gay men.[59] And fifteen years later, prisoner Donald Lee added his
opinion that "from the point of view of the out-and-out homosexual,
prison life is a paradise."[60]

In taking issue with this damaging characterization of prison life as a paradise for gay inmates, gay activists were forced to contend not only with mainstream representations of prison life but also with aspects of gay men's culture that eroticized prisoners and sex behind bars. Depictions of prison sex in novels and films no doubt held titillating appeal for audiences across a range of sexual orientations. Gay activist Ken Carpenter suggested provocatively that the idea of prison rape gripped the popular imagination because it "provides a script for powerful and forbidden sexual fantasies" and speculated that "this may explain some of its popularity as a literary scene."[61] The archetypal all-male space of the prison and its alluring association with dangerous masculinity held an especially important place in gay pornographic iconography, which enjoyed increasingly wider circulation with the loosening of censorship laws and the explosion of sexually explicit materials in the 1960s and 1970s. Following his release from prison and still traumatized by his experience of sexual assault, Stephen Donaldson was troubled by the eroticization of prison in gay culture, "with gay bars bearing names like The Cell Block, supposed replicas of cells built into them, and purported jailhouse scenes a mainstay of porno films, magazines, and books." These images, Donaldson insisted, "had little in common with reality; their creators didn't know what they were talking about."[62] The reality of prison life, Donaldson countered, "is no pornographer's fantasy."[63] "Despite the fact that there are hundreds of gorgeous men in here," gay porn writer and inmate Robert Boyd agreed, "it really is nicer out there."[64]

Some prisoners used much stronger language to persuade gay men and others of the dismal and often brutal conditions suffered by gay inmates: "Do not be fooled," one inmate wrote. "It is pure hell, the suffering, the abuses, the degradations, the indignities, the tortures, the horror, the sadistic punishments of both body and mind."[65] "Abuse to gays in prison isn't the word," another insisted; "It's Torture."[66] "People think that us gays have it made," yet another inmate wrote. "B.S. we are hassled hustled & some beaten up at times . . . for us gays in prison, even if it's all men, it's no picnic only hurt and sadness."[67]

Lesbians confronted different and differently damaging popular images of women's prisons, and they countered them in different ways. Lesbian activists in Los Angeles called for a boycott against the sponsors of *The Prisoner: Cell Block H*, a popular Australian television series about a women's prison syndicated in some U.S. cities, for depicting its main lesbian character Franky as "slovenly, psychotic and violent."[68] And while the sexually menacing and sadistic lesbian was a stock figure of women-in-prison films, lesbian and feminist activists drew attention to the much more real-istic threat posed by male guards. They organized most intensely around the case of Joan Little, a young African American woman charged with murdering a white jailer when he attempted to rape her in her Beaufort County, North Carolina, jail cell in August of 1974.[69] In her defense, Little explained that the prison guard, Clarence Alligood, entered her cell in his underwear armed with an ice pick, which she was able to wrest from him and used to stab him in order to escape. During her trial, Little's lawyers produced three other former prisoners to support their contention that Alligood had assaulted other women in his capacity as prison guard. Little presented a strong argument of self-defense and was ultimately acquitted in 1975. Her case was covered extensively in every lesbian and feminist publication of the period and attracted passionate support from high-profile activists including Angela Davis, Dick Gregory, Coretta Scott King, and Julian Bond. Bond attributed Little's success at defending her-self to the "centuries of repression and abuse against black women" that "welled up inside her that night."[70] Feminist and lesbian activists held up Joan Little's ordeal as symbolic of the condition of all women, in prison and out, who were vulnerable to sexual assault.

Lesbian and feminist prison activists revealed Little's case to be far from unique, citing evidence from women prisoners who reported routine harassment, sexual abuse, and sometimes sexual assault by male guards. Women prisoners had long been sexually vulnerable to male guards and wardens, and feminism provided new rhetorical tools and activist net-works to protest and publicize women's prison conditions. In 1975, over one hundred women prisoners incarcerated in a Florida state prison rioted to protest the "outrageous and unconstitutional abuses of prisoners by guards and the prison system itself, including sexual abuses by male cor-rections officers."[71] Women incarcerated in the New York state prison at Bedford Hills protested the employment of male guards, arguing that their presence in women's living areas deprived prisoners of all privacy. Bed-ford Hills guards, the feminist collective Women Free Women in Prison reported, "have been let loose on the floors where the general population lives." Because cell windows, showers, and bathrooms had no curtains or doors, "everything the women do becomes one huge peep show for the male guards."[72] Activists who advocated on behalf of Bedford Hills pris-oners made strategic use of language, inverting the popular association of lesbianism and prison sexual deviance by protesting the "many perver-sions in prison" perpetrated against female inmates by "degenerate" male guards.[73] Heterosexual harassment and rape of women prisoners by male guards, not lesbianism, was the true degeneracy in women's prisons, lesbian and feminist prison activists charged.

Challenging Discrimination Behind Bars

Gay activists challenged the damaging association of sexual violence with homosexual menace in representations of both men's and women's prisons. Committed as well to more material forms of prison activism, they did not have to look very hard to find evidence of an array of discriminatory practices and oppressive conditions suffered by gay and lesbian prisoners.

The blatant discrimination involved in segregating homosexual prisoners was one key focus of activism for both gay men and lesbians. A longstanding practice in men's prisons, segregation was justified by the claim on the part of prison administrators, articulated both vaguely and sweepingly, that homosexuals represented a threat to institutional order and security. By the 1970s, the segregation of gay inmates was newly promoted as a form of "protective custody" intended to shelter them from sexual harassment and assault. Gay men, especially effeminate ones, were often targets for humiliation, sexual exploitation, and sexual violence in prison, but many among them experienced their recourse of last resort—a request for protective custody, or "PC"—as compounding rather than relieving the conditions of their incarceration. Protective custody stamped gay men with the stigma of cowardice; it was also associated with the cardinal prison sin of informing, and placement in PC could brand gay men with the damning label of "snitch." Protective custody also submitted prisoners to a wide array of restrictions and penalties, and gay prisoners alerted activists to the lack of meaningful distinction between PC and punitive solitary detention. "While authorities state that protective custody is nonpunitive," two Angola prisoners wrote, "the reality is that there is absolutely no difference in the manner of treatment accorded the protection cases and the punishment cases."[74] Prisoners incarcerated in PC were often held in the same physical quarters as those in solitary confinement, and they suffered the same lack of access to social, recreational, vocational, and rehabilitative opportunities. As a consequence, gay prisoners were often unable to accrue "good time" credit or build a favorable prison record toward early parole or placement in work-release programs. One prisoner described the conditions of his confinement to a gay activist outside, writing, "I am here on what they are calling Protective Custody. It means I'm locked in a 9 × 4 cell 24 hours a day, 7 days a week and have no program of any kind." He added in understated conclusion, "I'm what you might call getting the shaft."[75]

In addition to these many deprivations, protective custody could also fail to be truly protective, and in some cases it singled out prisoners for abuse. One gay prisoner who was put in PC after having been stabbed while trying to defend himself in a rape attempt reported that "daily solid and liquid human waste was thrown on me as inmates passed my cell. Once my bed was set on fire while I was sleeping."[76] Another prisoner commented that the verbal abuse by guards in PC "is much worse than anywhere else in the prison."[77] "In short," one McNeil Island prisoner explained, "you are being punished for seeking protection of your life."[78]

Few women's prisons engaged in similar practices of segregating lesbians. But lesbian activists protested the policy of placing identifiable (typically butch) lesbians in a separate cellblock termed the "Daddy Tank" at the Sybil Brand Institute, the Los Angeles county jail for women. Selection for the Daddy Tank was reportedly made on the basis of physical appearance and deportment, segregating women, in one gay reporter's account, "with short hair cuts or no make up, those wearing trousers with flys [sic], jockey shorts, T-shirts or turned up socks, those who spread their legs when they sit, and those who hold a cigarette between thumb and forefinger."[79] Women were held in the Daddy Tank under harsh and restrictive maximum security conditions, regardless of whether they were awaiting trial or serving time and regardless of their offense. Conditions there were reportedly "three or four times worse" than in other sections of the jail.[80] Women confined in the Daddy Tank, lesbian activists charged, "have the least privileges; the filthiest jobs; get thrown in Lock Up without warning."[81] Physically separated from other women prisoners at all times, they were seated together when attending movies, prison shows, or church services, with "at least one or two rows of empty seats separating them from the others."[82]

In a demonstration held in mid-June of 1972, taking public relations advantage of the ironic Father's Day date, lesbian activists in Los Angeles picketed the Sybil Brand Institute to protest the discriminatory and punitive segregation policy represented by the Daddy Tank.[83] Although they refused to admit bowing to pressure, Sybil Brand officials modified the Daddy Tank into a medium-security "Daddy Dorm," in which inmates were housed in a dormitory rather than isolated in small single cells, were permitted access to an open dayroom, and were newly eligible for occupational classes and recreational programs. But some inmates denied any meaningful improvement in the still segregated conditions. One former

Daddy Tank resident reported that "they just pulled a few femmes out of the general population" in an effort to make the discriminatory punishment for gender nonconformity less obvious.[84]

Prisoners and their advocates also protested the discrimination against lesbian and gay inmates resulting from indeterminate sentencing laws and the routine denial and revocation of parole on the basis of homosexuality. The indeterminate sentence, a popular reform measure in the late nineteenth century that became the standard form of sentencing in the twentieth-century United States, gave courts wide discretion over sentencing lengths and allowed prison officials to hold prisoners beyond their minimum sentencing period for a variety of disciplinary reasons, homosexuality among them. Members of the San Francisco–based collective Join Hands, formed in 1972 and composed of gay men, some of whom were former prisoners, protested this practice in testimony before a state congressional committee hearing in 1974. "This negative discrimination is often for *no other reason* than the prisoner's sexuality," Join Hands members declared. To support their claims, Join Hands representatives quoted from a letter written by Eddie Loftin, a California prisoner who had recently been denied parole along with other gay men: "There was 7 gays that went to the parole board, and out of the 7 only one made parole. . . . That is a 'Hell' of a average." Parole boards, Loftin charged, "think that 'ALL' gay people are sick and need to be in a hospital." "I hope you don't mind tears on this letter," Loftin concluded; "I am crying."[85] Loftin died of a heart attack three months later, still awaiting parole at Folsom.

The discretionary power that indeterminate sentencing granted prison administrators meant that parole could also be denied to inmates on the basis of gender nonconformity. One prisoner at the California Men's Colony in San Luis Obispo complained that he was denied parole sixteen months following the termination of his sentence, "solely because I expressed my intention of having sexual reassignment surgery and hormonal treatment upon release." He was told that his parole would not be reconsidered "until I change my sexual identity."[86] Parole could also be revoked, and prisoners who had been released were consequently forced to hide their homosexuality and gender nonconformity to avoid reincarceration.

Outside and Inside: Queer Encounters

Gay activists arrived at their critique of incarceration in part through the politics of gay liberation and through radical politics more generally. They also did so, importantly, in conversation with gay and lesbian prisoners. Eager for genuine dialogue with prisoners, gay activists insisted that the direction of discussion not be simply one-way. The Join Hands collective advertised its newsletter as "a vehicle for gay prisoners to communicate with each other and to educate those of us on the outside as to what's coming down so that we can most effectively direct our support and action."[87] The Seattle-based lesbian-feminist collective that published the newsletter *Through the Looking Glass* on women's prison conditions in the Pacific Northwest likewise solicited the writing and creative work of women and lesbian prisoners, as did the feminist and lesbian journals *off our backs*, *Lesbian Connection*, and *Lesbian Tide*. Mike Riegle edited "The Other Side of the Wall," a monthly section of *Gay Community News* (*GCN*) devoted to publishing articles and letters written "*by prisoners* about their experiences being in and up against the prison system." In these pages, Riegle wrote, "prisoners speak for themselves for a change, instead of being the subject of others' writings, or forgotten altogether."[88]

The gay, lesbian, and feminist press served as a crucial conduit of information from the outside in and the inside out.[89] Prison officials routinely denied prisoners access to gay publications—the Federal Bureau of Prisons banned them formally in 1977—and getting them to prisoners was often a struggle.[90] Copies of *GCN*, sent free to prisoners who requested them, were often returned in unopened envelopes. One copy of *GCN* sent to an inmate in Huntsville, Texas was returned by the state's Department of Corrections, accompanied by a form with a checked box declaring the newspaper "detrimental to prisoner's rehabilitation because it would encourage deviate criminal sexual behavior."[91] An assistant warden of a federal prison informed *GCN* that "to permit those issues of your newspaper into our institution which condone or invite homosexual behavior is contrary to our mission, which is, to insure the safety and welfare of all persons assigned to our custody."[92] The feminist periodical *off our backs* was also prohibited in many prisons, deemed by an official at the federal women's prison at Alderson, West Virginia, in 1977 as "detrimental to the security, good order and discipline of this institution because of its advocation or support of homosexuality."[93]

Gay activists employed a variety of rhetorical and legal strategies to counter these arguments. One man wrote to the deputy warden of a Michigan women's reformatory to object to the notion that *Gay Community News* was "in any way salacious"; on the contrary, he wrote, "it is, if anything, rather plodding, knotty, and occasionally verging on the dull."[94] Others defended *GCN* and other gay publications as "newspapers of record" that charted the course of an important and growing political movement. They also mounted legal challenges to restrictions on publications as violations of the First Amendment rights of prisoners. After more than a decade of pressure on the part of activists and a successful lawsuit filed jointly by the National Gay Task Force, the Lambda Legal Defense and Education Fund, and the American Civil Liberties Union, the Federal Bureau of Prisons was forced to stipulate in 1980 that gay publications "of a news or informational nature, gay literary publications, and publications of gay religious groups" could be admitted to prison.[95] Despite this victory, gay and civil rights lawyers continued for years to argue on behalf of prisoners who were denied gay and lesbian publications.

For some prisoners, especially those who had been active in the movement before their incarceration, news of gay life and politics in the outside world offered by publications such as *Gay Community News*, the *Advocate*, *Gay Sunshine*, *Lesbian Tide*, *off our backs*, and *RFD*, as well as mimeographed newsletters like *Join Hands*, the *Gaycon Press Newsletter*, and *Cellmate*, could be a lifeline. One prisoner who claimed to have been among the "group of shouters" in the Stonewall riots wrote to *Join Hands* that he was "still shouting" and "will not stop. . . . If you are out in those streets, shout a little bit louder for us in here. If you listen really hard you can hear us shouting with you."[96] Another prisoner in New Mexico thanked Riegle for sending him copies of *GCN*, which enabled him to "maintain a modicum of pace with current events and grants some perspective to and mediates the negativity around me."[97] For a Wisconsin prisoner, receiving the *Advocate* "keeps me informed as to what is happening in the gay society."[98] Another expressed his appreciation to gay activists who demonstrated against the state penitentiary at Leavenworth, Kansas to protest the prison's ban on gay publications: "GAY LIB WAS HERE!" he exclaimed. "wow! Beautiful! Fantastic!! I wanted to hug every one of the protestors. . . . The Gay Community cared, and it felt good. Really great!" As a result, he wrote, "gays walked around here proud of the protestors and of themselves. . . . It's really hard to explain how much this means to gay inmates here."[99]

The value of gay publications to prisoners could be measured by tracking a single newspaper's circulation around an institution. "My own G.C.N.s make the rounds of gays on this floor, six of us," one prisoner wrote. "Then it go's upstairs to two more gays, then goes to another section of this prison for other gays to read."[100] Another Missouri prisoner counted "about half a dozen other gay men in this housing unit who are lined up to read each issue of *GCN* as I get them, so we are passing it around to everyone! We're building quite a readership here, I think."[101]

Members of that prison readership learned of gay demonstrations and pride marches, the election of Harvey Milk to San Francisco's Board of Supervisors in 1977 and his assassination the following year, Florida's Dade County anti–gay rights initiative, the defeat of California's Briggs initiative that would have banned gays and lesbians from teaching in public schools, and other news of the successes and setbacks of a growing movement. Reading in *RFD* about "the 100,000 gay march in San Francisco" in 1976 inspired one prisoner in the Washington State penitentiary to exclaim, "YEH-HOO! It opened my eyes to a new world, to know that gay brothers and sisters are out there doing what we want to do, but can't at this time."[102]

Perhaps less self-consciously but no less importantly, the gay press alerted readers to new homosexual norms and values. In the process, gay newspapers and journals not only informed readers of news of the movement but also instructed them in new ways to be gay. The new movement was accompanied by a new ethos—informed by the affirmation that gay was good and a call to gay pride, an imperative to "come out," a belief in sexual reciprocity and mutuality, a refusal of gay stereotypes, and a critique of gendered roles. Those new norms often collided with a sexual culture in prison that had a much longer history. In a 1976 *Advocate* article, gay prison activist David Rothenberg wrote that "gay pride and gay self acceptance . . . challenge the lifestyle and social structure of the prison population."[103] Prison sexual culture was characterized in women's prisons by butch-femme partnerships and in men's prisons by the participation of heterosexually identified men whose masculine gender presentation and penetrative role in sex with other men did not confer or connote a homosexual identity and by their asymmetrical and sometimes exploitative partnerships with other men who were sometimes feminized by association. Those sexual norms ran directly counter to the emerging norms of post-Stonewall urban gay life.

Prisons were far from impermeable to phenomena in the larger culture, and there is some evidence that the new norms of gay life were beginning to appear behind bars in the 1970s and 1980s. The demographic profile of the San Francisco jail would hardly have been typical, but one gay man imprisoned there reported in 1983 that "every conceivable Gay subculture" was represented on the jail's gay tier: "drag queens, muscle men, preppies, post-op transsexuals, hippie queers, rednecks, leather men, clones—the gamut."[104] "Just as the gay scene has changed in the free world," one prisoner wrote, "so in prison one finds a more militant gay who values his masculinity and refuses to be a female surrogate."[105] One Oklahoma prisoner, considerably further from the epicenter of gay culture, who identified as "not overly butch nor overly femme, I'm just me," wrote in 1976 about his defiance of prison gender norms in a relationship with another inmate: "We both agreed that neither of us was the dominant one. . . . Sometimes I would be in the passive role, sometimes Roger would." "The trouble started," he wrote, when straight prisoners started asking "'what could two whores do for each other?' The fact that two guys were making it to the exclusion of all straights rankled their souls."[106] Another prisoner at Vacaville wrote in 1977 that after "bounc[ing] in and out (mostly in) of the California prison system for close to 20 years," he had "at long last" begun to "break out of the restrictions of the almost mandatory stereotyping of sexual roles imposed on us here in the penal society by our peers."[107] When he stopped plucking his eyebrows and wearing tight pants, his noncompliance with prison gender norms incited a "battle" in which he had to "fight to prove my sincerity in demanding to be allowed to be myself" and to "put up with frequent threats of being stabbed."[108] One Lompoc inmate noted the "new trend" of what he termed "fag-on-fag" sex that emerged in the early 1980s, a trend that he blamed for disrupting "the sex life of straights" in the prison, his own included. "The basic penitentiary law was, no homosexuals can have sex with other homosexuals," he observed. "Regular guys can't compete with homosexuals," he added, because they could not abide sexual reciprocity: "Homos on homos get into sixty-nining. . . . We can't deal with that. That's tough to compete with."[109]

Some gay male prisoners resisted the feminizing demands of prison sexual culture, but many found the pressures of prison sexual norms and expectations overwhelming. That collision provoked frustration and anger on the part of some gay inmates who were forced to adjust to a sexual code that differed markedly from the one taking shape outside. Those accustomed to gay life on the street "must set aside their 'old self' and make way for a new personality" on coming to prison, one inmate wrote.[110] A California prisoner explained, "you don't have gays here. . . . There are 'men' and 'women.' The 'men' are 'straight' and the 'women' are queer, punks, fags, etc. All of the labels that the gays on the outside fight against. . . . It's a real bummer of a trip. . . . These things merely serve to make things difficult for those who are gay and proud."[111] Another wrote to members of New York's Gay Activists Alliance that, in prison, "there is no such animal as a 'Gay.' You must be a punk, a queer, a faggot, a dick-sucker. . . , a bitch, a whore—but you *may not be Gay,* and *certainly cannot be proud!*"[112] Still another complained, "There simply is no room in the prison environment for a man who likes other men. The only relationship that can be understood and accepted is a man and his 'girl.'"[113]

Some lesbian prisoners voiced similar frustration with the dissonance of gay life behind bars and the one taking shape outside. While women prisoners tended to organize their relationships along gendered lines, many lesbian feminists criticized butch-femme roles as imitative of heterosexuality and supportive of traditional and oppressive gender roles, and those criticisms found their way into prisons in the 1970s. One inmate told an interviewer in 1973 that "there's a lot more role playing" at California's Terminal Island prison "than out on the street" and that she felt forced to participate, because people say, "Oh, look at the new daddy that's in." "I've never been a daddy in my life!" She added, "But as long as you walk with an aggressive walk, then they tag you as a daddy and that's what you're gonna be." When she was "out on the streets," she had always had "an equal relationship" with girlfriends, she reported, "but when you come in the penitentiary, you gotta be one of the two."[114] She did note, however, that "now that Women's Liberation has come around, it's changed a little bit. Like I've noticed that more girls are accepting you being a woman instead of being a male image or a butch or a dyke."[115] Another California prisoner used the terminology of lesbian feminism in referencing "women loving women relationships" but complained that in prison, "they take on all the fucked up aspects of male female relationships—the dominant/passive, the games, the possessiveness, the jealousies, the role playing."[116]

The collision between new norms of gay liberation and lesbian feminism and those of prison sexual culture elicited a change in consciousness, or at least a new consciousness of appropriate sexual script, on the part of some prisoners. One inmate who had once adopted the gendered norms of prison sexual culture recalled self-critically in an interview with a gay activist that he had been "into a role thing, where I was a homosexual and [my partner] was a straight man." When asked, leadingly, if he had come to think differently, he replied, "Oh, yeah. My consciousness is entirely different now. I think that having to play those roles was extremely oppressive for many of us."[117] Allen Young observed what he characterized as the consciousness-raising effects of his correspondence with Eddie, "a gay brother" convicted of a "crime against nature" and serving a sentence at the Bridgewater State Prison in Massachusetts. When Eddie responded to an ad placed in a Boston weekly by the Rhode Island Gay Alliance soliciting contact with prisoners, Young wrote to him, and he and Eddie exchanged dozens of letters. In the process, Young noted, Eddie became "very turned on by his contact with the gay liberation movement, . . . pick[ing] up the gay-feminist analysis he read in gay papers, and . . . applying it to the people and situations he knew."[118] Inmate Bobbie Lee White testified to the transformative power of receiving GCN while in prison. In learning about the gay movement outside, White explained, he had come to understand that "being gay is something more than having sex with the same sex."[119]

Some who suffered the oppressive conditions of prison life were inspired both by the gay movement and the prisoners' rights movement to organize on their own behalf. Some of those efforts appeared to be spontaneous responses to discrimination. An Illinois prisoner recounted that "we used to have this thing where many of the gay people would organize, and do strikes, and sit-ins, and shit like that, refuse to do any work."[120] Other groups emphasized support and consciousness-raising. La Toya Lewis, a male-to-female transsexual inmate in the New Mexico prison at Los Lunas, notified GCN of a group called "Gays in Prison," which held "rap sessions to help each other with the problems of everyday prison life," especially vulnerability to sexual violence.[121] Tyrone Gadson announced the start of "a self-help organization" at New Jersey's Rahway State Prison called the Gayworld Organization, for "gay inmates who are having adjustment problems with their gaylife in the institution," adding that "a lot of homosexual inmates are lost and they don't make it. Some of them end up in protective custody or try to kill themselves."[122] Gay prisoners in the Louisiana State prison at Angola formed the Self-Help Alliance Group (or SHAG) in 1984, to "help, promote, and assist this segment of the prison society which has, for so long, been ignored, ridiculed, and belittled" and to help develop the "creative talents of homosexuals."[123] The founders of SHAG proposed an orientation for gay men entering prison, to "indoctrinate homosexuals to the various lifestyles and atmosphere of the various prison environments" and to teach them to "conduct themselves . . . so that they can live in peace, without harassment."[124]

One of the first organizations of gay prisoners, a multiracial group formed in alliance with some straight inmates, was founded in 1977 at the Washington State Penitentiary at Walla Walla. Initiated by members of the George Jackson Brigade, a revolutionary guerrilla organization active in the Pacific Northwest in the mid-1970s convicted for several small bombings and bank heists, the group worked to protect gay and other vulnerable inmates from sexual harassment and violence. Members met the "chain" (the bus on which new inmates were transferred to the prison) each week and provided orientation to new prisoners to tutor them in the complexities of prison etiquette and warn them of prison dangers. They also worked to secure "safe cells" and provided escort services for "those men most likely to be raped, sold, pimped, and preyed on in the sexual meat market condoned by the administration."[125] Gay prisoners at Walla Walla boasted some remarkable successes. "The other day two prisoners 'sold' a gay cellmate to another prisoner," one prisoner wrote. "We moved into the situation and smashed the deal. The 'property' was moved into one of our cells and is under our escort."[126] They also worked to release gay prisoners from protective custody and helped integrate them safely into the general population.

The name that Walla Walla prisoners chose for their organization, Men against Sexism, articulated an analysis of prison sexual violence comprehensible to gay and lesbian activists and fully compatible with the ideological foundations of gay liberationist thought. In working toward an analysis of gay oppression, lesbians and gay men looked to sexism as a root cause, indicting in particular the patriarchal values, normative gender roles, and institutionalized heterosexuality nurtured and policed by the nuclear family. Gay Liberation Front activist Martha Shelley identified gay men and lesbians as "women and men who, from the time of our earliest memories, have been in revolt against the sex-role structure and nuclear family structure."[127] It was perhaps not surprising that lesbians would turn to radical feminism for analyses of their oppression. But gay male activists also located their oppression in the nuclear family's enforcement of normative masculinity. "Gay liberation is a struggle against sexism," Allen Young announced. "Within the context of our society, sexism is primarily manifested through male supremacy and heterosexual chauvinism."[128]

Those critiques informed Walla Walla's Men against Sexism, whose members challenged the hypermasculinist prison ethos they viewed as contributing to sexual violence. Ed Mead, one of the group's founders, echoed the critique of normative masculinity expressed in early gay liberation politics, insisting that "we all have our yin and yang, our masculine and feminine sides. We should give expression to each" (plate 13).[129] Members of the lesbian prison activist collective *Through the Looking Glass* were impressed with the work of Men against Sexism, noting approvingly that "they have been studying and working to develop a clear understanding of sexism in themselves, in Walla Walla, and in this society."[130] Among its activities, Men against Sexism sponsored screenings of anti-sexist films and ran workshops on subjects including "rape, masculinity, and homosexuality."[131]

Prisoners who called on feminist analyses of sexism in order to understand prison oppressions were readily comprehensible to gay activists outside. The language of gay oppression and pride used more generally by many other incarcerated activists resonated with and echoed the language used by activists outside. Gay activists could not help but be gratified by proclamations like inmate La Toya Lewis's that "it was a long fight to get where we are now, but now the Gay Men and Transsexuals (such as myself) can walk with pride that cannot be DIMINISHED!!!!!!!!"[132] A representative from the "gay collective" in the Florida prison at Raiford likewise proclaimed it time "for us gay people to realize that we are oppressed people" and appealed to others to "reach out and join hands with your oppressed brothers."[133] Indiana prisoners wrote to Black and White Men Together (BWMT) declaring their interest in starting a chapter of the organization behind bars and asking outside members to "please send the Starter's Kit."[134] In communicating their gratitude to outside allies, some prisoners echoed the language of gay kinship used by activists. One lesbian wrote that *GCN* offered her and other gay prisoners "a sense of belonging—of being part of a family. The family of gay and lesbian brothers and sisters."[135] Connections between activists and prisoners were also apparent in appreciative and comradely salutations in their correspondence. One inmate signed his letter to Riegle, "Sealed with a kiss of our gay struggle," another "In gay love and pride," and another to *GCN*, "Thanks Fellow Gays."[136]

For gay and lesbian activists working in solidarity with their "brothers" and "sisters" behind bars, the familial resemblance of some prisoners was striking. When those newly forged familial connections produced a shared language and shared assumptions, conversations between prisoners and activists were mutually comprehensible, productive, and gratifying. Finding (and in some cases, producing) likenesses among others took more effort. Gay activists forged critiques of sexism that condemned the forced gendered roles of prison sexual culture expressed most violently in sexual assault and coerced partnerships, but their ethos of sexual reciprocity and condemnation of gay stereotypes sometimes made it difficult to ally with those in men's prisons who identified as ladies, queens, and transsexuals and who often felt the brunt of prison misogyny most directly. Activists typically disavowed those distancing and judgmental attitudes, but they were sometimes perceived by prisoners and occasionally by prison officials. When Mattachine and Gay Activists Alliance members held a lecture

and rap session with men training to be correction officers in New York
City's penal facilities, one officer-in-training observed the masculine gender presentation of the activists and noted, "I think you should have had a
feminine homosexual on the panel," since "that is the kind we have to deal
with mainly in here."[137] Another trainee, perhaps referencing class and racial divisions between activists and prisoners as well as gender differences,
told the gay panelists: "I think you have a different frame of reference
coming in from the outside like you do. I think most of you would look
down on most of the homos, I mean homosexuals, we have in here."[138]

Not all gay activists, certainly, disparaged queens, in or out of prison.
But the 1970s ushered in a new understanding of gay identity and new
modes of gay self-presentation in which gender-transgressive queers
would be increasingly marginalized. The gay movement moved away
from its earlier embrace of gender transgression; many gay men embraced a clonish masculinity and lesbian feminists rejected butch-femme
styles they cast as relics of an earlier, apolitical time for a purportedly
gender-neutral androgyny.[139] Many prison queens who insisted on identifying as "gay" at a time when inclusion in that category was coming to
privilege gender normativity felt looked down on by gay activists from
the outside. One complained, "The gays outside are so wrapped up in
saying that drag queens are a disgrace to macho gays, . . . that they forget
. . . that we're all homosexuals and on top of that we're all oppressed."
He criticized Join Hands as a group that "wish[es] to continue bickering
about whether queens are acceptable to be part of the gay society and
if we should be cast out even further into oppression *by our own brothers
and sisters.*" In response to the *Join Hands* invitation to prisoners to help
define gay political strategy, this prisoner stated: "First of all you should
drop all your barriers about gays having to be macho."[140] Another who
identified as "a gay prisoner from Illinois" who was transferred to a small
male unit of a predominantly women's institution "because I have breasts
resulting from hormone treatment," addressed "all you gay brothers and
sisters out there," asking "why don't you give the queens a break? It's hard
enough on us being put down by straights."[141] And still another spoke to
the tensions between "queens" behind bars and "machos" outside: "Both
are Gay," he wrote. "This . . . should be the Unity point." This prisoner
urged gay activists to focus on "just being Gay brothers seeking to help
other Gay brothers."[142] Other prisoners felt pressured to conform to the
gendered expectations of gay men outside, shaped by the scripts of gay
pornography that eroticized prisoners as roughly masculine. "Just because
we are in prison," one wrote, "doesn't mean we are all supermen, macho,

hung like mules, etc., etc., etc." He added that he had been "forced to live these lies" in order to "keep the letters coming" from gay pen pals on the outside.[143]

Some observers described the presence of prison queens and butches and the differences between prison sexual culture and gay culture in temporal terms, as the clash between "primitive" and more evolved forms of sexual organization, or the meeting of a stubbornly retrograde sexual culture with a modern one. Casting prison sexual culture in an overtly developmental narrative, some characterized its gendered roles as evidence of a less enlightened homosexual past. To Wooden and Parker, the "prison sexual code, which works to feminize homosexuals, is directly opposed to the goals of the modern gay movement. A positive gay identity attempts to free men from the tyranny of rigid role-playing."[144] That tyranny was usually equated with gender deviance and most strongly with male effeminacy; masculinity, for gay men, was typically cast not as a "role" but, rather, as a reclamation of manhood and dignity long denied them and as a sign of gay modernity. Prison life, Wooden and Parker wrote, keeps gay men "bound to rigid stereotypic roles—the roles of the submissive, dependent, passive, and weak female—the same roles many in society have also rejected."[145] Prison gender norms, to Wooden and Parker, were signs that gay identity in prison "has remained at less advanced stages of development . . . compared to the gay subculture that is developing external to the prison environment."[146] Wooden and Parker contrasted prisoners' gendered pairings with relationships in the outside "gay community," which tend "*not* to be modeled along dichotomous male and female lines" and were characterized instead by "a bond between two self-affirming and masculine-defined gay men."[147] Their definition of modern gay men— those "who assume both active and passive roles and who display few if any effeminate mannerisms"—effectively removed prison queens from the category of "gay."[148]

The developmental explanation of prison sexual culture was deeply imbued with assumptions about the gender norms appropriate to modern gay identity. As in other iterations, this narrative of sexual primitivism and modernity was also deeply racialized. Those assumptions were laid bare in an account by gay journalist Randy Shilts, who arranged to be booked on fake traffic charges to observe gay life behind bars. After spending several nights in the jails' gay tiers, he felt that he had entered "not only another world but another era." The "queens' tanks" in San Francisco county jails, in Shilts's account, gave rise to their "own social system and stylized sex roles reminiscent of the gay world of two decades ago." In highlighting

racial and class difference in his representation of the gendered roles he
observed in jail as an anachronistic marker of same-sex desire, Shilts made
clear the racialized assumptions implicit in the developmental narrative of
modern gay identity.[149] Inmates of the San Francisco jails "brought back
to me what I had read about poor gays from black and Latin cultures.
Influenced by the more stringent sex roles of their own worlds, I found
these prisoners adopting feminine roles rather than the newer, masculine
gay-male roles of the educated white middle classes."[150]

Gender identity was sometimes a point of contention in advocacy efforts on behalf of gay prisoners, and emerging norms of gay masculinity
and sexual reciprocity sometimes created tension between gay activists
outside and queens and transsexuals behind bars. Gay and lesbian activists'
alliances with men incarcerated for sex with minors were also occasionally
strained, as they struggled over how and whether to accommodate men
who were attracted to boys into the larger movement. That ambivalence
was, in some cases, mutual. In a 1980 GCN article, Tom Reeves, founder
of the North American Man-Boy Love Association, offered an analysis
"of a serious oppression of gay men, among whose number I may some
day find myself."[151] But Reeves was dismayed to find that few of the 125
Massachusetts prisoners convicted of having sex with minors affiliated
with "the gay community." Some of them expressed their alienation from
that community in class and gender terms. One man told Reeves that the
gay life he knew about in Boston, "downtown, on Beacon Hill, faggots
dressed up like women, gay bars," had little to do with working-class life
in Revere where he grew up. Another told him, "I knew nothing about
gay organizations other than bars. If I had known, I would have thought
I didn't fit in."[152] Reeves found it gratifying, though, that more and more
of the men in prison for having sex with minors were "coming out":
"More of them are asking for subscriptions to GCN, more are identifying
as gay in prison, and more are seeking gay activist lawyers. . . . They are
beginning to define themselves as a gay population suffering a particularly
severe oppression."[153] Reeves and many others like him made a case for
their inclusion in the larger gay liberation movement, but gay advocacy
on behalf of men incarcerated for having sex with minors was always con-
tentious. The transformation of a movement for sexual liberation into
a movement for civil rights, requiring in turn a respectable homosexual
subject deserving of such rights, ultimately led to an effort to remove the
"pedophile" from the category homosexual.[154]

Before that point, however, in one California institution, men who had
been diagnosed as "disordered sex offenders," most charged with having

had sex with minors, were encouraged in a strikingly literal fashion to re-define and remake themselves as "gay." They were led in that remarkable effort by psychiatrist Michael Serber. A strong proponent and practitio-ner of behavior modification, Serber had earlier pioneered what he called shame aversion therapy, a technique that developed, he explained, as the incidental and fortuitous result of photographing a transvestite patient in the act of cross-dressing, which seemed to produce what Serber judged to be the usefully transformative shaming effects of social exposure.[155] The photography session was originally conceived as merely instrumental to the therapeutic plan. Serber had intended to project photographs of the patient dressed in women's lingerie while administering "painful electri-cal shocks to one of his extremities." But he found this later stage in the "therapy" to be unnecessary: the patient became "markedly anxious" and "unable to get sexually excited" while being photographed and reported that the experience had "completely 'turned him off'" and "changed his entire feeling about cross-dressing."[156] In Serber's later applications of the technique of shame aversion therapy, patients were ordered to cross-dress in front of a team of therapists. Serber also reported positively on the use of aversive conditioning to alter the behavior of homosexuals, noting that "homosexual practices were virtually eliminated and homosexual interest was substantially decreased," in patients who were administered electric shocks when aroused sexually.[157]

Serber came to disavow such therapies when his consciousness, along with that of many other psychiatrists and psychologists, was raised by gay liberationists who challenged the psychiatric profession's homopho-bic and pathologizing assumptions and practices.[158] After experiencing a Gay Activists Alliance "zap" at a meeting of the Association for Advance-ment of Behavior Therapy in New York in 1972, Serber introduced a new treatment and "retraining" program for inmates he termed "inadequate homosexuals"—most of them convicted of having sex with minors—sentenced to California's maximum-security hospital at Atascadero. One gay activist characterized Atascadero inmates as "closeted Gays on the street" who "have never experienced being Gay but have shared the com-mon trauma of feeling different and unaccepted."[159] Serber explained the goals of his program as working to retrain sex offenders "in the social skills most rewarding in the gay community while at the same time minimizing their problems in getting along in a generally hostile world."[160] Reporter Rob Cole translated Serber's social scientific language for readers of the *Advocate*, writing that Serber aimed "to teach adult males how to make it with each other instead of with young boys, and not get arrested."[161]

Toward that end, Serber renounced aversion therapy and instead led group discussions with inmates, exploring topics including "the problems of being gay in a predominantly straight society," "social alternatives for homosexuals," and "situations to be avoided in order not to be subsequently arrested."[162] To help Atascadero inmates learn social skills appropriate to modern gay life, Serber solicited members of the newly formed Gay Student Union at the California Polytechnic University to serve as instructors and "appropriate behavioral models." Cal Poly students led Atascadero inmates through imagined scenarios at a gay bar, coaching them in "specific verbal and nonverbal components of gay social interaction which served as a 'behavioral base' upon which further social skills could be built."[163] With the gay students as models, Atascadero inmate Tom Close explained that "we were taught cruising from eye contact to wrapup, and given the opportunity to practice our dancing skills."[164] (See plate 15.) "Phase 2" of Serber's program was devoted to consciousness raising, the first topic of which was titled "Gay is ____," calling on inmates to come to terms with homosexuality's negative associations and to arrive at more self-affirming definitions.[165] In the final phase of the program (and an important part of their treatment) inmates were encouraged to form and participate in a gay organization of their own, the Atascadero Gay Encounter, within the institution.[166] Minority identity group identification and political organization thus constituted the program's therapeutic denouement.

Serber's program replaced earlier "treatment" regimes at Atascadero and other prisons that were considerably more violent in their sexual pedagogy and more sexually normative in their aims. Stories had circulated for years in the gay press about the use of succinylcholine, a muscle-relaxing drug that produced a feeling of suffocation and was used along with nausea-inducing drugs in aversion therapy, as well as the use of electro-convulsive shock treatment as punishment for homosexual patients who "deviated" while in the hospital. One Atascadero inmate described the effects of the drug Proloxin, used in punitive aversion therapy: "It seems like your breathing is stopped. . . . Feels like you're dying. The doctors *tell* you you're dying. . . . You can't move anything. . . . You sweat. They tell you if you're ever caught having sex in here again, you won't get the antidote. You're froze. It's terrifying. You're helpless."[167] Reports of the use of drugs and darker rumors of the practice of lobotomy had earned Atascadero a reputation as the "Dachau for queers."[168] Inmates in other prisons told of similar "treatments" for homosexuality. Incarcerated Gay Activists Alliance member Albert Gay reported that he had been subjected to electroconvulsive shock "and other tortures" at the hands of prison doctors at Vacaville.[169] The suspicious death of one gay inmate in the Homosexual Unit at Vacaville enflamed gay activists, who charged that he was driven to suicide by cruel and inhumane treatment.[170]

Serber acknowledged that the history of treatment at Atascadero had "mainly centered around inadequate and sometimes cruel attempts at conversion to heterosexuality or asexuality," and he developed his treatment regime with considerably more humane and progressive aims.[171] Newly critical of the belief among psychiatrists that homosexuality was a psychopathic condition, Serber advanced "an alternative perspective of homosexuals," in line with the developing gay rights ideology, as "a minority group that should be provided meaningful social and psychological services in the criminal justice system."[172] "It is questionable that it is even possible to effect a change from complete homosexuality to complete heterosexuality," Serber wrote, "but even if it were possible to successfully effect complete change, does anyone have the right to revise a person's entire value system in an area of behavior that influences only himself and a consenting partner?"[173]

Serber's recognition that "a homosexual has the right to be a homosexual if he wants to" led the *Advocate* to call his program "revolutionary."[174] And surely his "retraining" program was appreciated by prisoners as more humane than earlier treatment regimes.[175] But Serber's program had a disciplinary purpose as well, however benevolently intentioned. Atascadero inmates were tutored in the new gay norms being forged in the 1970s. Those pedagogical aims were clearly recognized by Cole, who titled his article, "Lessons in Being Gay."[176]

The pedagogical impulses at work in Serber's program were evident in other aspects of gay prison activism as well. The Metropolitan Community Church (MCC), a nondenominational Christian church with largely gay congregations founded in 1968, began conducting services in prisons in 1972 and was very active in advocating on behalf of gay prisoners. In addition to holding services for prisoners—resisted in many prisons and requiring a long legal battle for the MCC's recognition as a legitimate church—the MCC developed pen pal and visitation programs for gay inmates and sometimes provided parole assistance, helping them find housing and employment on release.[177] Some of the MCC's literature made clear that among the church's missions in prison activism was inculcation in new gay norms and values. The MCC's *Prison Ministry Handbook* stated that "a person who is homosexual by nature, by inclination, and by behavior can benefit immensely by understanding what it is to be gay."[178] This illuminating line made clear that to be "homosexual" and to be "gay" were emerging as two different things—the first descriptive simply of a sexual orientation and the second embodying a set of norms and values, no less powerful for being only occasionally articulated explicitly.

The MCC's "Homosexual's Prayer," distributed in prison services, perhaps went the furthest in delineating those norms and exposing the MCC's missionary zeal in promoting them. In it, the MCC urged the homosexual prisoner to "be a Gay we can be proud of."[179] That self-improvement project involved coming to understand homosexuality as being "on a level higher than 'messing around.'"[180] The "bona fide homosexual," the MCC instructed, should be encouraged to "come to an understanding of how gay can be good and clean and ennobling"; that person, in the MCC's understanding, "becomes a whole lot healthier when he or she can say 'I am gay and I am proud.'"[181] This process involved, too, an acceptance of the minoritizing assumptions of the gay movement—the understanding of oneself as a "member of a minority," bound together with "brothers and sisters in a true family; bound together in a common cause"; and willing to "Thank God that I am a homosexual."[182]

While Serber's treatment program and the MCC's prison ministry suggested that there were proper ways to be gay, the MCC's reference to "bona fide homosexuals" suggested that some prisoners provoked more basic questions about who among the prison population, many of whom participated in homosexual sex, was truly "gay" to begin with (not just properly so). Gay activists were curiously silent about men who surely constituted the majority of participants in same-sex sex behind bars—jockers and punks—who had sex with other men without adopting (or, in the case of jockers, being ascribed) a gay identity, and who therefore could not be subsumed under the mantle of the gay minority. But in a section of the MCC's *Prison Ministry Handbook* tellingly titled "Who Is Gay?" the MCC warned those involved in prison ministry to "take note of special problems associated with sexuality in prisons," clarifying that "in prisons there may be homosexual behavior on the part of men and women who will never be 'gay' and who probably never will identify themselves with the gay community."[183] Because of circumstances the MCC described vaguely as "factors peculiar to homosexuality in prison," especially the "'old man–old lady' relationships that are common" behind bars, it recommended against performing the rite of Holy Union, practiced in MCC churches, in prison ministry work.[184] While some prisoners might, with some effort, be brought into the gay fold, the MCC suggested, others stretched the notion of gay kinship beyond the breaking point.

Anxiety about distinguishing "true" gays from their imposters arose most frequently around the subject of pen pal correspondence with prisoners. Many gay newspapers and journals supported pen pal initiatives with prisoners in the 1970s as a form of outreach and support, as part of the political project of connecting prisoners to gay men and lesbians outside and intended to let gay prisoners know that "they really are still part of the family."[185] "Remember that . . . those who submit their names for correspondence have a lot in common with those on the outside," *Advocate* editors wrote in 1973. "They are human, and they are oppressed."[186] "We've found . . . that prisoners are no different from us," the Join Hands collective wrote in soliciting prison pen pals. "We could be in jail too, just for being gay."[187] But by 1983, following reports of prisoners scamming gay pen pals out of money and gifts, the editor of the *Bay Area Reporter* prefaced the paper's prison pen pal request section with a cautionary note that "the paper in no way endorses or can stand behind the integrity of the letter writer. We . . . don't even know if they're Gay or not."[188] One reader warned, "Beware of the phony and non-gay that want to prey on us even from within the walls of Folsom, Pendleton, Michigan City, Travis, Lucasville, or wherever. They use OUR publications even as they sit in their jail cells as a means to get at the faggots."[189] One *Advocate* reader asked the editor of the pen pal section, "Isn't there any way you can weed out the non-gay mail order pimps from your list of prisoners who want mail?" writing that "your column is too good to be used by some tramp whose only aim is to 'use the queers.'" "Can't you screen these gays out," he asked, "or at least make sure they're gay?"[190]

Distinguishing between "real" and "phony" gays, however, was not always easy. A misunderstanding between prisoner Troy Lewis and *GCN*'s Mike Riegle illuminated some of the competing and unpredictable definitions of identity at work in interactions between prisoners and gays outside. Lewis had sent a pen pal request to *GCN*, in which he identified himself as "straight." When Riegle rejected the ad, specifying that the *GCN* pen pal section was for gay prisoners, Lewis responded in protest: "Well, Mike, I don't know how or what you consider the terms Gay, straight, etc . . . to be but my interpretation of straight is a homosexual that partake an *active* role playing (i.e. fucker) during the course of homosexuality, in contrast to 'a gay,'" who he defined as "a homosexual who partakes the *passive* role of homosexuality." "When I use the term 'straight,'" he concluded, "it doesn't exclude me from being homosexual too."[191] The self

understanding of some prisoners, in Lewis's case utterly confounding the
categories of the gay movement as well as those of the larger culture, was
difficult to assimilate into the sexual epistemology of even the most accommodating and expansive of gay activists.

Anxiety about the criminal as well as the sexual status of prisoners was
implicit in the many warnings about pen pal scams and "fake" gays. The
suspicions and prejudices of many gay men and lesbians who supported a
politics of prison advocacy were sometimes ignited when they were confronted with actual convicts. "Never have I seen one where the writer
reveals what he is in prison for," the editor of the *Bay Area Reporter* wrote
of prison pen pal ads in a warning to potential correspondents, "but when
they come from the maximum security prisons, I have to imagine the
reason is for more than jaywalking."[192] One reader wrote that "in fairness
to us readers, I think they should send a copy of their rap sheet to be published along with their letter. I'm sure most of those guys didn't get where
they are for helping grandmothers across the street."[193] One gay prisoner
wrote to the *Advocate* to complain that his pen pal stopped writing when
he told him that he was serving a sentence of ten years to life for armed
robbery.[194] Another reader warned that gay men who wrote to prisoners
were "ideal targets for everything from blackmail to murder."[195] One lesbian wrote to *GCN* in 1987 to "refuse to support the paper further as long
as it continues the asinine policy of supporting 'gay and lesbian' prisoners," her quotation marks raising questions about the authenticity of their
sexual identity. She added that she was "tired of seeing letters bitching
about how terrible prison is. They should have thought of that before
they committed a crime."[196] Comments like these reflected a marked shift
from the solidary position that "we are all prisoners," to a feeling of distance and disidentification, especially on the part of the predominantly
white, middle-class readers of gay magazines, from those behind bars.

Interest in gay advocacy on behalf of prisoners declined in the 1980s
and 1990s, evidenced by the discontinuation of prison pen pal projects,
often following exposés of scams perpetrated by prisoners on gay and lesbian correspondents and the dwindling coverage of prison issues in the
gay and lesbian press. In 1987, *RFD* renounced the Left's (and implicitly
its own) romanticized relationship with prisoners, which it traced to "a
certain resentment of authority which elevates the criminal to the rank
of hero." "The simple truth," *RFD* editors wrote, "is that most men in
prison are there because they belong there," adding that "some are truly
evil."[197] That change in position coincided with the transmutation of a
movement for sexual liberation into a movement dedicated to pursuing

equal rights and reflected a corresponding shift in the movement's commitments and priorities. Activist David Frey suggested as much, writing bluntly in 1980 that "the Gay Prisoner Activist is a role I see no future in." In part, Frey framed his objection to prison advocacy as a pragmatic calculation of winnable battles. "You cannot expect government institutions to allow magazines depicting illegal sex acts," Frey wrote, dismissing the long-standing fight against the prohibition of gay publications in prison. More broadly, Frey asserted, prison activism "serve[d] as a negative element in the overall debate" in the struggle for "Gay Rights." That struggle, Frey insisted, "must be a united one, with as little fragmentation as possible," and he worried that advocacy on behalf of the most stigmatized and marginalized members of the community threatened to fragment the "gay community." "Let's stay on the right path and keep Gay Rights a legislative issue," Frey urged. In his prescient conclusion that "legally sanctioned Gay marriage should be a primary concern for all of us," Frey anticipated the priorities of the gay and lesbian rights movement as they would evolve in later decades.[198]

Frey made these comments in 1980, a year before the ravages of the AIDS epidemic would begin to spur some gay men and lesbians toward more militant activism and radical social analysis. With few exceptions, however, gay and lesbian activists failed to take those forms of activism and analysis into work on behalf of prisoners.[199] In 1988, ACLU prison advocate Judy Greenspan recalled discussing prison AIDS activism with Mike Riegle, who "looked at me and said, 'Well, there's you and me.' . . . He was very depressed."[200] Riegle continued to work on behalf of prisoners until his own death from AIDS-related illness in 1992.[201]

: : :

Riegle called for gay men and lesbians to support prisoners as "the marginal people who get too far off the proper property/propriety line—the queer queers."[202] But prison sexual culture could be more capacious, heterogeneous, and troubling in its queerness than could be easily accommodated by an emerging gay rights politics. The community-building project of gay prison activism, radical in its vision and productive in many of its manifestations, confronted renegade sexual identifications and codes that mixed awkwardly and sometimes not at all with new visions, norms, and understandings of gay identity forged by activists. As Michel Foucault observed, even ostensibly liberatory discourses impose order through constructing norms of identity and practice. Activists struggled with the difficulty of assimilating some inmates into the gay and lesbian "family" being imagined into existence in the 1970s and 1980s. In so doing, they exposed the ironically normative and evangelizing impulses of gay liberation and of "modern" homosexuality more generally. Marked at various points by solidarity and meaningful connection across the divide of prison walls and, at others, by appropriation, pedagogy, misrecognition, and disidentification, the encounter of gay activists with prisoners illuminated the contours of new gay norms in the making.

In part, those new norms were advanced in the service of claims to respectability, as liberationist calls for sexual freedom and liberation gave way to liberal demands for gay rights and social inclusion. Anxiety about gay respectability was powerfully at work, certainly, in warnings about the criminal designs of prison pen pals, in ambivalence toward men attracted to minors, and in efforts to distinguish "modern" gay masculinity from the purportedly anachronistic stereotypes of gay male effeminacy. Questions of respectability, in prison activism as elsewhere, were bound up with questions of race. Racial difference, rarely marked or reflected directly on by lesbian and gay prison activists, shaped concerns about criminality in the 1970s and 1980s, as the mass incarceration of the late twentieth century and its disproportionate effects on people of color was beginning to gain momentum. Race was implicated, too, in the well-worn narrative of the sexually primitive and modern. Historian Lisa Duggan has recently charted the emergence of what she terms "the new homonormativity," marked by "a politics that does not contest dominant heteronormative assumptions and institutions but upholds and sustains them."[203] The story of gay prison activism, in part, locates and surveys some historical roots of that trend.

But more than respectability was at stake in these convergences and collisions between gay activists and prisoners. These encounters reveal a broader effort to shore up and stabilize the respectable homosexual subject and, in addition, to impose a gay paradigm posited as modern on a more multiform prison sexual culture and to enforce a homo/heterosexual binary system on the more complex set of identities and sensibilities of prisoners. As gay and lesbian activists would come reluctantly to understand, prison sexual culture exposed the limits of the range of dominant notions of sexuality presumed to be firmly in place by the late twentieth century and undermined presumptions of stable homosexuality as thoroughly as it did heterosexuality.

EPILOGUE

From their beginning, prisons were imagined to exist in a world apart. Indeed, separation from the outside world was fundamental to their design and central to their raison d'être, pursued in the belief that such forced disengagement would encourage habits of self-reflection and remorse in prisoners that might ultimately lead to their rehabilitation. Faith in prisons' rehabilitative powers waxed and waned over the course of the nineteenth and twentieth centuries. But as incarceration assumed its central place in the American criminal justice system and prisons proliferated, they came to be viewed as existing not only *in*, but *as* a world apart, nurturing strange, atavistic cultures, populated by prisoners who spoke their own often indecipherable language and lived by their own unique code.

The sexual aspects of that world attracted considerable attention beginning in the nineteenth century, from both within and beyond the prison and from both scholarly and popular quarters, and they continue to do so today. The participation in same-sex sex by prisoners who identified and were identified by others as healthy, upstanding, normal, or heterosexual (depending on the conceptual categories of the historical moment), stood as the most striking evidence of the profound alterity of prison life. Stories of masculine jockers devoted to prison wives, of men consolidating their heterosexual masculinity by forcing other men into sexual subordination, and of heterosexually married women with chil-

dren taking female husbands while behind bars suggested that the transformative power of prison culture was strong enough to rewrite the most
basic rules of the modern sexual order linking sexual desire and practices
to sexual identity and to defy its temporal march.

At the same time, many recognized that prison walls, however heavily fortified, could not seal the institution from the outside world. Prisons were acknowledged from their beginning to be porous. The nail file
smuggled in a cake is the iconic signifier of the prison's permeability, but
less material prison importations and exportations exposed the fiction of
a firm boundary demarcating inside and outside. People brought habits,
understandings, and expectations wrought from their pre-prison experience with them to prison, and they often returned to the outside world
with new ideas, perspectives, and even new identities forged behind bars.
Sexual ideas, attitudes, and understandings were among these prison importations and exportations.

Broader cultural preoccupations traversed prison walls as well. And as
I have shown, those concerns often attached themselves to the sexual life
of prisoners. A source of apprehension on its own terms, sex in prison was
also a useful proxy (as sex so often is) for wider-ranging anxieties. Stories of prison sex over the course of nearly two centuries distilled larger
cultural apprehensions not only about sexual instability but also about
male violence, male vulnerability, and male intimacy; about the weakness
of the national moral fiber; about interracial animosity, black anger, and
the politicization of African Americans; about the perceived durability
and danger of racialized underclass cultures; about women's autonomy
and criminality; and about changing gender roles and the instability of
gender identity, among others. Displacing those concerns onto prison sex
allowed them, at least in part, to be scrutinized at a safe remove and locked
behind bars.

HIV/AIDS in Prison

Any illusion that prisons were separate from the outside world was shat-
tered by the discovery of the first cases of prisoners diagnosed with the
disease complex that would come to be termed AIDS (Acquired Immunodeficiency Syndrome). In November of 1981, several prisoners in the
New York state prison system were diagnosed with a disease that had first
been identified and reported on by the Centers for Disease Control (CDC)
only five months earlier.[1] That discovery and its epidemic aftermath recast

and revivified anxieties about the relationship between the worlds behind and beyond bars.

In the wake of that finding, investigators attempted to measure the incidence of AIDS among prisoners. Those efforts were facilitated in 1984 by the identification of the Human Immunodeficiency Virus (HIV) as the cause of AIDS and, in the following year, by the development of a blood test capable of detecting the presence of antibodies to the virus. In late 1985, the National Institute of Justice, in cooperation with the American Correctional Association, began its first study of HIV/AIDS in the fifty state prison systems, the Federal Bureau of Prisons, and thirty-seven city and county jail systems.[2]

Conducted annually through 1997, those surveys revealed the distribution of prisoners with HIV/AIDS to be skewed dramatically by geographic region. Many U.S. prisons reported few cases of AIDS among prisoners through the first decade of the epidemic and some none at all. Fewer than 1 percent of prisoners in Alabama, Iowa, Kansas, Kentucky, Minnesota, Mississippi, Missouri, Nebraska, North Dakota, South Dakota, and Tennessee tested positive for the HIV virus in 1989.[3] Almost one-half of state and federal prisons and city and county jail systems reported ten or fewer cases in that year.[4] Other states, however, especially those in the urban, industrial regions of the Middle Atlantic and Northeast (primarily New York and New Jersey), reported high numbers.[5] In 1989, seven state and federal correctional systems accounted for almost 80 percent of total inmate AIDS cases.[6] And in those states, the rates of HIV infection among prisoners were alarmingly high. A study conducted in 1988 found that 17.4 percent of male prisoners and 18.8 percent of female prisoners tested anonymously in New York State, the second largest correctional system in the nation, were HIV positive.[7] In that year, AIDS became the leading cause of death among New York's prisoners, responsible for almost 60 percent of all prisoner fatalities.[8] Translated into real numbers, that meant that by the end of the 1980s, more than one thousand prisoners in New York had died from complications related to AIDS.[9]

At the end of 1996, fifteen years into what had become a global AIDS pandemic, the rate of confirmed AIDS cases among state and federal prison inmates was found to be six times higher than the "general population."[10] That deceptively benign and ostensibly neutral descriptor worked in insidious ways to dilute sexual, racial, and class differences among Americans and thereby to erase the disproportionately devastating effects of HIV/AIDS on poor communities of color, gay men, and injection drug users. It worked as well as to construct prisoners as a separate and stigma-tized class, virtually always already infected or likely to be infected, and to conjure prison as a nearly unique incubator of the disease.

But there was nothing exotic about HIV/AIDS in prison. The virus in its prison incarnation tracked its progression outside prison walls among injection drug users and people of color, groups long undercounted by the CDC and mistakenly associated with a "second wave" of the epidemic.[11] In prison and out, the virus followed lines of poverty, deprivation, drug use, and the high-risk sexual practices sometimes shaped by those condi-tions (including those that took place in the context of coercion as well as choices so compromised they were hardly choices at all). It is also impor-tant to note that the emergence of the AIDS epidemic, in prison and out, coincided almost exactly with the rising epidemic of mass incarceration in the United States. The average daily population of prison and jail inmates in the United States increased from just under 500,000 in 1980 to nearly 1.2 million in 1990 and to more than 2 million in 2000.[12] Much of that striking escalation could be traced to the nationwide policy of mandatory sentencing for drug offenders, as incarceration was deployed as the central tactic of the "War on Drugs." In 2001, 57 percent of federal prisoners were imprisoned for drug-related offenses, constituting a rise of 700 per-cent over the course of ten years.[13] The percentage of injection drug users among the inmate population through the 1980s and 1990s was variously estimated between 30 and 80 percent.[14]

Because of the combined effect of the War on Drugs, mass incarcera-tion, and the disproportionate arrest and incarceration of people of color (especially African Americans and Latinos) for drug-related offenses, the American prison population came to closely mirror a growing segment of the nation's HIV-infected population.[15] As a consequence of this per-fect storm of overdetermination, the numbers of prisoners with AIDS reflected the disproportionate rates of HIV infection among members of populations who were increasingly overrepresented in prison popula-tions. As the National Commission on AIDS made clear in its 1991 report, "By choosing mass imprisonment as the federal and state governments' response to the use of drugs, we have created a de facto policy of incarcer-ating more and more individuals with HIV infection."[16]

Despite these numbers, AIDS in prison did not capture significant or sustained media attention. In the 1980s and through the early 1990s, the media focused almost exclusively on AIDS as afflicting gay, primar-ily white, men, who were so closely associated with the disease syn-drome that it was originally termed Gay-Related Immune Deficiency, or

GRID.[17] The discovery of AIDS among prison populations did, however, lead to alarmed and sometimes panicked warnings within correctional and prisoner advocacy circles about its prevalence and dire predictions about its nearly inevitable spread. Because of the intimacy of incarceration and typically substandard medical care, prisons had long been associated with the transmission of communicable diseases, especially tuberculosis and hepatitis. The prevalence in prison of unprotected sex and the sharing of needles for both injecting smuggled drugs and for tattooing created what some investigators termed a "whirlpool of risk" for the transmission of HIV/AIDS.[18] In 1987, Alvin Bronstein, Executive Director of the American Civil Liberties Union's National Prison Project, declared AIDS "the most significant crisis facing America's prisons and jails in this century."[19] In that same year, Dr. Thomas Brewer, the chief medical officer for the Maryland Division of Correction, predicted a "whopping epidemic" of AIDS cases in the state's prisons.[20] In 1994, the Expert Committee on AIDS and Prisons likewise presaged an "impending disaster."[21]

Recognition of the urgency of the problem of AIDS in prison might have prompted prison officials to implement measures to minimize its devastating effects, stem its spread, and protect HIV-positive prisoners and those with AIDS from stigma and discriminatory treatment. Such measures would have included better health care in prisons and participation in new drug regimens and trials, education of officers and prisoners about the ways in which HIV could be transmitted and reassurance of the lack of risk through casual contact, and the availability of practical forms of risk reduction such as condoms and bleach for the cleaning of needles. Instead, responses to HIV/AIDS among prisoners echoed patterns and logics established long before the epidemic. Despite the widespread recognition that prisoners most often contracted HIV through injection drug use prior to incarceration, the disease was sexualized from its beginning through its close association with gay men. The overdetermination of both AIDS and prison with same-sex sex invited familiar scripts, established over the course of more than a century and traced in this book. As a consequence, prison AIDS panics were framed in registers well rehearsed over the course of at least a century and produced predictably blinkered responses.

Fears of contagion and contamination had long structured discourses of prison sex. With the emergence of the AIDS epidemic, those fears were literalized and amplified. In earlier periods, observers worried about the production of homosexuality in prison and the post-prison sexual consequences of incarceration. The introduction of HIV/AIDS gave new substance and urgency to anxieties about the consequences of prison sex to the larger culture. "Prison walls effectively restrain criminals," investigators warned in 1996, "but not the AIDS virus."[22] That concern could be expressed in ways that acknowledged prisoners as members of larger social worlds. "Prisoners are the community," the Joint United Nations Programme on HIV/AIDS stated in 1996. "They come from the community, they return to it. Protection of prisoners is protection of our communities."[23] But warnings of the spread of HIV/AIDS from the prison to the outside community were more often cast in panicked representations of the prison as an ideal "breeding ground," once for perversion and now for a literal and fatal disease intimately associated with perversion. A Syracuse newspaper characterized AIDS as being "produced in the state prison system at an alarming rate," as if the prison itself conjured the virus.[24] Anxieties about the spread of AIDS from prison into the larger community also promoted representations of urban communities of color as both criminal and diseased. "In city after city," journalist Brent Staples reported, "newly released felons return to a handful of neighborhoods where many households have some prison connection," creating "prison ZIP codes" that were "public health disaster areas and epicenters of blood borne diseases like hepatitis C and AIDS."[25]

While many pointed to the public health crisis posed by AIDS in prison, some recognized a unique opportunity for intervention. Because of the high turnover of prisoners, some noted, the criminal justice system might play an important public health role by treating HIV-infected prisoners and educating others to avoid infection behind bars and after release. Some characterized prisons as "optimal settings for the development, delivery, and study of AIDS education and prevention programs."[26] In outlining a public policy agenda for criminal justice, some recommended making more resources available for education, counseling, and early detection. Given the control they exercised over inmates' lives, prisons also offered unique opportunities for the treatment of HIV and AIDS. In some cases, HIV-infected prisoners received antiretroviral therapy for the first time while incarcerated—testimony to the failings and inequities of the American health care system rather than to the superiority of health care in prisons.[27] "Taking advantage of the period of confinement would serve both the individual and society by controlling communicable diseases in large urban communities," correctional health care specialists Jordan Glaser and Robert Greifinger wrote.[28]

Instead of capitalizing on such possibilities, however, prison officials sounded another familiar theme by maintaining the hopeful fiction that

they might respond to HIV and AIDS among prisoners simply by identifying and segregating those afflicted. In May 1987, President Ronald Reagan, close to the end of his second term in office and in his first ever public
speech on the epidemic, called for mandatory testing of federal prisoners
for the HIV virus in the interest of "protect[ing] uninfected inmates and
their families." [29] He did so over the objection of the U.S. surgeon general,
Dr. C. Everett Koop, as well as the protestations of many corrections experts, but with widespread support from many prison officers, politicians,
and the American public more generally. Although the National Association of State Corrections Administrators voted against mass mandatory
HIV testing of prisoners, most state correctional facilities employed testing protocols in some form. The first decade of the AIDS epidemic, especially, witnessed a rush to HIV testing in prisons. In 1989, sixteen state
and federal prison systems conducted mandatory HIV antibody screening
of all incoming inmates, all current inmates, and all inmates at the time
of their release. [30] Over the objections of civil liberties advocates and some
correctional authorities, who argued that testing compromised the confidentiality of inmates' medical records and could also make them vulnerable to ostracism, harassment, or even violence, prison officials proposed
that the protection of correctional staff and other inmates necessarily took
precedence over HIV-positive inmates' right to privacy. [31]

   Testing prison inmates en masse for HIV appealed to people's sense, in
leading prison AIDS investigator Theodore Hammett's words, that such
a protocol represented a "'magic bullet' for AIDS." [32] Large-scale testing
held out that hope, in part, because it seemed to promise the possibility
of cordoning off the threat. A growing number of prisons used the HIV-
antibody test to identify and segregate seropositive prisoners. While most
institutions segregated prisoners diagnosed with AIDS, some segregated
asymptomatic prisoners who simply tested positive for antibodies to the
HIV virus. The Colorado prison system was among the first to segregate
HIV-positive male prisoners in 1987, and others followed.

   Proponents argued that such segregation was protective rather than
punitive, but these policies had the same discriminatory impact suffered
by segregated gay and lesbian inmates, and by African Americans long
segregated in prison as well. Prisoners who were HIV-positive were often excluded from educational, vocational, and recreational activities, as
well as from prerelease programs that would allow them to accrue credits
necessary for early release. Prisoners diagnosed with AIDS in New Jersey,
for instance, were segregated in a "special medical unit" and were prohibited from participating in work-release programs, religious services,

and education courses.[33] Prisoners with AIDS in New York's Auburn prison were not allowed to eat in the mess hall or use the gymnasium.[34] In some institutions, HIV-positive prisoners were denied visitors altogether; other prisons allowed them only "noncontact" visits.[35] As a consequence, HIV-infected prisoners and prisoners diagnosed with AIDS were incarcerated under extraordinarily isolated, demoralizing, and discriminatory conditions. One Georgia prisoner wrote, "I was segregated in a cell with 'Beware' signs. They gave me reason to believe I was going to die shortly, and it broke me down mentally and emotionally."[36] As ACLU advocate Alvin Bronstein told prison officials in 1987, "You are punishing people for having a disease."[37]

The segregation of HIV-positive prisoners and prisoners with AIDS was also a stigmatizing brand, recalling the practices of segregating homosexuals and the use of punitive markers of sexual deviance imposed in many prisons. Compounding the stigma of segregation, prisons employed other identifying practices that compounded the stigmas and pains particular to this devastating disease. Women prisoners in Alabama who tested positive for HIV were required to wear surgical masks when outside their isolation cells. Seropositive male prisoners in Alabama were forced to use plastic utensils or disposable wooden ice cream sticks to eat their meals.[38] Perhaps the most disturbing example of discriminatory and undeniably punitive treatment was in New Orleans' Old Parish Prison, where HIV-positive prisoners and prisoners diagnosed with AIDS were required to wear "stun belts" during their transport to and from medical facilities. Typically used to control the most violent prisoners, these electroshock devices, when activated, caused muscle immobilization and excruciating pain. And as one critic noted, "The belt . . . acts as a visible status marker that encroaches on HIV-positive inmates' right to confidentiality and singles them out for further discrimination or abuse."[39]

Echoing earlier justifications for the segregation of gay prisoners, prison officials argued that segregation of HIV-positive prisoners was intended for their own protection. But in identifying the health status of prisoners and associating them with a dreaded and stigmatized disease, testing and segregation policies in prison could actually compromise prisoners' safety. Inmates reported death threats and violent attacks against HIV-positive prisoners.[40] In prison, one reporter found, "a rumor that an inmate carries the AIDS virus can pose almost as great a threat to his well-being as the disease itself."[41] Not surprisingly, the epidemic led to an upsurge in the ostracism, harassment, and sometimes violent intimidation of gay inmates suspected by default of being infected.[42]

The policies of mass testing and segregation followed by many prison systems in the mid-1980s led to the discriminatory treatment of prisoners with HIV/AIDS. Other preventive measures not taken in most prisons exacerbated the threat of HIV infection for all prisoners. Only a very small handful of prison and jail systems made condoms available to help prisoners protect themselves and their partners. Vermont and Mississippi provided condoms in their state prisons, as did municipal correctional systems in Washington, D.C., New York City, San Francisco, and Philadelphia. However, the vast majority of U.S. prisons and jails refused to do so. Condoms in most carceral institutions were (and are today) considered contraband, and getting caught with one was a serious, punishable offense. One Vacaville prisoner in 1992 reported a thriving "black market in condoms" at the prison but noted that "possession of them is cause for serious write-up and a loss of up to six months of time."[43]

Underlying the no-condom policy of most prisons was a long history of prohibitions against same-sex sex between prisoners and moralizing ideas about homosexuality. Prison officials argued that distributing condoms would implicitly condone prohibited and, in some jurisdictions (until *Lawrence v. Texas* struck down the criminal prohibition of homosexual sex in state sodomy statutes in 2003), illegal behavior. As Charles Colson, conservative evangelical Christian spokesman and chair of Prison Fellowship Ministries in Washington, D.C., argued in 1991, "There is only one reason to distribute condoms to inmates—and in the District, sodomy is as illegal as drug smuggling."[44] Thomas Coughlin, commissioner of New York's Department of Correctional Services, stated in 1988 that "allowing condoms could be interpreted as an endorsement of homosexual activity."[45] Some prison officials favored the prophylactic power of terror over that of condoms. "The approach I take," Coughlin stated, "is to remind inmates that not only are ['homosexual relations,' the use of needles, and the practice of tattooing] against the rules, but all three can now kill them because of AIDS."[46] Ronald Shansky, the medical director of the Illinois Department of Corrections, seconded this approach, stating plainly in 1987 that "we believe that . . . preying on the potential fears and anxieties of the inmates, is the best way of preventing the spread of this illness."[47] But as another group of investigators noted, "Denying prisoners access to condoms may be sentencing them to death."[48]

Some used understandings of rape in men's prisons, almost entirely conflated by the 1980s and 1990s with prison sex as a whole, to justify prisons' no-condom policy or to minimize the effects of denying condoms to prisoners. Following the trend of prison representations since the late 1960s, it proved considerably easier to conceive of sex between men in prison as nearly inevitably forced and violent. Even the most sympathetic and progressive thinking about AIDS in prison, almost by necessity, made reference to rape in prison and rarely if ever considered consensual sex behind bars. Few believed that prison rapists would place a high priority on protecting themselves or their unwilling partners with a condom. As prison activists noted in 1987, "Because rape is an irrational power trip and less a sexual act, it is doubtful fear of contracting AIDS would deter many assailants."[49] Urvashi Vaid, former staff attorney with the ACLU's National Prison Project and former executive director of the National Gay and Lesbian Task Force (NGLTF), insisted against the grain of many reports on AIDS in prison that sex in prison was "a fact of prison life" and that much of it was consensual. In commenting on HIV in prison, however, she emphasized the risks of nonconsensual sex, adding that "the epidemiology of AIDS, unfortunately, gives rapists little reason to modify their behavior," since the receptive participant in both anal and oral sex "bears the higher risk of contracting the virus."[50]

The concern about the connection between rape in prison and the transmission of AIDS was buttressed by several high-profile lawsuits by prisoners who claimed to have contracted AIDS as a consequence of prison rape.[51] It was heightened as well by the publication of a lengthy report titled "No Escape: Male Rape in Prison," published by the international human rights organization Human Rights Watch in 2001, which used surveys conducted over three years and interviews with over two hundred prisoners in thirty-four states to document violent rape as a regular feature of American prison life. This attention to prison rape lay the groundwork for the bipartisan legislation of the Prison Rape Elimination Act, signed into law by President George W. Bush in 2003 and motivated in large part by concern about the spread of HIV/AIDS in prison through sexual assault.[52] Brent Staples characterized the act as "at its heart, a public health law," promoting "sorely needed studies of disease transmission in the criminal justice system."[53]

A very few of the most progressive advocates of condoms in prisons made occasional recommendations, usually as an afterthought, for distributing dental dams in women's prisons. While AIDS in women's prisons gave rise to warnings about its transmission through lesbian sex and, according to some reports by women prisoners, intensified prohibitions against any physical contact between women, the virus was found to be only very rarely transmitted through sexual contact between women.[54] To those willing to grapple with the realities of women's prison condi-

tions, the epidemic drew attention away from the specter of prison lesbianism to the phenomenon of sexual relationships between women
prisoners and male guards, a long-standing but long submerged issue in
women's prisons. Those relationships were often coercive, sometimes violently so. Even when understood to be consensual, they inevitably took
place within the most dramatic inequities of power. Few were inclined to
draw attention to these relationships, however, especially in the context
of discussions of AIDS in prison.

In largely ignoring the conditions of women in prison, attention to
AIDS in prison mirrored in yet another way the long trend of thinking
about sex in prison over the course of nearly two centuries. Studies and
reporting on AIDS in prison were nearly uniformly focused on men, and
especially in the first decade of the epidemic, few even acknowledged the
plight of HIV-infected women in prison. This lack of attention was striking, ironic, and ultimately lethal, since studies showed that the rate of
HIV infection was slightly higher among women prisoners. At the end
of 1996, 3.5 percent of all female inmates were known to be HIV positive, as compared to 2.3 percent of male inmates.[55] The rate of increase in
the total number of cases of AIDS among prisoners was also observed to
be faster among women than men as early as 1988.[56] As with the case of
men, the geographic distribution of HIV/AIDS among women prisoners
was skewed dramatically by region. A study conducted in 1987 and 1988
revealed that almost 20 percent of women entering the New York state
prison system carried antibodies for HIV.[57] By 1990, AIDS was the leading cause of death for women prisoners as well as for men.[58] And in northeastern U.S. prisons more generally, 13 percent of women were found in
2000 to be HIV infected compared to 7.2 percent of men.[59]

Although incarceration rates among women were increasing dramatically during this period (nearly double the already high rates of incarceration for men by 1980), there were still far fewer women in American prisons and jails than men, and they comprised a relatively small percentage
of the total population of incarcerated people.[60] The number of women
in state and federal prisons increased eightfold from 1980 to 2005, from
around 12,300 to 107,500.[61] But those numbers were dwarfed by the
enormous numbers of incarcerated men. In 2005, there were well over 2
million men in the nation's prisons and jails.

That numerical differential goes some distance toward explaining the
relative lack of attention to HIV/AIDS among women prisoners. But the
nexus of race, class, and criminal status contributed in significant ways as
well to deflect attention from HIV-positive women in prison. Political

scientist Cathy Cohen and others have shown that women with AIDS received most attention when they could be cast as "innocent" victims, infected by a drug-using male partner, a deceiving bisexual lover, or through a blood transfusion.[62] Because so many women were incarcerated for sex work and drug use, they defied easy construction as innocent victims.[63]

In many ways, then, patterns of thinking and acting in response to HIV/AIDS in prison echoed past logics, panics, and efforts over the course of a long history to defuse the troubling implications of prison sexual culture. Widely sexualized in the larger culture, HIV/AIDS came to be closely associated with same-sex sex in prison. That overdetermined association gave rise to familiar scripts and responses, shaped over the course of more than a century.

At the same time, reckoning with the epidemic forced a reconsideration of the meaning of sex in prison and its practitioners, at least in some quarters. Much of that reconsideration was promoted by prisoners themselves, in peer education groups they initiated to respond to the AIDS epidemic. In the absence of commitment on the part of prison officials to AIDS education, prisoners organized peer education groups, sometimes with the official sanction of prison administrators, sometimes without, and sometimes in direct opposition to prison policy.[64] In addition to pressing for decent medical care, compassionate release for dying prisoners, and an end to punitive segregation, prisoner-led AIDS groups were devoted to safer sex education aimed at countering the fears and phobias that surrounded the epidemic. At the same time, they combated the fantasy, especially among male prisoners, that heterosexual identity granted immunity from HIV/AIDS. Prisoner-organized groups insisted that thinking about sexuality in terms of identity was insufficient when dealing with HIV/AIDS. Project Walk Tall, a Houston-based peer education program, taught prisoners that sexually transmitted diseases "are not limited to one sexual orientation."[65] "Remember, it's not how you label yourself—gay, straight, or bisexual—that's important," a pamphlet published by the ACLU with help from prisoners stated. "What you actually do or have done is what puts you at risk for AIDS."[66]

Nonidentitarian ways of thinking about sex promoted in prisoner-organized AIDS education groups ramified beyond prison walls. Their impact was reflected in the broader recognition in public health discourse and policy of "men who have sex with men," or MSM, an epidemiological category coined during the AIDS pandemic intended to convey that sexual practice, not sexual identity, correlated with risk for HIV/AIDS and to communicate information about risk beyond the group of men who identified as gay. More broadly, prisoner-initiated AIDS education organizations exposed what had been the case throughout this long history: the homo/heterosexual binary could not capture the complexity of human sexual desire, identification, and practice. Indeed, the emergence of HIV/AIDS proved that it was dangerous to think in those terms.

: : :

I opened this book by speculating about the value of cultivating historical curiosity about sexual expressions assumed either to have no history or to be historically out of sync with sexuality "as we know it." That sense of knowingness has led historians to assume that at least by the mid-twentieth century, a homo/heterosexual binary constituted the dominant if not universal way of thinking about sex. The responses to sex in prison—the complex, contradictory, and often bewildered efforts to explain it (and explain it away)—expose some of the work involved in creating that sexual ideology as dominant and in patrolling its borders. In part, I hope to have contributed to a critical history of a sexual ideology that announces itself as "modern" and has come to be taken for granted but is actually historically distinctive, circumscribed, and contested.

This history exposes some of the persistent challenges to that sexual ideology. Prison is but one locus from which modern sexuality has been confounded and destabilized by sexual acts, desires, and identities that failed (and fail) to map neatly onto categories of "gay" or "straight." Their long history suggests that the homo/heterosexual binary was not only "stunningly recent," as George Chauncey so provocatively and generatively proposed, but that it was also remarkably uneven and considerably less hegemonic and less coherent than historians have often assumed.[67] The phenomenon of sex in prison suggests the fundamental instability of the modern (and perhaps any) sexual regime, challenging not only the edifice of the sexual binary but also historians' ready acceptance of that binary as the truth of sexuality in the latter half of the twentieth century. The turn to a "modern" sexual model was never universal or complete. Multiple understandings of sex and gender overlapped in time and space and continue to do so. The long history of sex in prison underlines the complexity of desire and its enactments, behind bars certainly, but beyond them as well.

NOTES

INTRODUCTION

1. John Rosevear, "Time," in *Getting Busted: Personal Experiences of Arrest, Trial, and Prison,* ed. Ross Firestone (New York: Pyramid, 1973), 234.

2. George Harsh, *Lonesome Road* (New York: Norton, 1971), 111. In a speculative lecture in 1967, Michel Foucault proposed the concept of "heterotopias," which "more often than not" were "connected with temporal discontinuities." Foucault termed those spaces that housed people who transgressed norms, including prisons as well as rest homes and psychiatric hospitals, "heterotopias of deviation," characterized by their rupture of traditional time ("Of Other Spaces," trans. Jay Miskowiec, *Diacritics* 16 [1986]: 25). My concerns and questions in this book have been shaped by recent work on queer temporalities, including Judith Halberstam, *In a Queer Time and Place: Transgender Bodies, Subcultural Lives* (New York: New York University Press, 2005); Carolyn Dinshaw, *Getting Medieval: Sexualities and Communities, Pre- and Postmodern* (Durham, NC: Duke University Press, 1999); Carla Freccero, *Queer/Early/Modern* (Durham, NC: Duke University Press, 2006).

3. Michel Foucault, *The History of Sexuality*, vol. I, *An Introduction*, trans. Robert Hurley (New York: Pantheon, 1978), esp. 69–70, 77–80. For historical explorations of this phenomenon, see also David Halperin, *One Hundred Years of Homosexuality and Other Essays on Greek Love* (New York: Routledge, 1990); George Chauncey, *Gay New York: Gender, Urban Culture, and the Making of the Gay Male World, 1890–1940* (New York: Basic, 1994); Jeffrey Weeks, *Coming Out* (London: Pluto, 1977); John D'Emilio and Estelle B. Freedman, *Intimate Matters: A History of Sexuality in America* (New York: Perennial, 1989), esp. 171–235. For a reconsideration of Foucault and the acts-to-identity trajectory charted by historians of sexuality, see David Halperin, "Forgetting Foucault: Acts, Identities, and the History of Sexuality," *Representations* 63 (Summer 1998): 93–120.

4. Bérubé addresses this issue most directly in *Coming Out under Fire: The History of Gay Men and Women in World War II* (New York: Free Press, 1990), 191–93. See also John Costello, *Virtue under Fire* (Boston: Little, Brown, 1985), esp. 101–19. The military offers an especially interesting comparison with the prison, since the former is such an exalted site of citizenship, manliness, and patriotism, while the prison is a fundamentally stigmatized space associated with criminality and radical disfranchisement. That difference, I suspect, has contributed to the attractiveness of the military as a site of historical interest and the relative lack of appeal of the prison.

5. See Martha Vicinus, *Independent Women: Work and Community for Single Women, 1850–1920* (Chicago: University of Chicago Press, 1985), 187–210; Nancy Sahli, "Smashing: Women's Relationships before the Fall," *Chrysalis* 8 (Summer 1979): 17–27; Carroll Smith-Rosenberg, "The Female World of Love and Ritual: Relations between Women in Nineteenth-Century America," *Signs* 1 (Autumn 1975): 1–29; Helen Lefkowitz Horowitz, *Alma Mater: Design and Experience in the Women's Colleges from Their Nineteenth-Century Beginnings to the 1930s* (New York: Knopf, 1984), 166–67.

6. "The living world is a continuum in each and every one of its aspects," Kinsey and his associates wrote. "The sooner we learn this concerning human sexual behavior the sooner we shall reach a sound understanding of the realities of sex" (Alfred C. Kinsey, Wardell B. Pomeroy, and Clyde E. Martin, *Sexual Behavior in the Human Male* [Philadelphia: W. B. Saunders, 1948], 639). On Kinsey's efforts in this regard, see Jennifer Terry, *An American Obsession: Science, Medicine, and Homosexuality in Modern Society* (Chicago: University of Chicago Press, 1999), 301–4; Miriam G. Reumann, *American Sexual Character: Sex, Gender, and National Identity in the Kinsey Reports* (Berkeley: University of California Press, 2005), 166–83; Janice M. Irvine, *Disorders of Desire: Sex and Gender in Modern American Sexology* (Philadelphia: Temple University Press, 1990), 53–54.

7. Donald Clemmer, *The Prison Community* (Boston: Christopher Publishing House, 1940), 249, 256. Lee Bowker likewise stated that "female correctional subcultures . . . don't seem to have changed much over the years" (*Prisons and Prisoners: A Bibliographic Guide* [San Francisco: R & E Research Associates, 1978]), 46. In their 1982 study of sex in men's prisons, Wayne S. Wooden and Jay Parker declared "the situation in prison" to have remained "relatively unchanged" over the course of one hundred and fifty years (*Men behind Bars: Sexual Exploitation in Prison* [New York: Plenum Press, 1982], 205).

8. Thomas Mott Osborne, *Prisons and Common Sense* (Philadelphia: Lippincott, 1924), 89.

9. Victor F. Nelson, *Prison Days and Nights* (Boston: Little, Brown, 1933), 140.

10. Stephen "Donny" Donaldson, "A Million Jockers, Punks, and Queens: Sex among American Male Prisoners and Its Implications for Concepts of Sexual Orientation" (lecture delivered at Columbia University, February 4, 1993), SPR: Stop Prisoner Rape, http://www.spr.org/en/docs/doc_01_lecture.asp, accessed March 18, 2007.

11. Donald Tucker, "A Punk's Song: View from the Inside," in *Male Rape*, ed. Anthony M. Scacco (New York: AMS Press, 1982), 58.

12. For the formative examples of each of these arguments, see John D'Emilio,

"Capitalism and Gay Identity," in *Powers of Desire: The Politics of Sexuality*, ed. Ann Snitow, Christine Stansell, and Sharon Thompson (New York: Monthly Review Press, 1983): 100–113; Chauncey, *Gay New York*; Terry, *An American Obsession*.

13. Donna Penn has observed that "women's prisons have been largely overlooked as a valuable site for studying the historical construction of lesbianism" ("Queer: Theorizing Politics and History," *Radical History Review* 62 [Spring 1995]: 36). For important exceptions, see Estelle B. Freedman, "The Prison Lesbian: Race, Class, and the Construction of the Aggressive Female Homosexual, 1915–1965," *Feminist Studies* 22 (Summer 1996): 397–423; Sarah Potter, "'Undesirable Relations': Same-Sex Relationships and the Meaning of Sexual Desire at a Women's Reformatory during the Progressive Era," *Feminist Studies* 30 (Summer 2004): 394–415; Chauncey, *Gay New York*, 91–96.

14. Vernon A. Rosario, "Homosexual Bio-Histories: Genetic Nostalgias and the Quest for Paternity," in *Science and Homosexualities*, ed. Vernon A. Rosario (New York: Routledge, 1997), 7.

15. Halperin, *One Hundred Years of Homosexuality*, 39.

16. Jack Abbott, "On 'Women,'" *New York Review of Books* 28, no. 10 (June 11, 1981), 17, quoted in Halperin, *One Hundred Years of Homosexuality*, 38–39.

17. Halperin, *One Hundred Years of Homosexuality*, 38–39.

18. Norval Morris and David J. Rothman, eds., *The Oxford History of the Prison: The Practice of Punishment in Western Society* (New York: Oxford University Press, 1995), vii. Foucault proposes that because the prison "appeared so bound up and at such a deep level with the very functioning of society . . . it seemed to have no alternative, as if carried along by the very movement of history" (*Discipline and Punish: The Birth of the Prison*, trans. Alan Sheridan [New York: Pantheon, 1977], 232).

19. Important exceptions include Patricia O'Brien, *The Promise of Punishment: Prisons in Nineteenth-Century France* (Princeton, NJ: Princeton University Press, 1982), esp. 90–107; Ruth M. Alexander, *The "Girl Problem": Female Sexual Delinquency in New York, 1900–1930* (Ithaca, NY: Cornell University Press, 1995).

20. Halperin, *One Hundred Years of Homosexuality*, 38.

21. Postcolonial theorists, anthropologists, and historians have exposed the ethnocentrism in the developmental narrative that positions a primitive other against a modern us. Halperin, for instance, notes the "noxious political effects" of pronouncing some forms of sexual organization "modern" and others "primitive" or "backward" by comparison. Such a progress narrative, he writes, "not only promotes a highly invidious opposition between sexually advanced and sexually retrograde cultures but also fails to take account of the complexity of contemporary transnational formations of sexuality" ("Introduction: In Defense of Historicism," in *How to Do the History of Homosexuality* [Chicago: University of Chicago Press, 2002], 18, 14). On anthropologists' use of temporal terms to communicate cultural difference and cultural hierarchy, see Johannes Fabian, *Time and the Other: How Anthropology Makes Its Object* (New York: Columbia University Press, 1983).

22. Eve Kosofsky Sedgwick writes that "the topos of 'homosexuality as we know it today' . . . has provided a rhetorically necessary fulcrum point for the denaturalizing

work of the past done by many historians" but that the "unfortunate side effect of this move has been implicitly to underwrite the notion that 'homosexuality as we conceive of it today' itself comprises a coherent definitional field rather than a space of overlapping, contradictory, and conflictual definitional forces." Such projects, she argues, "risk reinforcing a dangerous consensus of knowingness about the genuinely *unknown.*" (*Epistemology of the Closet* [Berkeley: University of California Press, 1990], 44–45).

23. Martin F. Manalansan IV, *Global Divas: Filipino Gay Men in the Diaspora* (Durham, NC: Duke University Press, 2003). See also Richard Phillips, Diane Watt, and David Shuttleton, eds., *De-Centering Sexualities: Politics and Representations beyond the Metropolis* (New York and London: Routledge, 2000).

24. John Howard, *Men Like That: A Southern Queer History* (Chicago: University of Chicago Press, 1999), xviii.

25. Foucault, *Discipline and Punish.*

26. Frank Tannenbaum, "Prison Cruelty," *Atlantic Monthly* 125 (April 1920): 434.

27. Researchers used prisoners as subjects for a wide range of experiments. Radiation experiments were conducted on prisoners from the 1940s to the 1970s. In 1944, hundreds of inmates at Illinois's Stateville Prison were infected with malaria to aid researchers in finding a more effective means of treating troops in the Pacific during World War II (see Joseph E. Ragen and Charles Finston, *Inside the World's Toughest Prison* [Springfield, IL: Charles C. Thomas, 1962], 391–95; Nathan F. Leopold, Jr., *Life Plus 99 Years* [Garden City, NY: Doubleday, 1958], 305–55). Allen Hornblum documents the medical experimentation carried out in Philadelphia's Holmesburg Prison from the mid-1940s to the 1970s, testing the effects of cosmetics and chemical warfare agents, in *Acres of Skin: Human Experiments at Holmesburg Prison* (New York: Routledge, 1999). On the use of prisoners for human experimentation more generally, see Andrew Goliszek, *In the Name of Science: A History of Secret Programs, Medical Research, and Human Experimentation* (New York: St. Martin's Press, 2003); Susan Lederer, *Subjected to Science: Human Experimentation in America before the Second World War* (Baltimore: Johns Hopkins University Press, 1995).

28. Vernon C. Branham, foreword to *Mentality and Homosexuality* by Samuel Kahn (Boston: Meador Publishing Co., 1937), 6.

29. Kahn, *Mentality and Homosexuality*, 29.

30. Jonathan Ned Katz, *The Invention of Heterosexuality* (New York: Penguin, 1995). Foucault announced his plan to study "the emergence of the power of normalization" in a lecture delivered in 1975. (See Foucault, *Abnormal: Lectures at the Collège de France, 1974–1975*, trans. Graham Burchell [New York: Picador, 2003], 25–26). Almost ten years after Katz's call to historians to pursue this elusive and important subject, Annette Schlichter wrote that "there remains a wide range of work to be done to arrive at a more nuanced understanding of the construction of heterosexuality as an institution and an identity position" ("Queer at Last? Straight Intellectuals and Desire for Transgression," *GLQ: A Journal of Lesbian and Gay Studies* 10, no. 4 [2004]: 557).

31. Richard Dyer, "White," in *The Matter of Images: Essays on Representations* (London: Routledge, 1993), 141. Eve Kosofsky Sedgwick similarly acknowledges the "stubborn

barriers to making [heterosexuality] accountable, to making it so much as visible, in the framework of projects of historicizing and hence denaturalizing sexuality. The making historically visible of heterosexuality is difficult because under its institutional pseudonyms such as Inheritance, Marriage, Dynasty, Family, Domesticity, and Population, heterosexuality has been permitted to masquerade so fully as History itself—when it has not presented itself as the totality of Romance" ("Queer and Now," in *Tendencies* (Durham, NC: Duke University Press, 1993), 10–11.

32. Eli Lehrer, "The Most-Silent Crime," *National Review* (April 29, 2003); Jane Eisner, "Inmate Rape Is the Dirty Secret of a Nation Obsessed with Jails," *Philadelphia Inquirer* (April 26, 2001). In arguing for the Prison Rape Reduction Act of 2002, Virginia Congressman Frank R. Wolf, stated that "prison rape, to be sure, is not a dinner conversation issue. For years, no one—no one—has talked about it, much less acted on it" (U.S. Senate Committee on the Judiciary, *The Prison Rape Reduction Act of 2002: Hearing before the Committee on the Judiciary*, 107th Cong., 2d sess., July 31, 2002, Serial No. J-107-99 [Washington, DC: U.S. Government Printing Office, 2003], 3).

33. O'Brien, *The Promise of Punishment*, 9. Until recently, most histories of the prison have focused on its institutional and administrative aspects, the social forces that have shaped various penal systems, the history of prison reform, and changes in prison architecture rather than on the lives and experiences of prisoners.

34. Ann-Louise Shapiro, *Breaking the Codes: Female Criminality in Fin-de-Siècle Paris* (Stanford, CA: Stanford University Press, 1996), 50.

35. Donaldson, "A Million Jockers, Punks, and Queens," 2.

36. On the tradition of writing by prisoners, see H. Bruce Franklin, introduction to *Prison Writing in Twentieth-Century America*, ed. H. Bruce Franklin (New York: Penguin, 1998); W. B. Carnochan, "The Literature of Confinement," in *The Oxford History of the Prison*, ed. Morris and Rothman; Herman K. Spector, "What Men Write in Prison," *Tomorrow* 5 (December 1945); Miriam Allen DeFord, "Shall Convicts Write Books?" *The Nation* 131 (November 5, 1930): 495–97.

37. My use of *queer* here is informed by the many efforts to resist its reification as an umbrella-like sexual identity and by Carla Freccero's proposal in particular that we "allow it to continue its outlaw work as a verb and sometimes an adjective" (*Queer/Early/Modern*, 5). As legal theorist Martha Umphrey writes, "Queerness is about making the given seem strange" ("The Trouble with Harry Thaw," *Radical History Review* 62 [Spring 1995]: 19).

38. While the questions I take up are different from those addressed by recent critics and theorists of the contemporary prison and the mass incarceration of the last twenty years, this book is in conversation with and indebted to their work. See Ruth Wilson Gilmore, *Golden Gulag: Prisons, Surplus, Crisis, and Opposition in Globalizing California* (Berkeley: University of California Press, 2006); Michael Hames-Garcia, *Fugitive Thought: Prison Movements, Race, and the Meaning of Justice* (Minneapolis: University of Minnesota Press, 2004); Marc Mauer, *Race to Incarcerate* (New York: New Press, 1999); Angela Davis, *Are Prisons Obsolete?* (New York: Open Media, 2003).

CHAPTER 1

1. Prison Discipline Society (Boston), *Annual Report of the Board of Managers of the Prison Discipline Society*, vol. 4 (1829), 299.

2. Michel Foucault, *Discipline and Punish: The Birth of the Prison*, trans. Alan Sheridan (New York: Pantheon, 1977). The first generation of prison historians tended to characterize that shift as the result of progressive and humanitarian change that they viewed as characterizing the history of the prison more generally. See, for example, Harry Elmer Barnes and Negley K. Teeters, *New Horizons in Criminology: The American Crime Problem* (New York: Prentice-Hall, 1944); Orlando F. Lewis, *The Development of American Prisons and Prison Customs, 1776–1845* (Albany, NY: J. B. Lyon, 1922); Blake McKelvey, *American Prisons: A Study in American Social History Prior to 1915* (Montclair, NJ: Patterson Smith, 1936). Foucault, conversely, characterized that transition as heralding a new technology of power and surveillance and the consolidation of new disciplinary and coercive techniques that produced the self-disciplining subject. See also Charles Bright, *The Powers That Punish: Prison and Politics in the Era of the "Big House," 1920–1955* (Ann Arbor: University of Michigan Press, 1996); Michael Ignatieff, *A Just Measure of Pain: The Penitentiary in the Industrial Revolution, 1750–1850* (New York: Pantheon, 1978).

3. Thomas Mott Osborne, *Society and Prisons* (New Haven, CT: Yale University Press, 1916), 142.

4. Foucault observed that prison reform "does not . . . seem to have originated in a recognition of failure" but, rather, was "virtually contemporary with the prison itself: it constitutes, as it were, its programme" (*Discipline and Punish*, 234).

5. Prison Discipline Society (Boston), *Annual Report of the Board of Managers of the Prison Discipline Society*, vol. 1 (1826), n.p.

6. On punishment in the early American colonies, see David J. Rothman, *The Discovery of the Asylum: Social Order and Disorder in the New Republic* (Boston: Little, Brown, 1971), 3–56; Adam Jay Hirsch, *The Rise of the Penitentiary: Prisons and Punishment in Early America* (New Haven, CT: Yale University Press, 1992).

The question of how often sodomy was actually punished by death in colonial America is a subject of debate among historians. Richard Godbeer finds that early New Englanders were more willing to tolerate those who practiced sodomy and less willing than previously thought to prosecute it to the extent permitted by law. See Godbeer, *Sexual Revolution in Early America* (Baltimore: Johns Hopkins University Press, 2002), esp. 44–50, 104–15. See also Thomas A. Foster, *Sex and the Eighteenth-Century Man: Massachusetts and the History of Sexuality in America* (Boston: Beacon, 2006), 157.

7. This was less true in the South, where corporal punishments such as whipping continued well into the twentieth century and where penitentiaries remained peripheral to the criminal justice system throughout the nineteenth century. See Michael Stephen Hindus, *Prison and Plantation: Crime, Justice, and Authority in Massachusetts and South Carolina, 1767–1878* (Chapel Hill: University of North Carolina Press, 1980).

8. On the transcontinental and trans-American exchange of ideas about prison philosophy and architecture, see Patricia O'Brien, *The Promise of Punishment: Prisons in*

Nineteenth-Century France (Princeton, NJ: Princeton University Press, 1982); Rothman, *Discovery of the Asylum*, 94; Negley K. Teeters, *The Cradle of the Penitentiary: The Walnut Street Jail at Philadelphia, 1773–1835* (Philadelphia: Pennsylvania Prison Society, 1955), 1; Norman Johnston, *Forms of Constraint: A History of Prison Architecture* (Urbana: University of Illinois Press, 2000), 87, 144–47; Enoch Cobb Wines, *The State of Prisons and of Child-Saving Institutions in the Civilized World* (Cambridge: John Wilson & Sons, 1880), 22; Ricardo D. Salvatore and Carlos Aguirre, eds., *The Birth of the Penitentiary in Latin America: Essays on Criminology, Prison Reform, and Social Control, 1830–1940* (Austin: University of Texas Press, 1996).

9. Rothman, *Discovery of the Asylum*, 94. Confinement in jails, workhouses, and houses of correction all existed prior to early-nineteenth-century American prisons. Among the antecedents for the modern prison philosophy based on classification and segregation of prisoners and disciplined institutional life were the Hospice of St. Michele in Rome, established by Pope Clement XI in 1703 to house delinquent boys, and the Maison de Force, a house of correction established in Ghent in 1773. See Wines, *The State of Prisons*, 6–22; McKelvey, *American Prisons*, 3–4; Ignatieff, *A Just Measure of Pain*, 52–54; Norman B. Johnston, *The Human Cage: A Brief History of Prison Architecture* (New York: Walker, 1973), 8–13; Johnston, *Forms of Constraint*, chaps. 1–3; Foucault, *Discipline and Punish*, 121–24.

10. Foucault, *Discipline and Punish*, 200–202. For a detailed description of the Panopticon, see Janet Semple, *Bentham's Panopticon* (London: Oxford University Press, 1993).

11. On the emergence of the Pennsylvania and New York prison systems, see McKelvey, *American Prisons*; Lewis, *Development of American Prisons*; Fred E. Haynes, *The American Prison System* (New York and London: McGraw-Hill, 1939); Negley K. Teeters, *They Were in Prison: A History of the Pennsylvania Prison Society, 1787–1937* (Chicago: John C. Winston, 1937); Foucault, *Discipline and Punish*, 237–40; Rothman, *Discovery of the Asylum*; Michael Meranze, *Laboratories of Virtue: Punishment, Revolution, and Authority in Philadelphia, 1760–1835* (Chapel Hill: University of North Carolina Press, 1996); Ignatieff, *A Just Measure of Pain*; Johnston, *Forms of Constraint*, chap. 5; W. David Lewis, *From Newgate to Dannemora: The Rise of the Penitentiary in New York, 1796–1848* (Ithaca, NY: Cornell University Press, 1965); Wines, *State of Prisons*, 25–27.

12. Enoch Cobb Wines and Theodore W. Dwight, *Report on the Prisons and Reformatories of the United States and Canada* (Albany, NY: Van Benthuysen, 1867), 56.

13. Charles Dickens, *American Notes for General Circulation* (New York: Harper & Brothers, 1842; repr., Oxford: Oxford University Press, 1997), 99.

14. William Crawford, *Report on the Penitentiaries of the United States* (1835; repr., Montclair, NJ: Patterson Smith, 1969), 19.

15. Ibid.

16. Prison Discipline Society (Boston), *Annual Report of the Board of Managers of the Prison Discipline Society*, vol. 16 (1841), 40–41.

17. Correctional Association of New York, *Report of the Prison Association of New York*, vol. 25 (1869), 28.

18. Wines and Dwight, *Report on the Prisons and Reformatories*, 112. Concern about

segregating male and female prisoners and a movement on the part of female reformers to improve the conditions of incarcerated women led to the creation of separate women's prisons. Indiana was the first state to open a separate institution for women prisoners in 1873. Others followed soon after, modeled on the form of the "reformatory" and stressing rehabilitation rather than the harsh discipline of male institutions. See Estelle B. Freedman, *Their Sisters' Keepers: Women's Prison Reform in America, 1830–1930* (Ann Arbor: University of Michigan Press, 1981); Anne M. Butler, *Gendered Justice in the American West: Women Prisoners in Men's Penitentiaries* (Urbana: University of Illinois Press, 1997).

19. Correctional Association of New York, *Report of the Prison Association of New York*, vol. 2 (1845), 80.

20. New York State Legislature, *Report of the Select Committee Appointed by the Assembly of 1875 to Investigate the Causes of the Increase of Crime in the City of New York* (New York, 1876), 111.

21. Horace Woodroff, *Stone Wall College* (Nashville: Aurora Publishers, 1970), 25–26.

22. In many cases, male jailers may have been responsible for prison pregnancies. Reports of sexual abuse and assaults on women prisoners by male guards and wardens contributed to arguments for separate women's prisons. See Freedman, *Their Sisters' Keepers*; Nichole Hahn Rafter, *Partial Justice: Women, Prisons, and Social Control*, 2d ed. (New Brunswick, NJ: Transaction, 1990).

23. See Jody Greene, "Public Secrets: Sodomy and the Pillory in the Eighteenth Century and Beyond," *Eighteenth Century: Theory and Interpretation* 44 (June 2003): 203–32. I am indebted to Jonathan Goldberg's analysis of the indeterminacy of sodomy in "Sodomy in the New World: Anthropologies Old and New," *Social Text* 29 (1991): 46–56, and in "Introduction: That Utterly Confused Category," in *Sodometries: Renaissance Texts, Modern Sexualities*, ed. Jonathan Goldberg (Stanford, CA: Stanford University Press, 1992), 1–28. On the links between sodomy and bestiality, see John Murrin, "'Things Fearful to Name': Bestiality in Early America," *Pennsylvania History* 65, suppl. (1998): S8–S43. I am inspired as well by Foucault's observation that "silence itself—the things one declines to say, or is forbidden to name, the discretion that is required between different speakers—is less the absolute limit of discourse, the other side from which it is separated by a strict boundary, than an element that functions alongside the things said, with them and in relation to them within over-all strategies. There is no binary division to be made between what one says and what one does not say; we must try to determine the different ways of not saying such things" (*The History of Sexuality*, 1:27).

24. Teeters, *They Were in Prison*, 384.

25. See H. Tristram Englehardt, Jr., "The Disease of Masturbation: Values and the Concept of Disease," *Bulletin of the History of Medicine* 48 (1974): 234–48. On shifting understandings of masturbation in the eighteenth and nineteenth centuries, see Thomas W. Laqueur, *Solitary Sex: A Cultural History of Masturbation* (New York: Zone, 2003); Vernon Rosario, ed., *Solitary Pleasures: The Historical, Literary, and Artistic Discourses of Autoeroticism* (London: Routledge, 1995); Peter Lewis Allen, *The Wages of Sin: Sex and Disease, Past and Present* (Chicago: University of Chicago Press, 2000), chap. 5; E. H. Hare,

"Masturbatory Insanity: The History of an Idea," *Journal of Mental Science* 108 (January 1962): 2–25; Jean Stengers and Anne van Neck, *Masturbation: The History of a Great Terror* (New York: Palgrave, 2001); Alan Hunt, "The Great Masturbation Panic and the Discourses of Moral Regulation in Nineteenth- and Early-Twentieth-Century Britain," *Journal of the History of Sexuality* 8 (1998): 575–615; Lesley A. Hall, "Forbidden by God, Despised by Men: Masturbation, Medical Warnings, Moral Panic, and Manhood in Great Britain, 1850–1950," *Journal of the History of Sexuality* 2 (1992): 365–87; Michel Foucault, *Abnormal: Lectures at the Collège de France, 1974–1975*, trans. Graham Burchell (New York: Picador, 2003), 59–60. Robert H. MacDonald traces the early-eighteenth-century antecedents of these beliefs in "The Frightful Consequences of Onanism: Notes on the History of a Delusion," *Journal of the History of Ideas* 28 (July–September 1967): 423–31.

26. Prison Discipline Society (Boston), *Annual Report of the Board of Managers of the Prison Discipline Society*, vol. 14 (1839), 345.

27. Quoted in Murrin, "'Things Fearful to Name,'" 20.

28. Prison Discipline Society (Boston), *Annual Report of the Board of Managers of the Prison Discipline Society*, vol. 14 (1839), 345. If there were worries about the masturbatory tendencies of female prisoners akin to those of males, they were not articulated by the administrators or staff of women's institutions.

29. Dr. J. E. Pelham, quoted in Kenneth Lamott, *Chronicles of San Quentin: The Biography of a Prison* (New York: David McKay Co., 1961), 121.

30. *Journal of the Pennsylvania Prison Society* (1883), 33, quoted in Teeters, *They Were in Prison*, 386.

31. Correctional Association of New York, *Annual Report of the Prison Association of New York*, vol. 22 (1866), 274.

32. Prison Discipline Society (Boston), *Annual Report of the Board of Managers of the Prison Discipline Society*, vol. 15 (1840), 450.

33. Prison Discipline Society (Boston), *Annual Report of the Board of Managers of the Prison Discipline Society*, vol. 3 (1828), 158.

34. Gustave de Beaumont and Alexis de Tocqueville, *On the Penitentiary System in the United States, and Its Application in France; with an Appendix on Penal Colonies, and Also, Statistical Notes*, trans. Francis Lieber (Philadelphia: Carey, Lea & Blanchard, 1833), 4.

35. Teeters, *They Were in Prison*, 207.

36. Freedman, *Their Sisters' Keepers*, 19–20.

37. Rafter, *Partial Justice*, 4.

38. Freedman, *Their Sisters' Keepers*, 15.

39. J. B. Bittinger, "Responsibility of Society for the Causes of Crime," in *Transactions of the National Congress on Penitentiary and Reformatory Discipline, Held at Cincinnati, Ohio, October 12–18, 1870*, ed. E. C. Wines (Albany: Weed, Parsons, 1871), 287.

40. Bittinger, "Responsibility of Society for the Causes of Crime," 287.

41. Prison Discipline Society (Boston), *Annual Report of the Board of Managers of the Prison Discipline Society*, vol. 1 (1826), 30.

42. Wines and Dwight, *Report on the Prisons and Reformatories*, 316.

43. Correctional Association of New York, *Annual Report of the Prison Association of New York*, vol. 25 (1869), 8.

44. Rev. William C. Stoudenmire, "The Treatment of Prisoners—Past and Present," *Proceedings of the Annual Congress of the National Prison Association of the United States*, 1902 (1903), 53.

45. Julian Hawthorne, *The Subterranean Brotherhood* (New York: McBride, Nast & Co., 1914), 283.

46. Ibid.

47. "Promiscuous" is defined in Noah Webster's 1828 dictionary as "Mingled; consisting of individuals united in a body or mass without order; confused; undistinguished" (Webster, *An American Dictionary of the English Language* [1828; repr., New York: Johnson Reprint Corporation, 1970]).

48. Prison Discipline Society (Boston), *Annual Report of the Board of Managers of the Prison Discipline Society*, vol. 1 (1826), 30; Prison Discipline Society (Boston), *Annual Report of the Board of Managers of the Prison Discipline Society*, vol. 2 (1827), 66. See also *Annual Report of the Prison Association of New York*, vol. 2 (1845), 28; *Annual Report of the Prison Association of New York*, vol. 8 (1853), 17.

49. Wellington Scott, *Seventeen Years in the Underworld* (New York and Cincinnati: Abingdon, 1916), 24–25.

50. Josiah Flynt, *My Life* (New York: Outing, 1908), 82.

51. Prison Discipline Society (Boston), *Annual Report of the Board of Managers of the Prison Discipline Society*, vol. 16 (1841), 41.

52. Prison Discipline Society (Boston), *Annual Report of the Board of Managers of the Prison Discipline Society*, vol. 2 (1827), 65. In 1826, the Boston Prison Discipline Society alluded to "an elaborate report" that documented "the enormous evils arising from a promiscuous intercourse of villains of all ages and degrees of guilt" that had been "of very limited circulation; few men have known that such reports existed" (Prison Discipline Society [Boston], *Annual Report of the Board of Managers of the Prison Discipline Society*, vol. 1 [1826], 30). Jonathan Ned Katz identifies Dwight's report as "the earliest known document discussing homosexuality in this country's prisons" (*Gay American History: Lesbians and Gay Men in the U.S.A.* [New York: Avon, 1976], 42).

53. Louis Dwight, "Sodomy among Juvenile Delinquents" (Boston, April 25, 1826), reprinted in Katz, *Gay American History*, 42–43.

54. Ibid., 43.

55. Ibid., 44.

56. Freedman notes that, in 1850, women constituted only 3.6 percent of the total inmates in thirty-four state and county prisons (*Their Sisters' Keepers*, 11). Visiting in the early 1830s, William Crawford found only ninety-seven women in the penitentiaries of the seven most populous states and the District of Columbia. Fifteen years later, Dorothea Dix counted 167 female inmates in her prison tour of the eastern seaboard (Rafter, *Partial Justice*, 10). See Dorothea Lynde Dix, *Remarks on Prisons and Prison Discipline in the United States* (Boston: Munroe & Francis, 1845), 107–8. The number

of women convicted of crimes increased dramatically after 1860. See Freedman, *Their Sisters' Keepers*, 13.

57. Dix, *Remarks on Prisons and Prison Discipline in the United States*.

58. Margaret Otis, "A Perversion Not Commonly Noted," *Journal of Abnormal Psychology* 8 (June–July 1913): 113.

59. Ibid. My analysis is indebted to Siobhan Somerville's reading of Otis's account in *Queering the Color Line: Race and the Invention of Homosexuality in American Culture* (Durham, NC: Duke University Press, 2000), 34–37.

60. Otis, "A Perversion Not Commonly Noted," 115.

61. Ibid.,113. In 1923, director of the Bedford Hills psychopathic hospital, Edith R. Spaulding, attributed the infatuations of white girls for "colored" girls to the whites' substitution of color "for the masculine companionship they were temporarily denied" (Spaulding, *An Experimental Study of Psychopathic Delinquent Women* [Montclair, NJ: Patterson Smith, 1923], 273, quoted in Nichole Hahn Rafter, *Creating Born Criminals* [Urbana: University of Illinois Press, 1997], 181).

62. Otis, "A Perversion Not Commonly Noted," 114.

63. Sixteen years later, in 1929, psychiatrist Charles A. Ford also documented the attachments between white and black female inmates in "Homosexual Practices of Institutionalized Females," *Journal of Abnormal Psychology* 23 (January–March 1929): 442–48. In that same year, Clifford R. Shaw and Earl J. Myers wrote about attachments between white and black girls at the Illinois State Training School for Girls in "The Juvenile Delinquent," in *The Illinois Crime Survey*, ed. John W. Wigmore (Chicago: Blakely Printing Co., 1929), 720. See also Spaulding, *An Experimental Study of Psychopathic Delinquent Women*, 273; Lowell S. Selling, "The Pseudo Family," *American Journal of Sociology* 37 (September 1931): 247–53. A few years later, in 1934, federal inspector of prisons Joseph Fishman attributed interracial relations between women to white women's association of "masculine strength and virility with dark color" (*Sex in Prison: Revealing Sex Conditions in American Prisons* [New York: National Library Press, 1934], 29).

64. See Somerville, *Queering the Color Line*, 26–29, 64–67. On the nineteenth-century exclusion of black women from the category "true woman," see Hazel V. Carby, *Reconstructing Womanhood: The Emergence of the Afro-American Woman Novelist* (New York: Oxford University Press, 1987).

65. Estelle B. Freedman, "The Prison Lesbian: Race, Class, and the Construction of the Aggressive Female Homosexual, 1915–1965," *Feminist Studies* 22 (Summer 1996), 400–401. For a discussion of the criminological literature on race and sex in reform schools for girls, see also Kathryn Hinojosa Baker, "Delinquent Desire: Race, Sex, and Ritual in Reform Schools for Girls," *Discourse* 15 (Fall 1992): 49–68.

66. In her analysis of an investigation of the Bedford Hills women's reformatory in 1914, Sarah Potter argues that officials "pointed to working-class sexual passion, rather than homoeroticism, as inmates' underlying pathology" ("'Undesirable Relations': Same-Sex Relationships and the Meaning of Sexual Desire at a Women's Reformatory during the Progressive Era," *Feminist Studies* 30 [Summer 2004]: 395).

67. Rafter observes that many women's reformatories rejected older inmates on the grounds that they were "unlikely to reform" (*Partial Justice*, 36). Freedman notes that "inmates at the new prisons were often young morals offenders who fit the reformers' definitions of fallen women in need of aid" (*Their Sisters' Keepers*, 82).

68. Rafter, *Partial Justice*, 141.

69. On the disproportionate incarceration of African Americans throughout the nineteenth century, see Rafter, *Partial Justice*, 37, 141.

70. See Michael Moon, "'The Gentle Boy from the Dangerous Classes': Pederasty, Domesticity, and Capitalism in Horatio Alger," *Representations*, no. 19 (Summer 1987), 87–110; Kevin P. Murphy, "Socrates in the Slums: Homoerotics, Gender, and Settlement House Reform" in *A Shared Experience: Men, Women and Gender in U.S. History*, ed. Laura McCall and Donald Yacovone (New York: New York University Press, 1998); Murphy, *Political Manhood: Red Bloods and Mollycoddles and the Politics of Progressive Era Reform* (New York: Columbia University Press, 2008); David I. Macleod, *Building Character in the American Boy: The Boy Scouts, YMCA, and Their Forerunners, 1870–1920* (Madison: University of Wisconsin Press, 1983).

71. Prison Discipline Society (Boston), *Annual Report of the Board of Managers of the Prison Discipline Society*, vol. 4 (1829), 299. Early prison historian Orlando Lewis noted that a "rough basis of classification" was mandated by the Pennsylvania legislature in 1790, which provided that Philadelphia's Walnut Street prison be remodeled to separate "those who had been convicted of the more serious offenses, and those who had committed crimes of lesser severity" (*Development of American Prisons*, 25).

72. Otis, "A Perversion Not Commonly Noted," 113.

73. Ruth Alexander, *The "Girl Problem": Female Sexual Delinquency in New York, 1900–1930* (Ithaca, NY: Cornell University Press, 1995), 91. See also Freedman, *Their Sisters' Keepers*, 139–40; Rafter, *Partial Justice*, 152–53.

74. On the history of juvenile institutions, see Hastings H. Hart, *Preventative Treatment of Neglected Children* (New York: Charities Publication Committee, 1910); Robert S. Pickett, *House of Refuge: Origins of Juvenile Reform in New York State, 1815–1857* (Syracuse, NY: Syracuse University Press, 1969); Steven L. Schlossman, *Love and the American Delinquent: The Theory and Practice of "Progressive" Juvenile Justice* (Chicago: University of Chicago Press, 1977); Robert M. Mennel, *Thorns and Thistles: Juvenile Delinquents in the United States, 1825–1940* (Hanover, NH: University Press of New England, 1973); Joseph M. Hawes, *Children in Urban Society: Juvenile Delinquency in Nineteenth-Century America* (New York: Oxford University Press, 1971); Anthony Platt, *The Child Savers: The Invention of Delinquency* (Chicago: University of Chicago Press, 1969); and Barbara M. Brenzel, *Daughters of the State: A Social Portrait of the First Reform School for Girls in North America, 1856–1905* (Cambridge, MA: MIT Press, 1983).

75. Donald Lowrie, *My Life in Prison* (New York: Mitchell Kennerley, 1912), 57. See also Lamott, *Chronicles of San Quentin*, 146; Ed Morrell, *The Twenty-Fifth Man* (Montclair, NJ: New Era, 1924), 27–28.

76. See Elizabeth Lunbeck, "'A New Generation of Women': Progressive Psychiatrists and the Hypersexual Female," *Feminist Studies* 13 (1987): 513–43.

77. Otis, "A Perversion Not Commonly Noted," 116.

78. Ibid., 114. Randall Kennedy traces the origins of this expression to the Civil War era, when "Republicans' antislavery politics won them the appellation 'black Republicans' or 'nigger lovers'" (*Nigger: The Strange Career of a Troublesome Word* [New York: Pantheon, 2002], 25). The term remained in circulation, attached a century later to white civil rights protestors, and "continues to be heard amid the background noise that accompanies racial conflict" (Kennedy, *Nigger*, 27).

79. Some historians of early America have recently argued that as early as the eighteenth century, Americans conceived of sexual acts as reflective of an interiority and delineating a type of person. See Foster, *Sex and the Eighteenth-Century Man*, esp. 155–74; Foster, introduction to *Long before Stonewall: Histories of Same-Sex Sexuality in Early America*, ed. Thomas A. Foster (New York: New York University Press, 2007), 8–9; Richard Godbeer, "'The Cry of Sodom': Discourse, Intercourse, and Desire in Colonial New England," *William and Mary Quarterly*, 3d ser., 52 (April 1995): 259–86.

80. Dwight, "Sodomy among Juvenile Delinquents," 43.

81. Otis, "A Perversion Not Commonly Noted," 116.

82. In this way, the history of sexuality paralleled a history of criminality, first understood as a behavior (crime) and later as an identity (the criminal), though in both cases never as neatly differentiated and linear as that trajectory would suggest. See Foucault, "About the Concept of the 'Dangerous Individual' in Nineteenth-Century Legal Psychiatry," trans. Alain Baudot and Couchman, *International Journal of Law and Psychiatry* 1 (1978): 1–18; Foucault, *Abnormal*, esp. 89–92; Richard Quinney, *The Problem of Crime* (New York: Dodd, Mead, 1970), 59–60; Rafter, *Creating Born Criminals*; Marie-Christine Leps, *Apprehending the Criminal: The Production of Deviance in Nineteenth-Century Discourse* (Durham, NC: Duke University Press, 1992); Piers Beirne, *Inventing Criminology: Essays on the Rise of "Homo Criminalis"* (Albany: State University of New York Press, 1993); Peter Becker and Richard F. Wetzell, introduction to *Criminals and Their Scientists: The History of Criminology in International Perspective* (Cambridge: Cambridge University Press, 2006), esp. 6.

83. Ann Fabian documents the efforts of convicts, along with beggars, slaves, and soldiers, to "take advantage of the opportunities to represent themselves in print" and to write personal narratives. Fabian credits the nineteenth-century impulse to read and write personal narratives to "the growth of evangelical religion, the development of democratic politics, the rise of nationalism, the spread of print culture, and the expansion of the commercial relations of a capitalist society" (*The Unvarnished Truth: Personal Narratives in Nineteenth-Century America* [Berkeley: University of California Press, 2000], 2).

84. Ibid., 53.

85. At the same time, tours of actual prisons were growing in popularity. Seth W. Payne wrote in his autobiography that "while I write this, several lady and gentlemen visitors are peeking at me through the bars. They gave a quarter a piece to get in, and I am part of the show they paid to see. They seem inclined to get their money's worth at this one cage. I wonder if they wouldn't like to have me show my claws, stand on my head, roll over or give one of my peculiar savage yells. They must consider me a curious

animal—and I begin really to think so myself, else why am I thus caged" (*Behind the Bars* [New York: Vincent, 1873], 11).

86. John N. Reynolds, *A Kansas Hell; or, Life in the Kansas Penitentiary* (Atchison, KS: Bee Publishing Co., 1889), 9.

87. Joseph Kelley, *Thirteen Years in the Oregon Penitentiary* (Portland, n.p., 1908), 4.

88. *Report of the Prison Association of New York*, vol. 1 (1844), 42. See also Wines and Dwight, *Report on the Prisons and Reformatories*, 50.

89. Beaumont and Tocqueville, *On the Penitentiary System*, 8.

90. Payne, *Behind the Bars*, 116.

91. Frank Tannenbaum, "Prison Cruelty," *Atlantic Monthly* 125 (April 1920), 436.

92. Ibid., 436–37.

93. "My Life in the Penitentiary," *The Independent* 56 (February 4, 1904), 255.

94. Samuel Smith, *Inside Out; or, Roguery Exposed* (Hartford, CT: n.p., 1827), 45.

95. William C. Francis, *A Hell on Earth; or, A Story of Prison Life* (Kansas City, MO: Hudson-Kimberly, 1896), 1–2.

96. Andrew W. George, *The Texas Convict: Sketches of the Penitentiary, Convict Farm and Railroads, Together with Poems* (Charlotte, NC: n.p., 1895), 6.

97. Franklin Carr, *Twenty-Two Years in State Prisons* (Philadelphia: n.p., 1893).

98. John N. Reynolds, *The Twin Hells: A Thrilling Narrative of Life in the Kansas and Missouri Penitentiaries* (Chicago: Bee Publishing Co., 1890), 10.

99. Walter Wilson, *Hell in Nebraska: A Tale of the Nebraska Penitentiary* (Lincoln, NE: Bankers Publishing Co., 1913); Reynolds, *A Kansas Hell*; Reynolds, *The Twin Hells*; Francis, *A Hell on Earth*; Orange L. Pettay, *Five Years in Hell; or, The Ohio Penitentiary* (Coldwell, OH: Citizens' Press, 1883); Morgan K. Sipe, *Twenty-Nine Hundred and Forty-Four Days in Hell, and What I Saw and Heard: An Inside View of one of the Greatest Public Institutions in Kansas* (Galesburg, KS: printed by author, 1895); Thelma Roberts, *Red Hell: The Life Story of John Good, Criminal* (New York: Rae D. Henkle, 1934); O. J. Gillis, *To Hell and Back Again . . . or, Life in the Penitentiaries of Texas and Kansas* (Little Rock, AR: n.p., 1906).

100. Fabian, *Unvarnished Truth*, 54.

101. W. A. Coffey, *A Peep into the State Prison, at Auburn, New York, by One Who Knows* (Auburn, NY: n.p., 1839), 6.

102. J. Harrie Banka, *State Prison Life: By One Who Has Been There* (Cincinnati: Vent, 1871).

103. Julian Hawthorne, ed., *The Confessions of a Convict* (Philadelphia: Rufus C. Hartranft, 1893), 163.

104. Pettay, *Five Years in Hell*, 95.

105. Hawthorne, *Subterranean Brotherhood*, viii.

106. Ibid., viii.

107. Wilson, *Hell in Nebraska*, 78.

108. Jack London, "The 'Pen': Long Days in a County Penitentiary," *Cosmopolitan Magazine* 43–44 (August 1907), 375.

109. Ibid. 375.

110. Wilson, *Hell in Nebraska*, 79.

111. Ibid., 79.

112. Reynolds, *A Kansas Hell*, 70.

113. Ibid., 71.

114. Ibid.

115. Sipe, *Twenty-Nine Hundred and Forty-Four Days in Hell*, 60.

116. Carlo De Fornaro, *A Modern Purgatory* (New York: Kennerley, 1917), 175.

117. Ibid., 175.

118. Jonathan Ned Katz, *Love Stories: Sex between Men before Homosexuality* (Chicago: University of Chicago Press, 2001), 61.

119. On male homosociality in the nineteenth century, see E. Anthony Rotundo, *American Manhood: Transformations in Masculinity from the Revolution to the Modern Era* (New York: Basic, 1993); Susan Lee Johnson, *Roaring Camp: The Social World of the California Gold Rush* (New York: Norton, 2000), chaps. 2, 3; Katz, *Love Stories*; John Donald Gustav-Wrathall, *Take the Young Stranger by the Hand: Same-Sex Relations and the YMCA* (Chicago: University of Chicago Press, 1998).

120. George Thompson, *Prison Life and Reflections* (Oberlin, OH: J. M. Fitch, 1847), 138. On the practice of male bed-sharing in the nineteenth century, see Rotundo, *American Manhood*; Johnson, *Roaring Camp*, 174; Katz, *Love Stories*, 6–7.

121. Payne, *Behind the Bars*, 65.

122. Alexander Berkman, *Prison Memoirs of an Anarchist* (New York: Mother Earth Publishing Association, 1912; New York: Shocken, 1970), 324.

123. Ibid., 336.

124. Ibid., 440.

125. Katz, *Love Stories*, 90.

126. John H. King, *Three Hundred Days in a Yankee Prison: Reminiscences of War Life Captivity* (Atlanta: Jas. P. Davis, 1904), 94–95. On all-male dances in the diggings during the California Gold Rush, see Johnson, *Roaring Camp*, 171–73. See also Chris Packard, *Queer Cowboys and Other Erotic Male Friendships in Nineteenth-Century American Literature* (New York: Palgrave, 2005).

127. Lowrie, *My Life in Prison*, 117.

128. Eugene B. Block, "A Man-Sized Job," *Sunset* 57 (July 1926): 56. See also Lamott, *Chronicles of San Quentin*, 200.

129. Katz, *Love Stories*, 135–35.

CHAPTER 2

1. Alexander Berkman, *Prison Memoirs of an Anarchist*, quoting Oscar Wilde, *The Ballad of Reading Gaol* (1898).

2. Wilde, *Ballad of Reading Gaol*.

3. Chester Himes, "To What Red Hell?" *Esquire* (October 1934), 100–101, 122, 127.

4. Joan Henry, *Women in Prison* (Garden City, NY: Doubleday, 1952), 39–40.

5. Wilde, *The Ballad of Reading Gaol*, quoted in Victor F. Nelson, *Prison Days and Nights*

(Boston: Little, Brown, 1933), 147. Other examples of the use of this quote include Thomas Mott Osborne, *Within Prison Walls* (New York: D. Appleton & Co., 1916), 314; Benjamin Karpman, "Sex Life in Prison," *Journal of Criminal Law, Criminology, and Police Science* 38 (January–February 1948), 486; Barnes and Teeters, *New Horizons in Criminology*, 616; David Abrahamsen, *Who Are the Guilty? A Study of Education and Crime* (New York: Rinehart, 1952), 213; and Wayne S. Wooden and Jay Parker, epigraph to *Men behind Bars: Sexual Exploitation in Prison* (New York: Plenum Press, 1982), v.

6. Emma Goldman, "The State Prison at Jefferson City, Mo.," in *A Fragment of the Prison Experiences* (New York: n.p., 1919), 5.

7. Osborne, *Society and Prisons*, 143.

8. Ed Cohen, *Talk on the Wilde Side: Toward a Genealogy of a Discourse on Male Sexualities* (New York: Routledge, 1993), 1–2. See also Morris B. Kaplan, *Sodom on the Thames: Sex, Love, and Scandal in Wilde Times* (Ithaca, NY: Cornell University Press, 2005), 224–64; Alan Sinfield, *The Wilde Century: Effeminacy, Oscar Wilde and the Queer Moment* (London: Cassell, 1994). For a discussion of the coverage of the Wilde trail in Portland, Oregon, see Peter Boag, *Same-Sex Affairs: Constructing and Controlling Homosexuality in the Pacific Northwest* (Berkeley: University of California Press, 2003), 127–35.

9. Given the unspeakability of the charges levied against Wilde, Cohen argues that the name Oscar Wilde came to stand in for the new sexual type, the homosexual: "Indeed, as the condensation of Wilde's 'crimes' with his 'character' became ubiquitous in the first decades of this century, his given name alone came to designate a standard deviation from normative male sexuality" (*Talk on the Wilde Side*, 100).

10. Ibid., 184. See also Sinfield, *Wilde Century*, 3. E. M. Forster's character Maurice refers to himself as "an unspeakable of the Oscar Wilde sort" in *Maurice*, published posthumously in 1971 (quoted in Sinfield, *Wilde Century*, 3). Boag finds that the coverage of the Wilde trial in Portland, Oregon, was less reticent in specifying the particulars of the charges against Wilde (Boag, *Same-Sex Affairs*, 128).

11. Barnes and Teeters, *New Horizons in Criminology*, 616.

12. Charles N. Lathrop, *A Practical Program for Church Groups in Jail Work* (New York: National Council, Department of Christian Social Service, 1923), 15.

13. Frank Tannenbaum, *Crime and the Community* (Boston: Ginn, 1938), 429.

14. See Jennifer Terry, *An American Obsession: Science, Medicine, and Homosexuality in Modern Society* (Chicago: University of Chicago Press, 1999), 43; Hubert Kennedy, "Karl Heinrichs Ulrichs: First Theorist of Homosexuality," in *Science and Homosexualities*, ed. Vernon Rosario (New York: Routledge, 1997).

15. Erin Carlston examines the differences and disagreements among sexologists in "'A Finer Differentiation': Female Homosexuality and the American Medical Community, 1926–1940," in *Science and Homosexualities*, ed. Rosario.

16. See Terry, *An American Obsession*, esp. 42–43.

17. See Harry Oosterhuis, *Stepchildren of Nature: Krafft-Ebing, Psychiatry, and the Making of Sexual Identity* (Chicago: University of Chicago Press, 2000), 71.

18. That diagnosis was announced in Westphal's title, "Die conträre Sexualempfindung: Symptom eines neuropathischen (psychopathischen) Zustandes" [Contrary sexual

feeling: symptom of a nuropathic (psychopathic) condition], *Archiv für Psychiatric und Nervenkrankheiten* [Archives of Psychiatry and Nervous Diseases], 2, no. 1 (1870), 73–108.

19. James D. Steakley, "Per scientiam ad justitiam: Magnus Hirschfeld and the Sexual Politics of Innate Homosexuality," in *Science and Homosexualities*, ed. Rosario.

20. Havelock Ellis, *Studies of the Psychology of Sex*, vol. 2, *Sexual Inversion*, 3d ed. (Philadelphia: F. A. Davis Co., 1928), 310.

21. Richard von Krafft-Ebing, *Psychopathia Sexualis, with Especial Reference to Contrary Sexual Instinct: A Medico-Legal Study*, trans. Charles Gilbert Chaddock, 7th ed. (Philadelphia and London: F. A. Davis Co., 1893), vi.

22. Ibid., 187.

23. Foucault, *The History of Sexuality*, 1:43. For an important reconsideration of Foucault and the acts-to-identity trajectory charted by historians of sexuality, see David Halperin, "Forgetting Foucault: Acts, Identities, and the History of Sexuality," *Representations* 63 (Summer 1998): 93–120.

24. German physician and sexologist Iwan Bloch acknowledged this influence, noting that the experience of interviewing "a very large number of genuine homosexual individuals" convinced him that "true homosexuality as a congenital natural phenomenon is *far greater* than I had earlier assumed" (*The Sexual Life of Our Time: A Complete Encyclopedia of the Sexual Sciences* [New York: Falstaff, 1937], 489). Harry Oosterhuis observes that in formulating his analysis, Krafft-Ebing relied "on what 'perverts' were telling him" ("Richard von Krafft-Ebing's 'Step-Children of Nature': Psychiatry and the Making of Homosexual Identity," in *Science and Homosexualities*, ed. Rosario, 74). Oosterhuis credits this collaborative relationship with moving Krafft-Ebing toward a more positive and sympathetic appraisal of homosexuality (*Stepchildren of Nature*). Havelock Ellis also observed that, "in the last edition of his work, Krafft-Ebing was inclined to regard inversion as being not so much a degeneration as a variation, a simple anomaly, and acknowledged that his opinion thus approximated to that which had long been held by inverts themselves" (*Studies of the Psychology of Sex*, 2:70). Jay Prosser makes this point very powerfully in *Second Skins: The Body Narratives of Transsexuality* (New York: Columbia University Press, 1998). See also Jennifer Terry, "Theorizing Deviant Historiography," *differences* 3, no. 2 (1991): 55–74.

25. Ellis, *Studies in the Psychology of Sex*, 2:83.

26. Ibid.

27. Ibid., 2:83, 2:213.

28. Ibid., 2:215.

29. Ellis authored "The School-Friendships of Girls" himself, drawing on studies of romantic friendships among school girls in Italy, South America, and the United States. On Josiah Flynt's early studies of tramps, see Flynt, *My Life* (New York: Outing Publishing Co., 1908).

30. Krafft-Ebing, *Psychopathia Sexualis*, 7, 188.

31. Ibid., 188.

32. Magnus Hirschfeld, *Sexual Anomalies: The Origins, Nature, and Treatment of Sexual Disorders* (New York: Emerson, 1948), 192, 202–3.

33. Ellis, *Studies in the Psychology of Sex*, vol. II, 3rd ed., 83.

34. Halperin writes that "it is this incoherence at the core of the modern notion of homosexuality that furnishes the most eloquent indication of the historical accumulation of discontinuous notions that shelter within its specious unity" (Halperin, "How to Do the History of Male Homosexuality," *GLQ: A Journal of Lesbian and Gay Studies* 6, no. 1 [2000]: 107).

35. See Freud, *Three Essays on the Theory of Sexuality*, trans. James Strachey (1905; reprint, London: Imago Publishing Co., 1949), esp. 14–25. Some argue that the distinctions between sexologists and psychoanalysts were less clear, pointing to biological elements in Freud's theories and psychological aspects in the thinking of some sexologists. On the relationship of Freud to sexology, see Chris Waters, "Havelock Ellis, Sigmund Freud and the State: Discourses of Homosexual Identity in Interwar Britain," in *Sexology in Culture: Labeling Bodies and Desires*, ed. Lucy Bland and Laura Doan (Chicago: University of Chicago Press, 1998); Erin G. Carlston, "'A Finer Differentiation': Female Homosexuality and the American Medical Community, 1926–1940," in *Science and Homosexualities*, ed. Rosario; Terry, *An American Obsession*, 55–57.

36. Hirschfeld, *Sexual Anomalies*, 191–92.

37. Ibid., 238–39, 241.

38. Ellis, *Studies in the Psychology of Sex*, 2:83.

39. Krafft-Ebing, *Psychopathia Sexualis*, 320.

40. Ellis, *Studies in the Psychology of Sex*, 2:322.

41. Ibid., 2:26.

42. Ibid., 2:373–74.

43. Krafft-Ebing, *Psychopathia Sexualis*, 187.

44. Ellis, *Studies in the Psychology of Sex*, 2:25.

45. Number 1500, *Life in Sing Sing* (Indianapolis: Bobbs–Merrill, 1904), 169.

46. Oosterhuis observes that "the American medical establishment was as reluctant as the British one to deal with sexuality and acknowledge the existence of variant sexual behavior. Although some medical scientists were active in this field—for instance, Frank Lydston and James Kiernan . . . —such research was viewed with suspicion and considered unrespectable" (Oosterhuis, *Stepchildren of Nature*, 276). And Jennifer Terry observes that "writing about sexuality in any manner other than strictly proscribing it was discouraged in the United States. Authors met with publishers' refusals, censorship, public criticism, and even prosecution on obscenity charges" (*An American Obsession*, 76).

47. Randolph Winslow, "Report of an Epidemic of Gonorrhea from Rectal Coition," *Philadelphia Medical News* 49 (August 14, 1886): 180.

48. George J. Monroe, "Sodomy—Pederasty," *St. Louis Medical Era* 9 (1899–1900), 432.

49. The first major American study of homosexuals was conducted in the 1930s by the Committee for the Study of Sex Variants, a privately funded group of doctors and psychologists. See Terry, *An American Obsession*, 178–219; Henry L. Minton, *Departing from Deviance: A History of Homosexual Rights and Emancipatory Science in America* (Chi-

cago: University of Chicago Press, 2001), 36–57. On the 1930s sex crime panic, see Estelle B. Freedman, "'Uncontrolled Desires': The Response to the Sexual Psychopath, 1920–1960," *Journal of American History* 74, no. 1 (June 1987): 83–106; Andrea Friedman, "'The Habitats of Sex-Crazed Perverts': Campaigns against Burlesque in Depression-Era New York City," *Journal of the History of Sexuality* 7 (1996): 203–38; Terry, *An American Obsession*, 270–78.

50. Joseph Lewis French, ed., *Grey Shadows* (New York: Century, 1931), v.

51. See Herman K. Spector, "What Men Write in Prison," *Tomorrow* 5 (December 1945): 53–56; H. Bruce Franklin, introduction to *Prison Writing in Twentieth-Century America* (New York: Penguin, 1998). This wave of inmate writing produced a backlash and led to efforts to suppress it. Miriam Allen De Ford reported in 1930 in the *Nation* that "cells were searched all through San Quentin—not for narcotics or knives, but for manuscripts to be confiscated or destroyed" ("Shall Convicts Write Books?" *Nation* 131 [November 5, 1930]: 496).

52. Quoted in Jim Tully, *A Dozen and One* (Hollywood: Murray & Gee, 1943), 233.

53. Ernest Booth, preface to *Stealing through Life* (New York: Knopf, 1929).

54. Joseph F. Fishman, *Sex in Prison: Revealing Sex Conditions in American Prisons* (New York: National Library Press, 1934), 12. In this position, Fishman reported that he "visited over and over every penal institution of any importance in the U.S., Alaska, and Porto Rico [*sic*], and the majority of the country's 3500 jails" (*Sex in Prison*, 11). Later, Fishman became associate consultant in delinquency and penology at the Russell Sage Foundation. He resigned from that position in 1928 to become deputy commissioner of the New York City Department of Correction.

55. Kahn conducted his research in 1922–26 while he was psychiatrist for New York City's Department of Corrections. Kahn later served on the psychiatric staffs of Sing Sing Prison and the New York County Penitentiary.

56. Fishman, *Sex in Prison*, 5, 8.

57. Louis Berg, *Revelations of a Prison Doctor* (New York: Minton, Balch & Co., 1934), 138.

58. Fishman, *Sex in Prison*, 8.

59. Publisher's preface to Fishman, *Sex in Prison*, 6.

60. Joseph G. Wilson and Michael J. Pescor, *Problems in Prison Psychiatry* (Caldwell, ID: Caxton Printers, 1939), 196.

61. Berg, *Revelations of a Prison Doctor*, 139.

62. Charles A. Ford, "Homosexual Practices of Institutionalized Females," *Journal of Abnormal Psychology* 23 (January–March 1929): 443.

63. Maurice Chideckel, *Female Sex Perversion: The Sexually Aberrated Woman as She Is* (New York: Eugenics Publishing Co., 1938), 143.

64. Ibid., 136.

65. Lowell S. Selling, "The Pseudo Family," *American Journal of Sociology* 37 (September 1931): 248.

66. Chauncey, *Gay New York*, 47–48. See also Allen Drexel, "Before Paris Burned:

Race, Class, and Male Homosexuality on the Chicago South Side, 1935–1960," in *Creating a Place for Ourselves: Lesbian, Gay, and Bisexual Community Histories*, ed. Brett Beemyn (New York: Routledge, 1997).

67. Chauncey, *Gay New York*, 13.

68. Carlo de Fornaro, *A Modern Purgatory* (New York: Kennerley, 1917), 7.

69. Perry M. Lichtenstein, "The 'Fairy' and the Lady Lover," *Medical Review of Reviews* 27 (August 1921), 372.

70. Fishman, *Sex in Prison*, 60.

71. Ibid., 60.

72. Berg, *Revelations of a Prison Doctor*, 137.

73. Ibid., 152.

74. Ibid., 153.

75. Ibid.

76. Ibid., 153–54.

77. Ibid., 155–56.

78. Ibid., 140.

79. Fishman, *Sex in Prison*, 22.

80. Berg recommended segregating "the constitutional type, the one the man in the street recognizes under the optimistic title of 'fairy'" (*Revelations of a Prison Doctor*, 163). Fishman noted that the policy of segregating known homosexuals into separate wings of prisons was in place in "almost every big penitentiary" in the United States (*Sex in Prison*, 68–69).

81. Correctional Association of New York, *Report of the Prison Association of New York*, vol. 72 (1916), 120.

82. Ibid., 125.

83. Harry R. Hoffman, "Sex Perversion and Crime," *Archives of Neurology and Psychiatry* 3 (February 1920), 210.

84. Kahn, *Mentality and Homosexuality*, 23.

85. Ibid., 24.

86. Chauncey, *Gay New York*, 48.

87. In his discussion of New York City's Welfare Island prison, Chauncey noted as well that the sexual argot of the street and the sexual roles and expectations it delineated found an echo among prison populations. See ibid., 91–96.

88. John Loughery observes that many men interviewed in Samuel Kahn's 1937 study, *Mentality and Homosexuality*, were drawn from the urban working class, working before their arrest as "cooks, waiters, elevator operators, launderers, hospital orderlies, or stagehands" (*The Other Side of Silence: Men's Lives and Gay Identities: A Twentieth-Century History* [New York: Henry Holt, 1998], 34).

89. Hi Simons, "A Prison Dictionary (Expurgated)," *American Speech* 8, no. 3 (October 1933): 23.

90. Ibid., 32.

91. For other glossaries of prison terms, see Herbert Yenne, "Prison Lingo," *American Speech* 2 (March 1927): 280–82; George Milburn, "Convicts' Jargon," *American Speech*

6, no. 6 (August 1931): 436–42; Noel Ersine, *Underworld and Prison Slang* (Upland, IN: A. D. Freese & Son, 1933); J. Louis Kuethe, "Prison Parlance," *American Speech* 9, no. 1 (February 1934): 25–28; Clemmer, *The Prison Community*, 88–100; Rose Giallombardo, "Glossary of Prison Terms," in *Society of Women: A Study of a Women's Prison* (New York: John Wiley & Sons, 1966); Kay Johnson, "The Language of the Down People (a Glossary of Terms)," in *My Name Is Rusty: A Story of Lesbian Life behind Prison Bars* (New York: Castle Books, 1958). On prison argot, see Anthony Guenther, "The Language of Prison Life," in *Justice and Corrections*, ed. Norman Johnston and Leonard Savitz (New York: Wiley, 1978), 528–30.

92. Ersine, *Underworld and Prison Slang*.

93. Simons, "A Prison Dictionary," 23–24.

94. Nelson, *Prison Days and Nights*, 158.

95. Clifford R. Shaw, *Natural History of a Delinquent Career* (Chicago: University of Chicago Press, 1931), 189.

96. Berg, *Revelations of a Prison Doctor*, 148.

97. Ibid., 148.

98. Nelson, *Prison Days and Nights*, 158.

99. Goat Laven, *Rough Stuff: The Life Story of a Gangster* (London: Falcon Books, 1933), 185.

100. Berg, *Revelations of a Prison Doctor*, 148.

101. Ibid., 149.

102. Charles A. Ford, "Homosexual Practices of Institutionalized Females," *Journal of Abnormal Psychology* 23 (January–March 1929): 446.

103. Berg, *Revelations of a Prison Doctor*, 142. Josiah Flynt includes this expression in his glossary "The Tramp's Jargon," in which he defines an "ex-prushun" as "one who has served his apprenticeship as a 'kid' and is 'looking for revenge,' i.e. for a lad that he can 'snare' and 'jocker,' as he himself was 'snared' and 'jockered'" (*Tramping with Tramps: Studies and Sketches of Vagabond Life* [New York: Century Co., 1899], 396). See also James R. Winning, *Behind These Walls* (New York: Macmillan, 1933), 16.

104. Charles S. Wharton, *The House of Whispering Hate* (Chicago: Madelaine Mendlesohn, 1932), 39–40.

105. Jim Tully, *Shadows of Men* (Garden City, NY: Doubleday, Doran & Co., 1930), 264.

106. Berg, *Revelations of a Prison Doctor*, 147.

107. Ibid., 150.

108. Ibid., 151.

109. Wilson and Pescor, *Problems in Prison Psychiatry*, 202. Todd DePastino identifies hoboes as a "prominent part of a larger multiethnic, multiracial, and cross-class bachelor world flourishing in late-nineteenth- and early-twentieth-century American cities . . . whose preferences for male company included sex" (*Citizen Hobo: How a Century of Homelessness Shaped America* [Chicago: University of Chicago Press, 2003], 85). See also Boag, *Same-Sex Affairs*, 15–44; Josiah Flynt, "Homosexuality among Tramps," in *Studies in the Psychology of Sex*, vol. 2, ed. Havelock Ellis (1910; repr., New York: Random House,

1936), 359–67; Towne Nylander, "Tramps and Hoboes," *Forum* 74 (August 1925): 232; Frank C. Laubach, "Why There Are Vagrants: A Study Based upon an Examination of One Hundred Men," Ph.D. diss., Columbia University, 1916, 36; Kenneth L. Kusmer, *Down and Out on the Road: The Homeless in American History* (New York: Oxford University Press, 2002), 141–43; Thomas Minehan, *Boy and Girl Tramps of America* (New York: Gosset & Dunlap, 1934), 143.

110. Nels Anderson, *The Hobo: The Sociology of the Homeless Man* (Chicago: University of Chicago Press, 1923), 144; see also 137–39.

111. Jim Tully, *Beggers of Life* (New York: Albert & Charles Boni, 1924), 130–31.

112. Roberts, *Red Hell*, 63.

113. Flynt, "Homosexuality among Tramps," in *Sexual Inversion*, by Ellis, 36. See also, Flynt, *Tramping with Tramps*, 57–58.

114. Flynt, "Homosexuality among Tramps," 363.

115. Vagrancy was a common charge, of course, but Peter Boag finds a large number of transient men convicted of sexual charges. See Boag, *Same-Sex Affairs*, 22.

116. Jack London, "Pinched: A Prison Experience," *Cosmopolitan Magazine* 43–44 (July 1907): 264.

117. Simons, "A Prison Dictionary," 27.

118. Chester Himes, *The Quality of Hurt* (New York: Doubleday, 1972), 60.

119. Ibid., 61.

120. See "Critics of Cell Life," *Survey* 44 (1920): 151–52.

121. Berkman, *Prison Memoirs of an Anarchist*, 170.

122. Ibid., 173.

123. Wharton, *House of Whispering Hate*, 38.

124. Joseph F. Fishman, *Crucibles of Crime: The Shocking Story of the American Jail* (New York: Cosmopolis Press, 1923), 101.

125. Eugene Victor Debs, *Walls and Bars* (Chicago: Socialist Party, 1927), 147, 148.

126. Ibid., 147.

127. Ibid., 51.

128. Alice M. Propper, *Prison Homosexuality: Myth and Reality* (Lexington, MA: Lexington Books, 1981), 8.

129. A. McDonald, Superintendent, Chillicothe, Ohio, to Director, Bureau of Prisons, January 5, 1931, Bureau of Prison Records, National Archives, College Park, MD, box 612, file 4-8-3.

130. F. E. Wylie, "Reform by Surgery?" *Louisville Herald Post*, February 15, 1936, 3.

131. Ibid.

132. Oregon State Board of Control, F. W. Mulkey, chairman, *Report of the Commission to Investigate the Oregon State Penitentiary* ([Portland], OR: Oregon State Board of Control, 1917), 75. For discussion of the sex scandal that precipitated this investigation, see Boag, *Same-Sex Affairs*, 208–10.

133. The 1929 report of the Prison Association of New York reported on recent legislation in Idaho and North Dakota that authorized sterilization surgery on "moral degenerates and perverts" as well as the "feebleminded, insane, epileptic, and habitual

criminals." "The criminals who shall come under the operation of this law," the legislation specified, "shall be those who are . . . addicted to the practice of sodomy or the
crime against nature" (Correctional Association of New York, *Report of the Prison Association of New York*, vol. 85 [1929], 111, 112). On changes in Oregon's sterilization laws
following a homosexual scandal, see Boag, *Same-Sex Affairs*, 206–15.

134. Wilson and Pescor, *Problems in Prison Psychiatry*, 208.

135. Berg, *Revelations of a Prison Doctor*, 157. See also Shaw, *Natural History of a Delinquent Career*, 189.

136. Berg, *Revelations of a Prison Doctor*, 157.

137. Lewis E. Lawes, *Invisible Stripes* (New York: Farrar & Rinehart, 1938), 94.

138. Wilson and Pescor, *Problems in Prison Psychiatry*, 208.

139. Samuel Roth, *Stone Walls Do Not: The Chronicle of a Captivity* (New York: William
Faro, 1930), 260.

140. George Harsh, *Lonesome Road* (New York: W. W. Norton, 1971), 15, 52.

141. Berg, *Revelations of a Prison Doctor*, 160; see also Chauncey, *Gay New York*, 92.

142. Fishman claimed that the lockstep was abandoned because prison administrators believed that the close body contact it required promoted homosexuality (*Sex in
Prison*, 90).

143. Quoted in Ben Bagdikian, *Caged: Eight Prisoners and Their Keepers* (New York:
Harper & Row, 1976), xiii.

144. See Murphy, *Political Manhood*; Edgardo Rotman, "The Failure of Reform:
United States, 1865–1965," in *Oxford History of the Prison*, ed., Morris and Rothman;
David J. Rothman, *Conscience and Convenience: The Asylum and Its Alternatives in Progressive
America* (Boston: Little, Brown, 1980), 119–22.

145. Jack Black, *You Can't Win* (New York: Macmillan, 1926; repr., San Francisco:
Nabat/AK Press, 2000), 82.

146. George B. Wright, *Two Years' Experience as a Prisoner(!) in the United States Penitentiary at Leavenworth, Kansas* (Leavenworth: Leavenworth Bag Co., 1915), 67.

147. Edward Bunker, *Education of a Felon* (New York: St. Martin's, 2000), 110.

148. Angelo Herndon, *Let Me Live* (New York: Random House, 1937), 210.

149. Malcolm Braly, *False Starts: A Memoir of San Quentin and Other Prisons* (Boston:
Little, Brown & Co., 1976), 159.

150. Jean Harris, *They Always Call Us Ladies: Stories from Prison* (New York: Macmillan, 1988), 140.

151. Julius A. Leibert, *Behind Bars: What a Chaplain Saw in Alcatraz, Folsom and San
Quentin* (Garden City, NY: Doubleday, 1965), 25.

152. John N. Reynolds, *A Kansas Hell; or, Life in the Kansas Penitentiary* (Atchison, KS:
Bee Publishing Co., 1889), 13.

153. Ibid., 71.

154. Ted Ditsworth, *Out of the Depths of Hell* (New York: Vantage, 1974), 32.

155. American Correctional Association, *The American Prison: From the Beginning . . .
a Pictorial History* ([College Park, MD]: American Correctional Association, 1983), 126.

156. Berg, *Revelations of a Prison Doctor*, 141.

157. Evan Thomas, "Disciplinary Barracks: The Experience of a Military Prisoner at Fort Leavenworth," *Survey* 41 (February 1, 1919): 626.

158. Dean Harno to Burgess, May 9, 1927, 6, Ernest W. Burgess Papers, University of Chicago Archives, Special Collections Research Center, Chicago, Illinois, box 34, fol. 7.

159. Interview of Pontiac inmate by Landesco, August 23, 1927, in Ernest W. Burgess Papers, University of Chicago Archives, Special Collections Research Center, Chicago, Illinois, box 34, fol. 9.

160. Kahn, *Mentality and Homosexuality*, 24. Estelle Freedman notes that cutbacks in appropriations and increases in the number of women committed to prison in the early twentieth century resulted in serious overcrowding of women's prisons (*Their Sisters' Keepers*, 138–39).

161. See Anne Butler, *Gendered Justice in the American West: Women Prisoners in Men's Penitentiaries* (Urbana: University of Illinois Press, 1997).

162. On the development of the criminal justice system in the South, see Michael Stephen Hindus, *Prison and Plantation: Crime, Justice, and Authority in Massachusetts and South Carolina, 1767–1878* (Chapel Hill: University of North Carolina Press, 1980); David M. Oshinsky, *"Worse than Slavery": Parchman Farm and the Ordeal of Jim Crow Justice* (New York: Free Press, 1996); Mary Ellen Curtain, *Black Prisoners and Their World, Alabama, 1865–1900* (Charlottesville: University Press of Virginia, 2000); William Banks Taylor, *Down on Parchman Farm: The Great Prison in the Mississippi Delta* (Columbus: Ohio State University Press, 1999).

163. See Matthew J. Mancini, *One Dies, Get Another: Convict Leasing in the American South, 1866–1928* (Columbia: University of South Carolina Press, 1996); Alex Lichtenstein, *Twice the Work of Free Labor: The Political Economy of Convict Labor in the New South* (London: Verso, 1996).

164. Oshinsky, *"Worse than Slavery,"* 59. See also Harsh, *Lonesome Road*, 18; Mancini, *One Dies, Get Another*, 59–78.

CHAPTER 3

1. Bly originally published her account in the *New York World*. She later published it under the name Elizabeth Cochrane, *Ten Days in a Mad-House* (New York: Munro, 1887).

2. "Crime and Punishment: Prison Lids Blow off Revealing Ugly Secrets Which Challenge American Penal System," *News-Week*, February 3, 1934, 7.

3. Berg, *Revelations of a Prison Doctor*, 32.

4. "World's Worst," *Time*, February 5, 1934, 15. For accounts of the Welfare Island raid, see Berg, *Revelations of a Prison Doctor*, 210; Chauncey, *Gay New York*, 91–94; Loughery, *The Other Side of Silence*, 106; Lowell M. Limpus and Burr W. Leyson, *This Man La Guardia* (New York: Dutton, 1938), 378–81.

5. "Prison Gang Chiefs Served by Valets," *New York Times*, January 25, 1934, 3.

6. "Welfare Island Raid Bares Gangster Rule over Prison; Weapons, Narcotics Found," *New York Times*, January 25, 1934, 3.

7. "M'Cormick Raids Welfare Island," *New York Herald Tribune*, January 25, 1934, 9.

8. Sinfield, *The Wilde Century*. Laura Doan makes a similar point about the indeterminacy of female masculinity in the early twentieth century in *Fashioning Sapphism: The Origins of a Modern English Lesbian Culture* (New York: Columbia University Press, 2001).

9. "Welfare Island Raid Aids Prison Reform," *Literary Digest* 117 (February 3, 1934): 6.

10. "M'Cormick Raids Welfare Island," *New York Herald Tribune*, January 25, 1934, 9.

11. Frederick Woltman, "Sex Offenders Create Difficult Prison Problem Even Experts Can't Solve," *World-Telegram*, April 21, 1939), 1.

12. "Tammany Leader Linked to Jail Ring," *New York Times*, January 27, 1934, 2.

13. Chauncey, in *Gay New York*, documents the new visibility of gay life and culture in early-twentieth-century New York City, complete with gay neighborhood enclaves, widely publicized social events, and commercial establishments, as well as queer representation in literature and on the stage. On the "pansy craze," see Chauncey, *Gay New York*, esp. 301–29; Daniel Hurewitz, *Bohemian Los Angeles and the Making of Modern Politics* (Berkeley: University of California Press, 2007), 118–22; Eric Garber, "A Spectacle in Color: The Lesbian and Gay Subculture of Jazz Age Harlem," in *Hidden from History: Reclaiming the Gay and Lesbian Past*, ed. Martin Duberman, Martha Vicinus, and George Chauncey, Jr. (New York: New American Library, 1989), 318–33; Lillian Faderman, *Odd Girls and Twilight Lovers: A History of Lesbian Life in Twentieth-Century America* (New York: Penguin Books, 1992), 67–79; Kevin J. Mumford, *Interzones: Black/White Sex Districts in Chicago and New York in the Early Twentieth Century* (New York: Columbia University Press, 1997); David K. Johnson, "The Kids of Fairytown: Gay Male Culture on Chicago's Near North Side in the 1930s," in *Creating a Place for Ourselves: Lesbian, Gay, and Bisexual Community Histories*, ed. Brett Beemyn (New York: Routledge, 1997), 97–118; and Allen Drexel, "Before Paris Burned: Race, Class, and Male Homosexuality on the Chicago South Side, 1935–1960," in *Creating a Place for Ourselves*, ed. Beemyn, 119–44.

The Motion Picture Code, formally adopted in 1930, was the means by which the motion picture industry regulated itself. Establishing generally that "no picture shall be produced that will lower the moral standards of those who see it," the code stated explicitly that "sex perversion or any inference to it is forbidden." See Vitto Russo, *The Celluloid Closet: Homosexuality in the Movies* (New York: Harper & Row, 1981), esp. 31; Patricia White, *Uninvited: Classical Hollywood Cinema and Lesbian Representability* (Bloomington: Indiana University Press, 1999), xviii, 1–12; James Robert Parish, *Gays and Lesbians in Mainstream Cinema* (Jefferson, NC: McFarland and Co., 1993).

14. Berg, *Revelations of a Prison Doctor*, 156.

15. On the backlash against homosexuality in the late 1920s and 1930s, see Chauncey, *Gay New York*, 331–54; Terry, *An American Obsession*, 268–96; Andrea Friedman, *Prurient Interests: Gender, Democracy, and Obscenity in New York City, 1909–1945* (New York: Columbia University Press, 2000), 95–122.

16. "Just a Pansy," *Brevities*, February 12, 1934, 12.

17. George W. Henry and Alfred A. Gross, "The Homosexual Delinquent," *Mental Hygiene* 25, no. 3 (July 1941): 422. See also Morris G. Caldwell, "Group Dynamics in the Prison Community," *Journal of Criminal Law, Criminology and Police Science* 46 (1956): 652–53.

18. Henry and Gross, "The Homosexual Delinquent," 422.

19. Clinton T. Duffy and Al Hirschberg, *Sex and Crime* (Garden City, NY: Doubleday, 1965), 29.

20. David Halperin argues that "the hallmark of 'homosexuality,' in fact, is the refusal to distinguish between same-sex sexual partners or to rank them by treating them as more (or less) homosexual than the other," in *How to Do the History of Homosexuality* (Chicago: University of Chicago Press, 2002), 132. Other historians have located the emergence of this binary in the 1930s, 1940s, and 1950s. In his study of gay life and culture on Chicago's South Side, Allen Drexel finds that, "by the 1930s, this conceptual distinction between the practice of having sex with a 'fairy' and the identity of *being gay* was becoming blurred." Drexel discerns a new anxiety in this period among men who have sex with men but identify as "normal" ("Before Paris Burned," 125). Chauncey argues that the "hetero-homosexual binarism, the sexual regime now hegemonic in American culture, is a stunningly recent creation," taking shape only around the middle of the twentieth century (*Gay New York*, 13). Robert J. Corber and David C. Johnson both credit cold war homophobia for consolidating these ideas. See Corber, "Lesbian Visibility in *All About Eve*," *GLQ: A Journal of Lesbian and Gay Studies* 11 (2005): 6–7; David K. Johnson, *The Lavender Scare: The Cold War Persecution of Gays and Lesbians in the Federal Government* (Chicago: University of Chicago Press, 2004), 162–63. For discussions of the emergence of sexual object choice as the organizing principle of sexuality, see Chauncey, *Gay New York*, 99–127; Miriam G. Reumann, *American Sexual Character: Sex, Gender, and National Identity in the Kinsey Reports* (Berkeley: University of California Press, 2005), 176–77; Joanne Meyerowitz, *How Sex Changed: A History of Transsexuality in the United States* (Cambridge, MA: Harvard University Press, 2002), esp. 170–76; Hurewitz, *Bohemian Los Angeles*.

21. Henry and Gross, "The Homosexual Delinquent," 432. On the sexual self-conceptions of hustlers in this period, see Albert J. Reiss, Jr., "The Social Integration of Queers and Peers," *Social Problems* 9 (Fall 1961): 102–20.

22. Roth, *Stone Walls Do Not*, 260–61.

23. James Blake, *The Joint* (Garden City, NY: Doubleday, 1971), 66–67. On the segregation of homosexuals in men's prison, see Frederick S. Baldi, *My Unwelcome Guests* (New York: J. B. Lippincott, 1959), 98; Clinton T. Duffy and Dean Jennings, *The San Quentin Story* (Garden City, NY: Doubleday, 1950), 151; Wayne A. Oliver and Donald L. Mosher, "Psychopathology and Guilt in Heterosexuals and Subgroups of Homosexual Reformatory Inmates," *Journal of Abnormal Psychology* 73 (1968): 323; Clyde B. Vedder and Patricia G. King, *Problems of Homosexuality in Corrections* (Springfield, IL: Charles C. Thomas, 1967), vi; John H. Gagnon and William Simon, "The Social Meaning of Prison Homosexuality," *Federal Probation* 32 (March 1968): 27; William H. Haines and John J. McLaughlin, "Treatment of the Homosexual in Prison," *Diseases of the Nervous System* 13 (1952): 86–87; Richard W. Nice, "The Problem of Homosexuality in Corrections," *American Journal of Correction* 28 (May–June 1966), 31; Charles E. Smith, "The Homosexual Federal Offender: A Study of 100 Cases," *Journal of Criminal Law, Criminology and Police Science* 44 (1954): 590.

24. While few women's institutions seemed to practice the segregation of lesbian

prisoners, there were several recommendations that they do so. Joseph G. Wilson, chief medical officer of several prisons in the 1930s and 1940s, recommended that lesbians be segregated from general inmate populations, writing that "[the lesbian] should not be sent to a reformatory but to a prison where strict segregation can be enforced, and where she cannot corrupt others. It is better for society to let her rot alone, than to turn her loose to rot others" (*Are Prisons Necessary?* [Philadelphia: Dorrnace & Co., 1950], 219.) Among the charges made in the investigation of Miriam van Waters, superintendent of Massachusetts' Framingham Reformatory for Women in 1949 was that Van Waters "failed to segregate inmates with recorded homosexual tendencies from other inmates, both in work assignments and living quarters" ("Removal Notice with Reasons Given," February 14, 1949, p. 22, Van Waters Papers, Schlesinger Library, Cambridge, MA, box 22, fol. 251). Officials recommended that "'known' homosexual inmates to be isolated—and denied any 'special privileges" (Van Waters notes, "Possible Recommendations of Dwyer," June 1948, Van Waters Papers, box 22, fol. 248).

    25. Harvey Bluestone, Edward P. O'Malley, and Sydney Connell, "Homosexuals in Prison," *Corrective Psychiatry and Journal of Social Therapy* 12 (1966): 14.

    26. Joseph G. Wilson and Michael J. Pescor, *Problems in Prison Psychiatry* (Caldwell, ID: Caxton Printers, 1939), 201.

    27. Joseph E. Ragen and Charles Finston, *Inside the World's Toughest Prison* (Springfield, IL: Charles C. Thomas, 1962), 379.

    28. Leo Stanley and Evelyn Wells, *Men at Their Worst* (New York: Appleton-Century, 1940), 201.

    29. Nice, "The Problem of Homosexuality in Corrections," 31. Prison administrators were not alone in confronting this problem. The 1950 Senate Appropriations Committee hearings on the government employment of homosexuals and "other sex perverts" stated that "all homosexual males do not have feminine mannerisms, nor do all female homosexuals display masculine characteristics in their dress or actions," making it impossible to discern homosexuality from gender cues (U.S. Senate, Committee on Expenditures in Executive Departments, *Employment of Homosexuals and Other Sex Perverts in Government*, 81st Cong., 2d sess., 1950, S. Rep.241, 4). The armed forces experienced similar difficulties during the Second World War. See Allan Bérubé, *Coming Out under Fire: The History of Gay Men and Women in World War Two* (New York: Free Press, 1990).

    30. Lewis M. Terman and Catherine Cox Miles, *Sex and Personality: Studies in Masculinity and Femininity* (New York: McGraw-Hill, 1936), 7. On the Terman and Miles study, see Terry, *American Obsession*, 168–75; Henry L. Minton, *Departing from Deviance: A History of Homosexual Rights and Emancipatory Science in America* (Chicago: University of Chicago Press, 2002), 18. On the history of the understanding of the notion of gender as distinct from sex, see Meyerowitz, *How Sex Changed*, 98–129.

    31. Terman and Miles, *Sex and Personality*, 239.

    32. Ibid., 239–40.

    33. Ibid., 271.

    34. Ibid., 277.

    35. Ibid., 9.

36. Ibid., 242, 254.

37. Edward L. Walker, "The Terman 'M-F' Test and the Prison Classification Program," *Journal of Genetic Psychology* 59 (1941): 28.

38. Ibid., 37.

39. Charles E. Smith, "Some Problems in Dealing with Homosexuals in the Prison Situation," *Journal of Social Therapy* 2 (1956): 38.

40. Terman and Miles, *Sex and Personality*, 467–68.

41. Ibid., 78.

42. Terry, *An American Obsession*, 169.

43. Terman and Miles, *Sex and Personality*, 78.

44. See Edgardo Rotman, "The Failure of Reform: United States, 1865–1965," in *The Oxford History of the Prison*, ed. Morris and Rothman, 189; Julius A. Leibert, *Behind Bars: What a Chaplain Saw in Alcatraz, Folsom and San Quentin* (Garden City, NY: Doubleday, 1965), 7; John Irwin, *Prisons in Turmoil* (Boston: Little, Brown & Co., 1980), 38–40. On the influence of psychoanalysis in the culture more generally, see Nathan Hale, *The Rise and Crisis of Psychoanalysis in the U.S.: Freud and the Americans, 1917–1985* (New York: Oxford University Press, 1995); Ellen Herman, *The Romance of American Psychology: Political Culture in the Age of Experts* (Berkeley: University of California Press, 1995).

45. Malcolm Braly, *False Starts: A Memoir of San Quentin and Other Prisons* (Boston: Little, Brown & Co., 1976), 157–58.

46. Ibid., 160.

47. Ibid., 163–64.

48. Donald Clemmer, *The Prison Community* (Boston: Christopher Publishing House, 1940), 264. Clemmer clung to that assumption. Four years after the publication of this major study, Clemmer was brought to the penitentiary at Ashland, Kentucky, to diagnose civil rights activist Bayard Rustin. Clemmer reported that "Rustin presents . . . a classical picture of a constitutional homo—the invert type, the high voice, the extravagant mannerisms, the tremendous conceit, the general unmanliness of the inmate frame a picture . . . that it does not take a Freud to diagnose" (Clemmer, memo to Mr. Bennett and Mr. Loveland, September 25, 1944, Bureau of Prison Records, National Archives, College Park, MD, box 79, Notorious Offenders File). On identifying homosexuals among prison inmates, Wilson and Pescor wrote that "at the primary physical examination anatomical deviations from the average sex characteristics will of course be noted" (*Problems in Prison Psychiatry*), 204.

49. Kinsey et al., *Sexual Behavior in the Human Male*, 610.

50. See Estelle B. Freedman, "'Uncontrolled Desires': The Response to the Sexual Psychopath, 1920–1960," *Journal of American History* 74 (June 1987): 83–106; Chauncey, "The Post-War Sex Crime Panic," in *True Stories from the American Past*, ed. William Graebner (New York: McGraw-Hill, 1993), 160–78; Stephen Robertson, "Separating the Men from the Boys: Masculinity, Psychosexual Development, and Sex Crime in the United States, 1930s–1960s," *Journal of the History of Medicine and Allied Sciences* 56 (2001): 3–35; Terry, *An American Obsession*, 321–28.

51. Clemmer, *Prison Community*, 266.

52. V. C. Branham, foreword to *Mentality and Homosexuality* by Samuel Kahn (Boston: Meador Publishing Co., 1937), 5.

53. U.S. Senate, *Employment of Homosexuals and Other Sex Perverts in Government*; Johnson, *Lavender Scare*; John D'Emilio, "The Homosexual Menace: The Politics of Sexuality in Cold War America," in *Passion and Power: Sexuality in History*, ed. Kathy Peiss and Christine Simmons (Philadelphia: Temple University Press, 1989), 226–40.

54. See Johnson, *Lavender Scare*; Terry, *An American Obsession*, 334–47.

55. John Bartlow Martin, *Break Down the Walls* (New York: Curtis Publishing Co., 1951), 180.

56. Fishman, *Sex in Prison*, 28.

57. "Crime and Punishment: Prison Lids Blow off Revealing Ugly Secrets Which Challenge American Penal System," *News-Week* 3, no. 5 (February 3, 1934): 7.

58. Duffy and Hirshberg, *Sex and Crime*, 29.

59. Freedman, "'Uncontrolled Desires,'" 94; 97–98.

60. John D'Emilio cites one study in the 1950s that estimated that one out of five gay men had "encountered trouble at the hands of the police" (*Lost Prophet: The Life and Times of Bayard Rustin* [Chicago: University of Chicago Press, 2003], 194). See also D'Emilio, *Sexual Politics, Sexual Communities: The Making of a Homosexual Minority in the United States, 1940–1970* (Chicago: University of Chicago Press, 1983), 41–53, and "The Homosexual Menace," 226–40.

61. Karpman, "Sex Life in Prison," 482.

62. Duffy and Hirshberg, *Sex and Crime*, 177.

63. Ibid.

64. Katherine Sullivan, *Girls on Parole* (Westport, CT: Greenwood Press, 1956), 111.

65. Frank S. Caprio, *Female Homosexuality: A Modern Study of Lesbianism* (New York: Grove Press, 1954), 77.

66. Sara Harris, *Hellhole: The Shocking Story of the Inmates and Life in the New York City House of Detention for Women* (New York: E. P. Dutton & Co., 1967), 241.

67. Elizabeth Gurley Flynn, *The Alderson Story: My Life as a Political Prisoner* (New York: International Publishers, 1963), 163.

68. On the relationship of Freud to sexology, see Terry, *An American Obsession*, 43; Chris Waters, "Havelock Ellis, Sigmund Freud and the State: Discourses of Homosexual Identity in Interwar Britain," in *Sexology in Culture: Labeling Bodies and Desires*, ed. Lucy Bland and Laura Doan (Chicago: University of Chicago Press, 1998).

69. Robert M. Lindner, "Sexual Behavior in Penal Institutions," in *Sex Habits of American Men*, ed. Albert Deutsch (New York: Prentice Hall, 1948), 202.

70. Karpman, "Sex Life in Prison," 481. See also Vedder and King, *Problems of Homosexuality in Corrections*, 24.

71. Berg, *Revelations of a Prison Doctor*, 145.

72. See, for example, Arthur V. Huffman, "Sex Deviation in a Prison Community," *Journal of Social Therapy* 6 (1960): 172; Clemmer, *Prison Community*, 268–69.

73. Kinsey et al., *Sexual Behavior in the Human Male*, 224.

74. Victor F. Nelson, *Prison Days and Nights* (Boston: Little, Brown, 1933), 153–55.

75. Lou Torok, *The Strange World of Prison* (Indianapolis: Bobbs-Merrill, 1973), 95–96.

76. Virginia McManus, "My Experiences with Homosexuals in Women's Prison," *Confidential* 7, no. 4 (September 1959): 23, 52.

77. Haywood Patterson and Earl Conrad, *Scottsboro Boy* (New York: Doubleday, 1950), 83.

78. Ibid., 80, 83.

79. Paul Warren, *Next Time Is for Life* (New York: Dell, 1953), 74.

80. Donald Lee, "Seduction of the Guilty: Homosexuality in American Prisons," *Fact* 2 (November–December 1965): 57.

81. Jennifer Terry credits Kinsey's study with "pierc[ing] the *cordon sanitaire* that had marked a clear-cut difference between . . . heterosexuals and homosexuals" (Terry, *An American Obsession*, 303). In her history of the impact and significance of Alfred Kinsey's published studies of American sexual practice, Miriam Reumann identifies key questions that haunted postwar discussions of homosexuality more generally: "Experts wanted to know how many homosexuals existed in the present-day United States and whether their numbers were increasing. Was the homosexual a specific and recognizable kind of person, differentiated from the heterosexual by his or her body, sexual behavior, gender identity, or psychology?. . . . Ultimately, was homosexuality a stable and recognizable category, or, as more and more worried, were hetero- and homosexual behaviors so mingled that they could not be separated?" (*American Sexual Character*, 166–67). See also Terry, *An American Obsession*, 301–4; Loughery, *The Other Side of Silence*, 194; Stephanie H. Kenen, "Who Counts When You're Counting Homosexuals? Hormones and Homosexuality in Mid-Twentieth-Century America," in *Science and Homosexualities*, ed. Vernon Rosario (New York: Routledge, 1997).

82. Kinsey et al., *Sexual Behavior in the Human Male*, 623.

83. Kinsey et al., *Sexual Behavior in the Human Female* (Philadelphia: W. B. Saunders, 1953), 487.

84. Kinsey et al., *Sexual Behavior in the Human Male*, 650. See also 637, 639.

85. Wardell B. Pomeroy, *Dr. Kinsey and the Institute for Sex Research* (New York: Harper & Row, 1972), 201–2.

86. Ibid., 205.

87. See Jonathan Gathorne-Hardy, *Sex the Measure of All Things: A Life of Alfred C. Kinsey* (Bloomington: Indiana University Press, 1998), 326–27; Pomeroy, *Dr. Kinsey and the Institute for Sex Research*, 202; Paul H. Gebhard and Alan B. Johnson, *The Kinsey Data: Marginal Tabulations of the 1938–1963 Interviews Conducted by the Institute for Sex Research* (Philadelphia: W. B. Saunders Co., 1979), 28.

88. There is some question as to whether Kinsey actually recalculated his findings after omitting the sexual histories from prisoners. Kinsey biographer Jonathan Gathorne-Hardy writes that Kinsey assured critics that he had done so but that Kinsey associate Paul Gebhard "said at the time that they hadn't done this" (*Sex the Measure of All Things*, 326).

89. Kinsey et al., *Sexual Behavior in the Human Female*, 22. See also Gebhard and Johnson, *The Kinsey Data*, 2.

90. Gebhard and Johnson, *The Kinsey Data*, 28.

91. Pomeroy, *Dr. Kinsey and the Institute for Sex Research*, 202.

92. James Blake, *The Joint* (Garden City, NY: Doubleday, 1971), 320–31. Algren had met Blake, identified by Algren's biographer as "a writer, a piano player, and inept burglar," in a Chicago tavern, and he encouraged Blake's writing while Blake was in prison (Bettina Drew, *Nelson Algren: A Life on the Wild Side* [New York: Putnam's, 1989], 247). In 1956, Algren edited some of Blake's correspondence under the title "Letters from an American Prisoner," for publication in the *Paris Review* 13 (Summer 1956): 8–44.

93. Berg, *Revelations of a Prison Doctor*, 153.

94. Robert M. Lindner, "Sex in Prison," *Complex* 6 (1951): 18.

95. See, for example, David Abrahamsen, "Glossary of Prison Jargon," in *Who Are the Guilty?* 311–13; Giallombardo, "Glossary of Prison Terms"; M. Arc, "The Prison 'Culture'—from the Inside," *New York Times Magazine*, February 28, 1965, 52–58.

96. Kay Johnson, *My Name Is Rusty: A Story of Lesbian Life behind Prison Bars* (New York: Castle Books, 1958), 9–12.

97. Erving Goffman, *Asylums: Essays on the Social Situation of Mental Patients and Other Inmates* (Garden City, NY: Doubleday, 1961).

98. On the Chicago school's pioneering and largely overlooked sociological studies of sexuality, see Chad Heap, "The City as a Sexual Laboratory: The Queer Heritage of the Chicago School," *Qualitative Sociology* 26, no. 4 (Winter 2003): 457–87. John Irwin points out that "the prison was ideally suited for system or functionalist studies because, unlike the complex broader society, it was relatively small, contained, cohesive, and homogeneous. It appeared to parallel the isolated tribal societies that were the subject of the first functional analyses" (*Prisons in Turmoil*, 32–33).

99. Herbert A. Bloch, "Social Pressures of Confinement toward Sexual Deviation," *Journal of Social Therapy* 1 (April 1955): 123.

100. Ibid., 115.

101. Clemmer, *The Prison Community*, 270.

102. Arthur V. Huffman, "Sex Deviation in a Prison Community," *Journal of Social Therapy* 6 (1960): 176.

103. Percy R. Parnell, *The Joint* (San Antonio, TX: Naylor, 1976), 32.

104. Quoted in Dae H. Chang and Warren B. Armstrong, eds., *The Prison: Voices from the Inside* (Cambridge, MA: Schenkman, 1972), 65–66.

105. Robert H. Adleman, *Alias Big Cherry: The Confessions of a Master Criminal* (New York: Dial Press, 1973), 244.

106. Lee, "Seduction of the Guilty," 57–58.

107. Helen Bryan, *Inside* (Boston: Houghton Mifflin, 1953), 281.

108. Quoted in Rose Giallombardo, *The Social World of Imprisoned Girls: A Comparative Study of Institutions for Juvenile Delinquents* (New York: John Wiley & Sons, 1974), 244.

109. Piri Thomas, *Down These Mean Streets* (New York: Knopf, 1967), 262.

110. Christopher Teale, *Behind These Walls* (New York: Frederick Fell, 1957), 29.

111. Gresham M. Sykes, *The Society of Captives: A Study of a Maximum Security Prison* (Princeton, NJ: Princeton University Press, 1958). See also, Goffman, *Asylums*.

112. Ibid., 71.

113. Fred Cutter, "The Problem of Prison Sex," *Sexology* (July 1962), 824.

114. Berg, *Revelations of a Prison Doctor*, 143.

115. Robert Lindner, *Stone Walls and Men* (New York: Odyssey Press, 1946), 457.

116. Baldi, *My Unwelcome Guests*, 96.

117. Ibid., 96.

118. Richard Stiller, "Sex Practices in Prison," in *The Third Sex*, ed. Isadore Rubin (New York: New Book Co., 1961), 82.

119. George Deveureux and Malcolm C. Moss, "The Social Structures of Prisons and the Organic Tensions," *Journal of Criminal Psychopathology* 4 (October 1942): 317.

120. Harris, *Hellhole*, 60.

121. Bryan, *Inside*, 281.

122. Lee, "Seduction of the Guilty," 57.

123. Piri Thomas, *Seven Long Times* (New York: Praeger, 1974), 108.

124. George Sylvester Viereck, *Men into Beasts* (New York: Fawcett, 1952), 158–59.

125. Robert Neese, *Prison Exposures* (New York: Chilton Co., 1959), 52.

126. Russell H. Dinerstein and Bernard C. Glueck, Jr., "Sub-Coma Insulin Therapy in the Treatment of Homosexual Panic States," *Journal of Social Therapy* 3 (October 1955): 184.

127. See Martin, *Break Down the Walls*, 182; Daniel G. Moore, *Enter without Knocking* (Tucson: University of Arizona Press, 1969), 250; Duffy and Hirshberg, *Sex and Crime*, 4–5, 174–75; Barnes and Teeters, *New Horizons in Criminology*, 623; Vedder and King, *Problems of Homosexuality in Corrections*, vi–vii, 42; Stiller, "Sex Practices in Prison," 85; Joseph K. Balogh, "Conjugal Visitations in Prisons: A Sociological Perspective," *Federal Probation* 28 (September 1964): 52–58; Karpman, "Sex in Prison," 485; Cutter, "The Problem of Prison Sex," 823–24; Richard Stiller, "Conjugal Visits in Prison," *Sexology* (1959): 288–91.

128. Joseph G. Wilson, "Prison Sex Life," *Sexology* (October 1953), 161.

129. Barnes and Teeters, *New Horizons in Criminology*, 623.

130. See Columbus B. Hopper, *Sex in Prison: The Mississippi Experiment with Conjugal Visiting* (Baton Rouge: Louisiana State University Press, 1969); Hopper, "The Conjugal Visit at the Mississippi State Penitentiary," *Journal of Criminal Law, Criminology and Police Science* 53 (September 1962): 340–43; William Banks Taylor, *Down on Parchman Farm: The Great Prison in the Mississippi Delta* (Columbus: Ohio State University Press, 1999), 57–58; Nice, "The Problem of Homosexuality in Corrections," 31; David M. Oshinsky, *"Worse Than Slavery": Parchman Farm and the Ordeal of Jim Crow Justice* (New York: Free Press, 1996), 153–54.

131. Oshinsky, *"Worse Than Slavery,"* 154.

132. Duffy and Hirshberg, *Sex and Crime*, 175.

133. Ibid., 5.

134. Moore, *Enter without Knocking*, 250.

135. Eugene Zemans and Ruth Shonle Covan, "Marital Relationships of Prisoners," *Journal of Criminal Law, Criminology, and Police Science* 49 (May–June 1958): 50–57.

136. Columbus B. Hopper, "Conjugal Visiting: A Controversial Practice in Mississippi," *Criminal Law Bulletin* 3 (1967): 289.

137. Karpman, "Sex Life in Prison," 479; Bloch, "Social Pressures of Confinement toward Sexual Deviation," 123.

138. Minutes of the Fifteenth Session of the Conference of Women Superintendents of Girls' and Women's Correction Institutions, February 14–16, 1944, p. 21, Van Waters Papers, box 48, fol. 587.

139. Peter C. Buffum, *Homosexuality in Prisons* (Washington, DC: Govt. Printing Office, 1972), 20.

140. John Bartlow Martin, *My Life in Crime* (New York: Harper, 1952), 205.

141. See Eve Kosofsky Sedgwick, *Epistemology of the Closet* (Berkeley: University of California Press, 1990), 1.

142. Negley K. Teeters, *They Were in Prison: A History of the Pennsylvania Prison Society, 1787–1937* (Chicago: John C. Winston Co., 1937).

143. Tom Runyon, *In for Life: A Convict's Story* (New York: Norton, 1953), 102.

144. Quoted in Bruce Jackson, *In the Life: Versions of the Criminal Experience* (New York: Holt, Rinehart, & Winston, 1972), 269.

145. Lindner, "Sex in Prison," 11–12.

146. Lindner, *Stone Walls and Men*, 454.

147. Daniel Eisenberg observes that the Supreme Court criterion, imposed from 1957 to 1973, for determining if a work were to be denied First Amendment protection—that it be "utterly without redeeming social value"—"led . . . to the production of a large number of superficially non-fictional works, in which a skeleton of pseudo-scientific purpose was used as a means to present a series of erotic 'case histories.' To the extent that the primary purpose of these books was to arouse rather than to inform, they should be treated together with erotic fiction" (Eisenberg, "Toward a Bibliography of Erotic Pulps," *Journal of Popular Culture* 15 [Spring 1982]: 177–78).

148. Barnes and Teeters, *New Horizons in Criminology*; Norman Johnston et al., eds., *The Sociology of Punishment and Correction* (New York: John Wiley & Sons, 1962), also included excerpts from the studies of Donald Clemmer, Gresham Sykes, and others; James J. Proferes, *Prison Punk* (Washington, DC: Guild Press, 1969).

149. "I Lived in a Hell behind Bars," *True Confessions* (March 1954), 32+.

150. Ibid., 12.

151. Ibid., 50.

152. Ibid., 51.

153. Ibid.

154. Ibid., 52.

155. Ibid., 55.

156. Ibid., 54.

157. Johnson, *My Name Is Rusty*, 21.

158. Ibid., 63.

159. Ibid., 79, 84.

160. Ibid., 169.

161. Ibid., 22.
162. Ibid., 21.
163. Teale, *Behind These Walls*, 18.
164. Ibid., 50.
165. Ibid., 132.
166. Ibid., 131.
167. Ibid., 136.
168. Ibid., 222.

CHAPTER 4

Chapter 4's title is taken from Catherine I. Nelson, "A Study of Homosexuality among Women Inmates at Two State Prisons" (Ph.D. diss., Temple University, 1974), 143.

1. David A. Ward and Gene G. Kassebaum, *Women's Prison: Sex and Social Structure* (Chicago: Aldine, 1965); Giallombardo, *Society of Women*; Harris, *Hellhole*; Esther Heffernan, *Making It in Prison: The Square, the Cool, and the Life* (New York: John Wiley & Sons, 1972). Giallombardo published a book on imprisoned delinquent girls a few years later, *The Social World of Imprisoned Girls*.

2. *Prisoners in State and Federal Institutions* (Washington, DC: U.S. Department of Justice, Law Enforcement Assistance Administration, 1976–77). That number would double in a decade. In 1980, there were just over 12,000 women in U.S. state and federal prisons. By 1997, that number had increased to almost 80,000, comprising about 6.3 percent of all state and federal prisoners (Meda Chesney-Lind, "The Forgotten Offender," *Corrections Today* 60, no. 7 [December 1998]: 66; Barbara Owen, "Women and Imprisonment in the United States: The Gendered Consequences of the U.S. Imprisonment Binge," in *Harsh Punishment: International Experiences of Women's Imprisonment*, ed. Sandy Cook and Susanne Davies [Boston: Northeastern University Press, 1999], 81; Lori B. Girshick, *No Safe Haven: Stories of Women in Prison* [Boston: Northeastern University Press, 1999], 17; U.S. Department of Justice, Bureau of Justice Statistics, *Prisoners, 1925–1981* [Washington, DC: U.S. Department of Justice, December 1982], 2, and *Prisoners in 1988* [Washington, DC: U.S. Department of Justice, April 1989], 3).

3. Ward and Kassebaum, *Women's Prison*, v.

4. Giallombardo, *Society of Women*, 1.

5. Peter C. Buffum, *Homosexuality in Prisons* (Washington, DC: Government Printing Office, 1972), 20. Estelle B. Freedman points to the growing interest in lesbians in prison in the mid-twentieth-century United States in "The Prison Lesbian: Race, Class, and the Construction of the Aggressive Female Homosexual, 1915–1965," *Feminist Studies* 22 (Summer 1996): 397–423.

6. Charles A. Ford, "Homosexual Practices of Institutionalized Females," *Journal of Abnormal Psychology* 23 (January–March 1929): 444. One "colored matron" quoted in a 1929 investigation of the Illinois State Training School for Girls, conversely, reported that the "honey notes" passed between white and black inmates were filled with "the

filthiest, nastiest stuff you can imagine" (quoted in Clifford R. Shaw and Earl D. Meyers, "The Juvenile Delinquent," in *The Illinois Crime Survey*, ed. John W. Wigmore (Chicago: Blakely Printing Co., 1929), 720.

7. Margaret Otis compared the attachments between delinquent girls she observed in 1913 to "the ordinary form that is found among girls even in high-class boarding-schools," in "A Perversion Not Commonly Noted," *Journal of Abnormal Psychology* 8 (June–July 1913): 113.

8. Seymour L. Halleck and Marvin Hersko, "Homosexual Behavior in a Correctional Institution for Adolescent Girls," *American Journal of Orthopsychiatry* 32 (October 1962): 914.

9. Ibid., 911.

10. Quoted in Michela Robbins, "The Inside Story of a Girls' Reformatory," *Collier's* 30 (October 1953): 76.

11. Joseph G. Wilson, *Are Prisons Necessary?* (Philadelphia: Dorrnace & Co., 1950), 201.

12. Ibid., 209.

13. Abraham G. Novick, "The Make-Believe Family: Informal Group Structure among Institutionalized Delinquent Girls," *Casework Papers from the National Conference on Social Welfare* (New York: Family Service Association of America, 1960), 46.

14. See Otis, "A Perversion Not Commonly Noted"; Ford, "Homosexual Practices of Institutionalized Females," 442–48; Lowell S. Selling, "The Pseudo Family," *American Journal of Sociology* 37 (September 1931): 247–53; Theodora M. Abel, "Negro-White Interpersonal Relationships among Institutionalized Sub-Normal Girls," *American Journal of Mental Deficiency* 46 (1942): 325–39; Sylvan Keiser and Dora Schaffer, "Environmental Factors in Homosexuality in Adolescent Girls," *Psychoanalytic Review* 36 (July 1949): 283–95; Spencer Stockwell, "Sexual Experiences of Adolescent Delinquent Girls," *International Journal of Sexology* 7 (1953): 25–27; Halleck and Hersko, "Homosexual Behavior."

15. Ward and Kassebaum, *Women's Prison*, v.

16. Ibid.

17. Giallombardo, *Society of Women*, vii.

18. Kenneth M. Dimick, *Ladies in Waiting: Behind Prison Walls* (Muncie, IN: Accelerated Development, 1979), 87.

19. Sandee Bonham, as told to Gina Allen, "On the Women's Side of the Pen," *Humanist* 38 (September–October 1978): 30.

20. "Prisoners Fight Sex Rule," *off our backs* 10, no. 5 (May 1980): 7.

21. Catherine Angell and Laurie Hauer, Women's Prison Coalition, "Prison Life behind the Lavender 'H,'" *Lesbian Tide* (January–February 1977), 12.

22. See David A. Ward and Gene G. Kassebaum, "The Dynamics of Prison Homosexuality: The Character of the Love Affair," in *Observations of Deviance*, ed. Jack D. Douglas (New York: Random House, 1970), 104; Ward and Kasssebaum, *Women's Prison*, 88–89.

23. Quoted in Nelson, "Study of Homosexuality," 73.

24. Acknowledging the difficulty that researchers sometimes had in obtaining information from inmates on sex in prison, Rose Giallombardo recognized "the importance

of maintaining one's neutrality." "To eliminate possible identification with the staff," Giallombardo took measures to distance herself from the prison administration. She did not live on the institution grounds at the time of her study, and "insofar as it was possible for me to do so without actually living in a cottage, I tried to approximate the living existence of the inmate" (*Society of Women*, 194).

25. Nelson, "Study of Homosexuality," 142.

26. Halleck and Hersko, "Homosexual Behavior," 912. See also Linda Norris, "Comparison of Two Groups in a Southern State Women's Prison: Homosexual Behavior versus Non-Homosexual Behavior," *Psychological Reports* 34 (1974): 75. Alice M. L. Propper noted the difficulty for inmates in "answering the 'homosexual relations' question" and proposed "considering how heterosexuals might respond if someone asked them to write down the number of times they had heterosexual relations. There are a wide range of activities that could be counted or excluded" ("Importation and Deprivation Perspectives on Homosexuality in Correctional Institutions: An Empirical Test of Their Relative Efficacy" [Ph.D. diss., University of Michigan, 1976], 69).

27. Ward and Kassebaum restricted their definition of homosexual behavior to "kissing and fondling of the breasts, manual or oral stimulation of the genitalia and simulation of intercourse between two women," omitting kissing, handholding, and embracing (Ward and Kassebaum, *Women's Prison*, 81). Some believed this definition led them underestimate the incidence of homosexuality among women prisoners (see Norris, "Comparison of Two Groups," 75).

28. Dimick, *Ladies in Waiting*, 87; Giallombardo, *Society of Women*, 151. Fran O'Leary, who served time in the Women's House of Detention and in California state prisons, estimated that 85 percent of the women in prison "participate in 'prison homosexuality'" (interview from *Fortune News*, in *In Prison: Writings and Poems about the Prison Experience*, ed. James E. Trupin (New York: Mentor, 1975), 137.

29. Nelson, "Study of Homosexuality," 143.

30. Giallombardo, *Society of Women*, 115. The degree to which lesbianism was an accepted and expected part of the inmate culture surely varied by institution. For instance, Propper found "no evidence of a subcultural acceptance of homosexuality" in the prison populations she studied (*Prison Homosexuality*, 72).

31. Ward and Kassebaum, *Women's Prison*, 93.

32. Quoted in Harris, *Hellhole*, 83.

33. Giallombardo, *Society of Women*, 116.

34. Ibid., 115–16.

35. Ibid., 142.

36. Nicole Hahn Rafter, *Partial Justice: Women, Prisons, and Social Control*, 2d ed. (New Brunswick, NJ: Transaction, 1990), 33–34; originally published as *Partial Justice: Women in State Prisons, 1800–1935* (Boston: Northeastern University Press, 1985). See also Freedman, *Their Sisters' Keepers*, 56–57; 68–71; Barbara M. Brenzel, *Daughters of the State: A Social Portrait of the First Reform School for Girls in North America, 1856–1905* (Cambridge, MA: MIT Press, 1983).

37. Brenzel, *Daughters of the State*, 69. In 1858, Lancaster's Superintendent and Chap-

lain's Report stated that "the conviction grows stronger in our minds of the safety and even expediency of having older and younger girls together in the same family, rather than to have them classified by age" (Superintendent and Chaplain's Report, State Industrial School for Girls at Lancaster, MA, Miriam van Waters papers, Schlesinger Library, Harvard University, Cambridge, MA, box 51, fol. 650, p. 4).

38. Bonham, as told to Allen, "On the Women's Side of the Pen," 30.

39. Selling, "The Pseudo Family," 248.

40. Ibid., 248.

41. Robbins, "Inside Story of a Girls Reformatory," 76.

42. Sidney Kosofsky and Albert Ellis, "Illegal Communication among Institutionalized Female Delinquents," *Journal of Social Psychology* 48 (August 1958): 159.

43. Wilson, *Are Prisons Necessary?* 209.

44. Ward and Kassebaum were an exception among observers of women's prisons, finding little evidence of families among prisoners at Frontera (*Women's Prison*).

45. See Selling, "The Pseudo Family," 250.

46. See Bonham, as told to Allen, "On the Women's Side of the Pen," 30.

47. Ibid.

48. Giallombardo, *Society of Women*, 171.

49. Quoted in Linda L. LeShanna, "Family Participation: Functional Response of Incarcerated Females," M.A. thesis, Bowling Green State University, 1969, 71.

50. Vergil L. Williams and Mary Fish, "Women's Prison Families," in *Justice and Corrections*, ed. Norman Johnston and Leonard Savitz (New York: John Wiley & Sons, 1978), 544. See also Giallombardo, *Society of Women*, 158.

51. Quoted in Giallombardo, *Society of Women*, 171.

52. Ibid., 159.

53. Circulating in women's prisons by the 1950s, the term "stud" was probably imported into prison slang from black working-class lesbian vernacular. Elizabeth Lapovsky Kennedy and Madeline Davis observe that in the African American community of Buffalo, New York, "'stud broad' and 'stud and her lady' were common terms" (*Boots of Leather, Slippers of Gold: The History of a Lesbian Community* [New York: Routledge, 1993], 7).

54. Quoted in Giallombardo, *The Social World of Imprisoned Girls*, 150. Gender role inconsistency was frowned upon in lesbian communities outside the prison, as well. See Kennedy and Davis, *Boots of Leather*, 212–13.

55. Quoted in Ward and Kassebaum, *Women's Prison*, 122.

56. Giollombardo, *Society of Women*, 172. See also Barbara Carter, "Reform School Families," *Society* 11 (1973): 41.

57. Giallombardo, *Society of Women*, 163.

58. Selling, "The Pseudo Family," 247, 253.

59. Williams and Fish, "Women's Prison Families," 551.

60. Propper, "Importation and Deprivation Perspectives," 4.

61. See Giallombardo, *Social World of Imprisoned Girls*, 226–33.

62. In Ward and Kassebaum's study of Frontera, for example, butch-femme partner-

ships were observed to take place without the appearance of any form of extended kinship structure (*Women's Prison*).

63. Kennedy and Davis, *Boots of Leather, Slippers of Gold*. Many middle-class lesbians in this period apparently had a more ambivalent relationship to butch/femme signification. See Katie Gilmartin, "'We Weren't Bar People': Middle-Class Lesbian Identities and Cultural Spaces," *GLQ: A Journal of Lesbian and Gay Studies* 3 (1996): 1–51.

64. Florence Monahan, *Women in Crime* (New York: Ives Washburn, Inc., 1941), 224.

65. Harris, *Hellhole*, 234.

66. Ward and Kassebaum, *Women's Prison*, 124.

67. See Harris, *Hellhole*, 234. During the time of Ward and Kassebaum's investigation of Frontera, they noted, "those women playing the masculine homosexual role were required to allow their hair to grow to a certain length" (*Women's Prison*, 83.)

68. Flynn, *The Alderson Story*, 87.

69. Giallombardo, *Social World of Imprisoned Girls*, 151.

70. Ibid., 221.

71. "The Unpleasantries of Pleasanton," *Through the Looking Glass* 4, no. 3 (March 1979): 12.

72. Giallombardo, *Society of Women*, 137; Vergil L. Williams and Mary Fish, *Convicts, Codes, and Contraband: The Prison Life of Men and Women* (Cambridge, MA: Ballinger, 1974), 107.

73. Giallombardo, *Society of Women*, 137.

74. Ibid., 137.

75. Ibid., 138.

76. Giallombardo, *The Social World of Imprisoned Girls*, 151.

77. Ibid., 137.

78. Ibid., 138.

79. Harris, *Hellhole*, 234.

80. Jean Harris, *They Always Call Us Ladies: Stories from Prison* (New York: Scribner's, 1988), 136. See also Carter, "Reform School Families," 39.

81. Ward and Kassebaum, *Women's Prison*, 105.

82. Leonard H. Gross, "Lesbians in Prison," *Sexology* 34 (February 1968): 481. See also Giallombardo, *Society of Women*, 149.

83. Ward and Kassebaum, *Women's Prison*, 105.

84. Giallombardo, *Society of Women*, 138.

85. Quoted in Giallombardo, *Social World of Imprisoned Girls*, 152.

86. Quoted in Ward and Kassebaum, *Women's Prison*, 108.

87. Monahan, *Women in Crime*, 231.

88. Ibid., 233.

89. Joanne Meyerowitz discusses female-to-male transsexuals (FTMs) who participated in the butch-femme social networks of working-class lesbian bars in the 1950s and 1960s, in *How Sex Changed: A History of Transsexuality in the United States* (Cambridge, MA: Harvard University Press, 2002), 195–96.

90. Harris, *They Always Call Us Ladies*, 137.

91. Florrie Fisher, *The Lonely Trip Back* (Garden City, NY: Doubleday, 1971), 141.

92. Tamsin Fitzgerald, *Tamsin* (New York: Dial Press, 1973), 130.

93. Quoted in Harris, *Hellhole*, 238.

94. Susan Stern, *With the Weathermen: The Personal Journal of a Revolutionary Woman* (Garden City, NY: Doubleday, 1975), 333.

95. Harris, *Hellhole*, 208–9.

96. Ward and Kassebaum, *Women's Prison*, 113.

97. Quoted in Giallombardo, *Social World of Imprisoned Girls*, 151.

98. Carter, "Reform School Families," 39.

99. Williams and Fish, "Women's Prison Families," 548.

100. Carter, "Reform School Families," 39.

101. Quoted in Harris, *Hellhole*, 240.

102. William G. Miller and Thomas E. Hannum, "Characteristics of Homosexually Involved Incarcerated Females," *Journal of Consulting Psychology* 27 (June 1963): 277.

103. Ward and Kassebaum, *Women's Prison*, 105.

104. See Giallombardo, *Society of Women*, 99.

105. On new ways of thinking about sex and gender in the mid-twentieth century, see Meyerowitz, *How Sex Changed*, 3–4, 98–129.

106. Giallombardo, *Society of Women*, 185. Ward and Kassebaum made a similar argument in *Women's Prison*, 70–71.

107. Giallombardo, *Social World of Imprisoned Girls*, 16.

108. See John Irwin and Donald Cressey, "Thieves, Convicts, and the Inmate Culture," *Social Problems* 10 (1962): 142–55.

109. Thomas W. Foster, "Make-Believe Families: A Response of Women and Girls to the Deprivation of Imprisonment," *International Journal of Criminology and Penology* 3 (1975): 73.

110. Williams and Fish, *Convicts, Codes, and Contraband*, 30.

111. Giallombardo, *Society of Women*, 186.

112. Williams and Fish, "Women's Prison Families," 546.

113. Giallombardo, *Society of Women*, 103; 133.

114. Williams and Fish, "Women's Prison Families," 545.

115. Giallombardo, *Society of Women*, 186.

116. Betty Friedan, *The Feminine Mystique* (New York: Norton, 1963). For revisionist historical studies of gender in the postwar United States that challenge the stereotype of domestic quiescence, see Joanne Meyerowitz, ed., *Not June Cleaver: Women and Gender in Postwar America, 1945–1960* (Philadelphia: Temple University Press, 1994).

117. On the decline of the domestic ideology of the Cold War era, see Elaine Tyler May, *Homeward Bound: American Families in the Cold War Era* (New York: Basic, 1988), 208–26.

118. On the postwar vilification of sexually deviant women, see Donna Penn, "The Sexualized Woman: The Lesbian, the Prostitute, and the Containment of Female Sexuality in Postwar America," in *Not June Cleaver*, ed. Meyerowitz, 358–81; May, *Homeward Bound*; Regina Kunzel, *Fallen Women, Problem Girls: Unmarried Mothers and the Profession-*

alization of Social Work (New Haven, CT: Yale University Press, 1993); Rickie Solinger, *Wake Up Little Susie: Single Pregnancy and Race before "Roe v. Wade"* (New York: Routledge, 1992); Leslie Reagan, *When Abortion Was a Crime: Women, Medicine, and Law in the United States, 1867–1973* (Berkeley: University of California Press, 1997).

119. Ward and Kassebaum, *Women's Prison*, 118.

120. Ibid., 75–76.

121. Ibid., 198.

122. Nelson, "Study of Homosexuality," 146.

123. Of the 119 inmates who responded to Nelson's questionnaire, 44 percent reported having had sexual relations with another women prior to incarceration. Of these women, 57 percent were black, 37 percent were white, and 6 percent were members of other unidentified racial groups (ibid.).

124. Ibid., 146.

125. Propper, "Importation and Deprivation Perspectives," 66. Propper was alone among this group in publishing her dissertation as *Prison Homosexuality: Myth and Reality* (Lexington, MA: Lexington Books, D.C. Heath & Co., 1981).

126. William A. Fitzgerald, "Pseudoheterosexuality in Prison and Out: A Study of the Lower Class Black Lesbian" (Ph.D. diss., City University of New York, 1977), 93.

127. Nelson, "Study of Homosexuality," 156.

128. Fitzgerald, "Pseudoheterosexuality," 188.

129. Ward and Kassebaum, *Women's Prison*, 103.

130. Ibid., 96.

131. Giallombardo, *Social World of Imprisoned Girls*, 212.

132. Quoted in Ward and Kassebaum, *Women's Prison*, 119.

133. Quoted in ibid., 121.

134. Ibid., 122.

135. Eronel, "Women, Women, Everywhere and No One to Get Wonderfully Permanently Perverted With," 1984, unpublished ms, Bromfield Street Educational Foundation papers (hereafter BSEF), box 13, fol. 42.

136. Quoted in Ward and Kassebaum, *Women's Prison*, 117.

137. Giallombardo, *Society of Women*, 150.

138. Ibid., 192.

139. Quoted in Ward and Kassesbaum, *Women's Prison*, 144. Giallombardo also recognized that, for inmates with few financial resources, "there may be an economic advantage in assuming a male role" (*Social World of Imprisoned Girls*, 150).

140. Ward and Kassebaum, *Women's Prison*, 112. See also Williams and Fish, *Convicts, Codes, and Contraband*, 108.

141. Gross, "Lesbians in Prison," 481.

142. Giallombardo, *Social World of Imprisoned Girls*, 152.

143. Quoted in ibid., 152.

144. Ibid., 123.

145. Williams and Fish, "Women's Prison Families."

146. O'Leary, interview in *In Prison*, 137.

147. See Peter C. Buffum, "Homosexuality in Female Institutions," in *Male Rape: A Casebook of Sexual Aggressions*, ed. Anthony M. Scacco, Jr. (New York: AMS Press, 1982), 165; Karpman, "Sex Life in Prison," 479; Bloch, "Social Pressures of Confinement toward Sexual Deviation," 123; Ward and Kassebaum, "Dynamics of Prison Homosexuality," 99; Leonard H. Gross, "Lesbians in Prison," *Sexology* 34 (February 1968): 479.

148. Ward and Kassebaum, "Dynamics of Prison Homosexuality," 99.

149. Gross, "Lesbians in Prison," 479.

150. Giallombardo, *Society of Women*, 151.

151. Buffum, *Homosexuality in Prisons*, 19.

152. Ibid., 21.

153. Quoted in Kathryn Watterson Burkhart, *Women in Prison* (New York: Doubleday, 1973), 376.

154. Harris, *Hellhole*, 84.

155. Quoted in Flynn, *The Alderson Story*, 163.

156. O'Leary, interview in *In Prison*, 137.

157. Ward and Kassebaum, *Women's Prison*, 156.

158. Quoted in Giallombardo, *Society of Women*, 147.

159. Quoted in Ward and Kassebaum, *Women's Prison*, 195.

160. Pat Singer, "Love in Prison," *off our backs* 2, no. 8 (April 1972): 8.

161. Ward and Kassebaum, *Women's Prison*, 190. See also Lee H. Bowker, *Prison Victimization* (New York: Elsevier, 1980), 49.

162. Giollambardo, *Society of Women*, 98.

163. Cottle, "Children in Jail," quoted in Bowker, *Prison Victimization*, 50.

164. Propper, *Prison Homosexuality*, 183.

165. *People v. Lovercamp*, 43 Cal.App.3d 823, 118 Cal.Rptr. 110. See Martin R. Gardner, "The Defense of Necessity and the Right to Escape from Prison—a Step towards Incarceration Free from Sexual Assault," *Southern California Law Review* 49, no. 1 (1975): 129–30; David Gilman, "New Ruling Allows Sexual Attack in Jail to Be Justification for Escape," *Corrections Magazine* 2, no. 5 (September 1976): 52–53.

166. Dorothy West, "I Was Afraid to Shut My Eyes," *Saturday Evening Post* 241 (July 13, 1968), reprinted in *Male Rape: A Casebook of Sexual Aggressions*, ed. Anthony M. Scacco, Jr. (New York: AMS, 1982), 171.

167. Gene Kassebaum, "Sex in Prison," *Sexual Behavior* 11 (January 1972): 39.

168. Quoted in Harris, *Hellhole*, 63.

169. Giallombardo, *Society of Women*, 102.

170. Ruby Leah Richardson, "'Criminal' Sexual Acts: Looking for Some Answers," *GCN* (June 12, 1982): 10. Lesbian prison activists similarly noted that "rape, or anything akin to how straight men intimidate and assault people sexually is virtually unknown in women's prisons—television to the contrary" ("Prison Life behind the Lavender 'H,'" 12–13).

171. For a fascinating analysis of "the conditions of lesbian representability" in classic cinema, see Patricia White, *Uninvited: Classical Hollywood Cinema and Lesbian Representability* (Bloomington: Indiana University Press, 1999).

172. Judith Mayne, *Framed: Lesbians, Feminists, and Media Culture* (Minneapolis: University of Minnesota Press, 2000), 128.

173. "'Caged' is a cross-section of life in women's prisons, as I have seen them," Kellogg wrote. "They are composite episodes as I have drawn them from true conditions in the four state institutions I visited" (Virginia Kellogg, "She Went to Prison to Get Film Material," April 1949, clipping, Miriam Van Waters papers, box 19, fol. 218).

174. For a history of the exploitation film genre, see Eric Schaefer, *Bold! Daring! Shocking! True! A History of Exploitation Film, 1919–1959* (Durham, NC: Duke University Press, 1999); Randall Clark, *At a Theater or Drive-In Near You: The History, Culture, and Politics of the American Exploitation Film* (New York: Garland, 1995).

175. Judith Mayne remarks that the number of women-in-prison films in this period is "truly mind-boggling" (*Framed*, 116). For discussions of the genre, see also Suzanna Danuta Walters, "Caged Heat: The (R)Evolution of Women-in-Prison Films," in *Reel Knockouts: Violent Women in the Movies*, ed. Martha McCaughey and Neal King (Austin: University of Texas Press, 2001), 106–23; Karlene Faith, *Unruly Women: The Politics of Confinement and Resistance* (Vancouver: Press Gang Publishers, 1993), 258–59; Judith Halberstam, *Female Masculinity* (Durham, NC: Duke University Press, 1998); James Robert Parish, *Gays and Lesbians in Mainstream Cinema* (Jefferson, NC: McFarland & Co., 1993); Bruce Crowther, *Captured on Film: The Prison Movie* (London: B. T. Batsford, 1989); Marsha Clowers, "Dykes, Gangs, and Danger: Debunking Popular Myths about Maximum-Security Life," *Journal of Criminal Justice and Popular Culture* 9, no. 1 (2001): 22–30; Anne Morey, "'The Judge Called Me an Accessory': Women's Prison Films, 1950–1962," *Journal of Popular Film and Television* 23 (Summer 1995): 80–87; Beverly Zalcock, *Renegade Sisters: Girl Gangs on Film* (London and San Francisco: Creation Books International, 1998), 19–38; Jim Morton, "Women in Prison Films," in *Incredibly Strange Films*, no. 10 (San Francisco: Re/Search Publications, 1986), 151–52; Beverly Zalcock and Jocelyn Robinson, "Inside Cell Block H: Hard Steel and Soft Soap," *Continuum* 9 (1996): 88–97.

176. Mayne, *Framed*, 120.

177. Ibid., 118.

178. Halberstam, *Female Masculinity*, 199. See also Freedman, "The Prison Lesbian."

179. Patricia White proposes a reading of Harper and Benton as the opposition of "two 'dyke' types in a struggle for control over the young heroine" (White, *Uninvited*, 189) On Agnes Moorehead's "queer career," see White, "Supporting Character: The Queer Career of Agnes Moorehead," in *Out in Culture: Gay, Lesbian, and Queer Essays on Popular Culture*, ed. Corey K. Creekmur and Alexander Doty (Durham, NC: Duke University Press, 1995): 91–114.

180. Halberstam, *Female Masculinity*, 201.

181. See Murphy, *Political Manhood*. See also Gene Fowler, "An Allegation in Lavender," in *The Great Mouthpiece* (New York: Grosset, 1931).

182. Estelle B. Freedman, *Maternal Justice: Miriam Van Waters and the Female Reform Tradition* (Chicago: University of Chicago Press, 1996), esp. 278–79. In the heat of public controversy, van Waters burned twenty-two years of correspondence with her compan-

ion, Geraldine Thompson. See Freedman, "'The Burning of Letters Continues': Elusive Identities and the Historical Construction of Sexuality," *Journal of Women's History* 9 (Winter 1998): 181–200.

183. Halleck and Hersko, "Homosexual Behavior," 911.

184. Quoted in Ward and Kassebaum, *Women's Prison*, 142.

185. Morton reports that *The Big Doll House* was made for $125,000 and grossed millions ("Women in Prison Films," 152).

186. Walters, "Caged Heat," 115.

187. Ibid. On the interracial male buddy genre, see Robyn Wiegman, *American Anatomies: Theorizing Race and Gender* (Durham, NC: Duke University Press, 1995), 115–46.

188. Some critics see women-in-prison films as celebrations of female bonding, female rage, and female revolt. See Mayne, *Framed*, 115–16; Walters, "Caged Heat."

189. Walters, "Caged Heat," 119.

CHAPTER 5

1. Alan J. Davis, "Sexual Assaults in the Philadelphia Prison System and Sheriffs' Vans," *Trans-Action* 6 (December 1968): 9.

2. Of the 60,000 inmates who passed through the Philadelphia prison system from June 1966 to July 31, 1968, 3,304 were interviewed for Davis's study. Davis speculated that "if all 60,000 inmates had been interviewed . . . 1800 additional assaults would have come to light" (ibid., 8). Prisoners' concerns that reporting sexual assaults would be futile were well-founded. Davis found that of the ninety-six sexual assaults reported to prison authorities, only forty resulted in internal discipline against the aggressors and only twenty-six incidents were reported to the police for prosecution.

3. Ibid., 11, 13.

4. Ibid., 9.

5. Donald Tucker, "The Account of the White House Seven," in *Male Rape*, ed. Anthony M. Scacco, Jr. (New York: AMS Press, 1982), 38. (Stephen Donaldson was born Robert Anthony Martin, but he began to go by the name Stephen Donaldson in college in the mid 1960s, according to some accounts as a pseudonym for his involvement in the early gay liberation movement, and he used it throughout his public career. His account of his 1973 rape was initially published under another pseudonym, Donald Tucker.)

6. See Paul Hodge and William A. Elsen, "War Protester Tells of Rape at D.C. Jail," *Washington Post*, August 25, 1973, C:1; Tucker, "Account of the White House Seven."

7. See Anthony M. Scacco, Jr., *Rape in Prison* (Springfield, IL: Charles C. Thomas, 1975); Carl Weiss and David James Friar, *Terror in the Prisons: Homosexual Rape and Why Society Condones It* (New York: Bobbs-Merrill, 1974); Bowker, *Prison Victimization*; Daniel Lockwood, *Prison Sexual Violence* (New York: Elsevier, 1980); "Catalogue of Savagery," *Time* 92 (September 20, 1968): 54; Leo Carroll, *Hacks, Blacks, and Cons: Race Relations in a Maximum Security Prison* (Lexington, MA: D. C. Heath, 1974); Peter L. Danziger, "Sexual Assaults and Forced Homosexual Relationships in Prison: Cruel and Unusual Punishment," *Albany Law Review* 36 (1971): 428–38; Peter L. Nacci and Thomas R.

Kane, "Sex and Sexual Aggression in Federal Prisons," *Federal Probation* 48 (March 1984): 46–53; Wilbert Rideau and Billy Sinclair, "Prison: The Sexual Jungle," in *Male Rape*, ed. Scacco; John Haggerty, *Sex in Prison* (New York: Ace Books, 1975); Wayne S. Wooden and Jay Parker, *Men behind Bars: Sexual Exploitation in Prison* (New York: Plenum Press, 1982).

   8. Davis, "Sexual Assaults," 15. See also Scacco, *Rape in Prison*; Scacco, "The Scapegoat Is Almost Always White," in *Male Rape*, ed. Scacco, 91–103; Aryeh Neier, "Sex and Confinement," *Civil Liberties Review* 5, no. 2 (July–August 1978): 6–7; C. Scott Moss, Ray Hosford, and William R. Anderson, "Sexual Assault in a Prison," *Psychological Reports* 44 (1979): 826; Lockwood, *Prison Sexual Violence*; Lockwood, "The Contribution of Sexual Harassment to Stress and Coping in Confinement," in *Coping with Imprisonment*, ed. Nicolette Parisi (Beverly Hills, CA: Sage Publications, 1982); Carroll, *Hacks, Blacks, and Cons*, 182; Howard Levy and David Miller, *Going to Jail: The Political Prisoner* (New York: Grove, 1971), 131; Bowker, *Prison Victimization*, 8–10; Allan Wolper, "Young, Jailed, and White," *Soho Weekly News*, January 19, 1978; Jim Hogshire, *You Are Going to Prison* (Port Townsend, WA: Breakout Publications, 1999), 76–77; Jim Johnson, *Crime around the Clock* (New York: Vantage, 1968), 168–69; Wooden and Parker, *Men behind Bars*, 135; Clemens Bartollas, Stuart J. Miller, and Simon Dinitz, "The White Victim in a Black Institution," in *Treating the Offender: Problems and Issues*, ed. Marc Riedel and Pedro A. Vales (New York: Praeger, 1977), 97–108.

   9. Carroll, *Hacks, Blacks, and Cons*, 182.

   10. Johnson, *Crime around the Clock*, 168.

   11. David Rothenberg, "Prisoners," in *The Sexually Oppressed*, ed. Harvey L. Gochros and Jean S. Gochros (New York: Association, 1977), 225.

   12. Weiss and Friar, *Terror in the Prisons*, x.

   13. Donald Tucker, "A Punk's Song: View from the Inside," in *Male Rape*, ed. Scacco, 58.

   14. Berg, *Revelations of a Prison Doctor*, 148.

   15. Haywood Patterson and Earl Conrad, *Scottsboro Boy* (New York: Doubleday, 1950), 81–82.

   16. Robert M. Lindner, "Sex in Prison," *Complex* 6 (1951): 10.

   17. John Herbert, *Fortune and Men's Eyes* (New York: Grove Press, 1967). Helen Eigenberg and Agnes Baro find that most of the men's prison films they surveyed that were made between 1962 and 2000 included at least one scene of an attempted or completed male rape and that in the majority of the movies with rape scenes, the rapes or rape attempts are central to the plot ("If You Drop the Soap in the Shower You Are on Your Own: Images of Male Rape in Selected Prison Movies," *Sexuality and Culture* 7, no. 4 [Fall 2003]: 56–89).

   18. Miguel Piñero, *Short Eyes* (New York: Hill & Wang, 1975). *Short Eyes* was nominated for six Tony Awards. It won the New York Critics Circle Award and an Obie Award for the "best play of the year." In 1977, *Short Eyes* was made into a film, which was shot in the Manhattan Men's House of Detention known as the Tombs.

   19. Carl Corley's *Jail Mate* (San Diego: Greenleaf, 1971), for example, included a

foreword attributed to "The Final Report of the Task Force on Homosexuality," which educated readers on the concept of "situational homosexuality," observing that "there are individuals in whom a heterosexual preference is predominant but who will, under certain circumstances (such as imprisonment) become involved in homosexual behavior" (1). Daniel Eisenberg points out that the Supreme Court criterion for determining if a work were to be denied First Amendment protection, imposed from 1957 to 1973—"that it be 'utterly without redeeming social value' (86 S. Ct. 977)—led during this period to the production of a large number of superficially nonfictional works in which a skeleton of pseudo-scientific purpose was used as a means to present a series of erotic 'case histories'" (Eisenberg, "Toward a Bibliography of Erotic Pulps," *Journal of Popular Culture* 15 [Spring 1982]: 177–78). Authors of erotic fiction in this period resorted to similar strategies.

20. James R. Rudolph, "Evaluation of Screening Procedure for Preventing Sexual Assault in San Francisco Jails," July 28, 1978, 1, John De Cecco papers, GLBT Historical Society, San Francisco, box 72, fol. 1. The two-year project, the Sexual Assault and Violence Evaluation Project (SAVE), received over $400,000 from the National Rape Center of the U.S. Department of Health, Education, and Welfare.

21. "Catalogue of Savagery," *Time* 92 (September 20, 1968), 54. Linda Charlton also referenced Herbert's play, as well as the work of Jean Genet, in "The Terrifying Homosexual World of the Jail System," *New York Times*, April 25, 1971, 40.

22. Richard S. Jones and Thomas J. Schmid, "Inmates' Conceptions of Prison Sexual Assault," *Prison Journal* 69 (1989): 55.

23. Quoted in ibid., 54.

24. Ken Carpenter, "Men, Sex, and Imprisonment," *Gay Community News*, March 6, 1982, 5.

25. Berg, *Revelations of a Prison Doctor*, 150.

26. Sykes, *The Society of Captives*, 96–97.

27. Edward H. Peeples, Jr., and Anthony M. Scacco, Jr., "The Stress Impact Study Technique: A Method for Evaluating the Consequences of Male-on-Male Sexual Assault in Jails, Prisons, and Other Selected Single-Sex Institutions," in *Male Rape*, ed. Scacco, 249.

28. David Rothenberg, "Sexual Assaults in the Prisons," *Fortune News*, September 1976, 1.

29. Inez Cardozo-Freeman, *The Joint: Language and Culture in a Maximum Security Prison* (Springfield, IL: Charles Thomas, 1984), 399.

30. Davis, "Sexual Assaults," 13.

31. *Ruffin v. The Commonwealth*, 62 Va. 795, 796 (1871).

32. Edgardo Rotman, "The Failure of Reform: United States, 1865–1965," in *The Oxford History of the Prison*, ed. Morris and Rothman, 191. See also John Midgley, "Prison Litigation, 1950–2000: Hands Off, Hands On, Gloves On," in *Prison Nation: The Warehousing of America's Poor* (New York and London: Routledge, 2003); Michael B. Mushlin, *Rights of Prisoners* (New York: Shepard's/McGraw-Hill, 1993), 7–9; "Note—Beyond the Ken of the Courts: A Critique of Judicial Refusal to Review the Complaints of Convicts," *Yale Law Journal* 72 (January 1963): 506–58.

33. See Henri M. Yaker, "The Black Muslims in the Correctional Institution," *Welfare Reporter* 13 (October 1962): 158–65; Eric Cummins, *The Rise and Fall of California's Radical Prison Movement* (Stanford, CA: Stanford University Press 1994), 65–73; Irwin, *Prisons in Turmoil*, 67–70; Joseph T. Hallinan, *Going up the River: Travels in a Prison Nation* (New York: Random House, 2001), 25–27; James B. Jacobs, *Stateville: The Penitentiary in Mass Society* (Chicago: University of Chicago Press, 1977), 58–64.

34. 378 U.S. 546 (1964). See Cummins, *Rise and Fall*, 65–73; Irwin, *Prisons in Turmoil*, 67–70; Yaker, "Black Muslims in the Correctional Institution"; James B. Jacobs, *Stateville: The Penitentiary in Mass Society* (Chicago: University of Chicago Press, 1977), 58–64; Ronald Berkman, *Opening the Gates: The Rise of the Prisoners' Movement* (Lexington, MA: D. C. Heath, 1979), 46–55; Kathleen Moore, "Muslims in Prison: Claims to Constitutional Protection of Religious Liberty," in *The Muslims of America*, ed. Yvonne Yazbeck Haddad (New York: Oxford University Press, 1991).

35. *Kish v. County of Milwaukee*, 441 F. 2d 901, 905 (7th Cir. 1971).

36. *People v. Lovercamp*, 42 Cal. App. 3d. 823, 118 Cal. Rptr. 110 (1974).

37. *People v. Harmon*, 52 Mich. App. 482–484, 1974, quoted in David Gilman, "New Ruling Allows Sexual Attack in Jail to Be Justification for Escape," *Corrections Magazine* 2, no. 5 (September 1976): 52.

38. See, for example, *Holt v. Sarver*, 309 F. Supp. 362 (E.D. Ark. 1970), in which the court determined that "the cumulative impact of certain intolerable conditions such as abuses from the 'trustee' system, fear of homosexual attacks, fights and stabbings, debasing living conditions, and other abuses, constituted cruel and unusual punishment as prohibited by the eighth amendment" (Danziger, "Sexual Assaults," 430–31). A Louisiana federal court made a similar decision in *Hamilton v. Schiro*, Civil No. 69–2443 (E.D. La., June 26, 1970).

39. Martin R. Gardner, "The Defense of Necessity and the Right to Escape from Prison—a Step Towards Incarceration Free from Sexual Assault," *Southern California Law Review* 49, no. 1 (1975): 142–43.

40. On the efforts of prisoners to gain judicial redress for sexual assault or the threat of sexual violence, see Danziger, "Sexual Assaults," 428–38; Michael Graubart Levin, "Flight, Flee, Submit, Sue: Alternatives for Sexually Assaulted Prisoners," *Columbia Journal of Law and Social Problems* 18 (1985): 505–30; Gardner, "The Defense of Necessity and the Right to Escape from Prison"; Gilman, "New Ruling," 51–53.

41. Irwin, *Prisons in Turmoil*, 110.

42. Jacobs, *Stateville*, 162, 172.

43. Irwin, *Prisons in Turmoil*, xiv. Michael Ignatieff agrees that among the causes of increasing violence in prisons after 1970 was prisoner militancy and guard intransigence (*A Just Measure of Pain*, xi–xii).

44. Irwin, *Prisons in Turmoil*, 181.

45. Ibid., 5.

46. Billy McCune, *The Autobiography of Billy McCune* (San Francisco: Straight Arrow Books, 1973), 135.

47. Irwin, *Prisons in Turmoil*, 55–56.

48. Bill Sands, *My Shadow Ran Fast* (Englewood Cliffs, NJ: Prentice-Hall, 1964), 47.

49. Billy Wayne Sinclair and Jodie Sinclair, *A Life in the Balance: A Journey from Murder to Redemption Inside America's Worst Prison System* (New York: Arcade, 2000), 97.

50. Ibid., 121.

51. Maguire, "Racism II," in *Inside: Prison American Style*, ed. Robert J. Minton (New York: Random House, 1971), 69.

52. Eugene Delorme, quoted in Cardozo-Freeman, *The Joint*, 382–83. On the increase of violence between prisoners in California prisons, see Bowker, *Prison Victimization*, 24–25.

53. Richard H. Shoblad, *Doing My Own Time* (Garden City, NY: Doubleday, 1972), 175.

54. Quoted in Norman E. Smith and Mary Ellen Batiuk, "Sexual Victimization and Inmate Social Interaction," *Prison Journal* 69, no. 2 (Fall–Winter 1989): 35.

55. Howard Levy and David Miller, *Going to Jail: The Political Prisoner* (New York: Grove, 1971), 162.

56. More harsh mandatory sentencing and "three strikes and you're out" laws followed. In 1976, California Governor Jerry Brown passed a series of criminal sentences that abandoned parole. A federal law passed in 1986 established mandatory five- and ten-year prison terms for drug dealing, resulting in a massive increase in the prison population and a disproportionate prosecution of African Americans. Hallinan identifies the Sentencing Reform Act, passed by Congress in 1984, which eliminated parole for all federal crimes committed on or after November 1, 1987, as "the sea change" that would "spark an unprecedented boom in the nation's prison population" (*Going up the River*, 38–39). As a consequence, the U.S. prison population tripled between 1980 and 1995, from around 500,000 to 1.5 million. On the rise in incarceration rates beginning in the 1970s, see Marc Mauer, *Race to Incarcerate* (New York: New Press, 1999); Alex Lichtenstein, *Twice the Work of Free Labor: The Political Economy of Convict Labor in the New South* (London: Verso, 1996); Eric Schlosser, "The Prison-Industrial Complex," *Atlantic Monthly*, December 1998, 51–77; Ruth Wilson Gilmore, *Golden Gulag: Prisons, Surplus, Crisis, and Opposition in Globalizing California* (Berkeley: University of California Press, 2006).

57. Patrick A. Langan, John V. Fundis, and Lawrence A. Greenfeld, *Historical Statistics on Prisoners in State and Federal Institutions, Yearend 1925–86* (Washington, D.C.: U.S. Department of Justice, Bureau of Justice Statistics, May 1988); Mauer, *Race to Incarcerate*.

58. Ted Morgan, "Entombed," *New York Times Magazine*, February 17, 1974, 17.

59. Dale E. Smith, "Crowding and Confinement," in *The Pains of Imprisonment*, ed. Robert Johnson and Hans Toch (Beverly Hills, CA: Sage Publications, 1982), 45.

60. Quoted in Dae H. Chang and Warren B. Armstrong, eds., *The Prison: Voices from the Inside* (Cambridge, MA: Schenkman, 1972), 49.

61. Jack Henry Abbott, "In Prison," *New York Review of Books*, June 26, 1980, 35.

62. Philip Berrigan, *Prison Journals of a Priest Revolutionary* (New York: Holt, Rinehart & Winston, 1970), 39.

63. Bagdikian, *Caged*, xvi.

64. Presley Middleton, quoted in *Prison*, ed. Jamie Shalleck (New York: Grossman, 1972), 245.

65. Rubin "Hurricane" Carter, *The Sixteenth Round: From Number 1 Contender to #45472* (New York: Viking, 1974), 162.

66. Donaldson to Mitchell Karp, March 9, 1982, Stephen Donaldson Papers (hereafter Donaldson papers), New York Public Library, fol. 4, box 3.

67. See Nacci and Kane, "Sex and Sexual Aggression," 46; Mike Misenheimer, "Sex," in *Eye for an Eye*, ed. H. Jack Griswold, Mike Misenheimer, Art Powers, and Ed Tromanhauser (New York: Holt, Rinehart & Winston, 1970), 170; Hogshire, *You Are Going to Prison* (Port Townsend, WA: Breakout Publications, 1999), 70; Norval Morris, "The Contemporary Prison: 1965–Present," in *The Oxford History of the Prison*, ed. Morris and Rothmann, 232; Charles Alverson, "The Jail Jungle," *Wall Street Journal*, February 25, 1969, 1, 17.

68. Rothenberg, "Sexual Assaults in the Prisons," 6.

69. Misenheimer, "Sex," 170.

70. Rothenberg, "Sexual Assaults in the Prisons," 6.

71. "Cook County Horrors," *Time* 90 (December 15, 1967): 76.

72. Quoted in Chang and Armstrong, eds., *The Prison: Voices from the Inside*, 49.

73. Donald Cressey, foreword to *Prisons in Turmoil* by Irwin, vii.

74. Sinclair, *A Life in the Balance*, 103.

75. Jon Wildes, "To Be Young, Gay, and Behind Bars," *Village Voice* 23 (January 9, 1978): 1.

76. Levy and Miller, *Going to Jail*, 153.

77. Ibid., 154.

78. Jack Henry Abbott, *In the Belly of the Beast: Letters from Prison* (New York: Random House, 1981), 79–80. Sociologist Lee Bowker devoted a chapter of his book on prison victimization to documenting the direct involvement by penitentiary staff and administrators in orchestrating, watching, and profiting from the rape of prisoners. See Bowker, *Prisoner Victimization*, esp. 108–10.

79. Gustave de Beaumont and Alexis de Toqueville, *On the Penitentiary System in the United States, and Its Application in France; with an Appendix on Penal Colonies, and Also, Statistical Notes*, trans. Francis Lieber (Philadelphia: Carey, Lea & Blanchard, 1833), 93. As early as 1826, one-sixth to one-third of inmates in the United States were black, depending on the state (Prison Discipline Society [Boston], *Annual Report of the Board of Managers of the Prison Discipline Society*, vol. 1 [1830], 24–25).

80. James Jacobs calculates that in 1973, states with a majority or near majority of black prisoners were Alabama (48%), Delaware (60%), Florida (49%), Georgia (64%), Illinois (58%), Louisiana (71%), Maryland (74%), Michigan (58%), Mississippi (63%), New Jersey (50%), New York (58%), North Carolina (54%), Ohio (46%), Pennsylvania (57%), South Carolina (59%), and Virginia (59%) ("Race Relations and the Prison Subculture," in *New Perspectives on Prison and Imprisonment* [Ithaca, NY: Cornell University Press, 1983], 68).

81. Jacobs, *Stateville*, 160.

82. Law Enforcement Assistance Administration, U.S. Department of Justice, *Census of Prisoners in State Correctional Facilities 1973* (1976).

83. Segregation was the rule in most prisons before this period—de jure in the South and de facto in the North. See Jacobs, "Race Relations and the Prison Subculture."

84. Quoted in Bagdikian, *Caged*, 112–13.

85. Berrigan, *Prison Journals of a Priest Revolutionary*, 34.

86. Quoted in Drew Leder, *The Soul Knows No Bars: Inmates Reflect on Life, Death, and Hope* (Lanham, MD: Rowman & Littlefield, 2000), 76.

87. Irwin, *Prisons in Turmoil*, 87–107.

88. Bunker, *Education of a Felon*, 264.

89. Jacobs, "Race Relations and the Prison Subculture," 67. See also James Jacobs, "Stratification and Conflict among Prison Inmates," in *Justice and Corrections*, ed. Norman Johnston and Leonard Savitz (New York: John Wiley & Sons, 1978); John Irwin, *The Felon* (Englewood Cliffs, NJ: Prentice-Hall, 1970), 80–82.

90. Sinclair, *A Life in the Balance*, 125.

91. Quoted in Jackson, ed., *In the Life*, 269.

92. Irwin, *Prisons in Turmoil*, 5.

93. Ibid.

94. Lee Carroll, "Race, Ethnicity, and the Social Order of the Prison," in *The Pains of Imprisonment*, ed. Robert Johnson and Hans Toch (Beverly Hills, CA: Sage Publications, 1982), 183.

95. Piri Thomas, *Seven Long Times* (New York: Praeger, 1974), 103.

96. Ibid.

97. Sinclair, *A Life in the Balance*, 109, 101.

98. Jacobs, *Stateville*, 157.

99. John Irwin documented the emergence of "white lowrider groups" in prison who "called themselves Nazis and tattooed swastikas on their bodies" and began to appear in the late 1960s (*Prisons in Turmoil*, 75).

100. Malcolm L. Little, Jr., "Sexual Exploitation in Prison," *Gay Community News*, October 3, 1981, 7.

101. Jacobs, "Stratification and Conflict among Prison Inmates," 583.

102. Scacco, *Rape in Prison*, 47–48.

103. Don Horan, quoted in *The Prison*, ed. Chang and Armstrong, 208; Cameron Slates quoted in ibid., 230.

104. Cameron Slates, quoted in ibid., 228.

105. Quoted in Wooden and Parker, *Men behind Bars*, 191–92.

106. Scacco, *Rape in Prison*, 56.

107. Ibid.

108. Carroll, "Race, Ethnicity, and the Social Order of the Prison," 194.

109. Scacco, *Rape in Prison*, 61.

110. Lee Carroll, "Humanitarian Reform and Biracial Sexual Assault in a Maximum Security Prison," *Urban Life* 5 (January 1977): 433.

111. Weiss and Friar, *Terror in the Prison*, 73.

112. Quoted in Carroll, "Humanitarian Reform," 422.

113. Quoted in Haggerty, *Sex in Prison*, 33.

114. Levy and Miller, *Going to Jail*, 145.

115. Ibid., 146.

116. Ibid., 158.

117. Ibid., 147.

118. Quoted in Willard Gaylin, *In Service of Their Country: War Resisters in Prison* (New York: Viking, 1970), 294.

119. Quoted in ibid., 35.

120. Susan Brownmiller, *Against Our Will: Men, Women, and Rape* (New York: Simon & Schuster, 1975), 15.

121. Ibid., 258–59, 265–67.

122. Ibid., 258.

123. Abbott, *In the Belly of the Beast*, 78.

124. Davis, "Sexual Assaults," 16.

125. Bowker, *Prison Victimization*, 7.

126. Weiss and Friar, *Terror in the Prisons*, 72.

127. Wilbert Rideau and Billy Sinclair, "Prison: The Sexual Jungle," in *Male Rape*, ed. Anthony M. Scacco, Jr. (New York: AMS Press, 1982), 4.

128. George Whitmore, review of *Terror in the Prisons* by Carl Weiss and David James Friar, *Advocate*, March 26, 1975, 20.

129. Scacco, *Rape in Prison*, 62.

130. Daniel Patrick Moynihan, *The Negro Family: The Case for National Action* (Washington, DC: Department of Labor, 1965). For an analysis of the social science literature on the "damaged black psyche," see Daryl Michael Scott, *Contempt and Pity: Social Policy and the Image of the Damaged Black Psyche, 1880–1996* (Chapel Hill: University of North Carolina Press, 1997).

131. Levy and Miller, *Going to Jail*, 139–40; Carroll, *Hacks, Blacks, and Cons*, 182.

132. Scacco, *Rape in Prison*, 71.

133. Davis, "Sexual Assaults," 16.

134. Ibid., 16.

135. Scacco, *Rape in Prison*, 75–76.

136. Susan Brownmiller added support for this argument as well. In her discussion of race and rape, Brownmiller claimed that the effects of racial discrimination placed many of the "legitimate" expressions of male dominance beyond their reach: "Corporate executive dining rooms and climbs up Mount Everest are not usually accessible to those who form the subculture of violence. Access to a female body—through force—is within their ken" (*Against Her Will*, 194).

137. Bowker, *Prison Victimization*, 10.

138. Carroll, "Humanitarian Reform," 433–34.

139. Scott, *Contempt and Pity*.

140. See Auli Ek, *Race and Masculinity in Contemporary American Prison Narratives* (New York: Routledge, 2005), 52–54.

141. Irwin and Cressey, "Thieves, Convicts, and Inmate Culture," 142–55.

142. Cressey, foreword to *Prisons in Turmoil* by Irwin, ix–x.

143. Lockwood, *Prison Sexual Violence*, 105.

144. Roderick A. Ferguson details how "canonical sociology," from early twentieth century on, has "imagined African American culture as the site of polymorphous gender and sexual perversions and associated those perversions with moral failings typically" (*Aberrations in Black: Toward a Queer of Color Critique* [Minneapolis: University of Minnesota Press, 2004], 20).

145. Scacco, *Rape in Prison*, viii.

146. Ibid., 35.

147. See Kinsey et al., *Sexual Behavior in the Human Male*, 383; Paul Gebhard, John H. Gagnon, Wardell B. Pomeroy, and Cornelia V. Christenson, *Sex Offenders: An Analysis of Types* (New York: Harper & Row, 1965), 127. Kinsey felt he had too few sexual histories of African Americans to comment on them in this report, but he wrote that "it is impossible to generalize concerning the behavior of a whole race." He did note that "preliminary findings" suggested that "there are as many patterns of behavior among Negroes of different social levels as there are among whites" (*Sexual Behavior in the Human Male*, 393).

148. Wardell Baxter Pomeroy, "Sex in Prison," 16, speech given during Federal Wardens' Institute at University of Colorado, June 26, 1962, Kinsey Institute.

149. Buffum, *Homosexuality in Prisons*, 23–24.

150. Scacco, *Rape in Prison*, 78.

151. Huffman, "Sex Deviation in a Prison Community," 180.

152. Davis, "Sexual Assaults," 15.

153. "Project S.A.V.E.," John DeCecco Papers, Gay, Lesbian, Bisexual, and Transgender Historical Society of Northern California, San Francisco, box 62, fol. 1. A two-year study, Project SAVE was located at the Center for Homosexual Education, Evaluation, and Research at the San Francisco State University.

154. Inmate interviews, DeCecco papers, box 80, fol. 5.

155. Ibid., box 75, fol. 4.

156. Ibid., box 83, fol. 2.

157. Ibid., box 78, fol. 5.

158. Ibid., box 86, fol. 4.

159. Ibid., box 79, fol. 1.

160. Ibid., box 84, fol. 2.

161. Ibid., box 76, fol. 6.

162. Ibid., box 86, fol. 4.

163. Ibid., box 87, fol. 1.

164. Ibid., box 75, fol. 2.

165. Ibid., box 77, fol. 1.

166. Ibid., box 78, fol. 1.

167. Ibid., box 79, fol. 1.

168. Ibid., box 87, fol. 1.

169. Ibid., box 80, fol. 3.

170. Ibid., box 74, fol. 4.

171. Ibid., box 76, fol. 4.

172. Ibid., box 79, fol. 3.

173. Daniel Lockwood found "little empirical evidence" to support the position that "blacks rape whites for revenge" in his 1974–75 study of sexual aggressors and targets of aggressors incarcerated in three New York state prisons (*Prison Sexual Violence* [New York: Elsevier, 1980], 106).

174. Davis, "Sexual Assaults," 15.

175. Carroll, *Hacks, Blacks, and Cons*, 187.

176. Ibid., 180.

177. Donaldson to Phil, January 22, 1983, Donaldson papers, fol. 24, box 1.

178. Lee, "Seduction of the Guilty," 59.

179. Tarry Dobson to *Gay Community News*, July 2, 1992, Bromfield Strut Educational Foundation Records, Northeastern University, Boston, Massachusetts (hereafter BSEF), box 13, fol. 44.

180. Davis, "Sexual Assaults," 13.

181. Donaldson, "Hooking Up: Protective Pairing for Punks," pamphlet, http://www.spr.org/en/ps_hookingup.asp (accessed 4/17/07).

182. Stephen Donaldson, "A Million Jockers, Punks, and Queens: Sex among American Male Prisoners and its Implications for Concepts of Sexual Orientation" (lecture delivered at Columbia University, February 4, 1993, http://www.spr.org/en/stephendonaldson/doc_01_lecture.html), 18.

183. Donaldson, "Hooking Up," 2.

184. Abbott, *In the Belly of the Beast*, 80.

185. Danny Owen to Mike Riegle, April 29, 1984, BSEF, box 13, fol. 42.

186. Tucker, "A Punk's Song," 69.

187. Donaldson, "Hooking Up," 7.

188. Stephen Donaldson, "Letter from a Prison Punk," *RFD*, no. 67 (Fall 1991), 14. Born Robert Anthony Martin, Donaldson wrote under several pseudonyms, including Donald Tucker and Donny the Punk. Donaldson encouraged readers to believe that these names referred to different people. Writing "A Million Jockers, Punks, and Queens" under the name Stephen Donaldson, he recommended Donald Tucker's "A Punk's Song" as "the only systematic account from a punk's perspective" ("A Million Jockers, Punks, and Queens," 6).

189. Tucker, "A Punk's Song," 64.

190. Ibid., 65.

191. See ibid., 65, 73, 76; Donaldson to Dan Dennis, August 8, 1981, Donaldson papers, box 1, fol. 22; Donaldson, diary entry, June 22, 1981, Donaldson papers, box 7, fol. 19. Donaldson wrote that he ventured into the gay sadomasochism scene after his release from prison, "only to discover a charade in which the actors had to resort to symbols like

licking boots and calling someone 'Master' in order to represent a dominance which had no reality to it." "Gay men failed to satisfy me," he wrote; "I just couldn't find in them the strength which to me spelled protection. . . . Emotionally, they just weren't credible as Men" (Tucker, "A Punk's Song," 73).

192. Donaldson, "A Million Jockers, Punks, and Queens," 6.

193. Edward Sagarin, "Prison Homosexuality and Its Effect on Post-Prison Sexual Behavior," *Psychiatry* 39 (August 1976): 247. A professor of sociology at the City College of New York and president of the American Society of Criminology, Sagarin also wrote *The Homosexual in America: A Subjective Approach* in 1951 under the pseudonym Donald Webster Cory. That book provided a first-person account of the growing gay subculture and the experience of stigmatization and discrimination, critiqued the popular notion of a "cure" for homosexuality, and held out "a vision of a future of greater tolerance and understanding" for gay men and lesbians as an "unrecognized minority" (See Loughery, *Other Side of Silence*, 195).

194. Wooden and Parker, *Men behind Bars*, 21.

195. Jack H. Abbott, "On 'Women,'" *New York Review of Books* 28 (June 11, 1981): 1.

196. Ibid., 1.

197. Quoted in Lockwood, *Prison Sexual Violence*, 124.

198. Lee, "Seduction of the Guilty," 57.

199. Donaldson, "Hooking Up," 5.

200. See Wooden and Parker, *Men behind Bars*, 157; Donaldson, "Hooking Up," 10.

201. Quoted in Cardozo-Freeman, *The Joint*, 378.

202. Andreas Schroeder, *Shaking It Rough: A Prison Memoir* (Toronto: Doubleday, 1976), 45.

203. Pomeroy, "Sex in Prison," 12–13.

204. Edward Bunker, *The Animal Factory* (New York: Viking, 1977), 86.

205. Edwin Johnson, "The Homosexual in Prison," *Social Theory and Practice* 1 (1971): 92; Boyd, *Sex behind Bars*, 57, quoted in George Lester Kirkham, "Homosexuality in Prison," in *Studies in the Sociology of Sex*, ed. James M. Henslin (New York: Appleton-Century-Crofts, 1971), 346.

206. Kirkham, "Homosexuality in Prison," 346.

207. Carroll, *Hacks, Blacks, and Cons*, 78.

208. Ibid., 80–81. See also Wooden and Parker, *Men behind Bars*, 22–23, 73–74.

209. Leonard J. Berry, *Prison* (New York: Grossman, 1972), 250.

210. Pomeroy, "Sex in Prison," 12–13.

211. Kinsey and his research associates actively solicited such materials. "We would be delighted if you would keep confiscated erotic material for us," Paul Gebhard wrote to San Quentin's associate warden, L. S. Nelson, in 1958. "We appreciate your cooperation; when we ultimately begin a study of sexual adjustment within institutions, such confiscated material will prove of great worth" (Gebhard to Nelson, April 22, 1958, Prison Collection, Kinsey Institute).

212. Robert Raymond Hazel (Dorothy H.) to Charles Headrick, December 24, 1961, San Quentin, Prison Collection, Kinsey Institute, fol. 46.

213. Johnny to Billy, 1954, ibid., fol. 48-A.

214. Eddie to "Darling," June 2, 1950, ibid., fol. 48-B

215. Quoted in Jackson, *In the Life*, 378.

216. Cardozo-Freeman, *The Joint*, 384.

217. Quoted in Jackson, *In the Life*, 376.

218. Quoted in ibid., 371.

219. Danny Owen to Mike Riegle, April 29, 1984, BSEF, box 13, fol. 42.

220. Mickey to Pauline, April 6, 1951, San Quentin, Prison Collection, Kinsey Institute, fol. 48-A.

221. Gil to "My Darling," October 11, 1950, ibid., fol. 48-B.

222. Ibid.

223. Johnny to Tina, 1954, San Quentin, Prison Collection, Kinsey Institute, fol. 48-B.

224. Wardell to Donaldson, October 25, 1990, Donaldson papers, box 6, fol. 6.

225. Wardell to Donaldson, December 4, 1990, ibid.

226. Quoted in Jackson, *In the Life*, 373; 375.

227. Scacco, preface to *Male Rape*, ed. Scacco, viii.

CHAPTER 6

1. An FBI program, COINTELPRO was aimed at investigating and disrupting dissident political organizations within the United States. See David Cunningham, *There's Something Happening Here: The New Left, the Klan, and FBI Counterintelligence* (Berkeley: University of California Press, 2004); Ward Churchill and Jim Vander Wall, *The Cointelpro Papers: Documents from the FBI's Secret War against Dissent in the U.S.*, 2d ed. (Boston: South End Press, 2002).

2. Flynn, *The Alderson Story*, 15.

3. Ibid., 16.

4. Karla Jay, "Remembering the House of D," *Lesbian Tide* 3 (November 1973): 10. See also Audre Lorde, *Zami: A New Spelling of My Name* (Freedom, CA: Crossing Press, 1982), 206.

5. Joan Nestle, "Stone Butch, Drag Butch, Baby Butch," in *A Restricted Country* (Ithaca, NY: Firebrand, 1987), 77.

6. Donn Teal, *The Gay Militants: How Gay Liberation Began in America, 1969–1971* (New York: Stein & Day, 1971), 328. The Women's House of Detention was also a site of protest for activists in the early women's liberation movement. See Karla Jay, *Tales of the Lavender Menace: A Memoir of Liberation* (New York: Basic, 1999), 103–5.

7. Howard Blum, "Gays Take on the Cops: From Rage to Madness," *Village Voice*, September 3, 1970, 42, 44. For an account of this march, see Daniel Hurewitz, *Stepping Out: Nine Walks through New York City's Gay and Lesbian Past* (New York: Henry Holt, 1997), 23–24.

8. Blum, "Gays Take on the Cops," 44. See also Frank J. Prial, "Protest March by Homosexuals Sparks Disturbance in 'Village,'" *New York Times*, August 30, 1970, 49; C. Gerald Fraser, "'Gay Ghettos' Seen as Police Targets," *New York Times*, August 31, 1970, 28; Hurewitz, *Stepping Out*, 23–24.

9. "Gays Protest Brutality in N.Y.C. Prisons," *Advocate*, April 14, 1971, 20.

10. John C. Mitzel, "Boston's Week Includes March to Jail, Capital," *Advocate*, July 10, 1972, 14.

11. Deanna I. Sava to Jeannie, *Advocate*, June 6, 1973, 32.

12. The phrase "what's outside is inside too" is Mike Riegle's ("Sexual Politics of 'Crime': Inside and Out," *GCN*, December 10, 1983, 4).

13. On the relationship of the radical left and the prisoners' rights movement, see Eric Cummins, *The Rise and Fall of California's Radical Prison Movement* (Stanford, CA: Stanford University Press 1994); John Irwin, *Prisons in Turmoil* (Boston: Little, Brown & Co., 1980); Lee H. Bowker, *Prisoner Subcultures* (Lexington, MA: D.C. Heath & Co., 1977); Daniel Glaser, "Politicization of Prisoners: A New Challenge to American Penology," *American Journal of Correction* 33 (November–December 1971): 6–9.

14. "Gays Support SQ Six" (speeches given at San Quentin Six Rally, San Francisco, October 4, 1975), mimeographed ms., BSEF, box 13, fol. 5.

15. Allen Young, "Out of the Closets, into the Streets," in *Out of the Closets: Voices of Gay Liberation*, ed. Karla Jay and Allen Young (1972; repr., New York: New York University Press, 1992), 16.

16. John D'Emilio cites one study in the 1950s that estimated that one out of five gay men had "encountered trouble at the hands of the police" (John D'Emilio, *Lost Prophet: The Life and Times of Bayard Rustin* [Chicago: University of Chicago Press, 2003], 194). See also John D'Emilio, *Sexual Politics, Sexual Communities: The Making of a Homosexual Minority in the United States, 1940–1970* (Chicago: University of Chicago Press, 1983), 40–53, and "The Homosexual Menace: The Politics of Sexuality in Cold War America," in *Passion and Power: Sexuality in History*, ed. Kathy Peiss and Christine Simmons (Philadelphia: Temple University Press, 1989), 226–40.

17. See D'Emilio, *Sexual Politics, Sexual Communities*, 70; 157; Hurewitz, *Bohemian Los Angeles*, 232–37; 261–63; Nan Alamilla Boyd, *Wide Open Town: A History of Queer San Francisco to 1965* (Berkeley and Los Angeles: University of California Press, 2003), 172–73; Molly McGarry and Fred Wasserman, *Becoming Visible: An Illustrated History of Lesbian and Gay Life in Twentieth-Century America* (New York: Viking, 1998).

18. "Behind Bars," *RFD*, no. 10 (Winter 1976), 26.

19. Ibid.

20. Riegle, "Sexual Politics of 'Crime,'" 4.

21. Ibid.

22. "The Lesbian and Gay Prisoner Project," pamphlet, BSEF, box 13, fol. 49.

23. Mike Riegle, "A Brief History of *GCN*'s 'Prison Project,'" *GCN*, October 3, 1981, 8.

24. "BWMT/MACT and Gay Prisoners," flyer, n.d., BSEF, box 12, fol. 37.

25. League for Lesbian and Gay Prisoners, pamphlet, n.d., BSEF, box 12, fol. 37.

26. Scacco, *Rape in Prison*, viii.

27. The association of prison rape with homosexuality influenced the decision to exempt prisoners from the California Assembly Bill 489 passed in 1975 that revoked the state's sodomy laws and legalized private sexual acts between consenting adults. During debate over the bill, one gay journalist reported, "The ugly specter of so-called 'homo-

sexual rape' and 'homosexual prostitution' reared its collective head," and the bill was amended to exclude from decriminalization those confined in state prisons and other detention facilities (Pete Dunham, "California Gays Indicted," *Join Hands* 5 [August–September 1976]: 1).

28. Scacco, *Rape in Prison*, 4. See also Rideau and Sinclair, "Prison: The Sexual Jungle," 20.

29. Scacco, *Rape in Prison*, 4.

30. See Gresham M. Sykes, *The Society of Captives: A Study of a Maximum Security Prison* (Princeton, NJ: Princeton University Press, 1958), 96; George Lester Kirkham, "Homosexuality in Prison," in *Studies in the Sociology of Sex*, ed. James M. Henslin (New York: Appleton Century-Crofts, 1971), 334.

31. Accounts in the 1960s and 1970s seemed less concerned about the sexual futures of straight-women-turned-jailhouse femmes by prison butches. See Giallombardo, *The Social World of Imprisoned Girls*, 244–45; Ward and Kassebaum, *Women's Prison*, 103.

32. Weiss and Friar, *Terror in the Prisons*, 74. See also Jules Quentin Burstein, *Conjugal Visits in Prison: Psychological and Social Consequences* (Lexington, MA: D. C. Heath & Co. 1977), 18; Linda Charlton, "The Terrifying Homosexual World of the Jail System," *New York Times*, April 25, 1971, 40, reprinted in Gene Kassebaum, "Sex in Prison," *Sexual Behavior*, vol. 11 (January 1972).

Stephen Donaldson resisted this notion, writing, "I never accepted the notion that penetration meant a loss of masculinity. . . . I just never saw the fact that I had been fucked as having anything to do with my sexual identity . . . the notion that penetration = loss of masculinity is the Big Lie and is responsible for most of the psychological anguish which male rape victims feel" (Donaldson to Uriah SteppenWolf, May 9, 1985, Stephen Donaldson papers, New York Public Library, Rare Books and Manuscript Division, box 5, fol. 29).

33. Bowker, *Prison Victimization*, 17.

34. "Homosexuality in Prison," in "Playboy Forum," *Playboy* 14 (May 1967): 147; "Sodomy Factories," *Playboy* 14 (August 1967): 146; "Sodomy Factories," *Playboy* 15 (January 1968): 59–60; "Sodomy Factories" and "An Ex-Prisoner's Tale," *Playboy* 15 (March 1968): 45–46; "Sodomy Factories," *Playboy* 15 (September 1968): 82; "Sodomy Factories," *Playboy* 16 (December 1969): 82.

35. Torok, *The Strange World of Prison*, 9, 97.

36. Carter, *The Sixteenth Round*, 162.

37. Ibid., 170–71.

38. See, for example, Ray D. Johnson, *Too Dangerous to Be at Large* (New York: Quadrangle, 1975), 76; Ed Morris, *Born to Lose* (New York: Mason & Lipscomb, 1974), 31; Peter Remick, *In Constant Fear: The Brutal True Story of Life within the Walls of the Notorious Walpole State Prison, as Told to James B. Shuman* (New York: Reader's Digest Press, 1975), 13; Robert H. Adleman, *Alias Big Cherry: The Confessions of a Master Criminal* (New York: Dial, 1973), 245; Eddie Harrison and Alfred V. J. Prather, *No Time for Dying* (Englewood Cliffs, NJ: Prentice-Hall, 1973), 80–82.

39. Davis also distinguished between "innocent victims of homosexual rape" and

"male prostitutes," who, he wrote, occupied "opposite end[s] of the spectrum" ("Sexual Assaults in the Philadelphia Prison System and Sheriff's Vans," *Trans-Action* 6 [December 1968]: 13).

40. Burstein, *Conjugal Visits in Prison*, 18.

41. Wooden and Parker, *Men behind Bars*, 99.

42. Davis, "Sexual Assaults," 13.

43. As an undergraduate student at Columbia University, Donaldson (born Robert Martin) was one of the founders in 1967 of the Student Homophile League, the first gay student organization in the United States, and was involved in organizing a youth caucus of the North American Conference of Homophile Organizations (NACHO), the first national meeting of gay organizations. In 1972, Donaldson appealed his dishonorable discharge from the Navy on the grounds of "suspected homosexual involvement," arguing that "homosexual activity on the part of heterosexual Navy sailors is widespread" and implying that he participated in sex as "straight trade" (see Martin to Bella Abzug, February 16, 1972, Donaldson papers, box 1, fol. 1). Wayne Dynes, Donaldson's close friend and coauthor, wrote that Donaldson's bisexual identification "had something of a forced, theatrical quality. . . . Although he had sex with women from time to time, it is clear that his deepest erotic feelings came from his experiences with young men" (Wayne Dynes, "Stephen Donaldson [Robert A. Martin]: 1946–96," in *Before Stonewall: Activists for Gay and Lesbian Rights in Historical Context* [New York: Harrington Park Press, 2002], 270).

44. Donaldson to JD, January 17, 1974, Donaldson papers, fol. 1, box 3.

45. Donaldson's many pseudonyms, in Dynes's estimation, showed "a remarkable capacity for reinvention of self" (Dynes, "Stephen Donaldson," 266). They could also serve as a strategic and selective closeting device. Donaldson wrote to the gay magazine the *Advocate* under his given name, Bob Martin, in 1976, about the difficulty he experienced participating in gay life after being raped in prison (Bob Martin to the *Advocate*, June 30, 1976, 32). When writing under the names Stephen Donaldson, Donny the Punk, or Donny Tucker, Donaldson often insinuated that he was heterosexual by distinguishing his own identity as punk from that of prison queens, fags, and other gay men. In "A Punk's Song," for instance, Donaldson wrote that following his prison rape, he "sought to fathom my changed feelings toward men, thinking I must be bisexual (my erotic feelings for women remaining apparently unchanged) (Tucker, "A Punk's Song," 72). In another letter to the editor of a gay periodical, Donaldson criticized an article published in the previous issue: "Hell, it is bad enough for a boy to get gang-raped into a sex role he would not otherwise get into, without some self-righteous gay coming along to slag him off—we have to put up with enuf of that shit from the rapists without the gays, who should be (and usually are) our allies, joining in, just 'cos we happen to like women out on the street" (Donny the Punk to editor, *RFD*, no. 31 [Summer 1982], 15).

46. Donaldson, "A Million Jockers, Punks, and Queens," 17.

47. Pete Dunham, "California Gays Indicted," *Join Hands* 5 (August–September 1976): 1.

48. Carl Wittman, "A Gay Manifesto," in *Out of the Closets*, ed. Jay and Young, 335,

originally published as "Refugees from Amerika: A Gay Manifesto," *San Francisco Free Press*, December 22, 1969–January 7, 1970.

49. Young, "Out of the Closets, into the Streets," 16.

50. Ken Carpenter, "Men, Sex and Imprisonment," *GCN*, March 6, 1982, 5.

51. Young, "Out of the Closets, into the Streets," 16.

52. Wittman, "Gay Manifesto," 335.

53. Quoted in Wooden and Parker, *Men behind Bars*, 224.

54. Carpenter, "Men, Sex, and Imprisonment," 5.

55. Henry Lucas, "We Must Unify," BSEF, box 12, fol. 37.

56. Samuel Roth, *Stone Walls Do Not: The Chronicle of a Captivity* (New York: William Faro, 1930), 261.

57. Florence Monahan, *Women in Crime* (New York: Ives Washburn, Inc., 1941), 226.

58. Robert Lindner, *Stone Walls and Men* (New York: Odyssey Press, 1946), 458.

59. John Bartlow Martin, *Break Down the Walls* (New York: Curtis Publishing Co., 1951), 178.

60. Donald Lee, "Seduction of the Guilty: Homosexuality in American Prisons," *Fact* 2 (November–December 1965): 58–59.

61. Carpenter, "Men, Sex and Imprisonment," 5.

62. Tucker, "A Punk's Song," 72.

63. Donaldson to Morty Manford, May 18, 1983, Donaldson Papers, box 3, fol. 12. Donaldson noted that few if any of the "numerous gay pornographic books and videos featuring an incarceration setting" were written by former prisoners and that they were "generally wildly inaccurate in depicting sexual reciprocity" ("A Million Jockers, Punks, and Queens," 6). At the same time, Donaldson wrote "true-life sexual stories" with clearly pornographic appeal for gay publications (see Donaldson to French Wall, *Guide*, March 3, 1991, Donaldson papers, box 1, fol. 24).

64. Boyd, *Sex behind Bars*, 17. Boyd specialized in publishing nonfiction writing, much of it by prisoners, and claimed that his books "aren't porn, they're history" (Boyd McDonald to Donaldson, June 2, 1983, Donaldson papers, box 3, fol. 15). In soliciting writing from Stephen Donaldson, Boyd wrote that "porn is ideal; my work is real, and more exciting than the ideal" (Boyd McDonald to Donaldson, June 17, 1983, Donaldson papers, box 3, fol. 15).

65. Anthony T. Smith to *GCN* Prisoners Rights Project, January 16, 1984, BSEF, box 13, fol. 42.

66. Denver V. Sassoon to *GCN*, n.d., BSEF, box 13, fol. 44.

67. Ronald Cronick, "A Letter from a Gay Inmate," *Moto*, vol. 1 (December 1974), in Robert G. DeSantis papers, Gay and Lesbian Historical Society of Northern California, San Francisco Public Library, San Francisco, California, box 1, fol. 20.

68. "Prisoner Boycott Called," *Lesbian Tide* 9 (September–October 1979): 14.

69. Little's name was often misspelled as "Joanne" or "Joann." Christina Greene offers a fascinating analysis of Little's case in "'She Ain't No Rosa Parks!' Representations of Black Womanhood in the 1974–75 Joan Little Murder-Sexual Assault Case" (paper

presented at the Berkshire Conference of Women Historians, Claremont, California, June 2005).

70. Julian Bond, "Self-Defense against Rape: The Joanne Little Case," *Black Scholar* 6 (March 1975): 29.

71. "Florida," *off our backs* 6 (May 1976): 12.

72. Women Free Women in Prison, "Male Prison Guards," *off our backs* 7 (March 1977): 7.

73. "Aftermath at Bedford Hills," *off our backs* 9 (April 1979): 15. See also "Who's Who at Bedford Hills: Sexual Harassment by Male Guards," *No More Cages* 3 (May–June 1982): 11.

74. Rideau and Sinclair, "Prison: The Sexual Jungle," 23.

75. Ron Rose to DeSantis, May 19, 1974, DeSantis papers, box 1, fol. 16.

76. "Still More on P.C.," *Join Hands*, clipping, n.d., in BSEF, box 13, fol. 2.

77. Christopher Lemmond, "Protection," *RFD*, no. 15 (Spring 1978), 42.

78. Jon Wildes, "To Be Young, Gay, and Behind Bars," 21.

79. Don Jackson, "The Daddy Tank," *Gay Sunshine* 1 (1972): 3.

80. "Women Hit Jail Treatment," *Advocate*, July 10, 1972, 14.

81. "We Mean Business," *Lesbian Tide* 1 (July 1972): 1.

82. "No Touching, No Human Contact—in Cell Block 4200," *Lesbian Tide* 6 (November–December 1976): 7.

83. "We Mean Business," *Lesbian Tide* 1 (July 1972): 1.

84. Jeanne Cordova, "Prison Reform—New Freedoms for Daddy-Tanked Lesbians," *Lesbian Tide* 7 (March–April 1977): 6.

85. Join Hands Testimony, 1974, mimeographed ms., GLBT Historical Society, "Prisoners" file, 1.

86. Jack Hoffman to editor, *RFD*, no. 10 (Winter 1976), 29.

87. *Join Hands* subscription form, GLBT Historical Society, San Francisco, "Prisoners" file.

88. Riegle, "A Brief History of GCN's 'Prison Project,'" *GCN* 9 (October 3, 1981): 8.

89. Prison projects like the one started by Boston's *Gay Community News* were initiated to forge connections between gay prisoners with gay men and lesbians on the outside. The periodical *RFD* included a section titled "Brothers behind Bars," devoted to letters and pen pal requests from prisoners. In 1972, a group of gay men in San Francisco, some former prisoners, formed the Join Hands collective and published a newsletter "to bring together members of the 'free' community with gay prisoners through correspondence and visiting" (*Join Hands* subscription form, GLBT Historical Society, San Francisco, California). The primary aim of *Join Hands*, the first issue stated, was to "give gay men in prison a link with gay people on the outside through letter-writing and visiting" (*Join Hands*, no. 1 [1976]: 1). The *Gaycon Press Newsletter*, also published in San Francisco, printed articles, short stories, poetry, and graphics by gay prisoners, provided information on the status of prison life for gay men and lesbians, and listed gay publications that were available free to prisoners. The Metropolitan Community Church (MCC), a non-

denominational Christian church with largely gay congregations founded in 1968, began conducting services in prisons in 1972 and published the *Cellmate* newsletter.

90. See "Prisons Ban Gay Press," *off our backs* 7 (February 1977): 5.

91. Publication Review and Denial Notification, October 18, 1983, BSEF, box 12, fol. 11.

92. Larry D. May, Assistant Warden, to Mike Riegle, December 19, 1985, BSEF, box 13, fol. 4.

93. Editorial statement, *off our backs* 7 (May 1977): 1.

94. Michael Patrick O'Conner to Adria Libolt, Deputy Warden, Cassidy Lake Technical School, Chelsea, Michigan, September 29, 1988, BSEF, box 13, fol. 18.

95. *National Gay Task Force, et al. v. Norman Carlson* (Civil Action no. 77-0809). See Wooden and Parker, *Men behind Bars*, 224; "Federal Prisons to Admit Gay Publications," National Gay Task Force press release, October 22, 1980. *National Gay Task Force, et al. v. Norman Carlson* (1980) (U.S. District Court for the District of Columbia, [Civil Action no. 77-0809) stipulated that "sexually explicit material which by its nature or content poses a threat the security, good order, or discipline of the institution or facilitates criminal activity" may be excluded, but that "sexually explicit material does not include material of a news or information type" (quoted in Nan Hunter to Wallace H. Cheney, General Counsel, Federal Bureau of Prisons, March 20, 1990, BSEF, box 12, fol. 1).

96. "Still More on P.C.," *Join Hands*, clipping, n.d., in BSEF, box 13, fol. 2.

97. Alan Greene to Mike Riegle, April 16, 1984, BSEF, box 13, fol. 42.

98. Wilbert Leonard Thomas, letter to the editor, *Advocate*, August 18, 1972, 28.

99. Calvin L. Keach, "Gay Demo against Prison Censors," *Join Hands* 5 (August–September 1976): 2.

100. Louis to Mike Riegle, March 22, 1983, BSEF, box 13, fol. 42.

101. Danny Owen to Mike Riegle, January 27, 1984, BSEF, box 13, fol. 42.

102. Buddy L. to editor, *RFD*, no. 10 (Winter 1976), 29.

103. David Rothenberg, "Gay Prisoners: Fighting Back behind the Walls," *Advocate*, June 16, 1976, 11.

104. Mike Hippler, "Where the Boys Are: Gay Inmates at San Bruno Jail," *Bay Area Reporter*, December 29, 1983, 14.

105. Frank O'Rourke, "Prisons: The Nature of the Beast," *Honcho*, August 1983, 61.

106. Jack Childers, letter to editor, *Join Hands* 1 (1976): 2.

107. Chuck Hill to editor, *RFD* 13 (Fall 1977), 38.

108. Ibid.

109. Quoted in Mark Fleisher, *Warehousing Violence* (Newbury Park, CA: Sage Publications, 1989), 164.

110. Charles McLaughlin, "Homosexual Living behind the Walls," unpublished ms., n.d., BSEF, box 13, fol. 44.

111. Letter to editor, *Join Hands*, 1 (1976): 2.

112. William Kissinger, "View from Within," in New York Gay Activists Alliance newsletter, no title, n.d., in International Gay Information Center Archives, New York Public Library, ephemera, "Prison File."

113. Wildes, "To Be Young, Gay, and Behind Bars," 21.

114. Jeanne Cordova, "Inside Terminal Island," *Lesbian Tide* 2 (January 1973): 18.

115. Ibid., 18–19.

116. "The Unpleasantries of Pleasanton," *Through the Looking Glass* 4 (March 1979): 13.

117. "Sissy in Prison: An Interview with Ron Vernon," in *Out of the Closets*, ed. Jay and Young, 107.

118. Young, "Gay Prison Tragedy," *Gay Sunshine*, no. 20 (February 1974), 2.

119. Bobbie Lee White, "Learning to Understand," *GCN*, January 23, 1982, 9.

120. "Sissy in Prison," 104.

121. Billy LaToya Lewis to *GCN*, n.d., BSEF, box 13, fol. 44.

122. Flyer, "New American Cult Gay World Behavior Notice," April 20, 1983, BSEF, box 13, fol. 42.

123. "Self-Help Alliance Group," n.d. [1984?] BSEF, box 13, fol. 42.

124. Ibid.

125. Quoted in Wooden and Parker, *Men behind Bars*, 220. On Men against Sexism, see "Men against Sexism," *Through the Looking Glass* 2 (December 1977): 18; Daniel Burton-Rose, "The Anti-Exploits of Men against Sexism, 1977–78," in *Prison Masculinities*, ed. Don Sabo, Terry A. Kupers, and Willie London (Philadelphia: Temple University Press, 2001); Rick English, "Men against Sexism," *RFD*, no. 14 (Winter 1977): 49; John McCoy, *Concrete Mama: Prison Profiles from Walla Walla* (Columbia: University of Missouri Press, 1981), 92, 136–37; "Men against Sexism: Past, Present, and Future," *Join Hands* 13 (January–March 1978): 6.

126. Rick English, "Walla . . . Men against Sexism," *Join Hands* 12 (November–December 1977): 5.

127. Martha Shelley, "Gay Is Good," in *Out of the Closets*, ed. Jay and Young, 32. On the importance of an analysis and critique of sexism to gay liberation ideology, see John D'Emilio, "Still Radical after All these Years: Remembering *Out of the Closets*," in *The World Turned: Essays on Gay History, Politics, and Culture* (Durham, NC: Duke University Press, 2002); and D'Emilio, "After Stonewall," in *Making Trouble: Essays on Gay History, Politics, and the University* (New York: Routledge, 1992); Terence Kissack, "'Freaking Fag Revolutionaries': New York's Gay Liberation Front, 1969–1971," *Radical History Review* 62 (Spring 1995): 104–34; Marc Stein, *City of Sisterly and Brotherly Love: Lesbian and Gay Philadelphia, 1945–1972* (Chicago: University of Chicago Press, 2000), 322–23; John Loughery, *The Other Side of Silence: Men's Lives and Gay Identities: A Twentieth-Century History* (New York: Henry Holt, 1998), 327.

128. Young, "Out of the Closets," 7.

129. Quoted in McCoy, *Concrete Mama*, 137.

130. "Men Against Sexism," *Through the Looking Glass* 2 (December 1977): 18.

131. English, "Walla . . . Men against Sexism," 5. Walla Walla inmates were not alone in attributing the oppression experienced by gay prisoners to sexism. Another prisoner attributed homophobia in the several federal prisons where he had been an inmate to "Straight Male Sexism, which . . . reproduces the non-prison world's paradigm of

women's oppression" (Jon Staten Wildes, untitled article, in New York Gay Activists Alliance newsletter, n.d., in International Gay Information Center Archives, Rare Books and MS Division, New York Public Library, ephemera, "Prison File.")

132. Billy LaToya Lewis to *GCN*, n.d., BSEF, box 13, fol. 44.

133. Henry Lucas, "We Must Unify," BSEF, box 12, fol. 37.

134. Johnny Crawford to *BWMT Quarterly* 11 (Fall 1981): 34.

135. Mike Riegle and prisoner friends, "Why Does *GCN* Have a Prisoner Project?" BSEF, box 12, fol. 37.

136. Curly to Mike Riegle, January 29, 1986, BSEF, box 13, fol. 42; William D. Concannon to editor, *GCN* 7 (July 12, 1980): 4; Denver V. Sassoon to *GCN*, n.d. BSEF, box 13, fol. 44.

137. "Jail Guard Trainees Hear from Gays," *Advocate*, November 22, 1972, 14.

138. Ibid.

139. Joanne Meyerowitz, *How Sex Changed: A History of Transsexuality in the United States* (Cambridge, MA: Harvard University Press, 2002), 235, 237–38, 258. See also Aaron H. Devor and Nicholas Matte, "One Inc. and Reed Erickson: The Uneasy Collaboration of Gay and Trans Activism, 1964–2003," *GLQ: A Journal of Lesbian and Gay Studies* 10 (2004): 179–209; Dallas Denny, "You're Strange and We're Wonderful: The Relationship between the Gay/Lesbian and Transgendered Communities," *TransSisters* (Autumn 1994), 21–23; Kissack, "Freaking Fag Revolutionaries," 123. Kissack underlines the importance of masculinist affirmations in New Left politics and "the extent to which sexualized codes of masculinity were a highly charged component of sixties' discourse," in which gay liberationists took part, in "Freaking Fag Revolutionaries," 111–12; Richard Meyer, "Gay Power Circa 1970: Visual Strategies for Sexual Revolution," *GLQ: A Journal of Lesbian and Gay Studies* 12, no. 3 (2006): 454–55.

140. Tracy, letter to editor, *Join Hands* 1 (1976): 2.

141. "Hard Times for Queens," *Join Hands* 5 (August–September 1976): 3.

142. M. Darrell Hay, letter to editor, *Join Hands* 2 (February–March, 1976): 1.

143. "Mr. Cuddles Talks about Letter Writing," *Join Hands* no. 2 (February–March, 1976): 7.

144. Wooden and Parker, *Men Behind Bars*, 144.

145. Ibid., 145.

146. Ibid., 219.

147. Ibid., 160, 161.

148. Ibid., 3.

149. For discussions of the intersection of white identity and homonormativity, see Roderick A. Ferguson, "Race-ing Homonormativity: Citizenship, Sociology, and Gay Identity," in *Black Queer Studies: A Critical Anthology*, ed. E. Patrick Johnson and Mae G. Henderson (Durham, NC: Duke University Press, 2006); Martin F. Manalansan IV, "In the Shadows of Stonewall: Examining Gay Transnational Politics and the Diasporic Dilemma," *GLQ: A Journal of Lesbian and Gay Studies* 2, no. 4 (1995): 425–38.

150. Randy Shilts, "Locked up with the Jailhouse Queens," *San Francisco Chronicle*, April 7, 1978, 12. Marlon Ross characterizes the narrative of development and under-

development as "intrinsic to the project of queer history and theory," in "Beyond the Closet as Raceless Paradigm," in *Black Queer Studies: A Critical Anthology*, ed. E. Patrick Johnson and Mae G. Henderson (Durham, NC: Duke University Press, 2005), esp. 163.

151. Tom Reeves, "The Hidden Oppression: Gay Men in Prison for Having Sex with Minors," *GCN*, December 13, 1980, 8.

152. Ibid., 9.

153. Ibid., 11.

154. On the transition from a gay liberation movement to gay rights, see D'Emilio, "After Stonewall."

155. Michael Serber, "Shame Aversion Therapy," *Journal of Behavior Therapy and Experimental Psychiatry* 1 (1970): 213.

156. Ibid., 213.

157. Michael Serber and Joseph Wolpe, "Behavior Therapy Techniques," in *Sexual Behavior: Social, Clinical, and Legal Aspects*, ed. H. L. P. Resnick and Marvin E. Wolfgang (Boston: Little Brown, 1972), 247.

158. See Henry L. Minton, *Departing from Deviance: A History of Homosexual Rights and Emancipatory Science in America* (Chicago: University of Chicago Press, 2002), 256–64.

159. Don Altimus to Mike Riegle, October 7, 1982, BSEF, box 12, fol. 52.

160. Join Hands Testimony at California State Senate Committee on Penal Institutions Hearings, December 5, 1974, ms, 9, in GLBT Historical Society.

161. Rob Cole, "Behind Bars: Lessons on Being Gay," *Advocate*, June 20, 1973, 1.

162. Join Hands Testimony, 9.

163. Michael Serber and Claudia G. Keith, "The Atascadero Project: Model of a Sexual Retraining Program for Incarcerated Homosexual Pedophiles," *Journal of Homosexuality* 1, no. 1 (Fall 1974): 95.

164. Tom Close, "A Patient's View: A Strange New World," *Advocate*, June 20, 1973, 2.

165. Ibid., 2.

166. Close explained that Atascadero Gay Encounter (AGE) "is administratively a facet of the Sexual Reorientation Program but is open to all homosexual and bisexual patients in the hospital who are 18 or over. The club is designed for specific therapeutic purposes and is an integral part of many patients' formal program. AGE will become the voice of the gay patient as well as his conscience. As acting president, I am striving to achieve our four purposes:

- Becoming more aware and accepting of our sexual identity.
- Informing members and others in the hospital about gay culture.
- Providing opportunities to meet other Gays in social settings.
- Providing useful information to members about where to go and whom to go to after release from the hospital." (Ibid., 35)

Beginning in 1976, the group published their own newsletter, *Voice of AGE*.

167. John Lastala, "Atascadero, Dachau for Queers?" *Advocate*, April 26, 1972, 12.

168. Ibid., 11–13. See also Michael Selber, "View from the Garbage Heap: The Plight of the Sex Offender," *Los Angeles Advocate*, November 1968, 6–9; Rob Cole, "Or

Is Somebody Having Nightmares?" *Advocate*, April 26, 1972, 11–13; Serber and Keith, "Atascadero Project," 93; Don Jackson, "Abuse at Prison Hospital," *Bay Area Reporter* 2, no. 8 (April 15, 1972): 1–4; Estelle B. Freedman, "'Uncontrolled Desires': The Response to the Sexual Psychopath, 1920–1960," *Journal of American History* 74, no. 1 (June 1987): 99.

169. Jackson, "Abuse at Prison Hospital," 3.

170. Ibid., 2.

171. Serber and Keith, "Atascadero Project," 93.

172. Ibid., 87.

173. Ibid., 90.

174. Ibid., 87.

175. "Needless to say," Serber and Keith wrote, "the patients are more than grateful to receive a service that does not include stripping them of their homosexuality and personal dignity" ("Atascadero Project," 94). Greg M., the President of Atascadero Gay Encounter, wrote in appreciation of "the liberal attitude toward homosexuals" at Atascadero, adding, "Can you imagine how much more difficult this situation would be if therapists were trying to make us go straight?" (Greg M., "The President's Corner," *Voice of AGE* 4, no. 1 [January 1978]: 2).

176. Cole, "Behind Bars, Lessons on Being Gay," 1.

177. A class-action suit was brought by California inmates in 1973 to allow the MCC into prisons. In a decision handed down on May 20, 1975, in the U.S. District Court of Northern California, the court ruled that the MCC was a bona fide church and that denial of MCC religious services to prisoners who request them was an infringement of their constitutional rights guaranteed by the First Amendment. See "Court Allows MCC in Prisons, *GCN*, June 14, 1975, 1; "Gay Church Allowed in Prisons," *Lesbian Tide* 4 (July–August 1975): 19. On the MCC, see Kay Tobin and Randy Wicker, *The Gay Crusaders* (New York: Coronet, 1972), 19–22; Troy D. Perry, with Charles L. Lucas, *The Lord Is My Shepherd and He Knows I'm Gay* (Los Angeles: Nash Publishing, 1972); Troy D. Perry, with Thomas L. P. Swicegood, *Don't Be Afraid Anymore: The Story of Reverend Troy Perry and the Metropolitan Community Churches* (New York: St. Martin's Press, 1990).

178. Richard R. Mickley, *Prison Ministry Handbook*, 2d ed. (Los Angeles: Universal Fellowship Press, 1976), 7. The slogan on the cover page of the first few issues of *Voice of AGE*, the newsletter published by prisoners at Atascadero—"Homosexuality Means Much More"—echoed this sentiment (see, for example, *Voice of AGE*, vol. 1, no. 7 [July 1, 1976].)

179. Deacon Tom Purcell, "The Homosexual's Prayer," DeSantis papers, box 1, fol. 16.

180. Mickley, *Prison Ministry Handbook*, 33.

181. Ibid., 33, 7.

182. Purcell, "The Homosexual's Prayer."

183. Mickley, *Prison Ministry Handbook*, 8.

184. Ibid., 31.

185. "MCC Launching 'Prison Lifeline' Letters Program," *Advocate*, January 31, 1973, 14.

186. Jeanne Barney and David Bridell, "Mail Regulations Eased at CMC," *Advocate*, July 4, 1973, 38.

187. "Join Hands," *Gay Sunshine*, no. 1 (1972), 1.

188. "Open Forum," *Bay Area Reporter*, June 30, 1983, 6.

189. Lary Holvey, "Pen Pal Caution," *Bay Area Reporter*, August 11, 1983, 9.

190. Teddy to Jeannie, *Advocate*, July 4, 1973, 38. Some prisoners acknowledged that some among them used pen pal relationships to scam gay men. Exploiting the generosity of gay pen pals, one prisoner acknowledged, like that of "lonely women," was "one of the oldest games in the joint" (Hogshire, *You Are Going to Prison*, 90). One Michigan prisoner wrote to *GCN* offering to help gay men "sort the fakes from the real thing" (David Sidener to *GCN*, n.d., BSEF, box 13, fol. 42).

191. Troy Lewis to Mike Riegle, October 10, 1986, BSEF, box 13, fol. 42.

192. "Open Forum," *Bay Area Reporter*, June 30, 1983, 6.

193. "Prison Pen Pals on the March," *Bay Area Reporter*, June 30, 1983, 9.

194. M.B. to Jeannie, *Advocate*, October 10, 1974, 31.

195. Letter to the Editor, *GCN*, January 10–16, 1988, 4.

196. "A Concerned Lesbian Subscriber," letter to the editor, *GCN*, December 13–19, 1987, 4.

197. "Joint Venture," *RFD*, no. 13 (Spring 1987), 65.

198. David Frey, "You Are a Criminal Too," *RFD*, no. 27 (Summer 1980), 8.

199. The AIDS Coalition to Unleash Power (ACT-UP) of San Francisco had a small but thriving Prison Issues Group in the early 1990s that "was able to galvanize activists across the state to come together and fight for the rights of prisoners" (Elihu Rosenblatt, *Criminal Injustice: Confronting the Prison Crisis* [Boston: South End Press, 1996], 89). See also Dawn Schmitz, "Activists Demand PWA Rights on the Inside," *GCN*, April 19–May 8, 1992, 1, 3.

200. Rebecca Lavine, "A Great Need," *GCN*, December 1–17, 1991, 7.

201. Riegle's work as *GCN* office manager and his struggle with HIV/AIDS was memorably chronicled by his friend and *GCN* colleague Amy Hoffman in *Hospital Time* (Durham, NC: Duke University Press, 1997).

202. Mike Riegle, "The March: A Focus on 'Justice' (as 'Political' Finally!)—and Still Gay/Lesbian Prisoners Are Invisible," *GCN*, October 11, 1987, 4.

203. Lisa Duggan, *The Twilight of Equality? Neoliberalism, Cultural Politics, and the Attack on Democracy* (Boston: Beacon, 2003), 50. See also Duggan, "The New Homonormativity: The Sexual Politics of Neoliberalism," in *Materializing Democracy*, ed. Russ Castronovo and Dana D. Nelson (Durham, NC: Duke University Press, 2002): 173–94.

EPILOGUE

1. The complex of diseases that would become known as AIDS was first recognized on June 5, 1981, by the CDC in their journal, *Morbidity and Mortality Weekly Report* (June 5, 1981). The Centers for Disease Control announced that between November 1981

and October 1982, ten AIDS cases were reported among inmates of New York State correctional facilities (*Morbidity and Mortality Weekly Report* [January 7, 1983], 700).

2. Theodore M. Hammett, *AIDS in Correctional Facilities: Issues and Options* (Washington, DC: National Institute of Justice, 1986).

3. Saira Moini and Theodore M. Hammett, *1989 Update: AIDS in Correctional Facilities* (Washington, DC: National Institute of Justice, 1990), 14. On the regional skewing of HIV/AIDS among prisoners, see also David Dugdale and Ken Peterson, "The Prevalence of HIV Seropositivity and HIV-Related Illness in Washington State Prisoners," *Prison Journal* 69 (Spring–Summer 1989): 33–38; Nancy Neveloff Dubler and Victor W. Sidel, "AIDS and the Prison System," in *A Disease of Society: Cultural and Institutional Responses to AIDS*, ed. Dorothy Nelkin, David P. Willis, and Scott V. Parris (Cambridge: Cambridge University Press, 1991), 71–83; Rosemary L. Gido, "Inmates with HIV/AIDS: A Growing Concern," in *Prison Sex: Practice and Policy*, ed. Christopher Hensley (Boulder, CO: Lynne Rienner, 2002): 101–10; and Gido, "A Demographic and Epidemiological Study of New York State Inmate AIDS Mortalities, 1981–1987," *Prison Journal* 69 (Spring–Summer 1989): 27–32; Carol Polych and Don Sabo, "Sentence—Death by Lethal Infection: IV-Drug Use and Infectious Disease Transmission in North American Prisons," in *Prison Masculinities*, ed. Don Sabo, Terry A. Kupers, and Willie London (Philadelphia: Temple University Press, 2001); Jamie Lillis, "Dealing with HIV/AIDS Positive Inmates," *Corrections Compendium* 18, no. 6 (June 1993): 1–3.

4. Moini and Hammett, *1989 Update*, 12.

5. In 1986, a study conducted by the ACLU's National Prison Project and the National Institute of Justice found that over 70 percent of AIDS cases were found in New York, New Jersey, and Pennsylvania prisons. (Hammett, *AIDS in Correctional Facilities: Issues and Options*).

6. Moini and Hammett, *1989 Update*, 12.

7. Dubler and Sidel, "AIDS and the Prison System," 75; Nancy N. Dubler et al., "Management of HIV Infection in New York State Prisons," *Columbia Human Rights Law Review* 21 (1990): 364. In 1993, the District of Columbia reported that 20 percent of its prison population tested positive for HIV (Lillis, "Dealing with HIV/AIDS-Positive Inmates," 1).

8. Theodore M. Hammett, *1988 Update: AIDS in Correctional Facilities* (Washington, DC: National Institute of Justice, 1969), 9. In September 1988, there were 689 inmate deaths attributed to AIDS in the New York state correctional system (Gido, "A Demographic and Epidemiological Study," 27).

9. James E. Lawrence and Van Zwisohn, "AIDS in Jail," in *American Jails: Public Policy Issues*, ed. Joel A. Thompson and G. Larry Mays (Chicago: Nelson-Hall, 1991), 118.

10. About fifty-four in ten thousand prison inmates had confirmed cases of AIDS, compared to nine in ten thousand persons in the U.S. population overall (Theodore M. Hammett et al., *1996–1997 Update: HIV/AIDS, STDs, and TB in Correctional Facilities* [Washington, DC: National Institute of Justice, 1999], 9). The rate of increase in seropositivity, however, was found to be slower in prisons than in the general population. In

October 1988, confirmed AIDS cases among prisoners had increased 309 percent since 1985. But, as Hammett reported in 1988, "that staggering increase is still less than the 407 percent increase in confirmed AIDS cases among the general population during the same time period" (Hammett, *1988 Update*, iii). The rate of increase of HIV seropositivity among prisoners between 1985 and 1986 was 61 percent, compared with 79 percent for the nation as a whole; between 1986 and 1987, the increase in AIDS cases in prison was 59 percent, compared with 61 percent for the nation as a whole.

11. See Cathy J. Cohen, *The Boundaries of Blackness: AIDS and the Breakdown of Black Politics* (Chicago: University of Chicago Press, 1999), 130–31, 134–39.

12. Sourcebook of Criminal Justice Statistics Online, http://www.albany.edu/ sourcebook/pdf/6282005.pdf; Jordan B. Glaser and Robert B. Griefinger, "Correctional Health Care: A Public Health Opportunity," *Annals of Internal Medicine* 118, no. 2 (January 1993): 139.

13. U.S. National Commission on AIDS, *HIV Disease in Correctional Facilities* (Washington, DC: U.S. National Commission on AIDS, 1991); Polych and Sabo, "Sentence— Death by Lethal Infection," 175. In her recent study of California prisons, Ruth Gilmore calculates that "drug commitments to federal and state prisons surged 975 percent between 1982 and 1999" (*Golden Gulag: Prisons, Surplus, Crisis, and Opposition in Globalizing California* [Berkeley: University of California Press, 2006], 18).

14. See Dubler et al., "Management of HIV Infection," 365; Ronald L. Braithwaite, Theodore M. Hammet, and Robert M. Mayberry, *Prisons and AIDS: A Public Health Challenge* [San Francisco: Jossey-Bass, 1996], 21; Cathy Potler, *AIDS in Prison: A Crisis in New York State Corrections* (New York: Correctional Association of New York, June 1988), 6.

15. Investigators Ronald L. Braithwaite, Theodore M. Hammet, and Robert M. Mayberry report that, in the 1980s, "African Americans represented approximately 12 percent of the total population of the United States but accounted for 48 percent of all inmates in state correctional facilities. From 1990 to 1993, the percentage of black inmates in federal and state prisons rose from 46.5 percent to 50.8 percent, and the percentage of Hispanic inmates nearly doubled from 7.7 percent to 14.3 percent" (*Prisons and AIDS*, 18). In some geographic regions, those numbers were dramatically higher. In 1988, African Americans and Latinos comprised about 80 percent of the more than 41,000 prisoners housed in the New York state corrections system (Potler, *AIDS in Prison*, 6). On the "differential sentencing" that resulted (and continues to result) in the disproportionate sentencing of people of color for drug-related offenses, see Marc Mauer, *Race to Incarcerate* (New York: New Press, 1999), 151–60; Braithwaite, Hammett, and Mayberry, *Prisons and AIDS*, 20–21; Rudolph Alexander, Jr., and Jacquelyn Gyamerah, "Differential Punishing of African Americans and Whites Who Possess Drugs: A Just Policy or a Continuation of the Past?" *Journal of Black Studies* 28 (September, 1997): 97–111; R. L. Austin and M. D. Allen, "Racial Disparity in Arrest Rates as an Explanation of Racial Disparity in Commitment to Pennsylvania's Prisons," *Journal of Research in Crime and Delinquency* 37 (May 2000): 200–220; David Cole, *No Equal Justice: Race and Class in the American Criminal*

Justice System (New York: New Press, 1999); D. B. Mustard, "Racial, Ethnic, and Gender Disparities in Sentencing: Evidence from the U.S. Federal Courts," *Journal of Law and Economics* 44 (April 2001): 285–314.

16. U.S. National Commission on AIDS, *HIV Disease in Correctional Facilities*, 10.

17. In 1982, the CDC introduced the term "AIDS" to describe the newly recognized syndrome. For an analysis of media attention granted to African Americans with HIV/AIDS, see Cohen, *Boundaries of Blackness*, esp. 149–85.

18. Polych and Sabo, "Sentence—Death by Lethal Infection," 173. Many investigators proceeded with the assumption that AIDS was readily transmitted in prison but with little evidence to support this supposition. Despite early warnings that prisons would become "breeding factories" for the AIDS virus, most evidence suggests that the overwhelming majority of prisoners with HIV were infected before they were incarcerated and that prison transmissions rates have been surprisingly low. While National Institute of Justice investigators reported that the transmission of HIV in prisons remained "a subject of widespread concern," available data suggested "little if any transmission" (Moini and Hammett, *1989 Update*, 25). In 1993, data from the Federal Bureau of Prisons indicated that of approximately ninety-eight thousand HIV tests, there were only fourteen seroconversions, and those occurred within the first six months of incarceration, suggesting that the inmates could have been infected before entering prison (Randy Martin, Sherwood Zimmerman, and Billy Long, "AIDS Education in U.S. Prisons: A Survey of Inmate Programs," *Prison Journal* 73, no. 1 [March 1993]: 104). A recent study of the state prison system in Georgia, covering the years between 1992 and 2005, found that very few HIV-infected prisoners acquired the virus while behind bars. The eighty-eight prisoners in the Georgia study who tested negative when they entered prison but became HIV-positive while incarcerated defied the most common patterns of thinking about sex in prison in several ways. Of the sixty-eight who were interviewed, forty-five reported having had sex while in prison, but half of them reported that their partners were male prison staff members, not other inmates. And nearly three-quarters of the HIV-positive Georgia prisoners who reported having sex with other men in prison described it as consensual (David Brown, "Few Men Found to Get HIV in Prison," *Washington Post*, April 21, 2006, A9).

19. Alvin Bronstein, testimony in Hearing before the Subcommittee on Courts, Civil Liberties, and the Administration of Justice of the Committee of the Judiciary, House of Representatives, 100th Cong., 1st sess., *AIDS and the Administration of Justice*, October 29, 1987.

20. Robert Barnes, "Prison Officials Fear AIDS Epidemic; Md. Legislators Criticize Lack of Mandatory Testing," *Washington Post*, September 30, 1987, A16.

21. Polych and Sabo, "Sentence—Death by Lethal Infection," 173.

22. Braithwaite, Hammett, and Mayberry, *Prisons and AIDS*, 29.

23. Quoted in Hammet et al., *1996–1997 Update*, 1.

24. Charles Horne, "We Need to Address AIDS in Prison," *Syracuse Post-Standard*, February 4, 1994, 24.

25. Brent Staples, "The Federal Government Gets Real about Sex behind Bars," *New York Times*, November 27, 2004, A34.

26. Martin, Zimmerman, and Long, "AIDS Education in U.S. Prisons," 103.

27. The delivery of medical care in prisons was wildly uneven and, in the majority of cases, grossly inadequate. Many reports showed that prisoners were often denied access to experimental treatments and adequate medical care. There was no uniform medical policy in prisons regarding the prescription of azidothymidine (AZT), the first drug approved for treatment of AIDS and HIV infection, for instance. One journalist reported that aerosolized pentamidine, approved by the FDA in early 1999 for the prevention of pneumocystis pneumonia, the leading cause of death from complications related to AIDS, was largely unobtainable in prison (see Donna Minkowitz, "Cruel and Unusual: AIDS in Prison," *Village Voice*, October 17, 1999), 16. In a Georgia case, *Hawley v. Evans*, plaintiffs sought availability of AZT for all HIV-infected prisoners. But the court held that the correctional system's more limited provision of AZT met medical standards and was therefore "constitutionally acceptable" (quoted in Moini and Hammett, *1989 Update*, 66). As a consequence, reports showed, prisoners with AIDS lived less than half as long as people with AIDS in the outside world (Minkowitz, "Cruel and Unusual," 16). See also Suzanne Daley, "AIDS Inmates Get Poor Health Care, Report Says," *New York Times*, May 13, 1988, B1–B2; Dubler and Sidel, "AIDS and the Prison System," 75. After the development of protease inhibitors in 1994, many state prisons continued to deny prisoners the expensive three-drug regimen (Anne-Marie Cusac, "'The Judge Gave Me Ten Years. He Didn't Sentence Me to Death': Prisoners with HIV Deprived of Proper Care," in *Prison Nation: The Warehousing of America's Poor*, ed. Herivel, Tara and Paul Wright [New York: Routledge, 2003], 196).

28. Glaser and Greifinger, "Correctional Health Care," 139.

29. President Ronald Reagan, Remarks at the American Foundation for AIDS Research Awards Dinner, May 31, 1987, http://www.reagan.utexas.edu/archives/speeches/1987/0531a.htm (accessed April 30, 2007).

30. Moini and Hammett, *1989 Update*, 45.

31. Inmates reported that a known diagnosis of HIV infection or AIDS "often leads to isolation and exclusion in the prison by other inmates and staff. Infected inmates are shunned, or attacked, or left to suffer alone with inadequate care" (Dubler and Sidel, "AIDS and the Prison System," 75).

32. Hammett, *1988 Update*, 29.

33. May Romano, "Plan for AIDS Testing in Prison Raises Questions," *New York Times*, December 17, 1989, sec. 12NJ, 1. AIDS activist Michael Slocum reported that "54 percent of state prison systems exclude people with asymptomatic HIV from a variety of prison work assignments; 46 percent limit participation in education programs; 23 percent limit participation in religious services, recreation, and law library usage. This exclusion is even more widespread for those diagnosed with AIDS" ("Living with HIV in Prison," n.d., in packet compiled by *GCN* Prisoner Law Project, BSEF papers, box 12, fol. 40. See also Urvashi Vaid, "Prisons," in *AIDS and the Law: A Guide for the Public*,

ed. Harlon L. Dalton, Scott Burris, and the Yale AIDS Law Project (New Haven, CT: Yale University Press, 1987), 241–43.

34. William LaRue, "Twice a Prisoner: AIDS Inmates Outcasts in Life, Prison," *Post-Standard*, April 5, 1987, E1.

35. Slocum, "Living with HIV in Prison."

36. Quoted in Bruce Lambert, "Prisons Criticized on AIDS Programs," *New York Times*, August 19, 1990, 16.

37. Alvin Bronstein, testimony in Hearing Before the Subcommittee on Courts, Civil Liberties, and the Administration of Justice of the Committee of the Judiciary, House of Representatives, 100th Cong., 1st sess., *AIDS and the Administration of Justice*, October 29, 1987, 38.

38. Chris Bull, "Alabama Suit Challenges Prison Testing and Isolation Policies," *Gay Community News*, June 26–July 2, 1988, 1.

39. "HIV-Positive Prisoners Forced to Wear Stun Belts," in *The Body: The Complete HIV/AIDS Resource* (http://www.thebody.com), September 1999, http://www.thebody.com/content/art30398.html#prisoners (accessed April 30, 2007).

40. Don Colburn, "AIDS in U.S. Prisons Mirrors Outside World; Not 'Escalating Wildly,' Experts Conclude," *Washington Post*, May 10, 1988, Z7.

41. Ibid.

42. Prisoners in New York's Auburn prison likewise reported violence against gay male prisoners to be "on the upswing" (Chris Bull, "Fighting AIDS in New York Prisons," *GCN*, January 24–30, 1988, 3). See also letter to editor, *Gay Community News*, March 6–12, 1988, 5; Harmeen Rowe, "AIDS behind Bars—a Prisoner's Concern," *U.S. News and World Report* (February 2, 1987), 7.

43. Dawn Schmitz, "Activists Demand PWA Rights on the Inside," *GCN*, April 19–May 8, 1992, 3.

44. Charles W. Colson, "Condoms: No Way to Control AIDS in Prison," *Washington Post*, June 26, 1991, A18.

45. Thomas A. Coughlin, "AIDS in Prisons: One Correctional Administrator's Recommended Policies and Procedures," *Judicature* 72 (1988): 66.

46. Ibid.

47. Ronald Shansky, testimony in Hearing before the Subcommittee on Courts, Civil Liberties, and the Administration of Justice of the Committee of the Judiciary, House of Representatives, 100th Congr., October 29, 1987, 32.

48. Dubler et al., "Management of HIV Infection," 390.

49. "AIDS MAY BE A BLESSING FOR SOME PRISONERS," press release from People Organized to Stop Rape of Imprisoned Persons, March 12, 1987, BSEF, box 12, fol. 40.

50. Vaid, "Prisons," 238.

51. See, especially, *LaRocca v. Dalsheim* (467 N.Y.S. 2d 302 [App. 1983]), *Blucker v. Washington*, ND. IL, no. 95C50110, 1994. See David M. Siegal, "Rape in Prison and AIDS: A Challenge for the Eighth Amendment Framework of Wilson v. Seiter," *Stanford Law Review* 44, no. 6 (July 1992): 1541–81.

52. When Senator Edward Kennedy introduced hearings on the Prison Rape Reduc-

tion Act of 2002, he noted that "infection rates for HIV, other sexually transmitted diseases, tuberculosis, and hepatitis C are far greater for prisoners than for the American population as a whole. Prison rape undermines the public health by contributing to the spread of these diseases and often gives a potential death sentence to its victims" (Senate Committee on the Judiciary, *Prison Rape Reduction Act of 2002*, Hearing before the Committee on the Judiciary, 107th Congr., 2d sess., 2002, 1). The Prison Rape Elimination Act of 2003 requires the Justice Department to collect data on prison rape and develop a national strategy for combating it.

53. Brent Staples, "The Federal Government Gets Real about Sex behind Bars," *New York Times*, November 27, 2004, A34.

54. Prisoner advocates reported that some women's institutions instituted a "severe clamp-down on relationships—including more disciplinary actions for kissing, hugging, and sitting on others' beds"—in response to the HIV/AIDS epidemic (Ann Bristow, Andrea Devine, and Denise McWilliams, "AIDS and Women in Prison," in packet compiled by *GCN* Prisoner Law Project, n.d., BSEF, box 12, fol. 40).

55. Hammett et al., *1996–1997 Update*, 10. This neglect of AIDS among women prisoners was part of a broader neglect of HIV/AIDS among women more generally. See Paula Treichler, "The Burdens of History: Gender and Representation in AIDS Discourse, 1981–1988," in *How to Have Theory in an Epidemic: Cultural Chronicles of AIDS* (Durham, NC: Duke University Press, 1999): 42–98.

56. Total female cases in U.S. correctional systems in 1998 "increased at a faster rate between 1987 and 1988 than total male cases (95 cases to 157 cases, for a 65% increase, as opposed to a 59% increase in male cases)" (Hammett, *1988 Update*, 11).

57. Theodore M. Hammett et al., "AIDS in Prisons in the USA," in *AIDS in Prison*, ed. Philip A. Thomas and Martin Moerings (Aldershot: Dartmouth, 1994), 140.

58. Kim Christensen, "Prison Issues and HIV: Introduction," in *Women, AIDS, and Activism*, ed. Marion Banzhaf et al. (Boston: South End Press, 1990), 139.

59. Gido, "Inmates with HIV/AIDS," 108.

60. From 1980 to 1989, the male prison population increased by 112 percent and the female population by 202 percent (Lawrence A. Greenfeld and Stephanie Minor-Harper, *Women in Prison* [(Washington, DC): U.S. Department of Justice, Office of Justice Programs, Bureau of Justice Statistics, Bureau of Justice Statistics Special Report, March 1991], NCJ-127991).

61. The Sentencing Project, "Factsheet: Women in Prison, from Bureau of Justice Statistics."

62. Cohen, *Boundaries of Blackness*, 324.

63. In 2000, drug offenders accounted for the largest source of the total growth among female inmates (35 percent), compared to 19 percent among male inmates (Allen J. Beck and Paige M. Harrison, *Prisoners in 2000* [(Washington, DC): U.S. Department of Justice, Office of Justice Programs, Bureau of Justice Statistics Bulletin, August 2001], http://www.ojp.usdoj.gov/bjs/pub/ascii/p00.txt [accessed March 31, 2007]).

64. The most publicized and perhaps best planned program was organized in 1988 by a diverse group of women incarcerated in the Bedford Hills Correctional Facility for

women in upstate New York. The AIDS Counseling and Education Program (ACE) was organized to offer education, to provide counseling, and to build a community of support for HIV-positive prisoners there. See Women of the ACE Program of the Bedford Hills Correctional Facility, *Breaking the Walls of Silence: AIDS and Women in a New York State Maximum-Security Prison* (Woodstock and New York: Overlook Press, 1998); Sue Rochman, "In an Unlikely Place, Women Offer Each Other AIDS Education and Love," in packet compiled by *GCN* Prisoner Law Project, n.d., BSEF, box 12, fol. 40. The Prisoner Education Project on AIDS (PEPA) was organized among male prisoners in New York's Auburn Correctional Institute. See Chris Bull, "Fighting AIDS in New York Prisons," *Gay Community News*, January 24–30, 1988, 1, 3; Martin, Zimmerman, and Long. "AIDS Education in U.S. Prisons," 103–29.

65. Sarah Etter, "HIV/AIDS Program Finds Success in Texas," *Corrections Connection Network News* (November 7, 2005), http://corrections.com/news/article.aspx?articleid =5959 (accessed April 30, 2007).

66. ACLU, National Prison Project, *AIDS and Prisons: The Facts for Inmates and Officers* (Washington, DC: American Civil Liberties Union Foundation, 1988), 23–24.

67. Chauncey, *Gay New York*, 13.

BIBLIOGRAPHY

MANUSCRIPT AND ARCHIVAL SOURCES

Columbia University Library, New York, New York
    Society for the Prevention of Crime Records
Cornell University, Ithaca, New York
    Human Sexuality Collection
Gay, Lesbian, Bisexual, Transgender Historical Society of Northern California,
San Francisco, California
    John DeCecco Papers
    Robert G. DeSantis Papers
Kinsey Institute for Research in Sex, Gender, and Reproduction, Bloomington,
Indiana
    Prison Collection
New York Public Library, New York, New York
    International Gay Information Center Archives
    Stephen Donaldson Papers
Northeastern University Library, Boston, Massachusetts
    Bromfield Street Educational Foundation Records
    Prisoner Newsletters Collection
Arthur and Elizabeth Schlesinger Library on the History of Women in America,
Harvard University, Cambridge, Massachusetts
    Miriam Van Waters Papers
    Massachusetts Society for Social Health Papers
University of Chicago Archives, Special Collections Research Center, Chicago,
Illinois
    Ernest W. Burgess papers
U.S. National Archives, College Park, Maryland
    U.S. Bureau of Prisons records

DISSERTATIONS AND THESES

Caffrey, Thomas A. "Assaultive and Troublesome Behavior among Adolescent Homosexual Prison Inmates." Ph.D. diss., City University of New York, 1974.

Fitzgerald, William A. "Pseudoheterosexuality in Prison and Out: A Study of the Lower Class Black Lesbian." Ph.D. diss., City University of New York, 1977.

Laubach, Frank C. "Why There Are Vagrants: A Study Based upon an Examination of One Hundred Men." Ph.D. diss., Columbia University, 1916.

LeShanna, Linda L. "Family Participation: Functional Response of Incarcerated Females." M.A. thesis, Bowling Green State University, 1969.

Mitchell, Arlene Edith. "Informal Inmate Social Structure in Prisons for Women: A Comparative Study." Ph.D. diss., University of Washington, 1969.

Nelson, Catherine I. "A Study of Homosexuality among Women Inmates at Two State Prisons." Ph.D. diss., Temple University, 1974.

Porter, Howard Kirk. "Prison Homosexuality: Locus of Control and Femininity." Ph.D. diss., Michigan State University, 1969.

Propper, Alice M. L. "Importation and Deprivation Perspectives on Homosexuality in Correctional Institutions: An Empirical Test of Their Relative Efficacy." Ph.D. diss., University of Michigan, 1976.

Sacks, Jerome G. "Troublemaking in Prison." Ph.D. diss., Catholic University of America, Washington, DC, 1942.

PERIODICALS

Advocate
Black and White Men Together Newsletter
Black and White Men Together Quarterly
Cellmate
Fortune News
Gay Community News
Gaycon Newsletter
Join Hands
Lesbian Connection
Lesbian Tide
National Association of Black and White Men Together Newsletter
No More Cages: A Bi-Monthly Women's Prison Newsletter
off our backs
RFD
Through the Looking Glass: A Women's and Children's Prison Newsletter
Voice of AGE: Atascadero Gay Encounter

GOVERNMENT DOCUMENTS

Buffum, Peter C. *Homosexuality in Prisons*. Washington, DC: Government Printing Office, 1972.

Hammett, Theodore M. *AIDS in Correctional Facilities: Issues and Options*. Washington,
DC: National Institute of Justice, 1986.

———. *AIDS in Correctional Facilities: Issues and Options*. 3d ed. Washington, DC:
National Institute of Justice, 1989.

———. *1986 Update: AIDS in Correctional Facilities*. Washington, DC: National Institute
of Justice, 1987.

———. *1988 Update: AIDS in Correctional Facilities*. Washington, DC: National Institute
of Justice, 1989.

Hammett, Theodore M., Patricia Harmon, and Laura M. Maruschak. *1996–1997 Update:
HIV/AIDS, STDs, and TB in Correctional Facilities*. Washington, DC: National
Institute of Justice, Center for Disease Control and Prevention, and Bureau of Justice
Statistics, 1999.

Langan, Patrick A., John V. Fundis, and Lawrence A. Greenfeld. *Historical Statistics on
Prisoners in State and Federal Institutions, Yearend, 1925–86*. Washington, DC: U.S.
Department of Justice, Bureau of Justice Statistics, May 1988.

Moini, Saira, and Theodore M. Hammett. *1989 Update: AIDS in Correctional Facilities*.
Washington, DC: National Institute of Justice, 1990.

United States. *Prison Rape Elimination Act of 2003*. Public Law 108–79. 108th Cong.,
September 4, 2003.

U.S. Congress. House. Committee on the Judiciary. *Prison Rape Reduction Act of 2003:
Hearing before the Subcommittee on Crime, Terrorism, and Homeland Security of the
Committee on the Judiciary*. 108th Cong.,1st sess. on H.R. 1707, April 29, 2003. Serial
No. 36. Washington, DC: U.S. Government Printing Office, 2003.

U.S. Congress. Senate. Committee on the Judiciary. *The Prison Rape Reduction Act of 2002:
Hearing before the Committee on the Judiciary*. 107th Cong., 2nd sess., July 31, 2002.
Serial No. J-107–99. Washington, DC: U.S. Government Printing Office, 2003.

PRIMARY SOURCES: BOOKS AND ARTICLES

Abbott, Jack Henry. *In the Belly of the Beast: Letters from Prison*. New York: Random
House, 1981.

———. "In Prison." *New York Review of Books*, June 26, 1980, 34–37.

———. "On 'Women.'" *New York Review of Books*, June 11, 1981, 1.

Abel, Theodora M. "Negro-White Interpersonal Relationships among Institutionalized
Sub-Normal Girls." *American Journal of Mental Deficiency* 46 (1942): 325–39.

Abrahamsen, David. "Study of 102 Sex Offenders at Sing Sing." *Federal Probation* 14
(September 1950): 26–32.

———. *Who Are the Guilty? A Study of Education and Crime*. New York: Rinehart, 1952.

Adleman, Robert H. *Alias Big Cherry: The Confessions of a Master Criminal*. New York:
Dial Press, 1973.

Akers, Ronald L., et al. "Homosexual and Drug Behavior in Prison: A Test of the
Functional and Importation Models of the Inmate System." *Social Problems* 21 (1974):
410–22.

Aldrich, Ann. *Carol in a Thousand Cities*. Greenwich, CT: Gold Medal Books/Fawcett, 1960.

Algren, Nelson. *Somebody in Boots: A Novel*. New York: Vanguard, 1935.

Allen, Clifford. "The Meaning of Homosexuality." *Medical World* 80 (1954): 9–16.

Allen, Edward L. *Idle Hours No. 8771: Prison Poems, Pictures, and Stories*. Erie, PA: Humane Workers' Society, 1912.

Allen, Gina. "On the Women's Side of the Pen." *Humanist* 38 (September–October 1978): 28–31.

Allen, John. *Assault with a Deadly Weapon: The Autobiography of a Street Criminal*. New York: Pantheon, 1977.

Altman, Dennis. *Homosexual Oppression and Liberation*. New York: New York University Press, 1993. First published 1971 by Outerbridge & Dienstfrey, New York.

Alverson, Charles. "The Jail Jungle." *Wall Street Journal*, February 25, 1969, 1, 17.

Anderson, Nels. *On Hoboes and Homelessness*. Chicago University Press, 1998.

Arc, M. "The Prison 'Culture'—from the Inside." *New York Times Magazine*, February 28, 1965, 52–58.

Ardelyan, John W., and Norman B. Rohrer. *Convict's Cry*. Chicago: Moody Press, 1970.

Arnold, Russell C. *The Kansas Inferno: A Study of the Criminal Problem*. Wichita: Wonderland, 1906.

Audett, James Henry. *Rap Sheet: My Life Story*. New York: William Sloane Associates, 1954.

Bagdikian, Ben. *Caged: Eight Prisoners and Their Keepers*. New York: Harper & Row, 1976.

Baird, Russell N. *The Penal Press*. Evanston, IL: Northwestern University Press, 1967.

Baldi, Frederick S. *My Unwelcome Guests*. New York: J. B. Lippincott, 1959.

Balogh, Joseph K. "Conjugal Visitations in Prisons: A Sociological Perspective." *Federal Probation* 28 (September 1964): 52–58.

Banka, J. Harrie. *State Prison Life: By One Who Has Been There*. Cincinnati: Vent, 1871.

Barnes, Harry Elmer. "The Contemporary Prison: A Menace to Inmate Rehabilitation and the Repression of Crime." In *The Future of Imprisonment in a Free Society*. Chicago: St. Leonard's House, 1965.

Barnes, Harry Elmer, and Negley K. Teeters. *New Horizons in Criminology: The American Crime Problem*. New York: Prentice-Hall, 1944.

Bartlett, Arthur C. "The Four-Eyed Kid: Austin MacCormick." *New Yorker*, May 26, 1934, 24–27.

Bartlett, George Leighton. *Thru the Mill*. St. Paul, MN: McGill-Warner, 1915.

Bartollas, Clemens, Stuart J. Miller, and Simon Dinitz. "The White Victim in a Black Institution." In *Treating the Offender: Problems and Issues*, edited by Marc Riedel and Pedro A. Vales. New York: Praeger, 1977.

Baskett, Edward Eugene. *Entrapped*. Westport, CT: Lawrence Hill, 1976.

Bathurst, Bill. *How to Continue*. San Francisco: Glide Publications, 1974.

Baulch, Lawrence. *Return to the World*. Valley Forge, PA: Judson Press, 1968.

Beaumont, Gustave de, and Alexis de Toqueville. *On the Penitentiary System in the United States, and Its Application in France; with an Appendix on Penal Colonies, and Also, Statistical Notes*. Translated by Francis Lieber. Philadelphia: Carey, Lea & Blanchard, 1833.

Beaver, Ninette, B. K. Ripley and Patrick Trese. *Caril*. Philadelphia: J. B. Lippincott, 1974.

Beck, Robert. *The Naked Soul of Iceberg Slim*. Los Angeles: Holloway House, 1971.

Behan, Brendan. *Borstal Boy*. New York: Knopf, 1959.

Behind Bars. New York: Star Distributors, 1980.

Bennett, De Robigne M. *From behind the Bars*. New York: Liberal and Scientific Publishing House, 1879.

Bennett, James V. *I Chose Prison*. New York: Knopf, 1970.

Benton, Roger, and Robert O. Ballow. *Where Do I Go from Here: The Life Story of a Forger*. New York: Lee Furman, 1936.

Berg, Louis. *Revelations of a Prison Doctor*. New York: Minton, Balch & Co., 1934.

Berger, Meyer. "The Tombs–I." *New Yorker*, August 30, 1941, 22–29.

———. "The Tombs–II." *New Yorker*, September 6, 1941, 34–46.

Berkman, Alexander. *Prison Memoirs of an Anarchist*. New York: Shocken, 1970. First published 1912 by Mother Earth Publishing Association.

Berrigan, Daniel. *America Is Hard to Find: Notes from the Underground and Letters from Danbury Prison*. New York: Doubleday, 1972.

———. *Lights on in the House of the Dead: A Prison Diary*. Garden City, NY: Doubleday, 1974.

Berrigan, Philip. *Prison Journals of a Priest Revolutionary*. New York: Holt, Rinehart & Winston, 1970.

———. *Widen the Prison Gates: Writing from Jails, April 1970–December 1972*. New York: Simon and Schuster, 1973.

Berry, Leonard J. *Prison*. Edited by Jamie Shalleck. New York: Grossman, 1972.

Bieber, Irving, et al., eds. *Homosexuality: A Psychoanalytic Study*. New York: Basic Books, 1962.

Black, Jack. *The Big Break at Folsom; A Story of the Revolt at Prison Tyranny*. 192? New York Public Library. Microform.

———. *You Can't Win*. San Francisco: Nabat/AK Press, 2000. First published 1926 by Macmillan.

Blake, James. *The Joint*. Garden City, NY: Doubleday, 1971.

———. "Letters from an American Prisoner." *Paris Review* 13 (Summer 1956): 8–44.

Bloch, Herbert A. "Social Pressures of Confinement toward Sexual Deviation." *Journal of Social Therapy* 1 (April 1955): 112–25.

Bloch, Iwan. *The Sexual Life of Our Time: A Complete Encyclopedia of the Sexual Sciences*. New York: Falstaff, 1937.

Block, Eugene B. "A Man-Sized Job." *Sunset* 57 (July 1926): 24–25, 56–58.

Bluestone, Harvey, Edward P. O'Malley, and Sydney Connell. "Homosexuals in Prison." *Corrective Psychiatry and Journal of Social Therapy* 12 (1966): 13–24.

Bond, Julian. "Self-Defense against Rape: The Joanne Little Case." *Black Scholar* 6, no. 6 (March 1975): 29–31.

Bonham, Sandee, as told to Gina Allen. "On the Women's Side of the Pen." *Humanist* 38 (September–October 1978): 30.

Booth, Ernest. "The Language of the Underworld." *American Mercury* 14 (May 1928): 78–81.

———. *Stealing through Life.* New York: Knopf, 1929.

———. *With Sirens Screaming.* Garden City, NY: Doubleday, 1945.

Bowker, Lee H. *Prisoner Subcultures.* Lexington, MA: D. C. Heath & Co., 1977.

———. *Prisons and Prisoners: A Bibliographic Guide.* San Francisco: R & E Research Associates, 1978.

———. *Prison Victimization.* New York: Elsevier, 1980.

———. *Women, Crime, and the Criminal Justice System.* Lexington, MA: D. C. Heath, 1978.

Boyd, Robert N. *Sex behind Bars.* San Francisco: Gay Sunshine Press, 1984.

Braly, Malcolm. *False Starts: A Memoir of San Quentin and Other Prisons.* Boston: Little, Brown & Co., 1976.

———. *Felony Tank.* New York: Fawcett, 1961.

———. *On the Yard.* Boston: Little Brown, 1967.

Branham, Vernon C. "Behavior Disorders in Prison." *Journal of Criminal Psychopathology* 1 (January 1940): 234–46.

Brent, William, and Milarde Brent. *The Hell Hole.* Yuma, AZ: Southwest Printers, 1962.

Brice, James R. *Secrets of the Mount-Pleasant State Prison, Revealed and Exposed.* Albany, NY: n.p., 1839.

Brockway, Zebulon Reed. *Fifty Years of Prison Service; an Autobiography.* New York: Charities Publication Committee, 1912.

Brown, Claude. *Manchild in the Promised Land.* New York: Macmillan, 1965.

Brown, Wenzell. *Prison Girl.* New York: Pyramid Books, 1958.

Browning, Frank. *Prison Life: A Study of the Explosive Conditions in America's Prisons.* New York: Harper, 1972.

Brownmiller, Susan. *Against Our Will: Men, Women, and Rape.* New York: Simon & Schuster, 1975.

Bruchac, Joseph, and William Witherup, eds. *Words from the House of the Dead: Prison Writings from Soledad.* Trumansburg, NY: Crossing Press, 1974.

Bryan, Helen. *Inside.* Boston: Houghton Mifflin, 1953.

Bubertson, Charles. *Fools and Rules: A Prison Odyssey.* New York: Vantage, 1973.

Buffum, Peter C. "Homosexuality in Female Institutions." In *Male Rape: A Casebook of Sexual Aggressions,* edited by Anthony M. Scacco, Jr. New York: AMS Press, 1982.

———. "Racial Factors in Prison Homosexuality." In *Male Rape,* edited by Anthony M. Scacco, Jr., 104–6. New York: AMS Press, 1982.

Bunker, Edward. *The Animal Factory.* New York: Viking, 1977.

———. *Education of a Felon.* New York: St. Martin's, 2000.

———. *Little Boy Blue.* New York: Viking, 1981.

———. "War behind Walls." *Harper's Magazine* 244 (February 1972): 39–47.

Burkhart, Kathryn Watterson. *Women in Prison.* New York: Doubleday & Co., 1973.

Burnham, Creighton Brown. *Born Innocent.* Englewood Cliffs, NJ: Prentice-Hall, 1958.

Burns, Robert E. *I Am a Fugitive from a Georgia Chain Gang.* New York: Vanguard, 1932.

Burns, Vincent G. *Out of These Chains*. Los Angeles: New World Books, 1942.

Burr, Levi S. *A Voice from Sing-Sing*. Albany, NY: n.p., 1833.

Burstein, Jules Quentin. *Conjugal Visits in Prison: Psychological and Social Consequences*. Lexington, MA: D. C. Heath & Co. 1977.

Butler, William R. *Behind Prison Walls: The Story of a Wasted Life*. Chicago: M. Stein, 1916.

Caldwell, Morris G. "Group Dynamics in the Prison Community." *Journal of Criminal Law, Criminology and Police Science* 46 (January–February 1956): 648–57.

Canizio, Frank, and Robert Markel. *A Man against Fate*. New York: Frederick Fell, 1958.

Cantine, Holly, and Dachine Rainer, eds. *Prison Etiquette*. Baersville, NY: Retort Press, 1950.

Cape, William Stanley. "Prison Sex: Absence of Choice." *Fortune News*, April 1974, 5.

Caprio, Frank S. *Female Homosexuality: A Modern Study of Lesbianism*. New York: Grove Press, 1954.

———. *The Sexually Adequate Female*. New York: Citadel Press, 1953.

Cardozo-Freeman, Inez. *The Joint: Language and Culture in a Maximum Security Prison*. Springfield, IL: Charles Thomas, 1984.

Carlton, Linda. "The Terrifying Homosexual World of the Jail System." *New York Times*, April 25, 1971, 40.

Carr, Franklin. *Twenty-Two Years in State Prisons*. Philadelphia: n.p., 1893.

Carroll, Leo. *Hacks, Blacks, and Cons: Race Relations in a Maximum Security Prison*. Lexington, MA: D. C. Heath, 1974.

———. "Humanitarian Reform and Biracial Sexual Assault in a Maximum Security Prison." *Urban Life* 5 (January 1977): 417–37.

Carter, Barbara. "Reform School Families." *Society* 11 (1973): 36, 39–43.

Carter, John. "Prison Life as I Found it." *Century Magazine* 80 (September 1910): 752–58.

Carter, Rubin "Hurricane." *The Sixteenth Round: From Number 1 Contender to #45472*. New York: Viking, 1974.

Cassel, Russell N., and Robert B. Van Vorst. "Psychological Needs of Women in a Correctional Institution." *American Journal of Corrections* 23 (January–February 1961): 22–24.

Cassity, John Holland. "Socio-Psychiatric Aspects of Female Felons." *Journal of Criminal Psychopathology* 3 (April 1942): 597–604.

"Catalogue of Savagery." *Time* 92 (September 20, 1968): 54.

Chandler, Edna Walker. *Women in Prison*. New York: Bobbs-Merrill, 1973.

Chaneles, Sol. *Losing in Place*. New York: Avon, 1972.

Chang, Dae H., and Warren B. Armstrong, eds. *The Prison: Voices from the Inside*. Cambridge, MA: Schenkman, 1972.

Chapin, Charles E. *Charles Chapin's Story; Written in Sing Sing Prison*. New York: Putnam, 1920.

Charlton, Linda. "The Terrifying Homosexual World of the Jail System." *New York Times*, April 25, 1971, 40.

Cheever, John. *Falconer*. New York: Knopf, 1977.

Chesney-Lind, Meda. "The Forgotten Offender." *Corrections Today* 60, no. 7 (December 1998): 66–73.

Cheyney, S. C. My *First Fourteen Months in the Ohio Penitentiary.* Columbus, OH: n.p., 1859.

Chideckel, Maurice. *Female Sex Perversion: The Sexually Aberrated Woman as She Is.* New York: Eugenics Publishing Co., 1938.

Chonco, Nobuhle R. "Sexual Assaults among Male Inmates: A Descriptive Study." *Prison Journal* 69, no. 1 (1989): 72–82.

Clark, Charles L. *Lockstep and Corridor: 35 Years of Prison Life.* Cincinnati, OH: University of Cincinnati Press, 1927.

Clark, Richard X. *The Brothers of Attica.* Edited by Leonard Levitt. New York: Links, 1973.

Cleaver, Eldridge. *Soul on Ice.* New York: Ramparts, 1968.

Clements, Carl B. "AIDS and Offender Classification: Implications for Management of HIV-Positive Prisoners." *Prison Journal* 69 (Fall–Winter 1989): 19–28.

Clemmer, Donald. *The Prison Community.* Boston: Christopher Publishing House, 1940.

———. "Some Aspects of Sexual Behavior in the Prison Community." *Proceedings of the American Correctional Association* (1958): 377–85.

Clines, Francis X. "State Aide Admits Failure of Albany Jail Inquiry." *New York Times,* April 29, 1975.

Cluchey, Rick. *The Cage.* San Francisco: Barbwire Press, 1970.

Coffey, W. A. *Inside Out; or, An interior View of the New York State Prison.* New York: n.p., 1823.

———. *A Peep into the State Prison, at Auburn, NY, by One Who Knows.* Auburn, NY: n.p., 1839.

Coggeshall, John M. "Ladies behind Bars: A Liminal Gender as Cultural Mirror." *Anthropology Today* 4 (August 1988): 6–8.

Cohen, Stanley, and Laurie Taylor. *Psychological Survival: The Experience of Long-Term Imprisonment.* New York: Pantheon, 1972.

Cole, Rob. "Atascadero Reformer Denies Aversion Used." *Advocate,* May 10, 1972, 16.

———. "Behind Bars, Lessons on Being Gay." *Advocate,* June 20, 1973, 1–2, 5.

———. "Or Is Somebody Having Nightmares?" *Advocate,* April 26, 1972, 11–13.

Comfort, Alex. "Institutions without Sex." *Social Work* 12 (April 1967): 107–8.

Cook, Charles A. *The Ways of Sin; or, Experiences of Convict Life.* Des Moines, IA: Patterson-Brown, 1894.

Cook, Jack. *Rags of Time: A Season in Prison.* Boston: Beacon Press, 1972.

"Cook County Horrors." *Time* 90 (December 15, 1967): 75–76.

Coons, William R. *Attica Diary.* New York: Stein & Day, 1972.

Cordones, Blake. "When the Gate Slams for the First Time." *Village Voice,* August 27, 1970, 5–6, 34–36.

Cordova, Jeanne, ed. "Inside Terminal Island California Federal Penitentiary." *Lesbian Tide* (January 1973): 3, 18–22.

Corley, Carl. *Jail Mate.* San Diego, CA: Greenleaf, 1971.

Cory, Donald Webster. "Homosexuality in Prison." *Journal of Social Therapy* 1 (1955): 137–40.

Coughlin, Thomas A. "AIDS in Prisons: One Correctional Administrator's Recommended Policies and Procedures." *Judicature* 72 (1988): 63–70.

Crawford, William. *Report on the Penitentiaries of the United States.* Montclair, NJ: Patterson Smith, 1969. First published 1835.

Cressey, Donald, ed. *The Prison: Studies in Institutional Organization and Change.* New York: Holt, Rinehart & Winston, 1961.

Cressey, Donald, and David A. Ward, eds. *Delinquency, Crime, and Social Process.* New York: Harper & Row, 1969.

"Crime and Punishment: Prison Lids Blow off Revealing Ugly Secrets Which Challenge American Penal System." *News-Week* 3, no. 5 (February 3, 1934): 7–9.

"Crime-Breeding Prisons." *Newsweek* 55 (April 25, 1960): 108, 110–12.

"Critics of Cell Life." *Survey* 44 (1920): 151–2.

Crowell, Vince. "Fags and Lesbians Are Running Wild in Today's Prisons." *Vice Squad* 6 (March 1966): 16–17, 33–37.

Curzon, Daniel. *Something You Do in the Dark.* New York: G. P. Putnam's Sons, 1971.

Cutter, Fred. "The Problem of Prison Sex." *Sexology* (July 1962): 822–25.

Danziger, Peter L. "Sexual Assaults and Forced Homosexual Relationships in Prison: Cruel and Unusual Punishment." *Albany Law Review* 36 (1971): 428–38.

Davidson, R. Theodore. *Chicano Prisoners: The Key to San Quentin.* New York: Holt, Rinehart & Winston, 1974.

Davis, Alan J. "Sexual Assaults in the Philadelphia Prison System and Sheriff's Vans." *Trans-Action* 6 (December 1968): 8–17.

Davis, Angela. *If They Come in the Morning.* New York: New American Library, 1971.

Davis, Lew M. "A Prisoner's Letter." *Survey* 32 (1914): 103–4.

Debs, Eugene Victor. *Walls and Bars.* Chicago: Socialist Party, 1927.

DeFord, Miriam Allen. "Shall Convicts Write Books?" *Nation* 131 (November 5, 1930): 495–97.

———. *Stone Walls.* New York: Chilton, 1962.

De Fornaro, Carlo. *A Modern Purgatory.* New York: Kennerley, 1917.

Delorme, Eugene. *Chief: The Life History of Eugene Delorme, Imprisoned Santee Sioux.* With Inez Cardozo-Freeman. Lincoln: University of Nebraska Press, 1994.

Deming, Barbara. *Prison Notes.* New York: Grossman Publishers, 1966.

Dennis, William. "The Rape of the 'Fish' Is Brutal." *Advocate*, August 14, 1974, 25, 29.

Deutsch, Albert. *Our Rejected Children.* Boston: Little, Brown & Co., 1950.

Deveureux, George, and Moss, Malcolm C. "The Social Structures of Prisons and the Organic Tensions." *Journal of Criminal Psychopathology* 4 (October 1942): 306–24.

Diaman, N. A. "On Sex Roles and Equality." In *Out of the Closets: Voices of Gay Liberation*, edited by Karla Jay and Allen Young. 1972. Reprint, New York: New York University Press, 1992. First published in *Zygote* (October 30, 1970).

Dickens, Charles. *American Notes for General Circulation.* New York: Harper & Brothers, 1842. Reprint, New York: Oxford University Press, 1997.

Dimick, Kenneth M. *Ladies in Waiting: Behind Prison Walls*. Muncie, IN: Accelerated Development, 1979.

Dinerstein, Russell H., and Bernard C. Glueck, Jr. "Sub-Coma Insulin Therapy in the Treatment of Homosexual Panic States." *Journal of Social Therapy* 3 (October 1955): 183–86.

Ditsworth, Ted. *Out of the Depths of Hell*. New York: Vantage, 1974.

Divans, Kenneth, and Larry M. West. "Prison or Slavery." *Black Scholar* 3 (October 1971): 6–12.

Dix, Dorothea Lynde. *Remarks on Prisons and Prison Discipline in the United States*. Boston: Munroe & Francis, 1845.

Donaldson, Stephen. "Hooking Up: Protective Pairing for Punks." http://www.spr.org/en/ps_hookingup.asp. Accessed March 18, 2007.

———. "Letter from a Prison Punk." *RFD*, no. 67 (Fall 1991), 13–17.

———. "A Million Jockers, Punks, and Queens: Sex among American Male Prisoners and Its Implications for Concepts of Sexual Orientation." Lecture delivered at Columbia University, February 4, 1993. http://www.spr.org/en/docs/doc_01_lecture.asp. Accessed March 18, 2007.

Doty, Sile. *The Life of Sile Doty*. Detroit: Alved, 1948.

Doyle, William. *Man Alone*. With Scott O'Dell. Indianapolis: Bobbs-Merrill, 1953.

Dressler, David, ed. *Readings in Criminology and Penology*. New York: Columbia University Press, 1964.

Dudding, Earl E. *Dudding's Prison Story: The Miracle at Moundsville*. n.p., 1915.

Duffy, Clinton T., and Al Hirschberg. *Sex and Crime*. Garden City, NY: Doubleday, 1965.

Duffy, Clinton T., and Dean Jennings. *The San Quentin Story*. Garden City, NY: Doubleday, 1950.

Duncan, Lee. *Over the Wall*. New York: Dutton, 1936.

Dunn, Barry. *Banged and Blown behind Bars*. San Diego, CA: Greenleaf, 1983.

Dwight, Louis. "Sodomy among Juvenile Delinquents" (Boston: April 25, 1826). In *Gay American History: Lesbians and Gay Men in the U.S.A.*, edited by Jonathan Ned Katz, 42–45. New York: Avon Books, 1976.

Dynes, Wayne R., and Stephen Donaldson, eds. *Homosexuality and Government, Politics, and Prisons*. New York: Garland, 1992.

Edwards, Edward W. *Metamorphosis of a Criminal*. New York: Hart, 1972.

Eigenberg, Helen. "Male Rape: An Empirical Examination of Correctional Officers' Attitudes toward Rape in Prison." *Prison Journal* 69 (1989): 39–56.

———. "Prison Staff and Male Rape." In *Prison Sex: Practice and Policy*, edited by Christopher Hensley. Boulder, CO: Lynne Rienner, 2002.

Eisner, Jane. "Inmate Rape Is the Dirty Secret of a Nation Obsessed with Jails." *Philadelphia Inquirer*, April 26, 2001.

Elgar, Thomas. *Convict Life; or, Penitentiary Citizenship in the Illinois State Penitentiary*. Rochester, NY: n.p., 1886.

Elli, Frank. *The Riot*. New York: Coward-McCann, 1966.

Ellis, Havelock. "Sexual Inversion in Women." *Alienist and Neurologist* 16, no. 2 (April 1895): 141–58.

———. *Studies in the Psychology of Sex*. Vol. 2, *Sexual Inversion*. 3d ed. Philadelphia: F. A. Davis Co., 1928.

Erickson, Gladys A. *Warden Ragen of Joliet*. New York: Dutton, 1957.

Ersine, Noel. *Underworld and Prison Slang*. Upland, IN: A. D. Freese & Son, 1933.

Eshelman, Byron E. *Death Row Chaplain*. Englewood Cliffs, NJ: Prentice-Hall, 1962.

Evans, Jeff. *Undoing Time: American Prisoners in Their Own Words*. Boston: Northeastern University Press, 2001.

"Ex-Convicts Recall Sexual Suppression." *Fortune News*, April 1974, 4.

Faith, Karlene, ed. *Soledad Prison: University of the Poor*. Palo Alto, CA: Science and Behavior Books, 1975.

Feurey, Joe. "Behind Prison Walls." *New York Post*, May 4, 1971.

Finley, James. *Memorials of Prison Life*. Edited by Rev. B. F. Tefft. Cincinnati. OH: Swormstedt & Powder, 1850.

Firestone, Ross, ed. *Getting Busted: Personal Experiences of Arrest, Trial, and Prison*. New York: Pyramid, 1973.

Fisher, Florrie. *The Lonely Trip Back*. Garden City, NY: Doubleday, 1971.

Fishman, Joseph F. *Crucibles of Crime: The Shocking Story of the American Jail*. New York: Cosmopolis Press, 1923.

———. *Sex in Prison: Revealing Sex Conditions in American Prisons*. New York: National Library Press, 1934.

Fishman, Joseph F., and Vee Terrys Perlman. "The Hardest Prison in the World to Manage." *Vanity Fair*, February 1933, 38–40.

Fitzgerald, Tamsin. *Tamsin*. New York: Dial Press, 1973.

Fleisher, Mark. *Warehousing Violence*. Newbury Park, CA: Sage Publications, 1989.

Flowers, R. Barri. *Female Crime, Criminals and Cellmates: An Exploration of Female Criminality and Delinquency*. Jefferson, N.C.: McFarland & Co., 1995.

Flynn, Elizabeth Gurley. *The Alderson Story: My Life as a Political Prisoner*. New York: International Publishers, 1963.

Flynn, Thomas. *Tales for My Brothers' Keepers*. New York: W. W. Norton, 1976.

Flynt, Josiah [pseud. F. Willard]. "Homosexuality among Tramps." Appendix A in *Studies in the Psychology of Sex*. Vol. 2, *Sexual Inversion*, by Havelock Ellis. 3d ed. Philadelphia, F.A. Davis Co., 1928.

———. *My Life*. New York: Outing Publishing Co., 1908.

———. *Tramping with Tramps: Studies and Sketches of Vagabond Life*. New York: The Century Co., 1899.

Ford, Charles A. "Homosexual Practices of Institutionalized Females." *Journal of Abnormal Psychology* 23 (January–March 1929): 442–48.

Foner, Philip S., and Sally M. Miller, eds. *Kate Richards O'Hare: Selected Writings and Speeches*. Baton Rouge: Louisiana State University Press, 1982.

Foster, Thomas W. "Make-Believe Families: A Response of Women and Girls to the

Deprivation of Imprisonment." *International Journal of Criminology and Penology* 3 (1975): 71–78.

Fowler, Gene. "An Allegation in Lavender." In *The Great Mouthpiece*. New York: Grosset, 1931.

Fox, Vernon B. *Violence behind Bars*. New York: Vantage Press, 1956.

Francis, William C. *A Hell on Earth; or, A Story of Prison Life*. Kansas City, MO: Hudson-Kimberly Publishing Co., 1896.

French, Joseph Lewis, comp. *Grey Shadows*. New York: Century Co., 1931.

French, Laurene. "Prison Sexualization: Inmate Adaptations to Psycho-sexual Stress." *Corrective and Social Psychiatry and Journal of Behavior Technology, Methods and Therapy* 25 (April 1979): 64–69.

Freud, Sigmund. *Three Essays on the Theory of Sexuality*. Translated by James Strachey. 1905. Reprint, London: Imago Publishing Co., 1949.

Friedman, Paul. "Sexual Deviations." In *American Handbook of Psychiatry*, edited by Silvano Arieti, 589–613. New York: Basic Books, 1959.

Gagnon, John H., and William Simon. "The Social Meaning of Prison Homosexuality." *Federal Probation* 32 (March 1968): 23–29.

Ganz, Marie. *Rebels: Into Anarchy—and Out Again*. With Nat J. Ferber. New York: Dodd, Mead & Co., 1920.

Garrett, Paul W., and Austin MacCormick, eds. *Handbook of American Prisons and Reformatories*. New York: National Society of Penal Information, 1929.

"Gay Penal Crusade." *Mattachine Times* (February 1974).

Gaylin, Willard. *In Service of Their Country: War Resisters in Prison*. New York: Viking, 1970.

Gebhard, Paul H. "A Comparison of White-Black Offender Groups." In *Sexual Behavior: Social, Clinical, and Legal Aspects*, ed. H. L. P. Resnick and Marvin E. Wolfgang. Boston: Little Brown, 1972.

Gebhard, Paul H., and Alan B. Johnson. *The Kinsey Data: Marginal Tabulations of the 1938–1963 Interviews Conducted by the Institute for Sex Research*. Philadelphia: W.B. Saunders Co., 1979.

Geis, Alex. *Jailhouse Queen*. El Cajon, CA: Publisher's Export Co., 1969.

George, Andrew W. *The Texas Convict: Sketches of the Penitentiary, Convict Farm and Railroads, Together with Poems*. Charlotte, NC: n.p., 1895.

Giallombardo, Rose. *The Social World of Imprisoned Girls: A Comparative Study of Institutions for Juvenile Delinquents*. New York: John Wiley & Sons, 1974.

———. *Society of Women: A Study of a Women's Prison*. New York: John Wiley & Sons, 1966.

Gilman, David. "New Ruling Allows Sexual Attack in Jail to Be Justification for Escape." *Corrections Magazine* 2, no. 5 (September 1976): 51–53.

"Girl Delinquent: Age Sixteen—an Undecorated Autobiography." *Harper's* 164 (April 1932): 551–59.

Girshick, Lori B. *No Safe Haven: Stories of Women in Prison*. Boston: Northeastern University Press, 1999.

Glaser, Daniel. "Politicalization of Prisoners: A New Challenge to American Penology." *American Journal of Correction* 33 (November–December 1971): 6–9.

Glaser, Jordan B., and Robert B. Griefinger. "Correctional Health Care: A Public Health Opportunity." *Annals of Internal Medicine* 118, no. 2 (January 1993): 139–45.

Goffman, Erving. *Asylums: Essays on the Social Situation of Mental Patients and Other Inmates.* Garden City, NY: Doubleday, 1961.

Goldman, Emma. *A Fragment of the Prison Experiences of Emma Goldman and Alexander Berkman.* New York: Stella Comyn, 1919.

Goodsell, James Nelson. "The Penal Press: Voice of the Prisoner." *Federal Probation* 23 (June 1959): 53–57.

Gray, Francis C. *Prison Discipline in America.* London: John Murray, 1848.

Greco, Marshall C., and James C. Wright. "The Correctional Institution in the Etiology of Chronic Homosexuality." *American Journal of Orthopsychiatry* 14 (1944): 295–308.

Gregory, George H. *Alcatraz Screw: My Years as a Guard in America's Most Notorious Prison.* Columbia: University of Missouri Press, 2002.

Gregory, Sasha. "Prison Head Talks with Gays: Meeting May Aid Lesbian Inmates." *Advocate*, August 2, 1972.

Gonnerman, Jennifer. "Love behind Bars." *Village Voice*, May 13, 1997, 47–50.

Good, Milton. *Twelve Years in a Texas Prison.* Amarillo, TX: n.p., 1935.

Goodell, Charles. *Political Prisoners in America.* New York: Random House, 1973.

Graeme, Roland. *Prison Sex.* New York: Surree, Ltd., 1980.

Griffiths, William E. *The Story of an Ex-Convict and the Horrors of Prison Life in the Penitentiary at Joliet, Illinois.* Atchison, KS: Home Printing Co., 1896.

Griswold, H. Jack, Mike Misenheimer, Art Powers, and Ed Tromanhauser. *An Eye for an Eye.* New York: Holt, Rinehart & Winston, 1970.

Gross, Leonard H. "Lesbians in Prison." *Sexology* 34 (February 1968): 478–81.

Guenther, Anthony. "The Language of Prison Life." *Justice and Corrections*, edited by Norman Johnston and Leonard Savitz, 528–30. New York: John Wiley & Sons, 1978.

Haggerty, John. *Sex in Prison.* New York: Ace Books, 1975.

Haines, William H. "Homosexuality." *Journal of Social Therapy* 1 (1955): 132–36.

Haines, William H., and John J. McLaughlin. "Treatment of the Homosexual in Prison." *Diseases of the Nervous System* 13 (1952): 85–87.

Halleck, Seymour L., and Marvin Hersko. "Homosexual Behavior in a Correctional Institution for Adolescent Girls." *American Journal of Orthopsychiatry* 32 (October 1962): 911–17.

Hammer, Max. "Homosexuality in a Women's Reformatory." *Corrective Psychiatry and Journal of Social Therapy* 4 (May 1965): 168–69.

———. "Hypersexuality in a Women's Reformatory." *Corrective Psychiatry and Journal of Social Therapy* 15 (1969): 20–26.

Hankins, Leonard. *Nineteen Years Not Guilty.* New York: Exposition Press, 1956.

The Hardened Criminal: Folsom Prison Convicts. Millbrae, CA: Celestial Arts, 1976.

Harper, Ida. "The Role of the 'Fringer' in a State Prison for Women." *Social Forces* 31 (October 1952): 53–60.

Harris, Jean. *They Always Call Us Ladies: Stories from Prison.* New York: Scribner's, 1988.

Harris, Mary B. *I Knew Them in Prison.* New York: Viking, 1936.

Harris, Sara. *Hellhole: The Shocking Story of the Inmates and Life in the New York City House of Detention for Women.* New York: E. P. Dutton & Co., 1967.

Harris, William C. *Prison Life in the Tobacco Warehouse of Richmond.* Philadelphia: George W. Childs, 1862.

Harrison, Eddie, and Alfred V. J. Prather. *No Time for Dying.* Englewood Cliffs, NJ: Prentice-Hall, 1973.

Harsh, George. *Lonesome Road.* New York: W. W. Norton, 1971.

Hassler, Alfred. *Diary of a Self-Made Convict.* Chicago: Regnery, 1954.

Hayner, Norman S. "Attitudes toward Conjugal Visits for Prisoners." *Federal Probation* 36 (March 1972): 43–49.

Haynes, Fred E. *The American Prison System.* New York and London: McGraw-Hill, 1939.

Hawthorne, Julian, ed. *The Confessions of a Convict.* Philadelphia: Rufus C. Hartranft, 1893.

———. *The Subterranean Brotherhood.* New York: McBride, Nast & Co., 1914.

Heard, Nathan. *House of Slammers.* New York: Macmillan, 1983.

———. *To Reach a Dream.* New York: Dial, 1972.

Heffernan, Esther. *Making it in Prison: The Square, the Cool, and the Life.* New York: John Wiley & Sons, 1972.

Heffernan, Esther, and Elizabeth Krippel. "A Coed Prison." In *Justice and Corrections*, edited by Norman Johnston and Leonard D. Savitz, 441–45. New York: John Wiley & Sons, 1978.

Henry, George W., and Alfred A. Gross. "The Homosexual Delinquent." *Mental Hygiene* 25, no. 3 (July 1941): 420–42.

Henry, Joan. *Women in Prison.* Garden City, NY: Doubleday, 1952.

Herbert, John. *Fortune and Men's Eyes.* New York: Grove Press, 1967.

Herndon, Angelo. *Let Me Live.* New York: Random House, 1937.

Hilaire, Frank. *Thantos.* New York: E. P. Dutton, 1971.

Himes, Chester. "Crazy in the Stir." *Esquire* 2 (August 1934): 28, 114, 117.

———. *The Quality of Hurt.* New York: Doubleday, 1972.

Hippler, Mike. "Where the Boys Are: Gay Inmates at San Bruno Jail." *Bay Area Reporter*, December 29, 1983, 14–16.

Hirschfeld, Magnus. *Sexual Anomalies: The Origins, Nature, and Treatment of Sexual Disorders.* New York: Emerson, 1948.

Hodge, Paul, and William A. Elsen. "War Protester Tells of Rape at D.C. Jail." *Washington Post*, August 25, 1973, C:1

Hoffman, Harry R. "Sex Perversion and Crime." *Archives of Neurology and Psychiatry* 3 (February 1920): 210.

Hoffman, Leon E. R. *A History of Blasted Hopes; or, Eleven Years in an Indiana States Prison.* Chicago: n.p., 1904.

Hogshire, Jim. *You Are Going to Prison.* Port Townsend, WA: Breakout Publications, 1999.

Holiday, Billie. *Lady Sings the Blues*. New York: Lancer Books, 1965.

Hopper, Columbus B. "Conjugal Visiting: A Controversial Practice in Mississippi." *Criminal Law Bulletin* 3 (1967): 288–99.

———. "Conjugal Visiting at the Mississippi State Penitentiary." *Federal Probation* 29 (June 1965): 39–46.

———. "The Evolution of Conjugal Visiting in Mississippi." *Prison Journal* 69 (Spring–Summer 1989): 103–9.

Horan, James D. *The Mob's Man*. New York: Crown, 1959.

Howarth, Joan W. "The Rights of Gay Prisoners: A Challenge to Protective Custody." *Southern California Law Review* 53 (1980): 1225–76.

Howe, Samuel Gridley. *An Essay on Separate and Congregate Systems of Prison Discipline; Being a Report Made to the Boston Prison Discipline Society*. Boston: William D. Ticknor & Co., 1856.

Huffman, Arthur V. "Problems Precipitated by Homosexual Approaches on Youthful First Offenders." *Journal of Social Therapy* 7 (1961): 216–22.

———. "Sex Deviation in a Prison Community." *Journal of Social Therapy* 6 (1960): 170–81.

Huncke, Herbert. *The Evening Sun Turned Crimson*. Cherry Valley, NY: Cherry Valley Editions, 1980.

Ibrahim, Azmy Ishak. "Deviant Sexual Behavior in Men's Prisons." *Crime and Delinquency* 20 (January 1974): 38–44.

"I Lived in a Hell behind Bars." *True Confessions* (March 1954), 32+.

Irwin, John. *The Felon*. Englewood Cliffs, NJ: Prentice-Hall, 1970.

———. *Prisons in Turmoil*. Boston: Little, Brown & Co., 1980.

Irwin, John, and Donald Cressey. "Thieves, Convicts, and the Inmate Culture." *Social Problems* 10 (Autumn 1962): 142–55.

Jackson, Bruce. *In the Life: Versions of the Criminal Experience*. New York: Holt, Rinehart, & Winston, 1972.

———. *Killing Time: Life in the Arkansas Penitentiary*. Ithaca, NY: Cornell University Press, 1977.

Jackson, Don. "The Daddy Tank." *Gay Sunshine* (1972): 3.

"Jail Guard Trainees Hear from Gays." *Advocate*, November 22, 1972, 3, 14.

Jay, Karla. "Remembering the House of D." *Lesbian Tide* (November 1973): 9–10, 26.

Jennings, Al, and Will Irwin. *Beating Back*. New York: D. Appleton, 1914.

Jensen, Gary, and Dorothy Jones. "Perspectives on Inmate Culture: A Study of Women in Prison." *Social Forces* 54 (1976): 590–603.

Johnson, Edwin. "The Homosexual in Prison." *Social Theory and Practice* 1, no. 4 (1971): 83–95.

Johnson, Jim. *Crime around the Clock*. New York: Vantage, 1968.

Johnson, Kay. *My Name Is Rusty: A Story of Lesbian Life behind Prison Bars*. New York: Castle Books, 1958.

Johnson, Lester Douglas. *The Devil's Front Porch*. Lawrence: University Press of Kansas, 1970.

Johnson, Ray D. *Too Dangerous to Be at Large*. With Mona McCormick. New York: Quadrangle, 1975.

Johnson, Robert, and Hans Toch, eds. *The Pains of Imprisonment*. Beverly Hills, CA: Sage Publications, 1982.

Johnston, James A. *Prison Life Is Different*. Boston: Houghton Mifflin, 1937.

Jones, Joe. *The Life Story of Joe (Daddy) Jones*. Waco, TX: Davis Brothers Publishing, 1932.

Jones, Oliver F. *Fifteen Years in a Living Hell*. Sanger, CA: n.p. 1944.

Jones, Richard S., and Thomas J. Schmid. "Inmates' Conceptions of Prison Sexual Assault." *Prison Journal* 69 (1989): 53–61.

Jones, Tonya Star. "What It's Like Being a Drag Queen in the Illinois Department of Corrections." In *Undoing Time: American Prisoners in Their Own Words*, edited by Jeff Evans. Boston: Northeastern University Press, 2001.

Kahn, Samuel. *Mentality and Homosexuality*. Boston: Meador Publishing Co., 1937.

———. *Sing Sing Criminals*. Philadelphia: Dorrance & Co., 1936.

Karpman, Benjamin. "Sex Life in Prison." *Journal of Criminal Law, Criminology, and Police Science* 38 (January–February 1948): 475–86.

Kassebaum, Gene. "Sex in Prison." *Sexual Behavior* 11 (January 1972): 39–45.

Kates, Elizabeth M. "Sexual Problems in Women's Institutions." *Journal of Social Therapy* 1 (October 1955): 187–91.

Keiser, Sylvan, and Dora Schaffer. "Environmental Factors in Homosexuality in Adolescent Girls." *Psychoanalytic Review* 36 (1949): 283–95.

Kellog, Virginia. "Inside Women's Prison." *Colliers* 125, no. 22 (June 3, 1950): 15, 37–41.

Kelley, Joseph. *Thirteen Years in the Oregon Penitentiary*. Portland, OR: n.p., 1908.

Kern, William, Jr. "Petition to the President of the U.S." *ONE* 14 (April –May 1966): 7–10.

King, Don. *Prisoner of Evil*. Detroit: Foremost Publishers, 1965.

King, John H. *Three Hundred Days in a Yankee Prison: Reminiscences of War Life Captivity*. Atlanta: Jas. P. Davis, 1904.

Kinsey, Alfred C., Wardell B. Pomeroy, and Clyde E. Martin. *Sexual Behavior in the Human Female*. Philadelphia: W. B. Saunders, 1953.

———. *Sexual Behavior in the Human Male*. Philadelphia: W. B. Saunders, 1948.

Kirkham, George Lester. "Homosexuality in Prison." In *Studies in the Sociology of Sex*, edited by James M. Henslin, 325–49. New York: Appleton Century-Crofts, 1971.

Klauck, Daniel L. *Everything Else . . .* Washington, DC: King Publications, 1976.

Knight, Etheridge. *Black Voices from Prison*. New York: Pathfinder Press, 1970.

Koscheski, Mary, Christopher Hensley, Jeremy Wright, and Richard Tweksbury. "Consensual Sexual Behavior." In *Prison Sex: Practice and Policy*, edited by Christopher Hensley, 111–31. Boulder: Lynne Rienner, 2002.

Kosofsky, Sidney, and Albert Ellis. "Illegal Communication among Institutionalized Female Delinquents." *Journal of Social Psychology* 48 (August 1958): 155–60.

Krafft-Ebing, Richard von. *Psychopathia Sexualis, with Especial Reference to Contrary Sexual*

Instinct: A Medico-Legal Study. Translated by Charles Gilbert Chaddock. 7th ed. Philadelphia and London: F. A. Davis Co., 1893.

Krebs, Richard Julius Herman [pseud. Jan Valtin]. *Bend in the River.* New York: Alliance, 1942.

Kromer, Tom. *Waiting for Nothing.* New York: Knopf, 1935.

Kuethe, J. Louis. "Prison Parlance." *American Speech* 9 (February 1934): 25–27.

Kwartler, Richard, ed. *Behind Bars: Prisons in America.* New York: Vintage Books, 1977.

Lamott, Kenneth. *Chronicles of San Quentin: The Biography of a Prison.* New York: David McKay Co., 1961.

Lane, Horace. *Five Years in State's Prison.* 3d ed. New York: n.p., 1835.

Lastala, John. "Atascadero: Dachau for Queers?" *Advocate,* April 26, 1972, 11–13.

Lathrop, Charles N. *A Practical Program for Church Groups in Jail Work.* New York: National Council, Department of Christian Social Service, 1923.

Laven, Goat. *Rough Stuff: The Life Story of a Gangster.* London: Falcon Books, 1933.

Lawes, Lewis E. *Invisible Stripes.* New York: Farrar & Rinehart, 1938.

———. *Life and Death in Sing Sing.* Garden City, NY: Doubleday, Doran & Co., 1928.

Leary, Timothy. *Jail Notes.* Lakewood, OH: Douglas Books, 1971.

Leder, Drew. *The Soul Knows No Bars: Inmates Reflect on Life, Death, and Hope.* Lanham, MD: Rowman & Littlefield, 2000.

Lee, Donald. "Seduction of the Guilty: Homosexuality in American Prisons." *Fact* 2 (November–December 1965): 57–61.

Lee, Eugene. *Yeggmen in the Shadows.* London: Arthur H. Stockwell, 1935.

Lehrer, Eli. "The Most-Silent Crime." *National Review,* April 29, 2003.

Leibert, Julius A. *Behind Bars: What a Chaplain Saw in Alcatraz, Folsom and San Quentin.* Garden City, NY: Doubleday, 1965.

Leinwand, Gerald, ed. *Prisons.* New York: Pocket Books, 1972.

Leopold, Nathan. *Life Plus Ninety-Nine Years.* Garden City, NY: Doubleday, 1958.

Levin, Michael Graubart. "Flight, Flee, Submit, Sue: Alternatives for Sexually Assaulted Prisoners." *Columbia Journal of Law and Social Problems* 18 (1985): 505–30.

Levy, Howard and David Miller. *Going to Jail: The Political Prisoner.* New York: Grove, 1971.

Lewis, Orlando F. *The Development of American Prisons and Prison Customs, 1776–1845.* Albany: J. B. Lyon, 1922.

Lichtenstein, Perry M. "The 'Fairy' and the Lady Lover." *Medical Review of Reviews* 27 (August 1921): 369–74.

Lieber, James. "The American Prison: A Tinderbox." *New York Times Magazine,* March 8, 1981, 26–35, 55–60.

Lillis, Jamie. "Dealing with HIV/AIDS Positive Inmates." *Corrections Compendium* 18, no. 6 (June 1993): 1–3.

Limpus, Lowell M., and Burr W. Leyson. *This Man La Guardia.* New York: Dutton, 1938.

Lindner, Robert M. *Rebel without a Cause: The Hypnoanalysis of a Criminal Psychopath.* New York: Grune & Stratton, 1944.

————. "Sex in Prison." *Complex* 6 (1951): 5–20.

————. "Sexual Behavior in Penal Institutions." In *Sex Habits of American Men*, edited by Albert Deutsch, 201–15. New York: Prentice Hall, 1948.

————. *Stone Walls and Men*. New York: Odyssey Press, 1946.

Lipton, Harry R. "Stress in Correctional Institutions." *Journal of Social Therapy* 6 (1960): 216–23.

Lockwood, Daniel. "The Contribution of Sexual Harassment to Stress and Coping in Confinement." In *Coping with Imprisonment*, edited by Nicolette Parisi. Beverly Hills, CA: Sage Publications, 1982.

————. *Prison Sexual Violence*. New York: Elsevier, 1980.

Loftin, Edward E., and Join Hands. "The Life and Death of a Gay Prisoner." In *After You're Out*, edited by Karla Jay and Allen Young. New York: Links, 1975.

London, Jack. "The 'Pen': Long Days in a County Penitentiary." *Cosmopolitan Magazine* 43 (August 1907): 373–80.

————. "Pinched: A Prison Experience" *Cosmopolitan Magazine* 43 (July 1907): 263–70.

Lorraine, Charles. *It Can Be Done*. New York: Vantage, 1973.

Love, F. W. *Jail Bait Boy*. San Diego: Greenleaf, 1976.

Loveland, Frank. "Classification in the Prison System." In *Contemporary Correction*, edited by Paul W. Tappan. New York: McGraw Hill, 1951.

Lowrie, Donald. *My Life in Prison*. New York: Mitchell Kennerley, 1912.

Lucky, Denver. "Punk or Snitch: Not Many in Jail Like a Homosexual." *Advocate*, October 13, 1971, 12.

Lynch, Dirk. *Hard behind Bars*. New York: Rough Trade 454, 1977.

MacCormick, Austin H. "Farewell to Welfare Island." *News Bulletin* 8 (August 1937): 1–2, 6–7.

Macdonald, A. R. *Prison Secrets: Things Seen, Suffered, and Recorded During Seven Years in Ludlow Street Jail*. New York: Acme, 1893. Reprint, New York: Arno Press, 1969.

Mackwood, J. C. "A Note on the Psychotherapeutic Treatment of Homosexuality in Prison." *Medical Press* 218 (September 1947): 217–19.

Manocchio, Anthony, and Jimmy Dunn. *The Time Game: Two Views of a Prison*. Beverly Hills, CA: Sage Publications, 1970.

Martin, Dannie M. "How AIDS Has Changed Life in the Pen." *San Francisco Chronicle*, August 12, 1989.

Martin, John Bartlow. *Break Down the Walls*. New York: Curtis Publishing Co., 1951.

————. *My Life in Crime*. New York: Harper, 1952.

McCook, John J. "Leaves from the Diary of a Tramp, V." *Independent* 54 (June 16, 1902): 332–37.

McCormick, Austin. "Behind the Prison Riots." In *Prisons in Transformation*, edited by Thorsten Sellin, 17–27. Special issue of *The Annals of the American Academy of Political and Social Science*. Philadelphia: American Academy of Political and Social Science, 1954.

McCoy, John. *Concrete Mama: Prison Profiles from Walla Walla*. Columbia: University of Missouri Press, 1981.

McCune, Billy. *The Autobiography of Billy McCune*. San Francisco: Straight Arrow Books, 1973.

McKelvey, Blake. *American Prisons: A Study in American Social History Prior to 1915*. Montclair, NJ: Patterson Smith, 1936.

McManus, Virginia. "My Experiences with Homosexuals in Women's Prison." *Confidential* 7, no. 4 (September 1959): 18–23, 52–55.

———. *Not for Love*. New York: G. P. Putnam's Sons, 1960.

McMurtrie, Douglas C. "Notes on Homosexuality: An Attempt at Seduction; An Example of Acquired Homosexuality in Prison; A Commentary on the Prevalence of Inversion in Germany." *Vermont Medical Monthly* 19 (1913): 66–68.

———. "Notes on Pederastic Practices in Prison." *Chicago Medical Recorder* 36 (January 1914): 15–17.

Melville, Samuel. *Letters from Attica*. New York: Morrow, 1972.

Mendenhall, George. "Life Could Be Worse in S.F. Jail." *Advocate*, January 17, 1973, 19.

Merrill, Liburn. "A Summary of Findings in a Study of Sexualism among a Group of One Hundred Delinquent Boys." *Journal of Delinquency* 3 (November 1918): 255–67.

Mickley, Richard R. *Prison Ministry Handbook*. 2d ed. Los Angeles: Universal Fellowship Press, 1976.

Milburn, George. "Convicts' Jargon." *American Speech* 6 (August 1931): 436–42.

Miller, William G., and Thomas E. Hannum. "Characteristics of Homosexually Involved Incarcerated Females." *Journal of Consulting Psychology* 27 (June 1963): 277.

Minkowitz, Donna. "Cruel and Unusual: AIDS in Prison." *Village Voice*, October 17, 1999.

Minton, Robert J., ed. *Inside: Prison American Style*. New York: Random House, 1971.

Mitchell, Roger S. *The Homosexual and the Law*. New York: Arco, 1969.

Molineux, Roland B. *The Room with the Little Door*. New York: Dillingham, 1903.

Monahan, Florence. *Women in Crime*. New York: Ives Washburn, Inc., 1941.

Monroe, George J. "Sodomy—Pederasty." *St. Louis Medical Era* 9 (1899–1900): 431–34.

Moore, Daniel G. *Enter without Knocking*. Tucson: University of Arizona Press, 1969.

Moore, Langdon W. *Langdon W. Moore, His Own Story of His Eventful Life*. Boston: n.p., 1893.

Moore, Winston E. "How to End Sex Problems in Our Prisons." *Ebony*, November 1976, 83–85, 92.

Moreno, J. L. *Who Shall Survive?* Beacon, NY: Beacon House, 1953.

Morgan, Dan J. *Historical Lights and Shadows of the Ohio State Penitentiary, and Horrors of the Death Trap*. Columbus, OH: Champlin Printing Co., 1893.

Morgan, Dominik. "Restricted Love." *Women and Therapy* 20 (1997): 75–84.

Morgan, Seth, and Edward Posada, eds. *About Time: An Anthology of California Prison Writings*. Santa Cruz, CA: Vacaville Prison Literary Workshop Program, 1980.

Morgan, Ted. "Entombed." *New York Times Magazine*, February 17, 1974, 14, 17–22.

Morrell, Ed. *The Twenty-Fifth Man*. Montclair, NJ: Globe Press, 1924.

Morris, Ed. *Born to Lose*. New York: Mason & Lipscomb, 1974.

Moss, C. Scott, Ray Hosford, and William R. Anderson. "Sexual Assault in a Prison." *Psychological Reports* 44 (1979): 823–28.

Murphy, Patrick C. *Behind Grey Walls*. Caldwell, ID: Caxton, 1920.

Murray, William. "Women in Prison." *Cosmopolitan* 17 (1972): 144–48.

Murtagh, John, and Sara Harris. *Cast the First Stone*. New York: McGraw-Hill, 1957.

Murton, Tom, and Joe Hyams. *Accomplices to the Crime*. New York: Grove Press, 1969.

"My Life in the Penitentiary." *Independent* 56 (February 4, 1904): 255–60.

Nacci, Peter L., and Thomas R. Kane. "The Incidence of Sex and Sexual Aggression in Federal Prisons." *Federal Probation* 47 (December 1983): 31–36.

———. "Sex and Sexual Aggression in Federal Prisons." *Federal Probation* 48 (March 1984): 46–53.

Nagel, William. *The New Red Barn: A Critical Look at the Modern American Prison*. New York: Walker, 1973.

National Society of Penal Information. *Handbook of American Prisons, Covering the Prisons of the New England and Middle Atlantic States*. New York: G. P. Putnam's Sons, 1925.

Neese, Robert. *Prison Exposures*. New York: Chilton Co., 1959.

Neier, Aryeh. "Sex and Confinement." *Civil Liberties Review* 5, no. 2 (July–August 1978): 6–16.

Nelson, Victor Folke. "Addenda to 'Junker Lingo.'" *American Speech* 8, no. 3 (October 1933): 33–34.

———. *Prison Days and Nights*. Boston: Little, Brown, 1933.

Nice, Richard W. "The Problem of Homosexuality in Corrections." *American Journal of Correction* 28 (May–June 1966): 30–32.

Nichols, Thomas L. *Journal in Jail*. Buffalo, NY: Dinsmore, 1840.

Norfolk Prison Brothers. *Who Took the Weight? Black Voices from Norfolk Prison*. Boston: Little, Brown & Co., 1972.

Norris, Clarence, and Sybil D. Washington. *The Last of the Scottsboro Boys: An Autobiography*. New York: G. P. Putnam's Sons, 1979.

Norris, Linda. "Comparison of Two Groups in a Southern State Women's Prison: Homosexual Behavior versus Non-Homosexual Behavior." *Psychological Reports* 34 (1974): 75–78.

Novick, Abraham G. "The Make-Believe Family: Informal Group Structure among Institutionalized Delinquent Girls." In *Casework Papers from the National Conference on Social Welfare*, 44–59. New York: Family Service Association of America, 1960.

Number 1500. *Life in Sing Sing*. Indianapolis: Bobbs-Merrill, 1904.

Nylander, Towne. "Tramps and Hoboes." *Forum* 74 (August 1925): 227–37.

"N.Y. Prisons Head Meets with Gays." *Advocate*, August 2, 1972, 6.

O'Brien, Edna V. *So I Went to Prison*. New York: Frederick A. Stokes, 1938.

O'Dare, Kain. *Philosophy of the Dusk*. New York: Century, 1929.

O'Hare, Kate Richards. *In Prison*. Seattle: University of Washington Press, 1976. First published ca. 1923 by Alfred A. Knopf.

Oliver, Wayne A., and Donald L. Mosher. "Psychopathology and Guilt in Heterosexuals and Subgroups of Homosexual Reformatory Inmates." *Journal of Abnormal Psychology* 73 (1968): 323–29.

Olivero, J. Michael, and James B. Roberts. "The Management of AIDS in Correctional

Facilities: A View from the Federal Court System." *Prison Journal* 69, no. 2 (Fall–Winter, 1989): 7–18.

O'Rourke, Frank. "Prisons: The Nature of the Beast." *Honcho*, August 1983, 59–62.

Osborne, Thomas Mott. *Prisons and Common Sense*. Philadelphia: J. Lippincott, 1924.

———. *Society and Prisons*. New Haven, CT: Yale University Press, 1916.

———. *Within Prison Walls*. New York: D. Appleton & Co., 1916.

Oswald, Russell G. *Attica: My Story*. New York: Doubleday, 1972.

Otis, Margaret. "A Perversion Not Commonly Noted." *Journal of Abnormal Psychology* 8 (June–July 1913): 113–16.

Paine, Lewis W. *Six Years in a Georgia Prison*. New York: n.p., 1851.

Pappas, Nick, ed. *The Jail: Its Operation and Management*. Washington, DC: Bureau of Prisons and University of Wisconsin, 1972.

Parisi, Nicolette, ed. *Coping with Imprisonment*. Beverly Hills, CA: Sage Publications, 1982.

Parker, Jack B., and Robert A. Perkins. "The Influence of Type of Institution on Attitudes toward the Handling of the Homosexual among Inmates." *Offender Rehabilitation* 2 (1978): 245–54.

Parnell, Percy R. *The Joint*. San Antonio: Naylor, 1976.

Patterson, Haywood, and Earl Conrad. *Scottsboro Boy*. New York: Doubleday, 1950.

Payne, Seth W. *Behind the Bars*. New York: Vincent, 1873.

Peeples, Edward H., Jr., and Anthony M. Scacco, Jr. "The Stress Impact Study Technique: A Method for Evaluating the Consequences of Male-on-Male Sexual Assault in Jails, Prisons, and Other Selected Single-Sex Institutions." In *Male Rape*, edited by Anthony M. Scacco, Jr., 241–78. New York: AMS Press, 1982.

Pell, Eve, ed. *Maximum Security: Letters from California's Prisons*. New York: Dutton, 1972.

Peretti, P.O. "Dysfunctions and Eufunctions of Prison Homosexuality: A Structural-Functional Approach." *Panminerva Medica* 21 (1979): 135–40.

Perry, Troy D. *Don't be Afraid Anymore: The Story of Reverend Troy Perry and the Metropolitan Community Churches*. With Thomas L. P. Swicegood. New York: St. Martin's Press, 1990.

———. *The Lord Is My Shepherd and He Knows I'm Gay*. With Charles L. Lucas. Los Angeles: Nash Publishing, 1972.

Petersen, David, and Marcello Truzzi, eds. *Criminal Life: Views from the Inside*. Englewood Cliffs, NJ: Prentice-Hall, 1972.

Petras, Herman. "Life behind Bars: Consenting Homosexuals." *Swank* 25, no. 9 (September 1978): 62–64, 94–95, 97–98, 104.

Pettay, Orange L. *Five Years in Hell; or, The Ohio Penitentiary*. Caldwell: Citizens' Press, 1883.

Philadelphia Society for Alleviating the Miseries of Public Prisons. *Remarks on Cellular Separation*. Philadelphia: n.p., 1861.

Philip, Cynthia Owen. *Imprisoned in America; Prison Communications: 1776 to Attica*. New York: Harper & Row, 1973.

Pileggi, Nicholas. "Inside Rikers Island." *New York*, June 8, 1981, 24–29.

Piñero, Miguel. *Short Eyes*. New York: Hill & Wang, 1975.

Planisheck, Florence Florenz. *Behind Prison Walls*. Boston: Meador Publishing Co., 1933.

Pollak, Otto. *The Criminality of Women*. Philadelphia: University of Pennsylvania Press, 1950.

Polsky, Howard W. *Cottage Six: The Social System of Delinquent Boys in Residential Treatment*. New York: John Wiley & Sons, 1962.

Pomeroy, Wardell B. *Dr. Kinsey and the Institute for Sex Research*. New York: Harper & Row, 1972.

"Portrait of a Lifer, by No. 77260." *American Mercury* 37 (February 1936): 175–82.

Powell, J. C. *The American Siberia; or, Fourteen Years' Experience in a Southern Convict Camp*. Philadelphia: H. J. Smith & Co., 1891. Reprint, New York: Arno Press, 1969.

Prisoner X. *Prison Confidential*. Los Angeles: Medco Books, 1969.

"Prison Gang Chiefs Served by Valets." *New York Times*, January 25, 1934, 1, 3.

"Prison Gangs Face a Federal Inquiry; Clean-Up Pressed." *New York Times*, January 26, 1934, 1.

Proferes, James J. *Prison Punk*. Washington, DC: Guild Press, 1969.

Propper, Alice M. "Love, Marriage, and Father-Son Relationships among Male Prisoners." *Prison Journal* 69, no. 2 (Fall–Winter 1989): 57–63.

———. *Prison Homosexuality: Myth and Reality*. Lexington, MA: Lexington Books, D. C. Heath & Co., 1981.

Raborg, Frederick. *Jail Rape*. San Diego, CA: Greenleaf, 1972.

Ragen, Joseph E., and Charles Finston. *Inside the World's Toughest Prison*. Springfield, IL: Charles C. Thomas, 1962.

Rankin, L. *No. 6847; or, The Horrors of Prison Life*. n.p., 1897.

Reasons, Charles E. "The Politicizing of Crime, the Criminal and the Criminologist." *Journal of Criminal Law and Criminology* 64 (March 1973): 471–77.

Reed, Nathaniel. *The Life of Texas Jack: Eight Years a Criminal, 41 Years Trusting in God*. Tulsa: Tulsa Printing Co., 1936.

Reeves, Tom. "The Hidden Oppression: Gay Men in Prison for Having Sex with Minors." *GCN*, December 13, 1980, 8–12.

Reinhardt, James Melvin. *Sex Perversion and Sex Crime*. Springfield, IL: Charles C. Thomas, 1957.

Reiss, Albert J., Jr. "The Social Integration of Queers and Peers." *Social Problems* 9 (Fall 1961): 102–20.

Remick, Peter. *In Constant Fear: The Brutal True Story of Life within the Walls of the Notorious Walpole State Prison*. As told to James B. Shuman. New York: Reader's Digest Press, 1975.

Rexroth, Kenneth. *An Autobiographical Novel*. New York: New Directions, 1969. First published 1966 by Doubleday.

Reynolds, John N. *A Kansas Hell; or, Life in the Kansas Penitentiary*. Atchison, KS: Bee Publishing Co., 1889.

———. *The Twin Hells: A Thrilling Narrative of Life in the Kansas and Missouri Penitentiaries*. Chicago: Bee Publishing Co., 1890.

Richardson, Jack. *The Prison Life of Harris Filmore*. Greenwich, CT: New York Graphic Society, 1963.

Rideau, Wilbert, and Billy Sinclair. "Prison: The Sexual Jungle." In *Male Rape*, edited by Anthony M. Scacco, Jr., 3–29. New York: AMS Press, 1982.

Robbins, Michela. "The Inside Story of a Girls' Reformatory." *Collier's* 30 (October 1953): 74–79.

Roberts, Thelma. *Red Hell: The Life Story of John Good, Criminal*. New York: Rae D. Henkle, 1934.

Rochman, Sue. "Iron Closets behind Bars: Lesbians Face Harsh Penalties in Prison." *Advocate*, February 26, 1991, 42–43.

Rodman, Benjamin. *A Voice from the Prison*. New Bedford, MA: Benjamin Lindsey, 1840.

Rogers, Paul T. *Saul's Book*. New York: Pushcart Press, 1983.

Rosevear, John. "Time." In *Getting Busted: Personal Experiences of Arrest, Trial, and Prison*, edited by Ross Firestone. New York: Pyramid, 1973.

Roth, Loren H. "Territoriality and Homosexuality in a Male Prison Population." *American Journal of Orthopsychiatry* 41, no. 3 (April 1971): 510–13.

Roth, Samuel. *Stone Walls Do Not: The Chronicle of a Captivity*. New York: William Faro, 1930.

Rothenberg, David. "Gay Prisoners: Fighting Back behind the Walls." *Advocate*, June 16, 1976, 10–11.

———. "Group Rip-Off: The Prison Rape!" *Advocate*, May 5, 1976, 9–11.

———, "Prisoners." In *The Sexually Oppressed*, edited by Harvey L. Gochros and Jean S. Gochros, 225–36. New York: Association, 1977.

———. "Sexual Assaults in the Prisons." *Fortune News*, September 1976, 1, 5–7.

Runyon, Tom. *In for Life: A Convict's Story*. New York: Norton, 1953.

Sagarin, Edward. "Prison Homosexuality and Its Effect on Post-Prison Sexual Behavior." *Psychiatry* 39 (August 1976): 245–57.

Salzman-Webb, Marilyn. "Empty the Women's Jails." *off our backs* 1, nos. 9–10 (Summer 1970): 2.

Sanders, Dennis. *Gay Source: A Catalog for Men*. New York: Berkley Publishing Corp., 1977.

Sands, Bill. *My Shadow Ran Fast*. Englewood Cliffs, NJ: Prentice-Hall, 1964.

———. *The Seventh Step*. New York: New American Library, 1967.

Scacco, Anthony M., Jr., ed. *Male Rape: A Casebook of Sexual Aggressions*. New York: AMS Press, 1982.

———. *Rape in Prison*. Springfield, IL: Charles C. Thomas, 1975.

———. "The Scapegoat Is Almost Always White." In *Male Rape*, edited by Anthony M. Scacco, Jr., 91–103. New York: AMS Press, 1982.

Schappes, Morris U. *Letters from the Tombs*. New York: Schappes Defense Committee, 1941.

Schroeder, Andreas. *Shaking It Rough: A Prison Memoir*. Toronto: Doubleday, 1976.

Scott, Wellington. *Seventeen Years in the Underworld*. New York and Cincinnati, OH: Abingdon Press, 1916.

Scudder, Kenyon J. *Prisoners Are People*. Garden City, NY: Doubleday, 1952.

Seale, Bobby. *Seize the Time: The Story of the Black Panther Party and Huey P. Newton*. New York: Vintage, 1968.

Selber, Michael. "View from the Garbage Heap: The Plight of the Sex Offender." *Los Angeles Advocate*, November 1968, 6–9.

————. "View from the Garbage Heap II." *Los Angeles Advocate*, December 1968, 6–10.

Sellin, Thorsten, ed. *Prisons in Transformation*. Special issue of *The Annals of the American Academy of Political and Social Science*. Philadelphia: American Academy of Political and Social Science, 1954.

Selling, Lowell S. "The Pseudo Family." *American Journal of Sociology* 37 (September 1931): 247–53.

Serber, Michael. "Shame Aversion Therapy." *Journal of Behavior Therapy and Experimental Psychiatry* 1 (1970): 213–15.

Serber, Michael, and Claudia G. Keith. "The Atascadero Project: Model of a Sexual Retraining Program for Incarcerated Homosexual Pedophiles." *Journal of Homosexuality* 1, no. 1 (Fall 1974): 87–97.

Serber, Michael, and Joseph Wolpe. "Behavior Therapy Techniques." In *Sexual Behavior: Social, Clinical, and Legal Aspects*, edited by H. L. P. Resnick and Marvin E. Wolfgang. Boston: Little Brown, 1972.

Serna, Idella. *Locked Down: A Lesbian Life in Prison*. Norwich, VT: New Victoria Publishers, 1992.

"Sex Life in Prison." Journal of the American Medical Association 138 (1948): 298.

"Sexual Hypocrisy." *Fortune News*, April 1974, 3.

Shaw, Clifford R. *The Natural History of a Delinquent Career*. Chicago: University of Chicago Press, 1931.

Shaw, Clifford R., and Earl D. Meyers. "The Juvenile Delinquent." In *The Illinois Crime Survey*, edited by John W. Wigmore. Chicago: Blakely Printing Co., 1929.

Shelley, Martha. "Gay Is Good." In *Out of the Closets: Voices of Gay Liberation*, edited by Karla Jay and Allen Young. 1972. Reprint, New York: New York University Press, 1992. First published in *Rat* (February 24, 1970).

Shelly, Gordon. *I Take the Rap*. New York: Frederick Fell, 1957.

Shilts, Randy. "Locked up with the Jailhouse Queens." *San Francisco Chronicle*, April 7, 1978, 12.

Shoblad, Richard H. *Doing My Own Time*. Garden City, NY: Doubleday, 1972.

Simons, Hi. "A Prison Dictionary (Expurgated)." *American Speech* 8, no. 3 (October 1933): 22–33.

Sinclair, Billy Wayne, and Jodie Sinclair. *A Life in the Balance: A Journey from Murder to Redemption inside America's Worst Prison System*. New York: Arcade, 2000.

Singer, Pat. "Love in Prison." *off our backs* 2, no. 8 (April 1972): 8

Sipe, Morgan K. *Twenty-Nine Hundred and Forty-Four Days in Hell, and What I Saw and Heard: An Inside View of One of the Greatest Public Institutions in Kansas*. Galesburg, KS: n.p., 1895.

"Sissy in Prison: An Interview with Ron Vernon." In *Out of the Closets: Voices of Gay*

Liberation, edited by Karla Jay and Allen Young. 1972. Reprint, New York: New York University Press, 1992.

Smith, Benjamin. *A Fugitive from Hell*. Joplin, MO: n.p., 1935.

Smith, Charles E. "The Homosexual Federal Offender: A Study of 100 Cases." *Journal of Criminal Law, Criminology and Police Science* 44 (1954): 582–91.

———. "Prison Pornography." *Journal of Social Therapy* 1 (1955): 126–28.

———. "Some Problems in Dealing with Homosexuals in the Prison Situation." *Journal of Social Therapy* 2 (1956): 37–45.

Smith, D. B. *Two Years in the Slave-Pen of Iowa*. Kansas City, MO: H. N. Farey & Co, 1885.

Smith, Dale E. "Crowding and Confinement." in *The Pains of Imprisonment*, edited by Robert Johnson and Hans Toch, 45–62. Beverly Hills, CA: Sage Publications, 1982.

Smith, Norman E., and Mary Ellen Batiuk. "Sexual Victimization and Inmate Social Interaction." *Prison Journal* 69, no. 2 (Fall–Winter 1989): 29–38.

Smith, Raymond Joseph. "Screaming for Change in Prison." *Gay Community News* 18, no. 43 (May 26, 1991): 5.

Smith, Samuel. *Inside Out; or, Roguery Exposed*. Hartford, CT: n.p., 1827.

Sobell, Morton. *On Doing Time*. New York: Scribner's, 1974.

Sorrentino, Joseph N. *Up from Never*. New York: Manor Books, 1973.

Spaulding, Edith R. *An Experimental Study of Psychopathic Delinquent Women*. Montclair, NJ: Patterson Smith, 1923.

Spector, Herman K. *San Quentiniana: Books Published by Officials and Inmates of San Quentin*. San Quentin: California State Prison at San Quentin, 1953.

———. "What Men Write in Prison." *Tomorrow* 5 (December 1945): 53–56.

Squire, Amos O. *Sing Sing Doctor*. Garden City, NY: Garden City Publishing Co., 1937.

Stanley, Leo, and Evelyn Wells. *Men at Their Worst*. New York: Appleton-Century, 1940.

Steiner, Jesse F., and Roy M. Brown. *The North Carolina Chain Gang: A Study of County Convict Road Work*. Chapel Hill: University of North Carolina Press, 1927.

Stern, Susan. *With the Weathermen: The Personal Journal of a Revolutionary Woman*. Garden City, NY: Doubleday, 1975.

Stiller, Richard. "Conjugal Visits in Prison." *Sexology* (1959): 288–91.

———. "Sex Practices in Prison." In *The Third Sex*, edited by Isadore Rubin, 82–85. New York: New Book Co., 1961.

St. John, Larry. *Prison Pluggers*. Santee, CA: Surree Ltd., 1976.

Stockwell, Spencer. "Sexual Experiences of Adolescent Delinquent Girls." *International Journal of Sexology* 7 (1953): 25–27.

"Stonewall Prison Program Wins Approval from State." *Advocate*, August 30, 1972, 16.

"The Story of a Black Punk." In *Prison Masculinities*, edited by Don Sabo, Terry A. Kupers, and Willie London. Philadelphia: Temple University Press, 2001.

Sullivan, Katherine. *Girls on Parole*. Westport, CT: Greenwood Press, 1956.

Sullivan, Richard M. "The Pros and Cons of Conjugal Visits in Prison Institutions." *Journal of Family Law* 9 (1970): 437–40.

Sutton, Charles. *The New York Tombs: Its Secrets and Its Mysteries*. New York: United States Publishing Co., 1874.

Swados, Felice. *House of Fury*. Garden City, NY: Doubleday, Doran & Co., 1941.

Sykes, Gresham M. *The Society of Captives: A Study of a Maximum Security Prison*. Princeton, NJ: Princeton University Press, 1958.

Sylvester, Sawyer F., John H. Reed, and David O. Nelson. *Prison Homicide*. New York: Spectrum Publications, 1977.

"Tammany Blocked Prison Clean-Up." *New York Times*, January 1, 1934, 3.

"Tammany Leader Linked to Jail Ring." *New York Times*, January 27, 1934, 2.

Tannenbaum, Frank. *Crime and the Community*. Boston: Ginn, 1938.

——. "Prison Cruelty." *Atlantic Monthly* 125 (April 1920): 432–44.

——. "The Professional Criminal." *Century* 110 (May –October, 1925): 577–88.

——. *Wall Shadows: A Study in American Prisons*. New York: G. P. Putnam's Sons, 1922.

Tarde, Gabriel, *Penal Philosophy*. Translated by Rapelje Howell. Boston: Little, Brown, & Co., 1912.

Tasker, Robert Joyce. *Grimhaven*. New York: Knopf, 1928.

Taylor, A. J. W. "The Significance of 'Darls' or 'Special Relationships' for Borstal Girls." *British Journal of Criminology* 5 (October 1965): 406–18.

Taylor, William Banks. *Down on Parchman Farm: The Great Prison in the Mississippi Delta*. Columbus: Ohio State University Press, 1999.

Teal, Donn. *The Gay Militants*. New York: Stein & Day, 1971.

Teale, Christopher. *Behind These Walls*. New York: Frederick Fell, 1957.

Teeters, Negley K. *The Cradle of the Penitentiary: The Walnut Street Jail at Philadelphia, 1773–1835*. Philadelphia: Pennsylvania Prison Society, 1955.

——. *They Were in Prison: A History of the Pennsylvania Prison Society, 1787–1937*. Chicago: John C. Winston Co., 1937.

Teeters, Negley K., and John D. Shearer. *The Prison at Philadelphia, Cherry Hill: The Separate System of Penal Discipline: 1829–1913*. New York: Columbia University Press, 1957.

Terman, Lewis M., and Catherine Cox Miles. *Sex and Personality: Studies in Masculinity and Femininity*. New York: McGraw-Hill, 1936.

Tewksbury, Richard. "Fear of Sexual Assault in Prison Inmates." *Prison Journal* 69 (Spring–Summer 1989): 62–71.

Third World Gay Revolution (Chicago) and Gay Liberation Front (Chicago). "Gay Revolution and Sex Roles." In *Out of the Closets: Voices of Gay Liberation*, edited by Karla Jay and Allen Young. 1972. Reprint, New York: New York University Press, 1992.

Thomas, Charles W. "Theoretical Perspectives on Prisonization: A Comparison of the Importation and Deprivation Models." *Journal of Criminal Law and Criminology* 68 (1977): 135–45.

Thomas, Evan. "Disciplinary Barracks: The Experience of a Military Prisoner at Fort Leavenworth." *Survey* 41 (February 1, 1919): 625–29.

Thomas, Mack. *The Total Beast*. New York: Simon & Schuster, 1970.

Thomas, Piri. *Down These Mean Streets*. New York: Knopf, 1967.

————. *Seven Long Times*. New York: Praeger, 1974.

Thompson, George. *Prison Life and Reflections*. Oberlin, OH: J. M. Fitch, 1847.

Thornton, Alice. "Pound of Flesh." *Atlantic Monthly* 135 (April 1925): 433–46.

Tiffin, Van. *Prison Tours and Poems; a Sketch of the Oregon State Penitentiary*. Salem, OR: n.p., 1904.

Timilty, Joseph. *Prison Journal: An Irreverent Look at Life on the Inside*. Boston: Northeastern University Press, 1997.

Tittle, Charles R. "Inmate Organization: Sex Differentiation and the Influence of Criminal Subcultures." *American Sociological Review* 34 (August 1969): 492–505.

Toch, Hans. *Living in Prison: The Ecology of Survival*. New York: Free Press, 1977.

Torok, Lou. *The Strange World of Prison*. Indianapolis: Bobbs-Merrill, 1973.

Touhy, Roger. *The Stolen Years*. Cleveland: Pennington Press, 1959.

Trainer, Russ. *Prison: School for Lesbians*. Van Nuys, CA: Triumph News Co., 1968.

Trupin, James E., ed. *In Prison: Writings and Poems about the Prison Experience*. New York: Mentor, 1975.

Tucker, Donald. "The Account of the White House Seven." In *Male Rape*, edited by Anthony M. Scacco, Jr., 30–57. New York: AMS Press, 1982.

————. "A Punk's Song: View from the Inside." In *Male Rape*, edited by Anthony M. Scacco, Jr., 58–79. New York: AMS Press, 1982.

Tully, Jim. *Beggars of Life*. New York: Albert & Charles Boni, 1924.

————. *A Dozen and One*. Hollywood: Murray & Gee, 1943.

————. *Shadows of Men*. Garden City, NY: Doubleday, Doran & Co., 1930.

Van Wormer, Katherine S. *Sex Role Behavior in a Woman's Prison, an Ethological Analysis*. San Francisco: R & E Research Associates, 1978.

Vedder, Clyde B., and Patricia G. King. *Problems of Homosexuality in Corrections*. Springfield, IL: Charles C. Thomas, 1967.

Vedder, Clyde B., and Dora B. Somerville. *The Delinquent Girl*. Springfield, IL: Charles C. Thomas, 1970.

Viereck, George Sylvester. *Men into Beasts*. New York: Fawcett, 1952.

Walker, Edward L. "The Terman 'M-F' Test and the Prison Classification Program." *Journal of Genetic Psychology* 59 (1941): 27–40.

Ward, David A., and Gene G. Kassebaum. "The Dynamics of Prison Homosexuality: The Character of the Love Affair." In *Observations of Deviance*, edited by Jack D. Douglas, 89–106. New York: Random House, 1970.

————. *Women's Prison: Sex and Social Structure*. Chicago: Aldine Publishing, 1965.

Ward, Jack L. "Homosexual Behavior of the Institutionalized Delinquent." *Psychiatric Quarterly Supplement* 32 (1958): 301–13.

Warren, Paul. *Next Time Is for Life*. New York: Dell, 1953.

Washington, Jerome. *Iron House: Stories from the Yard*. Fort Bragg, CA: QED Press, 1994.

Wattron, John B. "Validity of the Marsh-Hilliard-Liechti MMPI Sexual Deviation Scale in a State Prison Population." *Journal of Consulting Psychology* 22 (1958): 16.

We Are Attica: Interviews with Prisoners from Attica. New York: Attica Defense Committee, 1972.

Weaver, Flave J. *Six Years in Bondage and Freedom at Last*. Kansas City, MO: Chas. E. Brown, 1896.

"Welfare Island Raid Aids Prison Reform." *Literary Digest* 117 (February 3, 1934): 5–6.

"We Mean Business: Predicting the End of a So-Called Model Prison." *Lesbian Tide* (July 1972), 1.

Weinberg, S. Kirson. "Aspects of the Prison's Social Structure." *American Journal of Sociology* 47 (1942): 717–26.

Weiss, Carl, and David James Friar. *Terror in the Prisons: Homosexual Rape and Why Society Condones It*. New York: Bobbs-Merrill, 1974.

Weiss, Karel, ed. *The Prison Experience: An Anthology*. New York: Delacorte, 1976.

"'Welfare' Island." *Survey* 70 (February 1934): 48.

"Welfare Island Raid Bares Gangster Rule over Prison; Weapons, Narcotics Found." *New York Times*, January 25, 1934, 1.

Wells, Wesley Robert. *My Name Is Wesley Robert Wells*. San Francisco: San Francisco Civil Rights Congress, 1951.

Wentworth, L. J., E. E. Brodie, and F. W. Mulkey. *Report of the Commission to Investigate the Oregon State Penitentiary*. Portland, January 26, 1917.

West, Dorothy. "I Was Afraid to Shut My Eyes." *Saturday Evening Post*, vol. 241 (July 13, 1968). Reprinted in *Male Rape: A Casebook of Sexual Aggressions*, edited by Anthony M. Scacco, Jr. New York: AMS, 1982.

Westwood, Gordon. *Society and the Homosexual*. New York: E. P. Dutton & Co., 1953.

Wharton, Charles S. *The House of Whispering Hate*. Chicago: Madelaine Mendlesohn, 1932.

Wicker, Tom. *A Time to Die*. New York: Quadrangle, 1975.

Wierse, Paul. *Eighty-Eight Weeks in Purgatory; or, Life in the U.S. Penitentiary in Atlanta, Georgia*. Charleston: McFarlane, 1920.

Wildes, Jon. "To Be Young, Gay, and Behind Bars." *Village Voice* 23, no. 2 (January 9, 1978): 1, 21.

Williams, Vergil L., and Mary Fish. *Convicts, Codes, and Contraband: The Prison Life of Men and Women*. Cambridge, MA: Ballinger, 1974.

———. "Women's Prison Families." In *Justice and Corrections*, edited by Norman Johnston and Leonard Savitz, 541–52. New York, John Wiley & Sons, 1978.

Williamson, Roosevelt. "Prison Racism and Legal Slavery in America." *Gay Community News*, April 10, 1982, 7 + 9–10.

Wilson, Joseph G. *Are Prisons Necessary?* Philadelphia: Dorrnace & Co., 1950.

———. "Prison Sex Life." *Sexology* (October 1953): 161–64.

Wilson, Joseph G., and Michael J. Pescor. *Problems in Prison Psychiatry*. Caldwell, ID: Caxton Printers, 1939.

Wilson, Rob. "Homosexual Rape: Legacy of Overcrowding." *Corrections Magazine* 3 (March 1977): 10–11.

Wilson, Walter. *Hell in Nebraska: A Tale of the Nebraska Penitentiary*. Lincoln, NB: Bankers Publishing Co., 1913.

Wines, Enoch Cobb. *The State of Prisons and of Child-Saving Institutions in the Civilized World*. Cambridge, MA: John Wilson & Sons, 1880.

————, ed. *Transactions of the National Congress on Penitentiary and Reformatory Discipline.* Held at Cincinnati, Ohio, October 12–18, 1870. Albany: Weed, Parsons & Co., 1871.

Wines, Enoch Cobb, and Theodore W. Dwight. *Report on the Prisons and Reformatories of the United States and Canada.* Albany, NY: Van Benthuysen, 1867.

Winning, James R. *Behind These Walls.* New York: Macmillan, 1933.

Winslow, Randolph. "Report of an Epidemic of Gonorrhea from Rectal Coition." *Medical News* (Philadelphia) 49 (August 14, 1886): 180–82.

Wittman, Carl. "A Gay Manifesto." In *Out of the Closets: Voices of Gay Liberation*, edited by Karla Jay and Allen Young. 1972. Reprint, New York: New York University Press, 1992. First published as "Refugees from Amerika: A Gay Manifesto," *San Francisco Free Press*, December 22, 1969–January 7, 1970.

Wolper, Allan. "Young, Jailed, and White." *Soho Weekly News*, January 19, 1978.

Woltman, Frederick. "Sex Offenders Create Difficult Prison Problem Even Experts Can't Solve." *World-Telegram*, April 21, 1939.

"Women: 'Fears, Loneliness, Sexual Frustration.'" *Fortune News*, April 1974, 4, 7.

Women of ACE. "Prison Issues and HIV: Voices." In *Women, AIDS, and Activism*, edited by in Marion Banzhaf et al., 143–55. Boston: South End Press, 1990.

Women's Jail Collective. "Jailbreak." *off our backs* 1, no. 11 (September 30, 1970): 3.

Wood, Ed. *Young, Black and Gay.* San Diego, CA: Publishers Export Co., 1968.

Wood, Robert. "Homosexuals in Prison." *Sexology* (March 1956): 518–21.

Wood, Spike. *Jail House Sucker.* New York: Star Distributors, 1979.

Wooden, Wayne S., and Jay Parker. *Men behind Bars: Sexual Exploitation in Prison.* New York: Plenum Press, 1982.

Woodroff, Horace. *Stone Wall College.* Nashville: Aurora Publishers, 1970.

"World's Worst." *Time* 23 (February 5, 1934): 15–16.

Wright, George B. *Two Year's Experience as a Prisoner (!) in the United States Penitentiary at Leavenworth, Kansas.* Leavenworth, KS: Leavenworth Bag Co., 1915.

Wylie, F. E. "Reform by Surgery?" *Louisville Herald Post*, February 15, 1936, 3.

Yalom, Irvin D. "Group Therapy of Incarcerated Sexual Deviants." *Journal of Nervous and Mental Disease* 132 (1961): 158–70.

Yenne, Herbert. "Prison Lingo." *American Speech* 2, no. 6 (March 1927): 280–82.

Yoder, Robert M. "Trouble Shooter of the Big House." *Saturday Evening Post*, May 12, 1951, 19–21, 162–66.

Young, Allen. "Gay Prison Tragedy." *Gay Sunshine*, no. 20 (February 1974): 2–3.

————. "Out of the Closets, Into the Streets." In *Out of the Closets: Voices of Gay Liberation*, edited by Karla Jay and Allen Young. 1972. Reprint, New York: New York University Press, 1992.

Zemans, Eugene, and Ruth Shonle Covan. "Marital Relationships of Prisoners." *Journal of Criminal Law, Criminology, and Police Science* 49 (May –June 1958): 50–57.

Zeringer, B. D. "Sexual Assaults and Forced Homosexual Relationships in Prison: Cruel and Unusual Punishment." *Albany Law Journal* 36 (1972): 428–38.

Zuckerman, Stanley B. "Sex Literature in Prison." *Journal of Social Therapy* 1 (1955): 129–31.

SECONDARY SOURCES

Adam, Barry D. *The Rise of a Gay and Lesbian Movement*. Boston: Twayne, 1987.

Aguirre, Carlos. "The Lima Penitentiary and the Modernization of Criminal Justice in Nineteenth-Century Peru." In *The Birth of the Penitentiary in Latin America: Essays on Criminology, Prison Reform, and Social Control, 1830–1940*, edited by Ricardo D. Salvatore and Carlos Aguirre. Austin: University of Texas Press, 1996.

Alexander, Ruth M. *The "Girl Problem": Female Sexual Delinquency in New York, 1900–1930*. Ithaca, NY: Cornell University Press, 1995.

Allen, Peter Lewis. *The Wages of Sin: Sex and Disease, Past and Present*. Chicago: University of Chicago Press, 2000.

Almaguer, Tomas. "Chicano Men: A Cartography of Homosexual Identity and Behavior." *differences* 3 (Summer 1991): 75–100.

Anderson, Allen F. "AIDS and Prisoners' Rights Law: Deciphering the Administrative Guideposts." *Prison Journal* 69 (Spring–Summer 1989): 14–26.

Arnold, David. "The Colonial Prison: Power, Knowledge, and Penology in Nineteenth-Century India." In *Subaltern Studies* 8, edited by David Arnold and David Hardiman, 148–87. London: Oxford University Press, 1994.

Baker, Kathryn Hinojosa. "Delinquent Desire: Race, Sex, and Ritual in Reform Schools for Girls." *Discourse* 15 (Fall 1992): 49–68.

Barber, Stephen M., and David L. Clark. "Queer Moments: The Performative Temporalities of Eve Kosofsky Sedgwick." In *Regarding Sedgwick: Essays on Queer Culture and Critical Theory*, edited by Stephen M. Barber and David L. Clark. New York: Routledge, 2002.

Becker, Edith, Michelle Citron, Julia Lesage, and B. Ruby Rich. "Lesbians and Film." In *Out in Culture: Gay, Lesbian, and Queer Essays on Popular Culture*, edited by Corey K. Creekmur and Alexander Doty, 25–43. Durham, NC: Duke University Press, 1995.

Becker, Peter, and Richard F. Wetzell, eds. *Criminals and Their Scientists: The History of Criminology in International Perspective*. Cambridge: Cambridge University Press, 2006.

Bell, David, and Gill Valentine, eds. *Mapping Desire: Geographies of Sexualities*. London and New York: Routledge, 1995.

Bender, John. *Imagining the Penitentiary: Fiction and the Architecture of Mind in Eighteenth-Century England*. Chicago: University of Chicago Press, 1987.

Berkman, Ronald. *Opening the Gates: The Rise of the Prisoners' Movement*. Lexington, MA: D. C. Heath, 1979.

Bérubé, Allan. *Coming Out under Fire: The History of Gay Men and Women in World War Two*. New York: Free Press, 1990.

Betsky, Aaron. *Queer Space: Architecture and Same-Sex Desire*. New York: William Morrow, 1997.

Bland, Lucy, and Laura Doan, eds. *Sexology in Culture: Labeling Bodies and Desires*. Chicago: University of Chicago Press, 1998.

Blumberg, Mark. *AIDS: The Impact on the Criminal Justice System*. Columbus, OH: Merrill, 1990.

————. "Issues and Controversies with Respect to the Management of AIDS in Corrections." *Prison Journal* 69, no. 1 (Spring–Summer 1989): 1–13.

Boag, Peter. *Same-Sex Affairs: Constructing and Controlling Homosexuality in the Pacific Northwest.* Berkeley: University of California Press, 2003.

Boone, Joseph A., et al., eds. *Queer Frontiers: Millennial Geographies, Genders, and Generations.* Madison: University of Wisconsin Press, 2000.

Boyd, Nan Alamilla. *Wide Open Town: A History of Queer San Francisco to 1965.* Berkeley: University of California Press, 2003.

Bravmann, Scott. "Queer Historical Subjects." *Socialist Review* 25 (1995): 46–68.

————. *Queer Fictions of the Past: History, Culture, and Difference.* New York: Cambridge University Press, 1997.

Brenzel, Barbara M. *Daughters of the State: A Social Portrait of the First Reform School for Girls in North America, 1856–1905.* Cambridge, MA: MIT Press, 1983.

Bright, Charles. *The Powers That Punish: Prison and Politics in the Era of the "Big House," 1920–1955.* Ann Arbor: University of Michigan Press, 1996.

Bristow, Joseph. "Symond's History, Ellis's Heredity: *Sexual Inversion.*" In *Sexology in Culture: Labeling Bodies and Desires,* edited by Lucy Bland and Laura Doan. Chicago: University of Chicago Press, 1998.

Buffington, Robert M. *Criminal and Citizen in Modern America.* Lincoln: University of Nebraska Press, 2000.

Bullough, Vern. *Science in the Bedroom: A History of Sex Research.* New York: Basic Books, 1994.

Burton-Rose, Daniel. "The Anti-Exploits of Men against Sexism, 1977–78." In *Prison Masculinities,* edited by Don Sabo, Don, Terry A. Kupers, and Willie London. Philadelphia: Temple University Press, 2001.

Bussing, Sabine. *Of Captive Queens and Holy Panthers: Prison Fiction and Male Homoerotic Experience.* Frankfurt: Peter Lang, 1990.

Butler, Anne. *Gendered Justice in the American West: Women Prisoners in Men's Penitentiaries.* Urbana: University of Illinois Press, 1997.

Carlston, Erin G. "'A Finer Differentiation': Female Homosexuality and the American Medical Community, 1926–1940." In *Science and Homosexualities,* edited by Vernon A. Rosario. New York: Routledge, 1997.

Carnochan, W. B. "The Literature of Confinement." In *The Oxford History of the Prison: The Practice of Punishment in Western Society,* edited by Norval Morris and David J. Rothman. New York: Oxford University Press, 1998.

Casella, Eleanor Conlin. "Bulldaggers and Gentle Ladies: Archaeological Approaches to Female Homosexuality in Convict-Era Australia." In *Archaeologies of Sexuality,* edited by Robert A. Schmidt and Barbara L. Voss, 143–59. London and New York: Routledge, 2000.

Chauncey, George. *Gay New York: Gender, Urban Culture, and the Making of the Gay Male World, 1890–1940.* New York: Basic, 1994.

Christensen, Kim. "Prison Issues and HIV: Introduction." In *Women, AIDS, and Activism,* edited by Marion Banzhaf et al., 139–42. Boston: South End Press, 1990.

Christianson, Scott. *With Liberty for Some: 500 Years of Imprisonment in America*. Boston: Northeastern University Press, 1998.

Clark, Randall. *At a Theater or Drive-In Near You: The History, Culture, and Politics of the American Exploitation Film*. New York: Garland, 1995.

Clowers, Marsha. "Dykes, Gangs, and Danger: Debunking Popular Myths about Maximum-Security Life." *Journal of Criminal Justice and Popular Culture* 9, no. 1 (2001): 22–30.

Cohen, Cathy. *The Boundaries of Blackness: AIDS and the Breakdown of Black Politics*. Chicago: University of Chicago Press, 1999.

Cohen, Ed. *Talk on the Wilde Side: Toward a Genealogy of a Discourse on Male Sexualities*. New York: Routledge, 1993.

Collins, Patricia Hill. "Booty Call: Sex, Violence, and Images of Black Masculinity." In *Black Sexual Politics: African Americans, Gender, and the New Racism*, edited by Patricia Hill Collins. New York: Routledge, 2004.

Colvin, Mark. *Penitentiaries, Reformatories, and Chain Gangs: Social Theory and the History of Punishment in Nineteenth-Century America*. London: MacMillan, 1997.

Comfort, Megan, Olga Grimstead, Kathleen McCartney, Phillippe Bourgois, and Kelly Knight. "'You Can't Do Nothing in this Damn Place': Sex and Intimacy among Couples with an Incarcerated Male Partner." *Journal of Sex Research* 42 (February 2005): 3–12.

Conover, Ted. *Newjack: Guarding Sing Sing*. New York: Random House, 2000.

Crowther, Bruce. *Captured on Film: The Prison Movie*. London: B. T. Batsford, 1989.

Cummins, Eric. *The Rise and Fall of California's Radical Prison Movement*. Stanford, CA: Stanford University Press, 1994.

Curtin, Mary Ellen. *Black Prisoners and Their World, Alabama, 1865–1900*. Charlottesville and London: University Press of Virginia, 2000.

Cusac, Anne-Marie. "'The Judge Gave Me Ten Years. He Didn't Sentence Me to Death': Prisoners with HIV Deprived of Proper Care." In *Prison Nation: The Warehousing of America's Poor*, edited by Tara Herivel and Paul Wright. New York and London: Routledge, 2003.

Dandeker, Christopher. *Surveillance, Power, and Modernity: Bureaucracy and Discipline from 1700 to the Present Day*. New York: St. Martin's Press, 1990.

Davidson, Arnold. "Sex and the Emergence of Sexuality." *Critical Inquiry* 14 (Autumn 1987): 16–48.

Davis, Angela Y. "Rape, Racism, and the Myth of the Black Rapist." In *Women, Race, and Class*. New York: Random House, 1981.

Dellamora, Richard, ed. *Victorian Sexual Dissidence*. Chicago: University of Chicago Press, 1999.

D'Emilio, John. "Capitalism and Gay Identity." In *Powers of Desire: The Politics of Sexuality*, edited by Ann Snitow, Christine Stansell, and Sharon Thompson. New York: Monthly Review Press, 1983.

———. "The Homosexual Menace: The Politics of Sexuality in Cold War America." In

Passion and Power: Sexuality in History, edited by Kathy Peiss and Christine Simmons. Philadelphia: Temple University Press, 1989.

———. *Sexual Politics, Sexual Communities: The Making of a Homosexual Minority in the United States, 1940–1970*. Chicago: University of Chicago Press, 1983.

———. *The World Turned: Essays on Gay History, Politics, and Culture*. Durham, NC: Duke University Press, 2002.

D'Emilio, John, and Estelle B. Freedman. *Intimate Matters: A History of Sexuality in America*. New York: Perennial, 1989.

Denny, Dallas. "You're Strange and We're Wonderful: The Relationship between the Gay/Lesbian and Transgendered Communities." *TransSisters* (Autumn 1994): 21–23.

DePastino, Todd. *Citizen Hobo: How a Century of Homelessness Shaped America*. Chicago: University of Chicago Press, 2003.

Devor, Aaron H., and Nicholas Matte. "One Inc. and Reed Erickson: The Uneasy Collaboration of Gay and Trans Activism, 1964–2003." *GLQ: A Journal of Lesbian and Gay Studies* 10 (2004): 179–209.

Dinshaw, Carolyn. *Getting Medieval: Sexualities and Communities, Pre- and Postmodern*. Durham, NC: Duke University Press, 1999.

Dollimore, Jonathan. *Sexual Dissidence: Augustine to Wilde, Freud to Foucault*. Oxford: Clarendon, 1991.

Dorr, Lisa Lindquist. *White Women, Rape, and the Power of Race in Virginia, 1900–1960*. Chapel Hill: University of North Carolina Press, 2004.

Drew, Bettina. *Nelson Algren: A Life on the Wild Side*. New York: Putnam's, 1989.

Drexel, Allen. "Before Paris Burned: Race, Class, and Male Homosexuality on the Chicago South Side, 1935–1960." In *Creating a Place for Ourselves: Lesbian, Gay, and Bisexual Community Histories*, edited by Brett Beemyn. New York: Routledge, 1997.

Dubler, Nancy N., Catherine M. Bergmann, and Marvin E. Frankel. "Management of HIV Infection in New York State Prisons." *Columbia Human Rights Law Review* 21 (1990): 392–96.

Dubler, Nancy Neveloff, and Victor W. Sidel. "AIDS and the Prison System." In *A Disease of Society: Cultural and Institutional Responses to AIDS*, edited by Dorothy Nelkin, David P. Willis, and Scott V. Parris, 71–83. Cambridge: Cambridge University Press, 1991.

Dugdale, David, and Ken Peterson. "The Prevalence of HIV Seropositivity and HIV-related Illness in Washington State Prisoners." *Prison Journal* 69 (Spring–Summer 1989): 33–38.

Duggan, Lisa. *The Twilight of Equality? Neoliberalism, Cultural Politics, and the Attack on Democracy*. Boston: Beacon, 2003.

Dumm, Thomas L. *Democracy and Punishment: Disciplinary Origins of the United States*. Madison: University of Wisconsin Press, 1987.

Dynes, Wayne. "Stephen Donaldson (Robert A. Martin): 1946–96. In *Before Stonewall: Activists for Gay and Lesbian Rights in Historical Context*. New York: Harrington Park Press, 2002.

Eigenberg, Helen, and Agnes Baro. "If You Drop the Soap in the Shower You Are on Your Own: Images of Male Rape in Selected Prison Movies." *Sexuality and Culture* 7, no. 4 (Fall 2003): 56–89.

Eisenberg, Daniel. "Toward a Bibliography of Erotic Pulps." *Journal of Popular Culture* 15 (Spring 1982): 175–84.

Ek, Auli. *Race and Masculinity in Contemporary American Prison Narratives.* New York: Routledge, 2005.

Englehardt, H. Tristram Jr. "The Disease of Masturbation: Values and the Concept of Disease." *Bulletin of the History of Medicine* 48 (Summer 1974): 234–48.

Escoffier, Jeffrey. "Gay for Pay: Straight Men and the Making of Gay Pornography." *Qualitative Sociology* 26, no. 4 (Winter 2003): 529–53.

Fabian, Ann. *The Unvarnished Truth: Personal Narratives in Nineteenth-Century America.* Berkeley: University of California Press, 2000.

Faith, Karlene. *Unruly Women: The Politics of Confinement and Resistance.* Vancouver: Press Gang Publishers, 1993.

Ferguson, Roderick A. *Aberrations in Black: Toward a Queer of Color Critique.* Minneapolis: University of Minnesota Press, 2004.

———. "Race-ing Homonormativity: Citizenship, Sociology, and Gay Identity." In *Black Queer Studies: A Critical Anthology,* edited by E. Patrick Johnson and Mae G. Henderson. Durham, NC: Duke University Press, 2006.

Foster, Thomas A. *Sex and the Eighteenth-Century Man: Massachusetts and the History of Sexuality in America.* Boston: Beacon, 2006.

Foucault, Michel. *Abnormal: Lectures at the Collège de France, 1974–1975.* Translated by Graham Burchell. New York: Picador, 2003.

———. *Discipline and Punish: The Birth of the Prison.* Translated by Alan Sheridan. New York: Pantheon, 1977.

———. "Friendship as a Way of Life." In *Ethics: Subjectivity and Truth,* edited by Paul Rabinow, 135–40. New York: New Press, 1997.

———. "Of Other Spaces." Translated by Jay Miskowiec. *Diacritics* 16 (1986): 22–27.

———. "Prison Talk." In *Power/Knowledge: Selected Interviews and Other Writings, 1972–1977,* edited by Colin Gordon. New York: Pantheon, 1980.

Fradenburg, Louise, and Carla Freccero, eds. *Premodern Sexualities.* New York: Routledge, 1996.

Franklin, H. Bruce. "Hard Cell." *Village Voice,* July 27, 1982, 37–38.

———. *Prison Literature in America: The Victim as Criminal and Artist.* New York: Oxford University Press, 1989.

———, ed. *Prison Writing in Twentieth-Century America.* New York: Penguin, 1998.

Freccero, Carla. "Acts, Identities, and Sexuality's (Pre)Modern Regimes." *Journal of Women's History* 11, no. 2 (Summer 1999): 186–92.

———. *Queer/Early/Modern.* Durham, NC: Duke University Press, 2005.

Freedman, Estelle B. "'The Burning of Letters Continues': Elusive Identities and the Historical Construction of Sexuality." *Journal of Women's History* 9 (Winter 1998): 181–200.

————. *Maternal Justice: Miriam Van Waters and the Female Reform Tradition*. Chicago: University of Chicago Press, 1996.

————. "The Prison Lesbian: Race, Class, and the Construction of the Aggressive Female Homosexual, 1915–1965." *Feminist Studies* 22 (Summer 1996): 397–423.

————. *Their Sisters' Keepers: Women's Prison Reform in America, 1830–1930*. Ann Arbor: University of Michigan Press, 1981.

————. "'Uncontrolled Desires': The Response to the Sexual Psychopath, 1920–1960." *Journal of American History* 74, no. 1 (June 1987): 83–106.

Friedman, Andrea. "'The Habitats of Sex-Crazed Perverts': Campaigns against Burlesque in Depression-Era New York City." *Journal of the History of Sexuality* 7 (1996): 203–38.

Gardner, Martin R. "The Defense of Necessity and the Right to Escape from Prison—a Step towards Incarceration Free from Sexual Assault." *Southern California Law Review* 49, no. 1 (1975): 110–52.

Gathorne-Hardy, Jonathan. *Sex the Measure of All Things: A Life of Alfred C. Kinsey*. Bloomington: Indiana University Press, 1998.

Gibson, Margaret. "Clitoral Corruption: Body Metaphors and American Doctors' Constructions of Female Homosexuality, 1870–1900." In *Science and Homosexualities*, edited by Vernon A. Rosario. New York: Routledge, 1997.

Gido, Rosemary. "A Demographic and Epidemiological Study of New York State Inmate AIDS Mortalities, 1981–1987." *Prison Journal* 69 (Spring–Summer 1989): 27–32.

————. "Inmates with HIV/AIDS: A Growing Concern." In *Prison Sex: Practice and Policy*, edited by Christopher Hensley, 101–10. Boulder, CO: Lynne Rienner, 2002.

Gilmore, Ruth Wilson. *Golden Gulag: Prisons, Surplus, Crisis, and Opposition in Globalizing California*. Berkeley: University of California Press, 2006.

Goldberg, Jonathan, ed. *Queering the Renaissance*. Durham, NC: Duke University Press, 1994.

————, ed. *Reclaiming Sodom*. New York: Routledge, 1994.

Gustav-Wrathall, John Donald. *Take the Young Stranger by the Hand: Same-Sex Relations and the YMCA*. Chicago: University of Chicago Press, 1998.

Halberstam, Judith. *Female Masculinity*. Durham, NC: Duke University Press, 1998.

————. *In a Queer Time and Place: Transgender Bodies, Subcultural Lives*. New York: New York University Press, 2005.

Hall, Lesley A. "Forbidden by God, Despised by Men: Masturbation, Medical Warnings, Moral Panic, and Manhood in Great Britain, 1850–1950." *Journal of the History of Sexuality* 2 (January 1992): 365–87.

Hallinan, Joseph T. *Going Up the River: Travels in a Prison Nation*. New York: Random House, 2001.

Halperin, David M. "Forgetting Foucault: Acts, Identities, and the History of Sexuality." *Representations* 63 (Summer 1998): 93–120.

————. *How to Do the History of Homosexuality*. Chicago: University of Chicago Press, 2002.

————. "Is There a History of Sexuality?" *History and Theory* 28 (October 1989): 257–74.

————. *One Hundred Years of Homosexuality*. New York and London: Routledge. 1989.

Hames-Garcia, Michael. *Fugitive Thought: Prison Movements, Race, and the Meanings of Justice*. Minneapolis: University of Minnesota Press, 2004.

Hansen, Bert. "American Physicians' 'Discovery' of Homosexuals, 1880–1900: A New Diagnosis in a Changing Society." In *Framing Disease: Studies in Cultural History*, edited by Charles E. Rosenberg and Janet Golden. New Brunswick, NJ: Rutgers University Press, 1992.

Hartmann, Susan M. "Women's Employment and the Domestic Ideal in the Early Cold War Years." In *Not June Cleaver: Women and Gender in Postwar America, 1945–1960*, edited by Joanne Meyerowitz, 84–100. Philadelphia: Temple University Press, 1994.

Hawes, Joseph M. *Children in Urban Society: Juvenile Delinquency in Nineteenth-Century America*. New York: Oxford University Press, 1971.

Heap, Chad. "The City as a Sexual Laboratory: The Queer Heritage of the Chicago School." *Qualitative Sociology* 26, no. 4 (Winter 2003): 457–87.

Hekma, Gert. "The Homosexual, the Queen and Models of Gay History." *Perversions*, no. 3 (Autumn 1994): 119–38.

Hensley, Christopher, ed. *Prison Sex: Practice and Policy*. Boulder, CO: Lynne Rienner, 2002.

Herivel, Tara, and Paul Wright, eds. *Prison Nation: The Warehousing of America's Poor*. New York and London: Routledge, 2003.

Hindus, Michael Stephen. *Prison and Plantation: Crime, Justice, and Authority in Massachusetts and South Carolina, 1767–1878*. Chapel Hill: University of North Carolina Press, 1980.

Hirsch, Adam J. *The Rise of the Penitentiary: Prisons and Punishment in Early America*. New Haven, CT: Yale University Press, 1992.

Hoad, Neville. "Arrested Development or the Queerness of Savages: Resisting Evolutionary Narratives of Difference." *Postcolonial Studies* 3, no. 2 (2000): 133–58.

Hogan, Nancy Lynne. "The Social Construction of Target Populations and the Transformation of Prison-based AIDS Policy: A Descriptive Case Study." *Journal of Homosexuality* 32, nos. 3–4 (1997): 77–114.

Hopper, Columbus B. *Sex in Prison: The Mississippi Experiment with Conjugal Visiting*. Baton Rouge: Louisiana State University Press, 1969.

Hornblum, Allen. *Acres of Skin: Human Experiments at Holmesburg Prison*. New York and London: Routledge, 1999.

Horowitz, Helen Lefkowitz. *Rereading Sex: Battles over Sexual Knowledge and Suppression in Nineteenth-Century America*. New York: Knopf, 2002.

Howard, John. *Men Like That: A Southern Queer History*. Chicago: University of Chicago Press, 1999.

Humphreys, Laud. *Out of the Closets: The Sociology of Homosexual Liberation*. Englewood Cliffs, NJ: Prentice-Hall, 1972.

Hunt, Alan. "The Great Masturbation Panic and the Discourses of Moral Regulation in

Nineteenth- and Early-Twentieth-Century Britain." *Journal of the History of Sexuality* 8 (April 1998): 575–615.

Hurewitz, Daniel. *Stepping Out: Nine Walks through New York City's Gay and Lesbian Past.* New York: Henry Holt, 1997.

Ignatieff, Michael. *A Just Measure of Pain: The Penitentiary in the Industrial Revolution, 1750–1850.* New York: Pantheon Books, 1978.

———. "State, Civil Society, and Total Institutions: A Critique of Recent Social Histories of Punishment." In *Social Control and the State: Historical and Contemporary Essays*, edited by Stanley Cohen and Andrew Scull. New York: St. Martin's, 1983.

Irvine, Janice M. *Disorders of Desire: Sex and Gender in Modern American Sexology.* Philadelphia: Temple University Press, 1990.

Irwin, Robert McKee. "The Centenary of the Famous 41." In *The Famous 41: Sexuality and Social Control in Mexico, 1901*, edited by Robert McKee Irwin, Edward J. McCaughan and Michelle Rocio Nasser. New York: Palgrave, 2003.

Irwin, Robert McKee, Edward J. McCaughan, and Michelle Rocio Nasser, eds. *The Famous 41: Sexuality and Social Control in Mexico, 1901.* New York: Palgrave, 2003.

Jacobs, James B. *New Perspectives on Prisons and Imprisonment.* Ithaca, NY: Cornell University Press, 1983.

———. *Stateville: The Penitentiary in Mass Society.* Chicago: University of Chicago Press, 1977.

———. "Stratification and Conflict among Prison Inmates." In *Justice and Corrections*, edited by Norman Johnston and Leonard Savitz, 580–87. New York, John Wiley & Sons, 1978.

Johnson, David K. "The Kids of Fairytown: Gay Male Culture on Chicago's Near North Side in the 1930s." In *Creating a Place for Ourselves: Lesbian, Gay, and Bisexual Community Histories*, edited by Brett Beemyn. New York: Routledge, 1997.

———. *The Lavender Scare: The Cold War Persecution of Gays and Lesbians in the Federal Government.* Chicago: University of Chicago Press, 2004.

Johnson, Susan Lee. *Roaring Camp: The Social World of the California Gold Rush.* New York: Norton, 2000.

Johnston, Norman B. *Forms of Constraint: A History of Prison Architecture.* Urbana and Chicago: University of Illinois Press, 2000.

———. *The Human Cage: A Brief History of Prison Architecture.* New York: Walker, 1973.

Johnston, Norman, and Leonard D. Savitz, eds. *Justice and Corrections.* New York: John Wiley & Sons, 1978.

Jones, James H. *Alfred C. Kinsey: A Public/Private Life.* New York: W. W. Norton, 1997.

Kaplan, Morris B. *Sodom on the Thames: Sex, Love, and Scandal in Wilde Times.* Ithaca, NY: Cornell University Press, 2005.

Katz, Jonathan Ned. *Gay American History: Lesbians and Gay Men in the U.S.A.* New York: Avon Books, 1976.

———. *The Invention of Heterosexuality.* New York: Dutton, 1995.

———. *Love Stories: Sex between Men before Homosexuality.* Chicago: University of Chicago Press, 2001.

Keith, K. Wymand. *Long Line Rider: The Story of Cummins Prison Farm*. New York: McGraw-Hill, 1971.

Kenen, Stephanie H. "Who Counts When You're Counting Homosexuals? Hormones and Homosexuality in Mid-Twentieth-Century America." In *Science and Homosexualities*, edited by Vernon A. Rosario. New York: Routledge, 1997.

Kennedy, Elizabeth Lapovsky, and Madeline D. Davis. *Boots of Leather, Slippers of Gold: The History of a Lesbian Community*. New York: Routledge, 1993.

Kennedy, Hubert. "Karl Heinrichs Ulrichs: First Theorist of Homosexuality." In *Science and Homosexualities*, edited by Vernon A. Rosario. New York: Routledge, 1997.

Kessner, Thomas. *Fiorello H. La Guardia and the Making of Modern New York*. New York: McGraw-Hill, 1989.

Keve, Paul W. *Prisons and the American Conscience: A History of U.S. Federal Corrections*. Carbondale: Southern Illinois University Press, 1991.

Kissack, Terence. "Freaking Fag Revolutionaries: New York's Gay Liberation Front, 1969–1971." *Radical History Review* 62 (Spring 1995): 104–34.

Kupers, Terry A. "Rape and the Prison Code." In *Prison Masculinities*, edited by Don Sabo, Terry A. Kupers, and Willie London. Philadelphia: Temple University Press, 2001.

Laqueur, Thomas W. *Solitary Sex: A Cultural History of Masturbation*. New York: Zone, 2003.

Lawson, W. Travis, Jr., and Lena Sue Fawkes. "HIV, AIDS, and the Female Offender." *Federal Prisons Journal* 3 (Spring 1992): 27–32.

Leps, Marie-Christine. *Apprehending the Criminal: The Production of Deviance in Nineteenth-Century Discourse*. Durham, NC: Duke University Press, 1992.

Lewis, W. David. *From Newgate to Dannemora: The Rise of the Penitentiary in New York, 1796–1848*. Ithaca, NY: Cornell University Press, 1965.

Lichtenstein, Alex. *Twice the Work of Free Labor: The Political Economy of Convict Labor in the New South*. London: Verso, 1996.

Loughery, John. *The Other Side of Silence: Men's Lives and Gay Identities: A Twentieth-Century History*. New York: Henry Holt, 1998.

Lunbeck, Elizabeth. "'A New Generation of Women': Progressive Psychiatrists and the Hypersexual Female." *Feminist Studies* 13 (1987): 513–43.

MacDonald, Robert H. "The Frightful Consequences of Onanism: Notes on the History of a Delusion." *Journal of the History of Ideas* 28 (July–September 1967): 423–31.

Manalansan, Martin F., IV. *Global Divas: Filipino Gay Men in the Diaspora*. Durham, NC: Duke University Press, 2003.

Mancini, Matthew J. *One Dies, Get Another: Convict Leasing in the American South, 1866–1928*. Columbus: University of South Carolina Press, 1996.

Marotta, Toby. *The Politics of Homosexuality*. Boston: Houghton Mifflin, 1981.

Martin, Randy, Sherwood Zimmerman, and Billy Long. "AIDS Education in U.S. Prisons: A Survey of Inmate Programs." *Prison Journal* 73, no. 1 (March 1993): 103–29.

Massey, Dennis. *Doing Time in American Prisons: A Study of Modern Novels*. New York: Greenwood Press, 1989.

Mauer, Marc. *Race to Incarcerate*. New York: New Press, 1999.

May, Elaine Tyler. *Homeward Bound: American Families in the Cold War Era*. New York: Basic, 1988.

Mayne, Judith. *Framed: Lesbians, Feminists, and Media Culture*. Minneapolis: University of Minnesota Press, 2000.

McGarry, Molly, and Fred Wasserman. *Becoming Visible: An Illustrated History of Lesbian and Gay Life in Twentieth-Century America*. New York: Viking, 1998.

McKelvey, Blake. *American Prisons: A History of Good Intentions*. Montclair, NJ: Patterson Smith, 1977.

Meeker, Martin. *Contacts Desired: Gay and Lesbian Communications and Community, 1940s–1970s*. Chicago: University of Chicago Press, 2006.

Mennel, Robert M. *Thorns and Thistles: Juvenile Delinquents in the United States, 1825–1940*. Hanover, NH: University Press of New England, 1973.

Meranze, Michael. *Laboratories of Virtue: Punishment, Revolution, and Authority in Philadelphia, 1760–1835*. Chapel Hill: University of North Carolina Press, 1996.

Mercer, John. "In the Slammer: The Myth of the Prison in American Gay Pornographic Video." *Journal of Homosexuality* 47, nos. 3–4 (2004): 151–66.

Meyer, Richard. "Gay Power circa 1970: Visual Strategies for Sexual Revolution." *GLQ: A Journal of Lesbian and Gay Studies* 12, no. 3 (2006).

Meyerowitz, Joanne. "Beyond the Feminine Mystique: A Reassessment of Postwar Mass Culture, 1946–1958." In *Not June Cleaver: Women and Gender in Postwar America, 1945–1960*, edited by Joanne Meyerowitz, 229–62. Philadelphia: Temple University Press, 1994.

———. *How Sex Changed: A History of Transsexuality in the United States*. Cambridge, MA: Harvard University Press, 2002.

———, ed. *Not June Cleaver: Women and Gender in Postwar America, 1945–1960*. Philadelphia: Temple University Press, 1994.

Midgley, John. "Prison Litigation, 1950–2000: Hands Off, Hands On, Gloves On." In *Prison Nation: The Warehousing of America's Poor*, edited by Tara Herivel and Paul Wright. New York and London: Routledge, 2003.

Moore, Kathleen. "Muslims in Prison: Claims to Constitutional Protection of Religious Liberty." In *The Muslims of America*, edited by Yvonne Yazbeck Haddad, 136–56. New York: Oxford University Press, 1991.

Morey, Anne. "'The Judge Called Me an Accessory': Women's Prison Films, 1950–1962." *Journal of Popular Film and Television* 23 (Summer 1995): 80–87.

Morris, Norval. "The Contemporary Prison: 1965–Present." In *The Oxford History of the Prison*, edited by Norval Morris and David J. Rothman. New York: Oxford University Press, 1995.

Morris, Norval, and David J. Rothman, eds. *The Oxford History of the Prison: The Practice of Punishment in Western Society*. New York: Oxford University Press, 1995.

Morton, Jim. "Women in Prison Films." In *Incredibly Strange Films* no. 10, 151–52. San Francisco: Re/Search Publications, 1986.

Murphy, Kevin P. *Political Manhood: Redbloods, Mollycoddles and the Politics of Progressive-Era Reform*. New York: Columbia University Press, 2008.

———. "Socrates in the Slums: Homoerotics, Gender, and Settlement House Reform." In *A Shared Experience: Men, Women and Gender in U.S. History*, edited by Laura McCall and Donald Yacovone. New York: New York University Press, 1998.

Murray, Stephen O. "An African American's Representation of Internalized Homophobia during the Early 1930s: Chester Himes's *Cast the First Stone*." *Journal of Homosexuality* 34 (1997): 31–46.

Murrin, John. "'Things Fearful to Name': Bestiality in Early America." *Pennsylvania History* 65, special supplemental issue (1998): 8–43.

O'Brien, Patricia. "The Prison on the Continent: Europe, 1865–1965." In *The Oxford History of the Prison*, edited by Norval Morris and David J. Rothman. New York: Oxford University Press, 1995.

———. *The Promise of Punishment: Prisons in Nineteenth-Century France*. Princeton, NJ: Princeton University Press, 1982.

Okun, Peter. *Crime and the Nation: Prison Reform and Popular Fiction in Philadelphia, 1786–1800*. New York: Routledge, 2002.

Oosterhuis, Harry. "Richard von Krafft-Ebing's 'Step-Children of Nature': Psychiatry and the Making of Homosexual Identity." In *Science and Homosexualities*, edited by Vernon A. Rosario. New York: Routledge, 1997.

———. *Stepchildren of Nature: Krafft-Ebing, Psychiatry, and the Making of Sexual Identity*. Chicago: University of Chicago Press, 2000.

Oshinsky, David M. *"Worse Than Slavery": Parchman Farm and the Ordeal of Jim Crow Justice*. New York: Free Press, 1996.

Owen, Barbara. "Women and Imprisonment in the United States: The Gendered Consequences of the U.S. Imprisonment Binge." In *Harsh Punishment: International Experiences of Women's Imprisonment*, edited by Sandy Cook and Susanne Davies. Boston: Northeastern University Press, 1999.

Parish, James Robert. *Gays and Lesbians in Mainstream Cinema*. Jefferson, NC: McFarland & Co., 1993.

———. *Prison Pictures from Hollywood: Plots, Critiques, Casts, and Credits for 293 Theatrical and Made-for Television Releases*. Jefferson, NC: McFarland & Co., 1991.

Pell, Eve, ed. *Maximum Security: Letters from California's Prisons*. New York: Dutton, 1972.

Penn, Donna. "Queer: Theorizing Politics and History." *Radical History Review* 62 (Spring 1995): 24–42.

———. "The Sexualized Woman: The Lesbian, the Prostitute, and the Containment of Female Sexuality in Postwar America." In *Not June Cleaver: Women and Gender in Postwar America, 1945–1960*, edited by Joanne Meyerowitz, 358–81. Philadelphia: Temple University Press, 1994.

Phillips, Richard, Diane Watt, and David Shuttleton, eds. *De-Centering Sexualities: Politics and Representations beyond the Metropolis*. New York: Routledge, 2000.

Picatto, Pablo. "Interpretations of Sexuality in Mexico City Prisons: A Critical Version of Roumagnac." In *The Famous 41: Sexuality and Social Control in Mexico, 1901*, edited by Robert McKee Irwin, Edward J. McCaughan, and Michelle Rocio Nasser. New York: Palgrave, 2003.

Pinar, William F. *The Gender of Racial Politics and Violence in America: Lynching, Prison Rape, and the Crisis of Masculinity*. New York: Peter Lang, 2001.

Pisciotta, Alexander W. *Benevolent Repression: Social Control and the American Reformatory-Prison Movement*. New York: New York University Press, 1994.

Platt, Anthony. *The Child Savers: The Invention of Delinquency*. Chicago: University of Chicago Press, 1969.

Polych, Carol, and Don Sabo. "Sentence—Death by Lethal Infection: IV-Drug Use and Infectious Disease Transmission in North American Prisons." In *Prison Masculinities*, edited by Don Sabo, Terry A. Kupers, and Willie London. Philadelphia: Temple University Press, 2001.

Potter, Sarah. "'Undesirable Relations': Same-Sex Relationships and the Meaning of Sexual Desire at a Women's Reformatory during the Progressive Era." *Feminist Studies* 30 (Summer 2004): 394–415.

Querry, Ronald B. "Prison Movies: An Annotated Filmography 1921–Present." *Journal of Popular Film* 2 (Spring 1973): 181–97.

Rafter, Nichole Hahn. *Creating Born Criminals*. Urbana: University of Illinois Press, 1997.

———. *Partial Justice: Women, Prisons, and Social Control*. 2d ed. New Brunswick, NJ: Transaction, 1990. First published as *Partial Justice: Women in State Prisons, 1800–1935* (Boston: Northeastern University Press, 1985).

Retter, Yolanda. "Lesbian Activism in Los Angeles, 1970–1979." In *Queer Frontiers: Millennial Geographies, Genders, and Generations*, edited by Joseph A. Boone et al. Madison: University of Wisconsin Press, 2000.

Reumann, Miriam G. *American Sexual Character: Sex, Gender, and National Identity in the Kinsey Reports*. Berkeley: University of California Press, 2005.

Rierden, Andi. *The Farm: Life inside a Women's Prison*. Amherst: University of Massachusetts Press, 1997.

Rosario, Vernon A. "Homosexual Bio-Histories: Genetic Nostalgias and the Quest for Paternity." In *Science and Homosexualities*, edited by Vernon A. Rosario. New York: Routledge, 1997.

———, ed. *Science and Homosexualities*. New York and London: Routledge, 1997.

Ross, Marlon B. "Beyond the Closet as Raceless Paradigm." In *Black Queer Studies: A Critical Anthology*, edited by E. Patrick Johnson and Moe G. Henderson. Durham, NC: Duke University Press, 2005.

Rothman, David J. *Conscience and Convenience: The Asylum and Its Alternatives in Progressive America*. Boston: Little, Brown, 1980.

———. *The Discovery of the Asylum: Social Order and Disorder in the New Republic*. Boston: Little, Brown: 1971.

———. "Perfecting the Prison: United States, 1789–1865." In *The Oxford History of the Prison*, edited by Norval Morris and David J. Rothman. New York: Oxford University Press, 1995.

Rotman, Edgardo. "The Failure of Reform: United States, 1865–1965." In *The Oxford History of the Prison*, edited by Norval Morris and David J. Rothman. New York: Oxford University Press, 1995.

Russo, Vito. *The Celluloid Closet: Homosexuality in the Movies*. New York: Harper & Row, 1981.

Sabo, Don, Terry A. Kupers, and Willie London, eds. *Prison Masculinities*. Philadelphia: Temple University Press, 2001.

Sahli, Nancy. "Smashing: Women's Relationships before the Fall." *Chrysalis* 8 (Summer 1979): 17–27.

Salvatore, Ricardo D., and Carlos Aguirre, eds. *The Birth of the Penitentiary in Latin America: Essays on Criminology, Prison Reform, and Social Control, 1830–1940*. Austin: University of Texas Press, 1996.

———. "The Birth of the Penitentiary in Latin America: Toward an Interpretative Social History of Prisons." In *The Birth of the Penitentiary in Latin America: Essays on Criminology, Prison Reform, and Social Control, 1830–1940*, edited by Ricardo D. Salvatore and Carlos Aguirre. Austin: University of Texas Press, 1996.

Schaefer, Eric. *Bold! Daring! Shocking! True! A History of Exploitation Film, 1919–1959*. Durham, NC: Duke University Press, 1999.

Schlichter, Annette. "Queer at Last? Straight Intellectuals and Desire for Transgression." *GLQ: A Journal of Lesbian and Gay Studies* 10, no. 4 (2004): 543–64.

Schlosser, Eric. "The Prison-Industrial Complex." *Atlantic Monthly*, December 1998, 51–77.

Schlossman, Steven L. *Love and the American Delinquent: The Theory and Practice of 'Progressive' Juvenile Justice*. Chicago: University of Chicago Press, 1977.

Scott, Daryl Michael. *Contempt and Pity: Social Policy and the Image of the Damaged Black Psyche, 1880–1996*. Chapel Hill: University of North Carolina Press, 1997.

Sedgwick, Eve Kosofsky. *Epistemology of the Closet*. Berkeley: University of California Press, 1990.

———. *Tendencies*. Durham, NC: Duke University Press, 1993.

Shapiro, Ann-Louise. *Breaking the Codes: Female Criminality in Fin-de-Siècle Paris*. Stanford, CA: Stanford University Press, 1996.

Sinfield, Alan. *Gay and After*. London: Serpent's Tail, 1998.

———. "The Production of Gay and the Return of Power." In *De-Centering Sexualities: Politics and Representations beyond the Metropolis*, edited by Richard Phillips, Diane Watt, and David Shuttleton. New York: Routledge, 2000.

———. *The Wilde Century: Effeminacy, Oscar Wilde and the Queer Moment*. London: Cassell, 1994.

Smith-Rosenberg, Carroll. "The Female World of Love and Ritual: Relations between Women in Nineteenth-Century America." *Signs* 1 (Autumn 1975): 1–29.

Somerville, Siobhan B. *Queering the Color Line: Race and the Invention of Homosexuality in American Culture*. Durham, NC: Duke University Press, 2000.

Sommerville, Diane M. *Rape and Race in the Nineteenth-Century South*. Chapel Hill: University of North Carolina Press, 2004.

Spierenburg, Pieter. *The Prison Experience: Disciplinary Institutions and Their Inmates in Early Modern Europe*. New Brunswick, NJ: Rutgers University Press, 1991.

Steakley, James D. "Per scientiam ad justitiam: Magnus Hirschfeld and the Sexual Politics of Innate Homosexuality." In *Science and Homosexualities*, edited by Vernon A. Rosario. New York: Routledge, 1997.

Stein, Marc. *City of Sisterly and Brotherly Loves: Lesbian and Gay Philadelphia, 1945–1972*. Chicago: University of Chicago Press, 2000.

Storr, Merl. "Transformations: Subjects, Categories and Cures in Krafft-Ebing's Sexology." In *Sexology in Culture: Labeling Bodies and Desires*, edited by Lucy Bland and Laura Doan. Chicago: University of Chicago Press, 1998.

Sullivan, Larry E. *The Prison Reform Movement: Forlorn Hope*. Boston: Twayne, 1990.

Terry, Jennifer. *An American Obsession: Science, Medicine, and Homosexuality in Modern Society*. Chicago: University of Chicago Press, 1999.

Traub, Valerie. "The Rewards of Lesbian History." *Feminist Studies* 25, no. 2 (Summer 1999): 363–94.

Umphrey, Martha M. "The Trouble with Harry Thaw." *Radical History Review* 62 (Spring 1995): 8–23.

Vaid, Urvashi. "Prisons." In *AIDS and the Law: A Guide for the Public*, edited by Harlon L. Dalton, Scott Burris, and the Yale AIDS Law Project, 235–50. New Haven, CT: Yale University Press, 1987.

Vicinus, Martha. *Independent Women: Work and Community for Single Women, 1850–1920*. Chicago: University of Chicago Press, 1985.

Wacquant, Loic. "The Curious Eclipse of Prison Ethnography in the Age of Mass Incarceration." *Ethnography* 3–4 (December 2002): 371–97.

Walters, Suzanna Danuta. "Caged Heat: The (R)Evolution of Women-in-Prison Films." In *Reel Knockouts: Violent Women in the Movies*, edited by Martha McCaughey and Neal King. Austin: University of Texas Press, 2001.

Waters, Chris. "Havelock Ellis, Sigmund Freud and the State: Discourses of Homosexual Identity in Interwar Britain." In *Sexology in Culture: Labelling Bodies and Desire*, edited by Lucy Bland and Laura Doan. Chicago: University of Chicago Press, 1998.

Weiss, Robert P. "Humanitarianism, Labour Exploitation, or Social Control: A Critical Survey of Theory and Research on the Origins and Development of Prisons." *Social History* 12 (October 1987): 331–50.

White, Patricia. "Supporting Character: The Queer Career of Agnes Moorehead." In *Out in Culture: Gay, Lesbian, and Queer Essays on Popular Culture*, edited by Corey K. Creekmur and Alexander Doty, 91–114. Durham, NC: Duke University Press, 1995.

———. *Uninvited: Classical Hollywood Cinema and Lesbian Representability*. Bloomington: Indiana University Press, 1999.

Wriggins, Jennifer. "Rape, Racism and the Law." *Harvard Women's Law Journal* 6 (Spring 1983): 103–41.

Yaker, Henri M. "The Black Muslims in the Correctional Institution." *Welfare Reporter* 13 (October 1962): 158–65.

Zalcock, Beverly. *Renegade Sisters: Girl Gangs on Film*. London and San Francisco: Creation Books International, 1998.

Zalcock, Beverly, and Jocelyn Robinson. "Inside Cell Block H: Hard Steel and Soft Soap." *Continuum* 9, no. 1 (1996): 88–97.

Zedner, Lucia. "Wayward Sisters: The Prison for Women." In *The Oxford History of the Prison*, edited by Norval Morris and David J. Rothman. New York: Oxford University Press, 1995.

Abbott, Jack, 4, 6, 173, 182
Actors' Playhouse, 154
Adam's Rib (film), 142
adolescence: theories of, 90
Advocate (magazine), 207, 208, 217,
   219, 221, 222
African American men:
   homosexuality, pre-prison
   familiarity with, 277–78;
   incarceration of, 151, 165, 165–66;
   sexual relationships, primitive
   view of, 178. *See also* black
   masculinity; black men
African American prisoners:
   politicization of, 176; statistics of,
   286n80
African American sexual culture,
   289n144; and prison sex, 177
African American women:
   homosexual experiences of, 130,
   131; masculinity attributed to, 131
African Americans: in prison,
   305–6n15
*Against Our Will: Men, Women, and
   Rape* (Brownmiller), 172
AIDS (Acquired Immunodeficiency
   Syndrome), 303–4n1, 304n5,

306n17; among prisoners, 13, 226,
   227, 236, 306n18; cause of, 227;
   heterosexual identity, as immune
   from, 236; mass incarceration,
   rise of, 228; in poor communities,
   227–28; and sexual practice,
   236–37; sexualization of, 229
AIDS activism, 223
AIDS Coalition to Unleash Power
   (ACT-UP), 303n199
Alabama, 227; black prisoners in,
   286n80; surgical masks, use of
   in, 232
Albany Penitentiary, 35
Alcatraz, 83
Algren, Nelson, 93, 269n92
Alligood, Clarence, 202
Alpert, Jane, 191
American Civil Liberties Union
   (ACLU), 207, 236; and National
   Prison Project, 229, 234, 304n5
American Correctional Association,
   227
American Mercury (magazine), 56
American Notes (Dickens), 19
American prison system: critics of, 68
Anderson, Nels, 66